Śiva's Saints

Śiva's Saints

The Origins of Devotion in Kannada according to Harihara's Ragaḷegaḷu

GIL BEN-HERUT

OXFORD
UNIVERSITY PRESS

OXFORD
UNIVERSITY PRESS

Oxford University Press is a department of the University of Oxford. It furthers the University's objective of excellence in research, scholarship, and education by publishing worldwide. Oxford is a registered trade mark of Oxford University Press in the UK and certain other countries.

Published in the United States of America by Oxford University Press
198 Madison Avenue, New York, NY 10016, United States of America.

CIP data is on file at the Library of Congress
ISBN 978-0-19-087884-9

1 3 5 7 9 8 6 4 2

Printed by Sheridan Books, Inc., United States of America

For my parents,

for their endless love and support.

Elliava and Moshe Ben-Herut

Can one deny the existence of the child
simply because it assumes transformed features
as an adult?

P. B. DESAI, *Basaveśvara and His Times*, p. 272.

Contents

Acknowledgments

THIS BOOK IS the fruit of a protracted endeavor that spanned continents, with studies and research in the United States, India, Israel, and elsewhere. I am grateful to the many people without whom this book could not have been written. First, I wish to thank Laurie Patton, who inspired me on many levels—as a person, teacher, guide, and mentor. I am indebted to her for her foresight and guidance on this project from its earliest stages. I wish to thank Anne Monius, who taught me new things about scholarship, India, and friendship. I also wish to extend my gratitude to Jack Hawley, whose wisdom, intellectual acuity, and moral support were a guiding light in challenging moments.

My journey into the world of Kannada literature began with reading Sanskrit texts in Mysore with H. V. Nagaraja Rao, who was the first and primary inspiration for me to take my first course in Kannada studies. I consider myself fortunate to have known and worked with him. Although I did not know A. K. Ramanujan in person, his magisterial oeuvre about Kannada and other languages never ceased to inspire me as well.

I am fortunate to have had many generous and open-hearted Kannada teachers. Early on, the ever-cheerful Sudhanva Char taught me basic language skills. At the Central Institute for Indian Languages (CIIL) in Mysore, under the benevolent guidance of the late Lingadevaru Halemane, I was introduced for the first time to the structure of the Kannada language. As with Ramanujan and others, Halemane's premature passing was a great loss for all admirers of Kannada culture. I am grateful to my teachers at the CIIL: the late Talwar, Vijaya Lakshmi, and Shishira.

By good fortune (or was it as reward for meritorious past deeds?), I studied under Jyothi Shankar during the Advanced Kannada Academic Year program of the American Institute of Indian Studies (AIIS) in Mysore. I will always fondly cherish memories of the many hours I spent with Jyothi reading Harihara's texts. She has been a wonderful companion for walking an arduous path. I also wish to thank my other teachers of that memorable year: Akka Mahadevi, Shubha Chandra, and Poornima. Seeing Raja Lakshmi's unfazed smile during the breaks from intense learning sessions was always a comfort. The program by the AIIS was invaluable to my development in Kannada and shaped my research project in important ways. I thank Philip Lutgendorf, Martha Selby, Rebecca Manring, and Elise Auerbach for their continuous support and responsiveness. Equally supportive were the staff of the Delhi branch of the AIIS, headed by Purnima Mehta. I also thank Purushotham Bilimale for his help.

That unforgettable year also introduced me to R. V. S. Sundaram, who directed the Advanced Kannada Academic Year program. For months I sat daily for long, enlightening hours in Sundaram's cozy backroom study, with its four walls hidden by tall bookcases brimming with books in Kannada, Telugu, Tamil, Sanskrit, and English. That impression will linger in my memory forever. Sundaram introduced me to and guided me through the treasures of medieval Kannada literature. I cannot imagine this book being written without his guidance. For this and more I am deeply grateful.

I am grateful to several Kannada scholars who graciously offered their help and wisdom: the late L. Basavaraju, T. V. Venkatachala Shastry, M. Chidananda Murthy, N. S. Taranatha, Basavaraju Kalgudi, and Basavaraju Kodagunti. My conversations with M. M. Kalaburgi tragically ended with his horrific murder. I will never forget his towering figure and intellectual fervor. Manu Devadevan has been a wonderful companion for travelling in north Karnataka and into the past. Special thanks also to Prithvi Datta Chandra Shobhi. The long hours we spent together in his den, discussing religious matters and Kannada literature and reading primary and secondary materials, influenced my work greatly. Robert Zydenbos was incredibly helpful in thinking about Kannada literature and religion, and finding one's way in the culture and society of Karnataka, and I am thankful to him as well. Several people in the Kuvempu Institute of Kannada Studies at the University of Mysore and the Oriental Research Institute in Mysore were incredibly helpful and I am grateful to them.

I also wish to extend an especially hearty thank you to several people of the city of Mysore, who contributed to the magical sensation with which I lived during my research periods there: Rajalakshmi, Kuttu and Angeela Cariappa, John Gilbert, Flora Brajot, Suddha, Bharat Shetty, Ben and Rita, Anand, and Shrinivas. I cannot think of a better place to do research than the small heaven called Mysore.

I was fortunate to have, during my intellectual infancy in Tel Aviv University and the Hebrew University, gifted scholars and teachers such as David Shulman, Yigal Bronner, Yohanan Grinshpon, Alex Cherniak, and Ron Margolin, and I extend to them my deepest gratitude. My PhD studies at Emory University entailed learning from many people. I am indebted to them all. I was fortunate in having Velcheru Narayana Rao, an authority of rare magnitude on pre-modern South India, as my teacher and member of my dissertation committee. His sharp insights greatly contributed to my work. Sara McClintock has been a highly sensitive reader and a tremendous supporter of my project. Joyce Flueckiger, gifted with intellectual and many other human sensibilities, was and still is a warm, supporting, and candid interlocutor. I am also thankful to Paul Courtright, Tara Doyle, Gary Laderman, Julie Brown, Brian Croxall, Rachel Bowser, and Lisa Tedesco. Special thanks go to Jeffery and Eliana Lesser for their invaluable support during this period and after.

An important piece of my research was made possible through the Dissertation Completion Fellowship 2012–13 of the Bill and Carol Fox Center for Humanistic Inquiry (FCHI) at Emory University. I thank the director Martine Brownley and the coordinators Amy Erbil and Colette Barlow. I also extend special thanks to the associate director Brian Keith who gave me valuable professional advice and support at important moments.

I wish to thank Christian Novetzke, Richard Davis, Paula Richman, Leslie Orr, John Cort, Brian Hatcher, Gary Tubb, Leela Prasad, and Phyllis Granoff for stimulating intellectual conversations and providing helpful critical comments. John Nemec was incredibly forthcoming and supportive at certain moments during this project and I thank him deeply. Deven Patel, a true friend and comrade, was always present to support and help. I also wish to thank my friends and peers Brooke Dodson-Lavelle, Jenn Ortegren, Anita Crocitto, Harold Braswell, Harshita Mruthinti Kamath, Sarah Pierce Taylor, Dean Accardi, Anne Latowsky, Mani Rao, Aftab Jassal, Steven Vose, Eric Steinschneider, Patton Burchett, Daniel Raveh, Maya Tevet, Ori Tavor, Brian Pennington, Amy Alloco, and Peter Valdina. Udi Halperin and Luke Whitmore delivered warmth and understanding straight from the cold Himalayan peaks. Jon Keune, who in recent years became my close intellectual partner, spent many hours commenting on my writings and greatly contributed to this book. I am deeply grateful to Jeremy Sobel, the most special nonspecialist a scholar of India could wish for. With endless patience, precious insights, and—most of all—unwavering spirit, Jeremy read and commented on early drafts of this book. Celine Allen was incredibly involved and helpful through the final phases of the manuscript. I am deeply thankful for her bright comments and genuine, spirited support. Guy Golan was a wonderful interlocutor at the final moments as well. I also wish to thank Michael Fiden and Cynthia Read for all the help.

Since I graduated, the University of South Florida has been a wonderful academic home to me. I am thankful for the people of the Department of Religious Studies for their support, advice, and patience. All have been wonderful colleagues during this period. I send special thanks to Thomas Williams and Michael DeJonge for commenting on parts of this work. Special thanks are also in place for Eric Eisenberg, Elizabeth Bell, and Randy Larsen for their attentiveness and support. I also wish to thank David Jacobson, a friend and mentor.

Last but not least, I wish to thank my family for bearing with me throughout this project. To my mother and father Elliava and Moshe, my elder brother Adi and his wife Sunny, my two lovely daughters Sitar and Iyar, and to my wife and life-companion Snait, this could not have happened without your support.

Note on Transliteration and Translation

IN GENERAL, I have followed in this book the standard of ISO 15919 for transliterating Sanskrit and Kannada terms and names since it facilitates the Kannada differentiation between the short and long *e* and *o* vowels (e.g., "*dēśi*" and not "*deśi*"; "Gōrakṣa" and not "Gorakṣa"). For terms spelled differently in Kannada and Sanskrit, I have adhered to the Kannada form (e.g., "Pārvati" and not "Pārvatī"; "Kāḷidāsa" and not "Kālidāsa"). I have used italicization and lowercase for non-English words (e.g., "*bhakti*"), and have used non-italicization and uppercase for the initial letter in the following cases: for words that have been assimilated into English (e.g., "Brahmin" and "Vedas"), for literary genres (e.g., "Purāṇas"), for general terms pertaining to groups of people (a Bhakta, a Śaiva), and for anglicized forms of technical or abstract terms (Vīraśaivism). For "*ragaḷe*" in the sense of the meter, I have used italicization and lowercase, but for "Ragaḷe" in the sense of the poem written in that meter I have used non-italicization and uppercase for the initial letter. For publications in English by South Asian authors I have maintained the English form of their names (e.g., "M. Chidananda Murthy"), and for their Kannada publications I have transliterated them (e.g., "Eṃ. Cidānandamūrti").

All translations are my own unless otherwise noted. Word-by-word translations are annotated with the original Kannada citation, and summarized translations are annotated with a reference to the location in the original.

Introduction

UNDERSTANDING REQUIRES KNOWLEDGE of a subject, and paying attention to sources hitherto unexamined can result in new understanding. That is what this book sets out to do. It offers a rethinking of what we know about the origins of a South Asian religious tradition by analyzing a very early, little studied, but important collection of saints' biographies. The religious attitudes, values, and practices described in this text constitute a religious worldview, one that is complex but also well-reasoned and lucid, and—more important—one that substantively differs from commonly held notions about this particular religious tradition, notions based on later canonical texts.

The tradition discussed in this book is part of south-Indian Śivabhakti—a pervasive and mature religious culture centered on *bhakti* (devotion) to the Hindu god Śiva. The Śivabhakti strand discussed in this book is associated with the southwestern part of the Deccan plateau in India, in today's state of Karnataka, where the spoken language is Kannada. Members of the tradition today are referred to by two names. One is Vīraśaivas or "Heroes of Śiva," a name that conveys the impassioned religious sentiment promoted by the tradition. The other is Liṅgāyats or "Bearers of the *liṅga*," a name that attests to a distinct practice in this tradition of carrying the *liṅga*, which is Śiva's emblem, on one's body. The relation between the two names (whether they are synonymous or whether each signifies a separate tradition) is, historically speaking, complex, and in the public sphere of Karnataka today it has political implications as well.[1]

1. In this book I generally adhere to the former name, Vīraśaiva, following an admittedly imprecise scholarly trend. I do this only for the sake of clarity and do not consider the name Vīraśaiva more historically authentic than the name Liṅgāyat. Very recently, a heated debate

In the state of Karnataka, Vīraśaiva communities comprise between ten and fifteen million people, or about 20 percent of the population, and they are present in other regions of the South Asian peninsula as well.[2] In contemporary Kannada society, Vīraśaivas constitute an active religious community with a distinct—albeit polyphonic—social and political voice.[3] Vīraśaivas hold a unique place in Hindu society. They do not adhere to the hierarchical structures of Brahminical-centered society, nor do they acknowledge the priestly status of Brahmins. Vīraśaivas practice a distinct set of rituals, such as the previously mentioned carrying of a personal *liṅga* on their body, worshiping the *liṅga* individually as well as in groups, burying and not cremating their dead, and allowing widow remarriage.[4] Some Vīraśaiva communities are considered by the state of Karnataka to be OBC (Other Backward Classes), although this issue is contested.[5]

The focus of this book is not on contemporary Vīraśaivism but on a thirteenth-century collection of saints' lives, although some of the saints in that text figure significantly in contemporary debates about key issues regarding the political, social, and religious nature of the tradition as it is understood today. The thirteenth-century collection of saints' stories is untitled but is commonly referred to as the *Śivaśaraṇara Ragaḷegaḷu* ("Poems in the *Ragaḷe* Meter for Śiva's Saints," henceforth *Ragaḷegaḷu*),[6] and it was

---

has developed over the demand by some religious and political leaders that "Liṅgāyat religion" (*liṅgāyata dharma*) be recognized as distinct from Vīraśaivism and completely separate from Hinduism in an effort to receive religious minority status. The statewide conversation has been covered almost daily since June 15, 2017, in Kannada newspapers such as the *Prajāvāṇi*. It has also received nationwide coverage in English-language newspapers such as *The Hindu*. See, for example, Anonymous (2017); Pattanashetti (2017b, 2017a); Bageshree (2017).

2. Michael (2015). There are major Vīraśaiva centers in Śrīśailam, Varanasi, Kedarnath, and Ujjain (Nandimath 1979 [1942], 8–10).

3. See Chandra Shobhi (2005, 24–89). A recent article in the *Indian Express* demonstrates the political power Vīraśaivas have in today's politics in Karnataka as well as at the national level (Lal 2017).

4. For details on Vīraśaiva practices, see survey in McCormack (1973).

5. Chandra Shobhi (2005, 41–42). In very general terms, OBC is an official classification given by the government of India and its states to communities that have traditionally suffered economic and social discrimination.

6. *Ragaḷe* is the name of the meter in which this text was composed, and *gaḷu* is the neuter plural suffix in Kannada. Because this work is a collection of disparate poems, it has no fixed title in its original form. The title *Śivaśaraṇara Ragaḷegaḷu* is one among several used in scholarship; others include *Śivagaṇada Ragaḷegaḷu* ("Ragaḷes for Śiva's Attendants") or, simply, *Hariharana Ragaḷegaḷu* ("Harihara's Ragaḷes").

composed by Harihara, an accomplished Kannada poet who lived in the town of Hampi. Part of the text's historical significance has to do with the fact that it was the first written account of the devotees of the Kannada-speaking region. Therefore, it is the earliest testimony we have for how saintly figures considered by many to be the founders of Vīraśaivism were remembered. Despite (or perhaps because of) its chronological antecedence to the myriad subsequent retellings of these saints' stories, Harihara's text was almost completely forgotten by the tradition itself and by outsiders to the tradition. This book is the first English-language study dedicated to the religious significance of the *Ragaḷegaḷu* and more specifically to the manner in which *model devotional life* was understood by its author. In contrast to the later authors, Harihara allowed some of his protagonists to be imperfect and fallible, and some others to embrace mainstream temple worship and Brahminical customs. More broadly, the saints that populate the stories in Harihara's hagiographical accounts have diverse social backgrounds and multiple, syncretic ways of worshipping the god. Given this diversity, this collection of saintly stories is distinct from the more separationist and communalist historical memory of the saints. Therefore, the greater importance of paying attention to the *Ragaḷegaḷu* lies in the potential for correcting perceptions of this tradition's religious history by giving access to the tradition's earliest moment of self-representation.

"Canonical" Vīraśaivism

In order to appraise the distinctiveness and significance of Harihara's literary vision of devotional life in the *Ragaḷegaḷu*, a brief sketch of what is today thought of the tradition is required. Many modern scholars in the West and in India have based their understandings of this tradition on a historical memory of the Vīraśaiva progenitors, a group of devotees who lived in the southwestern Deccan during the twelfth century. These early devotees are usually presented in scholarship as revolutionary iconoclasts and social reformers who, as precursors to modern stances, eschewed the caste system and were egalitarian.[7] This inherited "myth of origins" revolves around one community that emerged in a city called Kalyāṇa, the regional

7. The association of Vīraśaivism with "democratic" values can be located already in V. Raghavan's famous lectures on *bhakti* (Hawley 2015, 26–27). For depictions of Vīraśaivism as egalitarian, see Chekki (2012); Ramaswamy (2007, 145–94; 1996); Schouten (1995); Ishwaran (1992, 1983).

capital of the Cālukya Empire, in a period when the city was ruled by a former feudal commander of the Cālukyas, Bijjaḷa II of the Kalacūri dynasty. According to the traditional and tragic story that was (and still is) retold in numerous texts and oral traditions, a large number of Śaivas gathered in Kalyāṇa around the leadership of Basavaṇṇa, the talented treasurer of King Bijjaḷa, and formed a society of devotees who openly transgressed caste and social barriers to form a classless society focused on personal belief, unmediated and open worship of the god, and a stringent work ethic. This radical and progressive social experiment was soon crushed by the king who, swayed by the conservative religious and social mainstream, expelled these Śaivas from his kingdom, leading to their dispersal throughout south India. Retaliation soon followed. King Bijjaḷa was assassinated. Kalyāṇa, which had been the brilliant capital of the Deccan for three centuries, was torn apart by political and social strife, ruined forever.

This brief sketch largely explains the attention the tradition continues to receive from the Western academy—it dramatically anticipates modern social and religious views. Max Weber was among the Western scholars to pay attention to the Vīraśaiva foundation story in his *Hinduismus und Buddhismus*, originally published in 1916. Despite the scarcity of translated material at the time, Weber provided an account of Basavaṇṇa's exploits in Kalyāṇa and using this as a basis,[8] he developed a sociological analysis of the early tradition, describing it as a "type of particularly sharp and principled 'protestant' reaction to the Brahmans and the caste order,"[9] which with time was assimilated into the Hindu social system of castes. Weber explained his reference to the activities of the twelfth-century devotees as "protestant" by several features that appeared to him as similar with those characterizing the Protestant religion: the religious egalitarianism propounded by the early devotees and their alleged rejection of traditional and elaborate worship practices and of the social hierarchy ("caste order" in Weber's words), and—somewhat less pronounced in Weber's analysis but clearly informing his understanding of the tradition—the centrality of faith-based personal morality and an uncompromising work ethic.

8. See the recounting of Basavaṇṇa's story in Kalyāṇa in Weber (1958, 304–5). Weber mentions the *Basava Purāṇa* as the story's source but adds that he could not read the untranslated materials, and it is difficult to determine whether he was referring to the Telugu original from the late thirteenth century or its Kannada translation from a century later (1958, 383n26).

9. Ibid., 19.

Weber's framing of the discussion about Vīraśaivism as the "Great Indian Reformation" anticipated much Western writing on the Vīraśaivas in the twentieth century, particularly during the 1980s and 1990s.[10] But the contemporary and prevalent Western understanding of the Vīraśaivas has been most significantly shaped by a literary study from the early 1970s, a book entitled *Speaking of Śiva*. Here, A. K. Ramanujan presented a masterful set of English translations of several hundred *vacanas* (devotional poems, pronounced as *va*-cha-na, literally "sayings") attributed to the early Śaiva devotees of the Kannada-speaking region. In *Speaking of Śiva*, Ramanujan offered an elegant, humane, and liberal portrayal of the early Kannada devotional tradition. With its two brief but encompassing appendices, one describing the theology and the other the society of the tradition, *Speaking of Śiva* became the unrivaled standard for introducing the Vīraśaivas, South Asian devotionalism, and even Hinduism more broadly to a variety of English-speaking audiences worldwide.[11] When R. Blake Michael writes in 2015 that "Ramanujan's little book is, as always, the best place to start,"[12] it is difficult not to agree with him.

The following *vacana* translated by Ramanujan is probably the most often-quoted poem associated with the Vīraśaivas in modern scholarship. Placed at the very beginning of Ramanujan's introduction to the tradition, this *vacana* demonstrates the overall appeal of Ramanujan's project:

> The rich
> will make temples for Śiva.
> What shall I,

10. See as examples Michael (1992, 1982) and Ishwaran (1983).

11. In the recent and detailed survey of scholarly literature about the Vīraśaiva tradition composed for Oxford Bibliographies by R. Blake Michael, he writes that Ramanujan's *Speaking of Śiva* "provides the most aesthetically pleasing and ethically motivating translations of selected *vachanas* available in English" (2015, 2) and adds: "This best-of-all introduction to Virashaivism is a remarkable coalescence of the poet's muse with the scholar's mind" (ibid.). In her 2004 novel *In Times of Siege*, award-winning author Githa Hariharan takes inspiration from the story of Basavaṇṇa and his poetry to portray a modern clash between a liberal intellectual group and a mob of violent and conservative Hindus. Hariharan uses Ramanujan's translations for all the *vacanas* quoted in her book (except for one that was translated by Ramanujan's student, Kamil V. Zvelebil) and writes in the acknowledgments: "In 1974, when I was a student in Bombay, a friend gave me a copy of Ramanujan's book, and this inspiring translation of medieval vachanas was my introduction to the poetry and ideas of Basava. Now, more than twenty-five years later, I find that my pleasure in these translations, and my gratitude for them, endures" (2003, 206).

12. Michael (2015, 8).

a poor man,
do?

My legs are pillars,
the body the shrine,
the head a cupola
of gold.

Listen, O lord of the meeting rivers,
things standing shall fall,
but the moving ever shall stay.
(*vacana* no. 820)[13]

This poem expresses the progressive social and religious attitudes that would be identified with Vīraśaivas as they came to be understood by outsiders to the tradition, both in India and abroad. It is an understanding that reflects the personal voice articulated in this *vacana*, a voice that resonates deeply with the sensibilities of the modern and progressive individual. This voice identifies itself with the socially and economically weak and with those who are usually absent from or marginalized by elitist pre-modern literary works. Socially, it seeks the individual's immediate, and spontaneous autonomy—an autonomy not simply disconnected from social ideals such as propriety and economic welfare but deliberately and radically opposed to them. Religiously, this poem expresses a living, interiorized, and embodied spiritual experience that is clearly contrasted with institutionalized and collective religion and with public ritual formalism. Its rhetorical power is due not only to the intrinsic qualities of the original *vacana* but also to Ramanujan's extraordinary poetic sensibilities, his bold choices for translating Kannada terms, and the unexpected line breaks he introduces to produce both dramatic effect and compelling cadence.[14]

13. Ramanujan (1973, 19).

14. See Ramanujan's reflections on his translation strategies in ibid., 13. Ramanujan's dramatic line breaking was unconventional in its time, and though his practice of translating key terms rather than transliterating them in the original (in the case of this *vacana*, Kūḍalasaṅgamadēva as "Lord of the Meeting Rivers," *jaṅgama* as "the moving," and *sthāvara* as "things standing") has been criticized over the years by some, his rare talent in translating *vacanas* is generally lauded to this day. See the recent monograph on Ramanujan's poetics by Rodríguez (2016).

Although it was not Ramanujan's intention, his depiction of the Vīraśaiva spirit in some of the major *vacanas* would become identified by many in the academy and outside it with the tradition as a whole and regarded as its religious "essence." Ramanujan's aim was to highlight a specifically compelling aspect of a pre-modern south-Indian tradition that would resonate well with modern spiritual and social attitudes.[15] Yet his book's exceptional appeal and popularity have tended to obfuscate the fuller and more complex history and nature of the Kannada tradition of Śiva devotion.[16] The fact is that there are persistent elements in the tradition's remembered history and vast literature that do not neatly fit into a clear geometry of liberal and progressive values. There are some thorny issues.

Even a cursory scholarly excavation of available resources about Vīraśaivas in the past and the present reveals the inconsistencies, gaps, and controversies that muddle the liberal narrative of "canonical" Vīraśaivism as it has been received through Ramanujan's work. For example, while the tradition is usually thought to have emerged in the twelfth century, some Vīraśaivas trace their roots to as early as the Indus Valley civilization, millennia prior to the Common Era, and minimize the historical significance and ingenuity of the twelfth-century devotees. Disagreement among Vīraśaiva scholars, public intellectuals, and religious leaders also prevails with regard to other aspects of the tradition. There is open disagreement about which texts constitute the core of the tradition's canon: is it the Kannada *vacana* poetry or a broader frame of reference including Sanskrit texts such as the Śaiva Āgamas? about the relation of the Vīraśaiva tradition to Brahminical orthodoxy and to Hinduism: is it a separate religion or an aspect of Brahminical and Vedic thought? about the early devotees' attitudes toward temple worship: did they reject or affirm it? toward caste: is the tradition anti-caste or caste-driven and hierarchical?

---

15. In the "Translator's Note" section of Ramanujan's book, he describes his choice of *vacanas* in personal, subjective, and vague terms (ibid., 12), and adds: "I can only hope that my needs are not entirely eccentric or irrelevant to the needs of others in the two traditions, the one I translate from and the one I translate into" (ibid., 13). Ramanujan's selection of *vacanas* to include (and those not to include) in the book, as well as the prefacing prose for each of the four saints included in the book, point to his modern sensibilities. For example, when describing the Kalyāṇa community, he writes: "A new community with egalitarian ideals disregarding caste, class and sex grew in Kalyāṇa, challenging orthodoxy, rejecting social convention and religious ritual" (1973, 63). The following discussion in this introduction and in Chapters 3 and 4 of this book complicate the depiction of Kalyāṇa in modern terms.

16. The incompleteness of Ramanujan's presentation of the tradition was directly addressed, probably for the first time, by Michael (1983, 309).

about women's roles in society: is it gender-equal or conservative and patriarchal? toward the religious community as a whole: is it inclusive and egalitarian or exclusive and elitist? and whether it should be classified as a "sect" or rather as a "church," to use the categories of classical Weberian studies? And while this list of antipodes appears exhaustive, or at least exhausting, it surely can be extended even further.[17]

The incongruities inherent within the Vīraśaiva tradition itself are acknowledged in some Western scholarship but are rarely dealt with, and discussions of their possible implications for our understanding of the tradition are even rarer. In 1983, for instance, R. Blake Michael published an article on the centuries-old institutional schism of Vīraśaivism into two major denominations, the more "protestant" Viraktas and the more "catholic" Gurusthalins (aka Pañcācāryas), noting that these two put forth competing ideals of what the tradition should be.[18] Michael's study deals primarily with the historical complexities that affected the Vīraśaiva tradition from the fourteenth century onward, but it did not open the way to fully consider the ways in which these historical reconfigurations would reshape historical memory of the twelfth-century movement and the *vacana* canon associated with it. This allows him to proceed without questioning Weber's and Ramanujan's understanding of how the tradition matured, according to which it moved away from its original core values as time passed. As Ramanujan put it, "in course of time, the heretics are canonized; temples are erected to them, Sanskrit hagiographies are composed about them. . . . They

17. In his recent entry on Vīraśaivas/Liṅgāyats in *Brill's Encyclopedia of Hinduism*, Michael addresses the tension inherent in describing the tradition. Early in the entry, right after presenting the usual descriptions of the tradition ("radically reformatory social movement . . . in favor of social equality . . . a gender-equality movement . . . comparable to Protestant Christianity's challenge to priestly domination from Rome"), Michael writes: "The full reality of Vīraśaivism also exhibits complex inter-mixtures of other, often contradictory characteristics. For example, in actual practice, Vīraśaivism has developed a social class system distinct from but, more or less, parallel to the caste system of broader Indian society. They have tried to free women from numerous social and cleanliness restrictions, but most have continued to live lives of ascribed social and family roles. And a network of holy places, attended by a hereditary lineage of priestly families, has served the religious needs of the laity as surely as have Brahmans for Hindus at large. . . . Even the name of the movement—Vīraśaiva or Liṅgāyat—and the aptness of its description as 'Hindu' reveal this complexity" (2011, 378–79, original references ommitted). See also Lal (2017).

18. Michael (1983). Also worth mentioning is the 1979 re-issue of S. C. Nandimath's *A Handbook of Vīraśaivism* with a new introduction by R. N. Nandi (Nandimath 1979 [1942]).

become, in retrospect, founders of a new caste, and are defied in turn by new egalitarian movements."[19]

This relatively stable historical understanding of early egalitarian Vīraśaivism was challenged for the first time in 1997, when Robert Zydenbos wrote an incisive book review in which he argued against a simplistic understanding of pre-modern Vīraśaivism as being democratic, egalitarian, or proto-feminist.[20] He also challenged the idea that an originally egalitarian somehow gone bad over time. Zydenbos called attention to the modern interest in presenting the early tradition in terms of a Western framework, and he called attention to *vacana*s that were associated with the progenitors of the tradition but did not cohere with the liberal and compelling vision sketched so masterfully by Ramanujan and others.

Prithvi Datta Chandra Shobhi's dissertation at the University of Chicago came on the scene in 2005 like a postmodern "big bang." Chandra Shobhi further destabilized the core narratives of "canonical" Vīraśaivism by casting doubt on the historicity of the canonical *vacana*s. He traced their earliest transmission in writing—through anthologies and other literary works—to the Vijayanagara era, about three centuries after they purportedly had been composed in oral form.[21] According to Chandra Shobhi, the fifteenth-century textual project of canonizing the *vacana*s was conducted on massive scale; as a result, in part, we have no access to their form beforehand. Chandra Shobhi also pointed to the political, institutional, and sectarian motivations that propelled the Viraktas, leaders of the Kannada Śivabhakti tradition in this period, to undertake a well-orchestrated project of framing the voices of the twelfth-century devotees in social and political terms that would resonate with new contexts of the fifteenth century. He wrote:

> The *virakta* ascetics from 15th century Vijayanagara produced the authoritative accounts of the Kalyāṇa of the 1160s, which form the

19. Ramanujan (1973, 36).

20. Zydenbos (1997). The issue of applying a modern vocabulary to pre-modern South Asia is dealt with differently in Novetzke (2016, 26–27), where Novetzke argues for what he terms (following others) "strategic anachronism."

21. With the exception of Dunkin Jalki's work, no study has yet considered the implications of this historical revision. An antecedent methodological gesture toward this line of thinking can be found in the classic study by El. Basavarāju in Kannada of Allama Prabhu's earliest *vacana* manuscripts (2001 [1960]); see especially pp. 29–38.

> basis of our historical consciousness of the movement. Since these ascetics were instrumental in collecting and interpreting *vacanas*, their accounts have come to be considered the contexts in which *vacanas* were [originally] uttered.[22]

Chandra Shobhi also discussed the creative process of editing, arranging, and publishing *vacanas* in modern printed editions, starting from the nineteenth century,[23] and he arrived at the conclusion that notions held today about twelfth-century "Vīraśaivas" by insiders and outsiders alike inevitably reflect later and quite massive revisions that took place at different moments in history. To demonstrate the validity of this claim, Chandra Shobhi pointed to the scheme of *ṣaṭsthalas*, the six-phase scale of spiritual progression in Vīraśaiva theology. The bulk of *vacana* collections and translations during the last two centuries, including Ramanujan's *Speaking of Śiva,* arrange the *vacanas* according to these six phases, so that every *vacana* is understood to have given expression to a specific spiritual disposition that the poet in question had achieved by the time of its composition.[24] The textual genealogy of the *ṣaṭsthalas*, however, goes back only to the fourteenth century, the time to which the Vīraśaiva text that introduces these *ṣaṭsthalas*, the Sanskrit *Siddhāntaśikhāmaṇi*, has been dated by most scholars. Consequently, Chandra Shobhi raised the question of whether it is possible to ignore their institutional and interpretive effect, as we attempt to understand what the original *vacanas*, whatever they were, were trying to say.[25]

Chandra Shobhi's project need not completely disconnect the *vacanas* from the twelfth-century movement to which they are attributed, however. The immense influence of the twelfth-century Kannada Śaivas and their *vacanas* on the region's history and culture seems, at least in my view, too substantial to be explained if we to accept such a radical historical revision wholesale. Yet, Chandra Shobhi's contextualizing of the *vacana* canonization at a considerably later period than the twelfth century does give rise to reservations regarding the viability of historical readings of

22. Chandra Shobhi (2005, 86).

23. Ibid., 101–16.

24. Ramanujan (1973, 65).

25. Chandra Shobhi (2005, 252–93). Dunkin Jalki's dissertation from 2009 was made known to me only recently and is not discussed in this book. However, it clearly furthers scholarly understanding of the vacanas' redescription during the colonial and post-independence eras.

vacanas as products of the earlier period.[26] We must recognize that the grammatical forms and lexical choices they display may actually reflect a later period than the time when Basavaṇṇa and others actually lived. Such potential disconnects also extend to theological terms, networks of saints and locales, and—perhaps most important—ideological claims made in the *vacanas*. In short, reconsideration of the early *vacanas*' textual authenticity inevitably affects our understanding of the origins of the Vīraśaiva tradition, if only because the *vacanas* are still the most commonly read source for its nascent moments.[27] I am reminded of an admonition made by Winand M. Callewaert with regard to the famous north-Indian *bhakti* poet Kabīr: "I can understand that a translator of Kabīr may look for a nice song without bothering about its authenticity. But let us not start writing commentaries on Kabīr and fifteenth century Banaras quoting those songs."[28] There is nothing sensational in noting that oral traditions change and that practitioners often fail to "register" those changes, but it is equally clear that the historical implications of this truism are not always fully acknowledged and accounted for, even in critical research.

A further significance of Chandra Shobhi's emphasis on the fact that the Viraktas flourished within the context of the Vijayanagara Empire lies in that this empire exercised an enormous influence on religious traditions throughout south India. The Vijayanagara court patronized religion mainly through networks of religious institutions called *maṭhas* (often translated as "monasteries"). This practice underscored the boundaries between religious sects and encouraged competition among them.[29] The Virakta *maṭhas* were outside the tight circles of power of the Vijayanagara court—certainly by the time of the empire's apex during the reign of

---

26. Although historical obscurities regarding the twelfth-century devotees and *vacanas* associated with them are glaring, they usually pass unnoticed. For example, Ramanujan and others situate the earliest *vacana* composer, Dēvara Dāsimayya, in the tenth century but assign most of the other *vacana* composers to the twelfth century, without considering the gap of two centuries between them (Ramanujan 1973, 11, 91–94; Basavarāju 2001 [1960]). This is problematic for several reasons that are outside the scope of this study. More recent studies in Kannada point, with substantial support, to the early twelfth century as the beginning of *vacanas*' oral composition. See Nāgabhūṣaṇa (2000).

27. See, for example, the discussion about Basavaṇṇa's life based on *vacanas* in Samartha (1977).

28. Kabir et al. (2000, vii). I second this assertion without committing to the subsequent effort to recover the "authentic" poems by Kabīr. Linda Hess's recent study of the oral tradition of Kabīr (2015) sheds light on some of the complexities involved. Also, see John S. Hawley's discussion of the anthologies of north-Indian *bhakti* poets (2005, 76–77).

29. Stoker (2016, 8).

King Kṛṣṇadēvarāya (1509–1529 CE)[30]—yet they were deeply influenced by the sectarian culture of the period. For the monastic institutions that identified with the local Śivabhakti tradition (as well as with other religious traditions), the competitive politico-religious culture generated new anxieties and concerns that prompted them to anchor their religious worldview in a collective remembered history. Thus, some institutions affiliated with Śaiva devotion—such as those connected with the Viraktas—took the Kannada devotional tradition in a new direction by realigning the collective memory of the twelfth-century devotees and the *vacana* poetry associated with them according to new constructions of collective self.[31] Moreover, the Viraktas were by no means the only ones to colonize the collective past of the twelfth-century devotees for the purpose of their own institutional agendas. The Gurusthalins mentioned earlier serve as another example of such appropriation, and the Ārādhyas of the Śaiva center at Śrīśailam yet another.[32] These various institutional lineages are interwoven in complex ways still mostly uncharted and little understood, yet it is evident that a critical unraveling of the appropriation of historical memory by various institutions during the Vijayanagara period is essential for an informed understanding of Vīraśaivism from that moment onward. In light of these uncertainties and the indelible influence of the Vijayanagara period on how the early tradition is remembered today, it becomes especially important to pay attention to regional Śaiva sources that predate that period. This book focuses on the earliest among them.

My book differs from studies that use the lyrical poetry of the *vacana*s as their main source by focusing instead on saints' stories produced at a very early stage of the tradition, roughly fifty years after the purported activity of the twelfth-century devotees. The poems in the *Ragaḷegaḷu* corpus are clearly distinguishable from the *vacana*s on several formal textual levels. First, the majority of the Ragaḷes are well-crafted narratives and not lyrical poems; they are considerably longer than the *vacana*s, with some having several hundred verses and others running to more than a thousand (some Ragaḷes are so long that they have been divided into chapters

30. Ibid., 7–10. See also Chandra Shobhi (2005, 116–37); Verghese (1995). In addition, there was a systemic linguistic disconnect between Kannada and literary production at the Vijayanagara court, which was mostly in Telugu, Tamil, and Sanskrit (Pollock 2001, 400–401).

31. See Devadevan (2016) on the religious history of the region.

32. Reddy (2014).

called *sthalas*). Second, the Ragaḷes strictly adhere to a standardized meter while also containing long prose sections. And third, unlike the *vacanas*, they were composed by a person skilled in the conventional, Sanskritized courtly idiom of classical Kannada poetry. All this separates the *Ragaḷegaḷu* from the early *vacanas*, placing it closer to other forms of written literature produced in Kannada. The *Ragaḷegaḷu* marks the starting point of a highly prolific and innovative tradition of writing biographies about local Śaiva devotees, a tradition that maintained a central position in Kannada literature for at least the following three centuries.

With the *Ragaḷegaḷu* as a guide, I would argue that the heterogeneity of this Kannada Śivabhakti tradition was inherent to it and, in addition, one of its most significant defining features from a very early stage. The *Ragaḷegaḷu* was composed during the first decades of the thirteenth century. Long before the Vijayanagara Empire with its sectarian politics—though, ironically, situated in the same city of Hampi—this text projected a catholic and inclusive thrust that was antithetical to the idea of a closed sect or a religious community. The *Ragaḷegaḷu* does celebrate the uncompromising flavor of Kannada devotionalism that we find in Basavaṇṇa's *vacana* no. 820, but at the same time it accommodates traditional norms and mainstream religious practices. According to the religious vision in this hagiographical collection, the fact of being a passionate or heroic devotee of the god Śiva could be enacted in manifold ways; to be adamant about one's faith led naturally to very individual forms of religious self-expression. This multiplicity challenges most of the going notions about "what Vīraśaivism really is."

A central assertion I make in this book, therefore, is that the author of the *Ragaḷegaḷu* understood the foundation of being a Śiva devotee in a way that is very different from what fifteenth-century Viraktas, modern Vīraśaiva formalists and separationists, and modern and progressive social activists have proclaimed. Judging by the *Ragaḷegaḷu*'s stories about the Kannada saints, there is no formal or correct manner to worship Śiva, nor a systematized theological framework to adhere to, nor a specific sectarian or social identity that distinguishes Śaiva devotees from non-devotees. The only unifying principle of the Śaiva characters who populate the *Ragaḷegaḷu* is an uncompromising dedication to Śiva—a stance that can be and is naturally expressed in many forms.

The pliable and open-ended treatment of core issues in the *Ragaḷegaḷu* can be seen, for example, in its descriptions of worship practices. Chapter 7 in the Ragaḷe that concerns Basavaṇṇa is dedicated to describing the collective worship of the *śivaliṅga*, an event held at the charismatic leader's private palace.[33] This passage depicts in detail how worship procedures—although sharing a basic grammar—vary greatly from one devotee to another. The overall message of the passage that one should be free to worship according to one's preference conforms to the familiarly accepted ideal of this tradition, namely that worship is essentially a personal matter that can unfold in personal ways, in contrast to formal and publicly orchestrated temple worship. But this passage is different from many others in the *Ragaḷegaḷu*, for they depict devotees of Basavaṇṇa's region and period as worshiping in a traditional temple.[34] The two modes of devotion—the spontaneous and personal on the one hand and the traditional and collective on the other hand—coexist in the *Ragaḷegaḷu* without any overarching unifying framework or attempt to reconcile them. This seminal text contains other incongruities pertaining to various aspects of devotional life as well. As our discussion proceeds, we will examine how the *Ragaḷegaḷu* offers us different perspectives on social status (Chapter 3), traditional Brahmanical orthodoxy (Chapter 4), courtly patronage (Chapter 5), and the religious other (Chapters 5 and 6). The picture that emerges is quite different from the "canonical" view of Vīraśaivism that has subsequently come to be embraced. There may be a reason why Harihara is so little read by the leading Vīraśaiva institutions today.

Śaraṇas, not Vīraśaivas

Broadening our horizon to consider texts by and about Kannada Śivabhaktas that are outside the *vacana* canon radically affects our knowledge of the early tradition. A key finding in this regard is that the words *vīraśaiva* and *liṅgāyata* are either completely missing or *hapax legomena* in non-*vacana* Kannada texts until the fourteenth century.[35] The profusive

33. Chapter 7 in the *Basavēśvaradēvara Ragaḷe* (Harihara and Suṅkāpura 1976, 53–59).

34. See Ben-Herut (2016).

35. The only written Kannada text prior to the fourteenth century that contains the words *vīraśaiva* and *liṅgāyata* is the early twelfth-century *Śīlamahatvada Kanda* ("A Poem in the *Kanda* Meter about the Glory of Proper Conduct") by Koṇḍaguḷi Kēśirāja, in which each word appears only once (Kēśirāja 1978, 59). Claims about the historical origins of Vīraśaivism are often influenced by contemporary political and social interests and contain obscure or incomplete historical information. Eṃ. Cidānandamūrti, a leading Kannada scholar who posits pre-Basavaṇṇa origins for the Vīraśaiva tradition, sees the single appearance of these terms in the *Śīlamahatvada Kanda* as indicative of the existence of a pre-Basavaṇṇa Vīraśaiva communal identity in Kannada (1989, 12–18; Chidananda Murthy 1983, 204–5). Eṃ. Eṃ. Kalaburgi,

use of *vīraśaiva* in written devotional literature in Kannada, then, starts relatively late—some two hundred years after the Kalyāṇa events. The issue is further complicated by the fact that the word *vīraśaiva* appears to have been imported from an extrinsic source—the Telugu *Basava Purāṇamu*, a text composed by the polyglot and prolific writer Pālkuriki Sōmanātha in the adjacent Andhra region. Although this text was created not much later than the *Ragaḷegaḷu*, its immense influence on the Kannada public memory of Basavaṇṇa and the early devotees—including the extensive use of the epithet *vīraśaiva*, so tightly connected with the tradition today—probably did not begin until a century later, when the Kannada poet Bhīmakavi translated the text in 1369. There is also a semantic complication. Whereas the Telugu poet Sōmanātha used in his *Basava Purāṇamu* the term *vīramāhēśvara* to refer to the twelfth-century Śaiva devotees, Bhīmakavi replaced this term in his Kannada translation with a cognate term, *vīraśaiva*. It is possible that Bhīmakavi's translational choice was inspired by the foundational Vīraśaiva text, the *Siddhāntaśikhāmaṇi* ("The Crown Jewel of Doctrines"), composed in Sanskrit, presumably not much earlier. That text argues, somewhat tortuously, that despite clear divergences in worship practices, there is actually no difference between Vīramāhēśvaras and Vīraśaivas.[36] Furthermore, the terminological rabbit hole of *vīraśaiva* runs deep also at the other end of the chronological line—perhaps as early as the ninth or tenth century—and in yet another Dravidian language, this time Tamil.[37]

---

another central figure in Kannada scholarship and a promoter of separation of Liṅgāyatism from Hinduism, argues against the application of the term *vīraśaiva* with regard to the twelfth-century Bhaktas and questions the authenticity of the single appearance of *vīraśaiva* in Kēśirāja's text (2010 [1998]-a, 197–98; 2010 [1998]-b). Examples of the ongoing debate in Kannada public discourse and scholarship with regard to when the term *vīraśaiva* started to appear, and what it designated prior to the thirteenth century, include Savadattimaṭha (2009) and the heated exchange of opinions in the op-ed pages of the *Prajāvāṇi* and the *Vijaya Karnāṭaka* in 2011 (Cidānandamūrti 2011b; Savadattimaṭha 2011; Kalaburgi 2011; Maridēvaru 2011; Cidānandamūrti 2011a). See also the earlier footnote in this introduction regarding the contemporary debate on the relation between the terms *vīraśaiva* and *liṅgāyata*.

36. The possibility of distinguishing between Śaivas and Māhēśvaras is clearly a cause for concern in the *Siddhāntaśikhāmaṇi*, as attested in verses 5.19–21, in which the author argues that there is no substantial difference between the two groups, even though the former worship god internally and the latter externally. The commentator Maritoṇṭadarāya's insistence on identifying *māhēśvara* with *vīraśaiva* and *śaiva* with *vīraśaiva* seems to further deepen the conceptual morass (Śivayogiśivācārya and Maritoṇṭadārya 2007, 99–101). Similar complexity can be evinced in Nijaguṇa Śivayōgi's *Vivēkacintāmaṇi* v. 2.266ff.

37. R. N. Nandi claims that the early canonical text for the Tamil Śaivas called *Tirumantiram* has the terms *vīramāhēśvara* and *ṣaṭsthala*, both of which are key in the theology laid out in

In short, the historical, linguistic, and geographical breadth of the term *vīraśaiva* goes far beyond and away from the twelfth-century Kannada devotees. It is exactly for this reason that the association of the signifier *vīraśaiva* and the signified memory of the twelfth century—an association that today is considered to be categorical—needs to be reconsidered. The appearance of the translated *Basava Purāṇa* in the late fourteenth century, with its heavy use of the term *vīraśaiva* for the first time in written Kannada (that is, with the exclusion of the *vacanas*), could indicate that it was only at this moment in history—or not much sooner—that *vīraśaiva* became synonymous with the memory of the twelfth-century devotees, as well as with the Kannada Śivabhakti tradition as a whole, with yet broader transregional networks of institutionalized forms of Śaivism such as those of the Pāśupātas and the Kāḷāmukhas, and with established Śaiva centers such as the one at Śrīśailam, headed by local Ārādhyas.

Even if we assume that the words *vīraśaiva* and *liṅgāyata* in Kannada written literature before the fourteenth century were actually penned by the purported authors, the fact that these words appear only rarely and sporadically indicates that the early devotional tradition in the Kannada-speaking region thought of itself in different terms. In this book my interest is deliberately restricted to this nascent phase, that is, to the Kannada Śivabhakti tradition *prior* to its association with Vīraśaivism.

In the *Ragaḷegaḷu* stories about the Kannada devotees, the terms *vīraśaiva* and *liṅgāyata*, like other familiar labels associated with Śaiva sects of this milieu, do not appear even once.[38] Instead, the author Harihara refers to devotees (whether *en masse* or as individuals) using the very general term *śivabhaktas*, a nondenominational label used across the subcontinent to refer to devotees of Śiva.[39] Harihara also interchangeably employs terms that are specific to the Kannada devotees: *nūtanapurātanas* (new elders),

---

the much later *Siddhāntaśikhāmaṇi* (Nandimath 1979 [1942], xxviii–xxix). Nandi, however, does not provide specific verse numbers in the *Tirumantiram*.

38. The Śaiva sects unmentioned in the Kannada stories in this text are Kāpālikas, Pāśupātas, Lākuḷīśas, and Kāḷāmukhas. On these traditions, see Lorenzen (1991, 1988).

39. In some cases, such as in the *Basavēśvaradēvara Ragaḷe* 7.2 (Harihara and Suṅkāpura 1976, 53), Harihara refers to the mass of devotees in his stories as *māhēśvaras*, but without prefixing the term with *vīra*. Read in context, it is clear that he uses *māhēśvara* in a general sense as synonymous with *śaiva* and not in a sect-specific sense.

jaṅgamas (roaming renouncers), *śivagaṇas* (Śiva's attendants), and *śaraṇas* (seekers of refuge [in Śiva]). The latter term is tightly linked by the later tradition to the twelfth-century devotees.[40]

Harihara's lexical choices just charted are clear and consistent, but I wish to note that in this study I refer to the early devotional culture of the Kannada-speaking region in the twelfth and thirteenth century as "Kannada Śivabhakti" and not as "Vīraśaiva/Liṅgāyata," not because of pedantic meticulousness about the absence of the latter terms from the *Ragaḷegaḷu* text but to signify in a deeper sense the way the early tradition thought of itself. Historically speaking, it makes more sense to refer to the twelfth-century devotees of the Kannada-speaking region as Śaraṇas than as Vīraśaivas, with the underlying premise that being a Śaraṇa meant something different from what we think that being a Vīraśaiva meant. The title of this book, "Śiva's Saints," reflects this claim, and I explain my choice to translate *śaraṇa* as "saint" below.

There are other lexical gaps in the *Ragaḷegaḷu* that have significance for our understanding of the early tradition. When Harihara mentions or cites devotional songs by famous *vacana* composers—and he does so only rarely—he refers to their literary output using the general term *gīte* (literally, "song") and not *vacana*.[41] In fact, the words *vacana* (in the particular sense of this poetic tradition) and *vacanakāras* (for *vacana* composers) are completely absent from Harihara's *Ragaḷegaḷu* as well as from other early works.[42] Similarly, when Harihara describes the settings in which the *vacana* composers met, he calls these settings *gōṣṭhis* (assemblies); he never mentions the *anubhava maṇṭapa*, a term that is today synonymous with the setting in which the early devotees assembled under the leadership of Basavaṇṇa in Kalyāṇa to

40. The word *śaraṇa* later came to signify also the fifth and high spiritual state in the *ṣaṭsthala* theological scheme.

41. Furthermore, Harihara's occasional mentioning of "songs of/about the elders" (*purātanagītegaḷu*) seems to refer to a previous devotional tradition outside the Kannada-speaking region (Ben-Herut 2015, 278). The only two Kannada devotees in the *Ragaḷegaḷu* who are minimally credited with composing poetry are Basavaṇṇa and Mahādēviyakka.

42. The first appearance of the term *vacana* with the specific sense of a devotional utterance associated with the twelfth-century Śivabhaktas is in Rāghavāṅka's *Siddharāma Cāritra* 4.73, 9.20, 9.27, 9.38 (Rāghavāṅka and Vivēka Rai 2004), although this and other sporadic appearances do not necessarily convey the later Vīraśaiva appreciation of *vacana* as a form of discourse or as a poetic genre. See also Devadevan (2016, 14n50); Basavarāju (2001 [1960], 24nA).

compose *vacanas*.[43] Yet another popular Vīraśaiva referent missing from Harihara's text is Cennabasava, who is known in other texts as Basavaṇṇa's nephew.[44]

These lexical inconsistencies have important implications regarding the multiple imaginings, at different points in history, of the twelfth-century Śaraṇas.[45] Although the diachronic evolution of the Kannada Śivabhakti public memory has yet to be studied in any thorough manner, it is evident that the memory of Kalyāṇa has consistently played a unique role in it. For example, the fourth version of the *Śūnyasampādane* from the early sixteenth century imagines the twelfth-century Kalyāṇa community of Śaivas as vibrant, diverse, and dynamic, a community that encouraged internal discussions and even polemics among its members regarding the nature of true faith and the religious practices of the nascent devotional tradition.[46] What is significant for our discussion is that, like many later retellings, the *Śūnyasampādane* clearly depicts a historical *community*, one that is geographically placed in Kalyāṇa and is defined by a shared set of attitudes, such as resistance to temple worship and to Brahminical supremacy. Shaped by the political and social conditions of their times, these later accounts use the public memory of the twelfth-century saints in order to describe a bounded community labeled "Vīraśaiva," a community whose concerns were contemporary and involved patronage and sectarian competition at the Vijayanagara court, the threat of institutional schisms, and the securing of social superiority for its clergy.

In contrast, the devotional world evinced in Harihara's narratives from the thirteenth century is far less bounded. There is no geographical

---

43. The later part of the *Basavēśvaradēvara Ragaḷe* is lost to us today, and it is theoretically possible that the term *anubhava maṇṭapa* is mentioned there. However, the absence of the term from any other Ragaḷe and the pervasive usage of *gōṣṭhi* suggests that *anubhava maṇṭapa* was either nonexistent or of little importance in Harihara's Śivabhakti milieu.

44. Cennabasava is mentioned in hagiographies for the first time early in Basavaṇṇa's life story in the *Basava Purāṇamu* (Somanātha, Narayana Rao, and Roghair 1990, 71–72).

45. The public memory of the Kalyāṇa Śaivas, led by Basavaṇṇa, remains central for the local culture well into modernity, with a plethora of artistic and scholarly retellings regardless of the absence of concrete historiographical data on the purported events. One indication of modern Vīraśaiva nostalgic attachment to Kalyāṇa is the late 1960s renaming of the site Kalyāṇa as "Basavakalyāṇa" (Chandra Shobhi 2005, 26). Leslie (1998) deals with modern artistic representations of the imagined Vīraśaiva community of Kalyāṇa. Eaton and Wagoner's recent historical reconstruction of the Cālukyas of Kalyāṇa incorporates the Vīraśaivas into this empire's disintegration (2014, 14).

46. Michael (1992).

center in which the community of devotees "lives." While Kalyāṇa is clearly central in Harihara's narratives, it by no means constitutes the early tradition's geographical hub in the manner imagined in later accounts. Two short examples demonstrate this: when the early sixteenth-century *Śūnyasampādane* presents Mahādēviyakka, a female devotee to whom numerous *vacanas* are attributed and one of the most popular of the early saints, the text's entry point to her life story is her arrival in Kalyāṇa and her meeting with the Kalyāṇa Śaivas, an event that occasions profound theological conversations between Mahādēviyakka and other members of this community. A similar geographical and communal thrust toward Kalyāṇa is evinced in the Telugu *Basava Purāṇamu*, which was produced in the late thirteenth century. When this text narrates the exploits of the zealous devotee Ēkānta Rāmayya, they occur in Kalyāṇa, and he even briefly meets Basavaṇṇa. In the accounts by Harihara for these two devotees, neither arrives in Kalyāṇa nor gets to shake hands with its devotees. It is evident, then, that Harihara was not invested in collecting all the twelfth-century saintly figures under Basavaṇṇa's leadership in Kalyāṇa, as later writers were inclined to do.

The communal uniformity of Kalyāṇa implied by the later retellings is inconsistent with the heterogeneous presentation of the Śaraṇas in the *Ragaḷegaḷu*. Although some of the saintly figures in the corpus are located in Kalyāṇa, others operate in different periods and locations, and their status and social roles are similarly disparate. One implication of this disparity is that, in contrast to later literary attempts to imagine the twelfth-century devotees as a tightly knit community physically centered in Kalyāṇa and around the charismatic leadership of Basavaṇṇa, the protagonists of Harihara's stories rarely come into contact with each other, and their religious practices, like their social backgrounds, are bewilderingly diverse, involving both the mainstream and the nontraditional. It becomes evident that, unlike the more sectarian or communal later accounts, the early thirteenth-century *Ragaḷegaḷu* was shaped by an opposite impulse of appealing to people from different strands of society without implying the necessity for a compulsory or radical shift in terms of social identity. In the *Ragaḷegaḷu*, the saintly protagonists can be traditional Brahmin priests as well as outcasts. They can be men or women, young or old. They worship their god inside the temple as well as outside it, in solitude or in community, at the palace or in the forest. Moreover, in the intricate literary universe of the *Ragaḷegaḷu*, the differences between devotees hailing from different social and religious backgrounds are not easily mediated and are sometimes settled in complicated and ad hoc ways.

Harihara acknowledges this in an episode in the *Ragaḷegaḷu* that will be discussed in detail in Chapter 4. The episode captures both the inevitable tensions that arise between the diverse characters who populate the *Ragaḷegaḷu* and Harihara's narrative creativity in attempting to mitigate those tensions. A Śaiva devotee who is a hunter and a meat-eater is paid a visit by a fellow Śaiva devotee who happens to be a vegetarian Brahmin, and they both begin by worshiping Śiva together. But when the host's wife presents the guest with the ceremonial consecrated food (*prasāda*), the Brahmin is dumbfounded, as the food is made of meat curries. The Brahmin does not touch it, and the hunter, understanding the Brahmin's predicament, addresses the god Śiva and tells him to turn the meat into rice dishes. Śiva—who in this tradition is quick to accede to his devotees' requests—promptly turns the meat curries into delicious sweet dishes, and the Brahmin, greatly relieved, happily consumes the food. Although the crisis is resolved with the hunter's injunction to the god to accommodate the Brahmin's vegetarian restrictions, this resolution can be read as conveying a deeper truth with regard to Harihara's imagined world of Śaiva saints, according to which no social affiliation or difference should impede devotees from worshiping their god and the god, in turn, being always attentive to the devotees' different needs, even when those needs are associated with the elite Brahminical culture. In sum, it is evident that social interaction in Harihara's *Ragaḷegaḷu*—even among fellow Śaiva devotees—is fraught with difference, contradiction, and incongruity.

The *Ragaḷegaḷu* stories convey the author's efforts to navigate this complicated social terrain by accommodating everyone and everything as long as it is grounded in open and uninhibited devotion to Śiva. Thus in the case of Brahmins, vegetarianism, orthodox and elite education, and other Brahminical practices are accommodated, while still other Brahminical practices, such as the social exclusion of Untouchables, are utterly rejected. Alternatively, practices associated with the lower reaches of society such as meat eating are accepted, as long as they are connected both ritually and rhetorically with devotion to the god Śiva. The seemingly contradictory affirmation of both vegetarianism and the consumption of meat in the episode about the hunter and the Brahmin exemplifies the complex nexus of conflicting attitudes and behaviors that are endorsed in the saints' stories of the *Ragaḷegaḷu*. Such inherent pliability calls for a thorough reconsideration of early Kannada devotionalism and can serve as a model for understanding tensions within the later tradition as well.

Kannada Devotional Literature in History

The prolific non-*vacana* literature produced in the devotional idiom of Kannada over the past eight hundred years includes: (1) lyrical poetry influenced by but formally and historically separated from the *vacana* canon; (2) a vast narrative (mostly hagiographic) literature, generally referred to as the Vīraśaiva Purāṇas; and (3) theological, discursive, doctrinal, and commentarial works. These texts were mostly composed in Kannada, but also in Sanskrit, Telugu, and later in Tamil. While scholarly interest in making available more of the tradition's materials through translations and new studies of primary materials is hardly new, access to them is still limited.[47] Except for the *vacanas*, the bulk of Kannada Śivabhakti literature remains beyond the reach of non-Kannadigas, with the exception of two works: the fourth edition of the early sixteenth-century *Śūnyasampādane*, which was translated into English about half a century ago,[48] and the *Basava Purāṇamu*, a Telugu text composed most probably a few decades after the *Ragaḷegaḷu* and translated into English by Velcheru Narayana Rao and Gene H. Roghair in 1990.[49] The brighter side of this picture is that studies of texts by Kannada Śivabhakti authors and a broader consideration of this massive literary oeuvre are now in the works. They are apt to alter the field in dramatic ways.

In his influential book, *The Language of the Gods in the World of Men: Sanskrit, Culture, and Power in Premodern India*, Sheldon Pollock uses the classical period of literary composition in Old Kannada—spanning roughly from the ninth to the twelfth centuries—as a historical case study of how vernacular literary expression was deployed in courts to

47. An appeal for more translations and studies of the primary materials was made more than four decades ago by Raymond Allchin (1971).

48. This translation appears in five volumes and was reprinted in 2007. See Siddhavīraṇāryaru et al. (2007 [1965–1972]).

49. Somanātha, Narayana Rao, and Roghair (1990). The translations of the Kannada *Śūnyasampādane* and the Telugu *Basava Purāṇamu* were each followed by a limited amount of academic study. The *Śūnyasampādane* was studied by Michael (1992) and the *Basava Purāṇamu* was reviewed by and referred to by David Shulman (1993a; 1993b, respectively). A third translation, this time from Sanskrit, that did not yield much scholarly attention is the *Siddhāntaśikhāmaṇi* (Śivayogiśivācārya and Mariтoṇṭadārya 2007).

serve the ends of political power, a process Pollock refers to by using the term "cosmopolitan vernacular."[50] Pollock argues that vernacularization (the process of developing indigenous literary practices in the vernacular) in South Asia was mainly the product of elitist and courtly cultures that were invested in political power and that had only limited interest in religious identity and content.[51] In accordance with this paradigm, Pollock's meticulous consideration of classical Kannada literature traces the development of the cosmopolitan vernacular in this language from the middle of the first millennium in epigraphy and from the ninth century in written texts. His analysis concludes in the twelfth century with the Vīraśaivas and their *vacanas*. As to further developments in Kannada literature, Pollock perceptively acknowledges the dramatic change brought forth by this devotional trend, acknowledging that the "Vīraśaivas' new standards of culture certainly contributed to the demise of [courtly] Kannada cosmopolitan vernacularity."[52] He comments on the subsequent emergence of Kannada literature as a non-cosmopolitan, highly localized, and religious idiom, although he does not go on to investigate it.[53] The subject matter of this book, chronologically speaking, picks up where Pollock's commanding work leaves off.

Since I examine a single text produced at an early stage in the history of devotional Kannada literature, my comments on the religious turn in this literature cannot be comprehensive. Yet even on the basis of Harihara and other poets who came to form part of his orbit, it is possible to locate an intermediate creative space that came to exist between two literary modes that are more familiar to us: representatives of the literary species Pollock has identified as the cosmopolitan vernacular and the world of the *vacanas*. This intermediate space marks a crucial stage in the history of Kannada composition, one that is oftentimes obfuscated by the radical nature of the *vacanas*. The emergence of the *vacanas* in contrast to the hegemonic literary practices of the time was so dramatic (and self-consciously so) that—as a literary event of interest to contemporary historians—it tends to overshadow the more long-term and dialectic process that Kannada

50. Pollock (2006, 330–79 and throughout). See also Pollock (1998).

51. Ibid., 423–30.

52. Ibid., 434.

53. Pollock writes: "The new vernacularism, then—noncosmopolitan, regional, *deśi* in outlook—combined a different, local way of poetry making with a different, local way of spiritual being" (ibid., 436).

literature underwent in response to the *vacanas*' literary challenge. There is no denying that the essential force behind non-elite Kannada literature was the twelfth-century *vacanas*, which Pollock incisively describes as "an attempt to replace the cosmopolitan idiom with one far more regionalized in everything from lexicon to syntax . . . a totally new literary form, or better, an antiform. . . a consciously decultured form of composition . . . an almost postliterary form of literature."[54] Yet an examination of the devotional literary field as it developed after the production of the *vacanas* complicates this claim. It suggests that the *vacanas* did not act alone but rather served in the subsequent memory of Kannada-speaking people as a more general *punctum archimedis* for the intellectual project of understanding non-elite and devotional literature in Kannada. As D. R. Nagaraj's insightful survey of Kannada literary history shows, devotional literature had a fuller and more fully interventionist role in the history of Kannada vernacularization than whatever might be postulated by focusing solely on the "antiform" of the *vacanas*.

Kannada devotional literature produced after the *vacanas* did not only draw on the constellation of existing literary practices Pollock has identified as the cosmopolitan vernacular but also responded to it in creative ways that, in turn, reshaped formal literary composition in Kannada from then on.[55] The cultural gravitation of courtly literary production from the linguistic register of Old Kannada (*haḷegannaḍa*), one heavily marked by the pan-Indian idiom of Sanskrit literature, to the simplified, non-elite style of composition associated with what has come to be called Middle Kannada (*naḍugannaḍa*) stretched beyond the *vacanas*. The ongoing production of *vacanas* was doubtless a part of this picture, but in many ways it unfolded elsewhere. The *vacanas*' exerted an important influence on the whole process, serving as a sort of literary avant-garde, but the non-*vacana* literature that started to appear from the thirteenth century onward (or possibly even a century earlier)[56] suggests that the *vacanas*' influence often exerted from a certain distance. Those who created the *vacanas*

54. Ibid., 433.

55. To my knowledge, Nagaraj (2003) remains to date the only attempt in English to think about Kannada literature from a comprehensive historical perspective, including the role of devotional literature in it. This field is lagging behind other regions and traditions in South Asia also in terms of applied methods of textual criticism, codicology, and so on.

56. I refer here to the poetry attributed to Koṇḍaguḷi Kēśirāja, who is discussed below and in Chapter 5.

from outside formal literary circles produced oral, un-versified, lyrical utterances of a particularly condensed sort, but other devotional poets—trained in classical, courtly idiom and informed in the scholarly discourse about literature—also searched for new ways of composing literature. This literature also carried some of the devotional messages that are prominent in the *vacanas*, but did so in other literary forms. What these poets composed was, indeed, written poetry, unlike what is suggested by the meaning of the term *vacana*—utterance. Their poetry was not just written but prosodically formulized and their compositions were often lengthy. In terms of both form and content, this new literature was deeply inspired by the rebellious vision of the *vacanas*, but it also shared some literary practices and conventions with the literary establishment, rebelling not from without but from within. Rather than representing a total breach in regard to earlier practices of literary expression, they continued trends from the courtly idiom at the same time as they disrupted them. Thus the innovations introduced by *bhakti* poets took hold in cultural circles far broader than those that came to be defined by the sectarian comradeships we identify today as devotional communities.

Perhaps the most striking example of this pattern is the ubiquitous *ṣaṭpadi* genre, a local mora-based meter associated with a written literature that persisted from the thirteenth century to the late pre-modern period. *Ṣaṭpadi* poetry recorded in writing what had evidently earlier been a style that flourished in oral performance. Its application to written literature was widely appreciated, as evinced by the popularity of Kumāravyāsa's *Karṇātabhāratakathāmañjari* and Lakṣmīśa's *Jaiminibhāratam*, two works that used *ṣaṭpadi* and which we know to have circulated in a broad range of cultural circles. The first poet known to have produced complete works in the *ṣaṭpadi* meter was Harihara's nephew, Rāghavāṅka, famous for composing literature that concerns Śiva and his followers. Notably, the opening section of Rāghavāṅka's masterpiece *Hariścandra Carite*, which stands apart from the main narrative, addresses both devotional matters and those pertaining to literary practices and conventions.[57] In verse 1.18, Rāghavāṅka writes: "Sowing this seed, I have grown the tree of my poetry. You devotees of Shiva, eminent scholars, renowned aesthetes, and great connoisseurs of art, nourish this tree with your keen reading, water it with your tears of artistic delight, bask in the shade of its lush branches

57. *Hariścandra Carite* vv. 14–31 in Rāghavāṅka and Viswanatha 2017, 14–29.

replete with shades of meaning, and reap sweet taste from the fresh fruit that it bears on every flourishing bough."[58] In this verse we can locate both a devotional and a literary appeal using an extended metaphor such as one might well find in Sanskrit narrative poetry. In such a manner, devotional poets did not always consider themselves separated from mainstream literary practices. To the contrary, they made those very practices serve new purposes.

This book focuses on Rāghavāṅka's uncle Harihara. He was among the very first literary figures to give voice to the devotional spirit within the boundaries of formal literary composition. And within the range of Harihara's literary oeuvre, we will fix our attention on the *Ragaḷegaḷu*, which marks a dramatic shift in compositional style by using a single, local, very simple Kannada meter, a colloquial style of language, and daily and immediate themes and characters. In Chapter 1 I will discuss in detail the *Ragaḷegaḷu*'s exceptional literary character.[59]

At the opposite pole of Harihara's oeuvre is his *Girijākalyāṇa* ("The Betrothal of the Mountain's Daughter"), a lengthy poem composed in the classical style of courtly epic (*mahākāvya, mahāprabandham*), which involves varying long meters and dense poetic articulation, a style generally associated with courtly literature in the cosmopolitan vernacular. Despite adhering to the classical style in his *Girijākalyāṇa*, Harihara also infuses into this work nontraditional and non-elite elements. Such is the case, for example, with Harihara's intensive use in this text of *oḷaprāsa* ("inner rhyming," or the use of rhymes within a verse's feet), a literary device that was uncommon in the classical medium.[60] Thus, the diversity in Harihara's literary production itself embodies the dramatic shift undergone by Kannada literature.

Harihara was aware of the literary change that were being forged in his time, and he forcefully argued for the need to compose poetry in a language that would be closer to colloquial speech. In the opening section of the *Girijākalyāṇa*, he advocates dropping the archaic distinction in literary Kannada between three different types of the phoneme /l/, while in the preceding verse, as if by contrast, he invokes literary concepts

58. Ibid., 19, I have slightly modified the translation of Vanamala Viswanatha.

59. In addition to the literary and devotional realms, the contribution of the *Ragaḷegaḷu* to the language in written media was significant. It received the attention of linguists and even yielded a monograph in English. See Saudattimath (1988).

60. Kurtakoṭi (1995, 158).

associated with Sanskrit poetics (*alaṅkāraśāstra*).[61] There are indications that Harihara's comments were not made in a cultural vacuum or to an imaginary interlocutor but rather were part of the contemporaneous poetic conversation that has heretofore been narrowly associated with court circles. We can get a sense of this by remembering that the famous Kannada grammarian Kēśirāja, writing apparently only a few decades after Harihara, argues for exactly the opposite of what Harihara had proposed, that is, the preservation of the threefold variation of /l/.[62] Obviously we have an ongoing literary back-and-forth. But the real historical significance of Harihara's innovations in the *Girijākalyāṇa* can be most clearly seen in its reception. This text received almost immediate attention and indeed recognition in the conservative, elite literary circles whose practices it seemed in important ways to challenge. The *Sūktisudhārṇavam*, an anthology of literature paradigmatic of courtly literary culture, which was produced at the Hoysaḷa court not long after the composition of the *Girijākalyāṇa*—indeed, by Kēśirāja's father—quotes verses from Harihara's text with evident approbation.[63] As noted by Nagaraj, these references to Harihara's work in a preeminently court-based text are indicative of a complex moment in Kannada literary history and can be read, to use Nagaraj's words, as "an effort to rebuild the critical consensus that was shattered during the twelfth century."[64] It is exactly this corrective effort that nurtured creativity and reoriented literary activity in the period that followed. Nagaraj also notes the telling absence of *vacana*s from this anthology, which he explains as "an omission confirming what is elsewhere suggested: that professional intellectuals did not consider the *vacana*s literature."[65] More to the point, perhaps, it valorizes the "intermediate space" of which I have spoken.

Clearly this brief example of intertextual exchanges at the crossroads of cosmopolitan and devotional literatures in Kannada suggests that more careful attention should be paid to cultural developments outside the courts than has often been done. As argued by Christian Novetzke in his recent book *The Quotidian Revolution*, which deals with the emergence of

---

61. See *Girijākalyāṇa* 1.32 and preceding verses in Harihara (1977, 29).

62. See *sūtra* 170 of the *Śabdamaṇidarpaṇa* and Pollock (2006, 375n99, 377).

63. The author of the *Sūktisudhārṇavam* was Mallikārjuna, the father of Kēśirāja and the brother-in-law of the Jain poet Janna (Nagaraj 2003, 364).

64. Ibid.

65. Ibid.

devotional literature in Marathi, there is a scholarly need to break away from a limited understanding of devotional literature as strictly "transcendent" and to recognize the broader social and cultural sphere in which it participated, including that of "power" per se.[66]

The above mentioned example of the *Sūktisudhārṇavam* shows that courts did not always ignore devotional literature. Likewise, early devotional literature in Kannada did not ignore the court but persistently imagined the court as an integral part of communal devotional life, and did so in complex ways. Basavaṇṇa's political career as the king's treasurer, so prominent in the public memory of the region, is in fact emblematic of a far larger trend to imagine the "political" from the vantage of the "transcendental," a trend that is mostly unknown to outsiders to this commemorative tradition and that gains particular force in Harihara's *Ragaḷegaḷu*. As many as ten out of the eighteen stories about Kannada devotees in the *Ragaḷegaḷu* directly involve the court and the figure of the king.[67]

The enhanced political sensibility in Harihara's text forces us to confront the issue of political power, in this case as it is perceived from a noncourtly point of view. A telling example of this leitmotif is the story about Koṇḍaguḷi Kēśirāja (not to be confused with the grammarian Kēśirāja mentioned above). As Harihara presents him, Kēśirāja is a Brahmin and devotee of Śiva who is made chief minister by a Kalyāṇa king called Permāḍirāya. As we shall see in detail in Chapter 5, there are some historical indications that the king to whom Harihara refers in this text was the important Cālukya king Vikramāditya VI, who according to inscriptions employed a high official named Kēśirāja. Furthermore, this Koṇḍaguḷi Kēśirāja, who preceded or was a contemporary of the earliest *vacana* composers, was the first to write devotional literature to Śiva in Kannada (albeit in traditional styles).[68]

But even apart from speculation about this early historical link between devotional literary production and the court, it is instructive to notice how Harihara's storyline about Kēśirāja interweaves the devotional

66. Novetzke (2016, 5–19).

67. The ten relevant Ragaḷes are: *Kēśirāja Daṇṇāyakara Ragaḷe, Kōvūra Bommatandeya Ragaḷe, Teluga Jommayyana Ragaḷe, Prabhudēvara Ragaḷe, Basavēśvaradēvara Ragaḷe, Bāhūra Bommatandeya Ragaḷe, Bhōgaṇṇana Ragaḷe, Mahādēviyakkana Ragaḷe, Śaṅkaradāsimayyana Ragaḷe, Rēvaṇasiddhēśvarana Ragaḷe.*

68. Kēśirāja Daṇṇāyaka is attributed with several works in the *kanda* meter. See Chapter 5.

with the political, as we see in the following sequence of events.[69] According to this Ragaḷe, the courtly position granted to Kēśirāja by the king comes with social status, power, and responsibility, and Kēśirāja carries out his duties with impressive success. The lucrative post also comes with financial resources and fiscal autonomy, benefits that do not diminish Kēśirāja's religious passion but rather enable him to increase his support of the local community of Śiva devotees. One day, he convenes a gathering of such devotees. As they tell stories about ancient followers of Śiva and worship the *liṅga,* they quickly become immersed in this activity. They are described by Harihara as ecstatic, their hair standing on end as they cry out with blissful joy. They disregard hunger, thirst, and fatigue. They are oblivious to speech, sight, directions, wind, the sky, and the earth. They forget the king, his court, and his politics. Time, whatever precedes and whatever proceeds, seconds, minutes, hours, day and night, inside and out, here and there—all has disappeared, for in the companionship of devotees nothing else matters. Suddenly, the king's servants appear at the assembly and tell Kēśirāja that the king wants to see him. Kēśirāja at first tries to ignore them, but they refuse to leave without him and persistently demand that he accompany them. This intrusion disrupts the Śiva assembly. Kēśirāja, deeply disturbed, declares to all present at the assembly: "Accumulation of wealth is an impediment to associating with saints, and submission to the court of a human king stabs me in the heart . . . O Lord, the presiding deity of Kalyāṇa . . . When you remove earthly wealth, the city's people will perform rituals for you and worship the multitudes of saints!"[70] Fuming, he sets out for the king's hall to confront him. In the remainder of the story, Kēśirāja renounces his riches and completely retires from politics, only to later reoccupy the same courtly position in response to the king's repeated pleas.

Despite the devotional heavy lifting in Kēśirāja's story, there is nothing anecdotal or off-hand about the courtly career he describes here—or, for that matter, about court life more generally. On the contrary, Harihara gives us a truly complicated treatment of worldly

69. The following narration is a summary of the first chapter in the *Kēśirāja Daṇṇāyakara Ragaḷe.*

70. From *Kēśirāja Daṇṇāyakara Ragaḷe* vv. 113–20 in Harihara and Suṅkāpura (1976, 187): *siriya saṅgam śaraṇasaṅgakke pageyāytu / naranōlagada parādhīnav iṟidantāytu . . . dēva kalyāṇadad hidaiva . . . sirihāṟihōge nimagarcaneya māḍutaven / śaraṇatati purajanaru mecce koṇḍāḍuven.*

power: the court takes up a central part of what this devotional poet chooses to narrate. Kēśirāja shows us a protagonist who resents his line of work, but who again and again resorts to it in order to provide financial and political support to the community of Bhaktas. In this literary universe, strikingly, the same intensity that characterizes the devotees' worship of Śiva also governs their interactions with powerful agents intrinsic to society itself, such as kings and leaders of other religious communities.

A consideration of such motifs leads us into the middle of a rich and diverse universe of devotional literature in Kannada that has often been obscured by the at times undeniably blinding brilliance of the *vacana* literature. My purpose in this book is to show how Harihara's *Ragaḷegaḷu* provides a critically important prism for more fully understanding the complex universe of pre-modern devotional Kannada literature.

Interpreting the Stories of the Saints in the Ragaḷegaḷu

I read the *Ragaḷegaḷu* as hagiography, a text consisting of narratives about the life stories of saints. Like other English writers, I am using the term "saint" for the Kannada term *śaraṇa,* which Harihara often uses in reference to the main characters and to the greater crowds of devotees they interact with.[71] P. B. Desai explains this term by quoting a Sanskrit verse from the *Śivarahasya* (verse number unspecified) that states: "The Śaraṇa is the body of Śiva made visible, and Śiva is to become a part of the Śaraṇa."[72] Danesh Chekki describes with some more detail the divine quality of the human Śaraṇa:

> Though having form, a śarana [*sic*] is, in fact, absolutely formless, seen but not seen, representing Lord Śiva, the timeless Absolute . . . The śarana engages in action, however, these actions are no longer those of the śarana, but of the Divine . . . The words of a śarana are holy words, and those who listen to the words of a śarana in reality listen to the Divine. The śarana lives in a divinized universe.[73]

71. Michael (2012), for example, translates *śaraṇa* as a "saintly devotee" (p. 178).

72. Desai (1968, 318): *śivāṅgaṁ śaraṇaḥ sākṣāt śaraṇāṅgaṁ śivo bhavet.*

73. Chekki (2003, 25–26).

This description corresponds well with the figures populating the *Ragaḷegaḷu*. As Śaraṇas, they embody divine qualities in a human framework.[74] They are in direct contact with the god, and their behavior on earth, from the perspective of the narrator, is axiomatically righteous and benevolent.

From a literary perspective, the cultural world in which the Śaraṇas operate in the *Ragaḷegaḷu* was not confined to a specific set of written texts in a particular language but was part of a larger imaginaire. My use of the term *imaginaire* follows what Laurie Patton defines in her work on early Sanskrit poetics as "a series of tropes and figures about which the public has general knowledge and would have basic associations."[75] Throughout my book, the term *imaginaire* is used to refer to the narrative universe of Kannada devotional culture, a universe with a symbolic vocabulary and grammar rooted in realities that extend beyond a particular literary work or even beyond a specific set of texts. In the case of the imaginaire that developed in the devotional culture to the god Śiva of the Kannada-speaking region, the sources for the "tropes and figures" with which it is populated are highly diverse and include saintly stories from an earlier, pan-Indian, and Sanskritic literary world, the Tamil Śaiva tradition, and several prolific local traditions. The *Ragaḷegaḷu* captures, for the first time in Kannada writing, this rich amalgam of religious lore and therefore marks a significant moment in the maturation of the devotional tradition in the Kannada-speaking region.

Since the saints' stories in the *Ragaḷegaḷu* are at the center of this book's analysis, reading them involves developing a strategy that can further our understanding of this text as representing general understandings of what devotional life entails, of values worth pursuing, and of practices of worship in the context of the composition of those saints' lives. In the words of Sascha Ebeling from his work on Tamil Śaivism:

> Discerning a particular theological (or ideological) intention may allow us to see the social *function* of the text, its "social logic". . . It may allow us to examine how larger (religio-)political issues are negotiated through the genre of hagiographical writing, for if hagiography was never written to chronicle reality, it was also never

---

74. See definition for "saint" in Zelliot and Mokashi-Punekar (2005, 12) and the discussion in the *Encyclopedia of Religion* (Cohn 2005, 8033).

75. Patton (2008, 54). See further discussion and additional references in note 16 (pp. 75–76).

> meant *only* to provide a pleasant, edifying story. It always served very real (and this is where the truth comes back in) ideological or political purposes, such as the negotiation of power and status amongst social groups or individuals.[76]

Such an approach to the hagiographical text allows us to extract insights about the intended audience of the text from the text itself.[77]

But there are also specific challenges to the reader of the *Ragaḷegaḷu*. Its devotional narratives tend to the hyperbolic and extreme, and therefore the question of how to interpret them gains specific importance. While saints' stories everywhere are by their very nature non-normative, the *Ragaḷegaḷu* and the narrative world of south-Indian Śaiva devotionalism to which it belongs use the transgressive potential inherent in any saintly discourse in particularly intense ways. When there is violence, either self-inflicted or aimed at the other, it is graphic and consuming. When conflict occurs, it is always brought to an ultimate, one-sided conclusion. Above all, when piety takes center stage, it is presented as uncompromising in its intensity and cost. As noted in various studies, there is a particular "harshness" to the literary expression of pre-modern south-Indian Śaivism.[78] This harshness runs through different levels, but as a foundational narrative idiom in the *Ragaḷegaḷu* stories it poses a real challenge to any attempt at understanding the role these stories play for their intended audiences.[79] What meaning can be attributed to and what sort of response (emotional, cognitive, normative, or other) is to be evoked by a story about a Śaiva devotee who swears to murder anyone in the way between him and Śiva's temple image and then actually proceeds to murder two unfortunate people, themselves Śaiva devotees? Or a story about a group of three hundred Śaivas who, in order to unite with the god in heaven, self-immolate inside a Śaiva

76. Ebeling (2010, 438, emphases in the original).

77. Novetzke (2016, 2008); Pechilis (2012); Ebeling (2010); Stewart (2010); Lutgendorf (1991); Hawley (1987) are examples of studies of the relation of a South Asian devotional canon to its audience in different historical contexts. See Brown (2015 [1981]); Cornell (1998); Ricœur and Wallace (1995); Kleinberg (1992) for examples of hagiographies outside South Asia.

78. The term "harsh" is adopted from David Shulman's work on the Tamil Śaiva saint Cuntarar, with Shulman's translation of *vaṉroṇṭaṉ* as "the harsh devotee" (Cuntarar and Shulman 1990, xvi). See also Monius (2004a, 2004b); Shulman (1993b); Hudson (1989).

79. See Laurie Patton's discussion on polysemy in Vedic hymns about violence (2007), especially p. 18.

temple?[80] The problem of meaning-generation in these extreme stories is compounded by the author's voice at these moments of cruelty and horror, since it is at such moments that the author's voice takes on an exceptionally celebratory tone, commending the protagonists' harsh actions. Thus, when the three hundred devotees slash off their limbs, Harihara depicts the incident as a holy act of worship. How were such moments, moments of basic human or even humanitarian crisis often colored by macabre overtones, understood by the intended audience for the text?

A helpful insight is provided in *Saints and Virtues*, a volume edited by John S. Hawley that explores saintly traditions from various religious cultures, South Asian and others.[81] In the introduction, Hawley speaks of a distinction between the saint's life as *example* and the saint's life as *exemplar*, a distinction that is useful for the purpose of establishing reading strategies for the *Ragaḷegaḷu*.[82] According to Hawley, in the case of the saint's life as *example*, a saint serves as an instance of something, such as a virtue or behavior, to be followed and imitated. In contrast, the reading of a saint's life as *exemplar* identifies behaviors that, while nonprescriptive and non-imitable, are nevertheless spiritually inspiring.

In discussing the saint's life as example, Hawley writes:

> The saintly example instantiates and thus clarifies general principles of morality and qualities of character that can be articulated as meaningful and understood as possible for all participants in a society or community of faith.[83]

Read this way, the saint's life can be understood as prescriptive, in the sense of demonstrating a particular sentiment or behavior to be imitated and followed by the text's audience. In this exemplifying role, the character of the saint might operate within a clear and given set of moral and normative criteria, at least according to the demands and ideals particular to the culture woven around his character.

---

80. The two stories I allude to here are the *Surigeya Cauḍayyana Ragaḷe* and the *Kōvūra Bommatandeya Ragaḷe* respectively.

81. Hawley (1987).

82. Indira V. Peterson (1994, 197) seems to gesture toward a similar Janus-faced reading of the characters of the Tamil Śaiva saints in the *Periya Purāṇam*.

83. Ibid., xvi.

A concrete illustration from the *Ragaḷegaḷu* of the prescriptive quality of the text is when Harihara describes how the female devotee Mahādēviyakka worships the *liṅga*.[84] Harihara provides a detailed description of Mahādēviyakka's personal ritual of worship of Śiva's small stone emblem, a ritual called *iṣṭaliṅga pūje*, which is one of the hallmarks of this particular devotional tradition. We find no mention of such a formalized ritual involving the devotee's personal emblem of the god anywhere in the subcontinent before the appearance of the twelfth-century Śaivas of the Kannada-speaking region, and it is reasonable to assume that in the context of the early thirteenth century, the estimated time of the composition of the *Ragaḷegaḷu*, this kind of ritual marked an innovative divergence from hegemonic and orthodox worship rituals. In light of this historical context, Harihara's detailed description of Mahādēviyakka's personal worship of the *liṅga* might have served, among other purposes, as a prescriptive passage. It provided for the immediate audience information on how an unorthodox ritual related to the personal *liṅga* should or could be performed, what steps were involved in the process, which instruments could be used for it and how they were to be used, as well as the appropriate internal mode involved in the performance of the ritual. In this sense, the *Ragaḷegaḷu* educates its immediate, assumed readers or listeners by portraying an innovative ritual that is seminal for the developing tradition. Such moments in the *Ragaḷegaḷu*, which project a clear sense of prescribed normative behavior for the community of devotees as they are imagined in the text, fit what Hawley identifies as the saint's role as setting an *example*.

As much as reading the *Ragaḷegaḷu* in a prescriptive mode has its historical and social logic, it would do violence to the text to use only a prescriptive approach or to apply such an approach comprehensively, since the text would then be reduced to a flat account that makes little historical or literary sense. No member of a religious community is encouraged to pluck out his or her eye the way the famous south-Indian hunter devotee Kaṇṇappa ("Venerable Mr. Eye") is remembered and commemorated for doing.[85] It is here that the second element in Hawley's distinction—the saint's life as *exemplar*—applies.

---

84. *Mahādēviyakkana Ragaḷe* 4.prose in Harihara and Suṅkāpura (1976, 196–97).

85. See Ulrich (2007, 249–50); Cox (2005); Monius (2004a); Vamadeva (1995); Peterson (1994); Hudson (1989). Harihara provides his own account of Kaṇṇappa in the *Kaṇṇappana Ragaḷe* (1995 [1968], 104–23).

As an *exemplar*, the saint does not represent a specific behavior or virtue to be emulated by the text's audience but rather something else. In Hawley's words, saints "can be seen as models, persons from whom one can learn patterns of life for which no principle or code can serve as an adequate representation."[86] In this second aspect of saintly character, the saint *embodies* a set of values and behaviors that are less clear and less easily imitated, since the saint represents a sort of perfection that is hard to follow.[87] Despite his or her essential inimitability, or perhaps because of it, the saint has an enormous effect on his or her audience. This effect, however, is not linear but oblique: it inspires the audience to hold certain positions and experience certain emotions that are communicated by the saint's extreme behavior.

Reading the figure of the saint as *exemplar* allows a meaning-generation reading strategy that is less hermetic and explicit than that of the earlier *example* approach. Rather than being prescriptive, it is inspirational and indirect. The audience to whom the saint's life is communicated is presented with a set of devotional attitudes meant for them to internalize without committing to the saint's extreme, uncompromising, sometimes even bizarre style of expression. Furthermore, members of the audience not only imbibe through the saint's transgressive behavior less specific internal modes and values but are also affected as spectators in a dramatic spectacle. Thus, for example, Kaṇṇappa's hideous act of plucking out his eye as an improvised offering to the god has, underneath its devotional meaning, a forceful and visceral effect. As the audience recognizes and admires the saint's uncompromising commitment, a commitment that could move any devotee to spontaneous, grandiose gestures of self-sacrifice (even if not as extreme and violent as Kaṇṇappa's), it also empathizes in a more basic sense with the intense emotions linked with the saint's gruesome actions. The presentation of the saint as *exemplar*, then, works at different levels and can produce various effects for the audience, all of which sidestep his direct prescriptive role as setting an example.

The saint's depictions as *example* and *exemplar* can operate simultaneously or alternate seamlessly. For example, in the brief passage about Kēśirāja and his fellowship mentioned above, Harihara quickly shifts

86. Hawley (1987, xiv).

87. The idea of the saint as "embodying" devotion is discussed in Pechilis (1999) and was recently explored in its more literal sense in Holdrege (2015).

between the two modes. He starts by describing the devotees' assembly in a concrete, easy-to-follow manner: they get together, worship the *liṅga*, tell each other stories, and sing songs by and about previous devotees. In the *Ragaḷegaḷu* corpus Harihara is clearly invested in providing a detailed and clear sense of Śiva assemblies, since he includes so many descriptions throughout the text (in Kēśirāja's story alone there are three spontaneous occurrences of Śiva assemblies) and in a highly detailed manner (with descriptions of the rituals involved, the stories and songs performed, and even the food prepared for the occasion). But the passage describing Kēśirāja's assembly quickly develops into the tale of a sharp political conflict between the saint and the king. As the story proceeds, the conflict will culminate with Kēśirāja deserting the court in protest and setting out stark naked to begin his life as a renouncer. This part of Kēśirāja's story, the spontaneous outcome of a volatile conversation between a king and his administrator, makes little sense if read as prescriptive, but it does make didactical sense in terms of its underlying inspirational message for the audience: to be wary of mundane commitments (especially those provoked by non-Śaivas) and their potentially detrimental effect on devotional activities, and to always try to adhere to a devotional compass, even if one is not the king's administrator.

The two modes—saint as *example* and as *exemplar*—should not be considered exhaustive or as precluding additional interpretations that might be less specific to religious discourse, such as literary (with attentiveness to the possibilities for expressing the human condition, interiority, and feeling in this particular historical context), cultural (work and general ethics, food customs), social (societal structures and interrelations, communal boundaries, family relations), and even archeological (how temples are visually imagined in the literary text). For example, the handling of Kēśirāja's political career is multilayered. Side by side with the overt rhetoric against court life mentioned above, the text as a whole also conveys an almost diametrically opposite—and apparently taken for granted—message regarding Kēśirāja's excellent skills in managing worldly affairs. Kēśirāja's administrative acumen, despite being secondary to the religious telos of his life story, generates a sense of affirmation or at least a recognition of the significance of this-worldly engagement. One cannot escape the underlying social message in the Ragaḷe about Kēśirāja regarding the normative value of excelling in whatever a person does, even in less desirable and non-religious realms (as long as it does not conflict with his or her devotional agenda).

A final word about interpreting the *Ragaḷegaḷu* in the context of the broader devotional culture of premodern south India: The application of a supple interpretive strategy, like the application of any interpretive strategy, can be argued for only by the interpreter's ability, in Umberto Eco's words, to "observe the rules of the game,"[88] i.e., the literary universe to which the text belongs.[89] In the case of Harihara's hagiographies, the "rules of the game" involve the broader imaginaire of Śaiva saints' lives from early second-millennium south India. The boundaries of this literary world—from the point of view of the modern interpreter—are fluid (for example, with regard to specific historical contexts of which we know too little, or with regard to the intricate, mirror-like interplay of oral and written forms that was essential to the development of this devotional culture and that poses particular methodological challenges for academic inquiry).[90] Nevertheless, it is possible to chart the literary contours and frames of reference for the imaginaire of early south-Indian and vernacular saints' lives. It started to evolve early, in the late centuries of the first millennium, and benefited from the influence of various languages endowed with a rich poetic heritage (primarily Tamil and Sanskrit, in addition to Kannada's own literary heritage and that of the neighboring Telugu-speaking region). It also relied on a fairly bounded (if not yet fully explored) compendium of ritual manuals (the Āgamas), and it enjoyed a discursive continuum with a vast corpus of Sanskrit narratives stretching back to the classical era.[91] I refer to these cultural repositories in the book whenever required.

The Structure of This Book

The first chapter of this book introduces the *Ragaḷegaḷu* by addressing the way the tradition commemorates this text and its author, the unique poetics that govern the text, and the relation between the text's form and its generation of meaning for its intended audiences. The chapter begins with a consideration of Harihara's literary innovations as they are acknowledged in his public memory. Then, through examination of some

88. Eco (1994, 10).

89. Eco writes: "Symbols are paradigmatically open to infinite meanings but syntagmatically, that is, textually, open only to the indefinite, but by no mean infinite, interpretations allowed by the context" (ibid., 21).

90. Hess (2015).

91. Ben-Herut (2015).

of the work's textual particularities, it underscores Harihara's contribution to Kannada literature in his *Ragaḷegaḷu* through the introduction of a new and simplified mode of literary expression (in terms of choice of meter, language register, and more) and of previously unfamiliar themes (such as characters from the margins of society).

The remainder of the book, from Chapter 2 to Chapter 6, is dedicated to a developing analysis of devotional-based themes in the *Ragaḷegaḷu*. The chapters are organized according to a movement from the personal and internal to the social and external. Chapter 2 considers the multiple ways in which the characters of the *Ragaḷegaḷu* embody the ideal of worshiping Śiva and seeks to identify the constitutive and recognizable component that is shared among the various model devotees that populate the corpus. I argue in the chapter that such a component can be located in the interiority of the Bhakta figure, an interiority that is indicated in the *Ragaḷegaḷu* through a specific set of key terms pertaining to the devotee's total commitment and expressed through actions that point to this uncompromising devotional stance.

After considering in Chapter 2 the interiority of the saint's devotion, the discussion moves outward to begin an exploration of realms external to the devotee. Chapters 3 and 4 deal with the ways in which different members of the imagined community of devotees in the *Ragaḷegaḷu* stories interact which each other. This part of the book highlights not only the social diversity of those considered by the text as Śiva's devotees but also Harihara's own recognition that this diversity poses real difficulties in terms of interactions between the devotees.

The book's third chapter examines the devotees' society as it is described in the saints' stories against the background of the tradition's ideal of egalitarianism. After noting Harihara's apparent lack of interest in social issues having to do with the greater society beyond the Śaiva community, I consider how, by addressing in complicated ways specific social areas such as work, wealth, and the roles of women, the *Ragaḷegaḷu* stories qualify certain aspects of the egalitarian ideal.

The fourth chapter addresses a specific theme within the larger discourse of social diversity, and that is Brahminism. Against contemporary understandings of Brahminism as completely antagonistic to (and antagonized by) Vīraśaivas, I read the relevant stories in the *Ragaḷegaḷu* as accommodating Brahmins who are also avid devotees of Śiva. In my approach I use a basic distinction between "Brahminness"—a birth-given condition that allows for the ceding of some traditional practices for maintaining devotional values when a social context generates conflict—and "Brahminism," which stands for the set of traditional and orthodox Brahminical values of social elitism and separation. Read with this distinction in mind, I argue, the *Ragaḷegaḷu* points to the wish of Harihara, himself a Brahmin, to guide the traditional male Brahmin in the unorthodox social terrain of *bhakti* while allowing him to maintain his traditional religious and social identity as a Brahmin.

The final two chapters of the book, Chapters 5 and 6, extend the movement outward by examining the story's figuration of the relationship Śivabhaktas maintain with people who are placed outside the canopy of Śaiva devotion, the political and religious "other." The acerbic tone Harihara adopts in relation to those seen as non-Śaivas (*bhavis*) serves in my analysis as a starting point for considering what the antagonistic character of the other entails for the literary construction of the Bhakta's self. Chapter 5 deals with interactions between devotees and the political other, such as kings and Brahmin ministers at kings' courts, and locates a complex message in Harihara's treatment of the court as a worldly and ethically corrupting arena but also a useful power center for the betterment of the society of devotees. In *Ragaḷegaḷu* stories that involve the court, the role of the "opponent other" is always taken up by Vaiṣṇava Brahmins, who are repeatedly depicted as corrupt and devious. The chapter concludes with a reflection on the possible social conditions that might have enabled Harihara to freely express his basically anti-court stance.

Chapter 6 deals with interactions with the religious other, namely Jains, outside the courts and most significantly at temples. This chapter highlights the ambiguity in Harihara's depictions of Jains, who are presented as utterly alien to Śaiva dispositions but also intimately close to them in terms of daily living. The different kinds of others to which I draw attention in Chapters 5 and 6 help shed light on the categorical difference between Harihara's treatment of the "opponent other" at the court and the "wholly other" at the temple: while some sort of reconciliation is possible with the former, the latter cannot be accommodated. However, Harihara's differentiation between the opponent other and the wholly other is further complicated by the text's distancing of the opponent other by his placement at the court in comparison to the more intimate presence of the wholly other in the mundane life of most Śaivas—at temples, in marketplaces, and even in the domestic sphere through interreligious marriages. Thus, Chapter 6 reads the aggressive alienation of Jains in the *Ragaḷegaḷu* stories against the text's silent admittance, at the same time, that social reality involves some amount of religious coexistence.

This book addresses the complex history of remembering the twelfth-century Śaiva devotees by providing, for the first time in English-language scholarship, access to the earliest source of the tradition's public memory. While the book does not provide answers to the question of what the twelfth-century saints *really* did, it reveals an incredibly rich portrayal of their lives as understood by a prominent and accomplished poet in the early thirteenth century, composed just a few decades after they purportedly lived. This book seeks to develop ways of understanding a complex hagiographical tradition, with its social and cultural motivations, concerns, and imagination, at the beginning stages of that tradition and before massive rewritings of its religious memory.

I

The Poetics of Bhakti

THE *RAGAḶEGAḶU* PLAYED a pivotal role in the development of devotional literature in Kannada and for more than one reason. The most obvious of these is thematic: the *Ragaḷegaḷu* introduced for the first time in written Kannada a dramatic universe populated by figures from different strands of society, including those traditionally considered marginal, and organized their social world according to a new value system based on devotion to the god Śiva. The *Ragaḷegaḷu* was the first expansive and cohesive account in written narrative form that was dedicated to describing the world of Śivabhaktas in the Kannada-speaking region, and it is difficult to overestimate the impact of this work on the remembered history of the Kannada Śaiva saints. The *vacanas*, short poems representing the voices of the saints themselves, had probably already been circulating orally for about a century before the *Ragaḷegaḷu,* and there are few written literary works prior to the *Ragaḷegaḷu* that can also be connected to this Śaiva religious idiom.[1] However, none of these early works present a coherent and detailed written account of a devotional universe as the *Ragaḷegaḷu* does.

But the innovative themes of the *Ragaḷegaḷu* were not its only original contribution to literary practices in Kannada. In the literature of South Asia and elsewhere, a text's form—its literary style, meter choices, language register, structure, authorial voice and texture, and so on—plays an active role in its meaning making. The *Ragaḷegaḷu* is not an exception to this: Harihara composed the *Ragaḷegaḷu* in a unique, almost *sui generis*

1. The early twelfth-century Koṇḍaguḷi Kēśirāja composed several theological works on Śaiva devotion in the standard discursive meter called *kanda*. Kereya Padmarasa composed in the early thirteenth century a Śaiva liturgical text called the *Dīkṣābōdhe* in the *ragaḷe* meter, probably under the direct influence of Harihara, who is traditionally remembered as his close friend.

form, which involved an unusual meter choice, innovative plotting, daily and non-literary language, and a unique structure. It is not coincidental that the Kannada literary tradition commemorates Harihara in ways that dramatize the unique poetic elements of the *Ragaḷegaḷu*.

In this chapter I consider the *Ragaḷegaḷu*'s pioneering role in a long-lasting and prolific literary production of saints' stories in Kannada. The chapter begins with a short introduction to the commemorative tradition of Harihara and the ways in which it resonates with the devotional characters in Harihara's own text. The chapter then turns to consider the poetics of the *Ragaḷegaḷu*, arguing that the nontraditional style with which Harihara composed the *Ragaḷegaḷu* is tightly connected with the devotional message he wished to convey to a new and non-elite audience for his work. Finally, I argue in the last section of the chapter that Harihara's literary innovation in the *Ragaḷegaḷu* paved the way for the golden age of Kannada written literature about the Śaiva saints, lasting roughly from the thirteenth to the sixteenth centuries.

Poet as Saint

Traditional accounts of poets' lives in South Asia rarely miss an opportunity to reflectively comment on the poet's own literary creation. Such is also the case with Harihara's life story as it was told by later poets, a story that hinges on themes that are already operative in his own literary works. The short diachronic discussion to follow highlights the similarities or homologisms between Harihara's life, as it was remembered in subsequent accounts, and the lives of the saints he wrote about, with the premise that an awareness of these similarities can shed light on features of a narrative tradition that was to remain central over a long period of time. In other words, the traditional accounts of Harihara's life are instructive for understanding deeper collective dispositions of the Kannada Śivabhakti tradition as they are manifested through recurring narrative patterns across stories from different eras and about different figures. Examples of such dispositions include an intense and intimate mode of devotion, a volatile relationship with the political center, transgressive etiquette, and miracle making—all of which are prominent in the hagiographies written by Harihara as well as central in the stories about Harihara's own life.

Historical facts relating to Harihara's life are scarce, even to the level of his dating. To demonstrate the complexities and obscurities involved in fixing Harihara temporally, I can briefly note the question regarding the identity of one Hoysaḷa king, named Narasiṃha Ballāḷa in the later Śivabhakti texts in Kannada, who, in an episode we shall explore below, is said to have had a brief acquaintance with Harihara. The lack of clarity here pertains to whether these texts refer to Narasiṃha I (r. 1152–1173), to Ballāḷa II (r. 1173–1220), or to Narasiṃha II (r. 1220–1234/5).[2] The obscurity that cloaks Harihara's dating is deepened by the difficulty involved in historically connecting Harihara with any of these kings; the author himself does not refer in any of his compositions to the Hoysaḷa courts, and there is no direct inscriptional or other "hard" evidence that connects them.[3] Since Harihara obviously lived after the Kannada figures he wrote about (figures who had operated during the twelfth century), and since quotations from Harihara's *Girijākalyāṇa* appear in the first Kannada anthology (the *Sūktisudhārṇavam,* firmly dated at 1245 CE),[4] it seems reasonable to assume that Harihara wrote the *Ragaḷegaḷu* in the early decades of the thirteenth century.

Obscurity also shrouds Harihara's peculiar name, which could have very different meanings in terms of the religious affiliation of this poet.[5] One way to translate "Harihara" is "Hari and Hara," (that is, Viṣṇu as well as Śiva), which is also the title of a cult led by *smārta* Brahmins in an attempt to reconcile competing Hindu-based sects in south India at the turn of the first millennium.[6] It is uncertain whether Harihara's parents

2. See epigraphical study of the two later kings in Kasdorf (2013, 46–60).

3. See Devadevan (2016, 14n49); Nāyaka, Veṅkaṭācala Śāstrī, and Sundaram (1977, 1255–60); Nilakanta Sastri (1976, 361–62); Cidānandamūrti (1970, 130). Compare these estimates with the rather theoretical and over-expansive one that places Harihara's activity sometime between 1145 and 1300 CE (Śivarudrappa 1976, 235). The earliest discussion in English about fixing a date for Harihara is from the middle of the twentieth century (Narasimhacharya 1988 [1934], 52–55). Ramanujan (1973) temporally locates the poet Harihara in the fifteenth century, roughly two centuries after the date accepted by all other scholars (p. 143). This misdate is repeated in Ramanujan, Dharwadker, and Blackburn (1999, 286). It is possible that Ramanujan conflated the thirteenth-century poet Hampeya Harihara with the fifteenth-century founder of Vijayanagara, also called Harihara and intriguingly situated in Hampi.

4. Narasiṃhācārya (2005 [1929], 433); Nagaraj (2003, 363–64). See list of verses quoted from the *Girijākalyāṇa* in the *Sūktisudhārṇavam* in Mallikārjuna and Anantaraṅgācār (1972, 417).

5. A different level of complexity with regard to the title "Harihara" involves the proliferation of different variations of this poet's name as they appear in various sources. Of the more popular variants are Haridēva, Harīśvara, Hariga, Hari, and Hariyaṇṇa Paṇḍita. These are sometimes used interchangeably in the same text. Often the names are preceded by the title Hampeya ("of Hampi"), which is his birthplace and the place where, according to tradition, he composed the *Ragaḷegaḷu.*

6. The origins of the Harihara cult in this region go back to the sixth century (Desai 1968, 115).

belonged to this anti-sectarian movement and thus named their son in a spirit of religious tolerance,[7] but it is fairly clear that Harihara did not end up promoting such values, judging from his fervent Śaiva authorial voice in the *Ragaḷegaḷu* and in other works.[8] In seeking thematic correspondence between the name Harihara and the religious persona of the poet, it is possible to consider a different explanation: the "destroyer (*hara*) of Hari" or—in a less harsh variation—Harīśvara, "the Lord (*īśvara*) of Hari." This explanation taps into a popular medieval Śaiva claim that Viṣṇu is a great Bhakta of Śiva and it coheres well with Harihara's anti-Vaiṣṇava temperament, which is often reflected in his work.[9] This etymology is provided by Harihara himself in three verses of his *Pampā Śataka*, in which the author claims that devotees call Śiva "Harihara" because Hari bows his head to Śiva's feet; because Śiva carries Viṣṇu as an ornament on his head; because Śiva, as Śarabha, killed Viṣṇu as Nṛsiṃha; and so on.[10] Still, Harihara does not directly attribute this explanation to his own name but to Śiva only.[11] There are other theories about Harihara's name,[12] and it is worth pointing out that a similar obscurity characterizes

7. Among Kannada literary historians, Si. Liṅgaṇṇa seems to be the only one to claim that Harihara's parents were *smārta*s and that they named their son to signify this harmonious concept (1979, 387).

8. A related but different explanation for Harihara's name points to a town called Harihara, in which there is a temple that celebrates the joined Vaiṣṇava-Śaiva tradition. Several traditional accounts report that the poet Harihara visited this town on his way from Dvārasamudra to Hampi, and that he released an evil demon (*brahmarākṣasa, ugrabhūta*) that had taken over the town's temple. This explanation is not consonant with the fact that all the traditional sources about Harihara's life specifically state that he was given his name at birth and not as a result of this incident. These sources also do not provide any alternative name the poet had prior to the miracle he allegedly performed in the town of Harihara. For detailed accounts about the ghost in the temple story, see Nāyaka, Veṅkaṭācala Śāstrī , and Sundaram (1977, 1266–67); Śivarudrappa (1976, 236, 238).

9. Dēvīrappa (1979, 30).

10. *Pampā Śataka* vv. 95–97 in Harihara and Basawanal (1969, 35).

11. Dēvīrappa (1979, 21).

12. Perhaps the most adventurous theory about the etymological origin for Harihara's name is the one offered by Eṃ. Eṃ. Kalaburgi, who thinks this name's lexical and cultural origin is Dravidian rather than Sanskritic. Kalaburgi suggests that Harihara's name is derived from a name of a local god called Paṟi (>Paṟiyala>Hariyala>Harihara). In a later article, Kalaburgi suggests a different explanation, according to which the origin of Harihara's name is Hereyāḷa, which is the crescent moon, an emblem of Śiva (Hereyāḷa >Hariyāḷa>Hariyala >Hariyara>Harihara) (2010 [1998], 433–34, 439–40). What is significant about Kalaburgi's musings is that he attempts to reclaim the epithet "Harihara" as thoroughly Dravidian rather than Sanskritic, while Harihara himself expresses no such linguistic puritanism in his own work.

Harihara's nephew Rāghavāṅka, who is depicted, like his uncle Harihara, as exclusively devoted to Śiva, but who nevertheless carries an ambiguously Vaiṣṇava epithet.[13] More significant than locating the "historical" and "correct" explanation for Harihara's name is the fact that the pre-modern tradition is not pressed to arrive at any definitive conclusion on this issue. Reflection about Harihara's name in pre-modernity is minimal and, in the hagiographies about them, Harihara and Rāghavāṅka are celebrated for their Śaiva zeal despite their accommodating names. Perhaps epithets in South Asian imaginaries are not always suggestive of deeper meaning.[14]

Harihara was an accomplished and prolific author. The innovative *Ragaḷegaḷu* is anomalous to his literary production, which, despite its overall thematic commitment to Śaiva devotionalism, was more in line with contemporaneous Kannada literary practices that in general made use of the Sanskritic, pan-Indian idiom. In this category are included the *Pampā Śataka*, the *Muḍigeya Aṣṭaka*, the *Rakṣā Śataka*, and what is acknowledged by many as Harihara's masterpiece, the *Girijākalyāṇa*, an eight-canto courtly epic written in the classical style of *campū*.[15] Despite the magnitude of Harihara's overall *oeuvre*, he is remembered by the Kannada literary tradition as the "*Ragaḷe* Poet" (*ragaḷeya kavi*), undoubtedly due to the poetic and thematic uniqueness of the *Ragaḷegaḷu* and its impact on future medieval Kannada poets.[16]

A detailed biography of Harihara's life was composed shortly after or perhaps during his life by his previously mentioned nephew, the famous

---

13. "Rāghavāṅka" denotes either a positive affiliation with the Raghu dynasty, which is connected to Viṣṇu in the classic imaginaire, or a negative one, since *aṅka* can be translated as "decoration" or as "affliction" (Kittel 1982, 17 s.v. *aṅka* 13 and 14). Some scholars, such as Kurtakoṭi (1995, 174–79), echo this obscurity. The name of Brahmaśiva, a Jain author from the twelfth century, is similarly ambiguous, though at the other end of sectarian divide. His evidently Hindu-centered name runs against the anti-Hindu polemics of his *Samayaparīkṣe* (Zydenbos 1985; Brahmaśiva 1958).

14. See Laurie Patton's brief reflection on translating epithets in the *Bhagavad Gītā* (2008, xxxvii–xxxviii).

15. The genre of courtly epic is called in Kannada literature *mahāprabandham* and in Sanskrit *mahākāvya*. On the latter term, see Bronner, Shulman, and Tubb (2014); Patel (2014, 6–7); Bronner (2010, 20–21). Another work attributed to Harihara but now lost is the *Śivākṣaramāle* (Narasiṃhācārya 2005 [1929], 257).

16. See, for example, in Ec. Dēvīrappa's introduction in Harihara and Dēvīrappa (1995 [1968], iv). Harihara's appellation "*Ragaḷe* poet" is judgmentally ambiguous, since the term *ragaḷe* also denotes in Kannada, in addition to the specific meter, the meaning of "nuisance" and "gabble" (Kittel 1982, 1326 s.v. *Ragaḷe*).

poet Rāghavāṅka. Unfortunately, this biography, titled *Hariharamahatva* ("Harihara's Greatness"), is no longer extant.[17] The available narratives about Harihara's life are taken from the later medieval Vīraśaiva Purāṇas in Kannada, the earliest being the *Padmarāja Purāṇa* (1385 CE).[18] A skeletal account of Harihara's life, based on these sources, begins in Kailāsa, Śiva's heavenly abode, when one of Śiva's attendants comes before Śiva and asks him to tell the stories of the attendants' great deeds on earth. Śiva responds: "There is none other than you who is fit for narrating my greatness. Go to earth and compose such stories in the *ragaḷe* meter. Then, return here." The attendant is consequently born as a human being in Hampi to two ardent devotees. He is named Harihara, undergoes a Śaiva initiation (*dīkṣe*) by a guru,[19] and grows up as a follower of the local manifestation of Śiva—Virūpākṣa.

It is significant that, before the inception of Harihara's professional career, even before his early childhood, all the way back to his prenatal life the author is firmly connected to the *Ragaḷegaḷu*. The most obvious reference is Śiva's explicit command to the attendant to compose on earth stories in the *ragaḷe* meter about the earthly incarnation of the god's attendants in their human form as Śaiva saints. The attention this narrative tradition pays to the particular (and unusual) meter in which the *Ragaḷegaḷu* was composed, and which provides to the entire work its title, clearly

17. Narasiṃhācārya (2005 [1929], 268).

18. This work, composed about a century and a half after Harihara's time, narrates the life of Harihara's contemporary and close friend Kereya Padmarasa, who is remembered as an administrator at the Hoysaḷa court. A more detailed account that directly builds on the now lost *Hariharamahatva* is Siddhanañjēśa's *Rāghavāṅka Carite* (*c.*1650 CE) (Śivarudrappa 1976, 237). Succinct accounts of Harihara's life appear in the *Cennabasava Purāṇa* (1578 CE) and the *Bhairavēśvarakāvyada Kathāsūtraratnākara* (1672 CE). For comprehensive and comparative discussions regarding Harihara's life, see Dēvīrappa (1979); Nāyaka, Veṅkaṭācala Śāstrī, and Sundaram (1977, 1245–81); Śivarudrappa (1976, 235–43). Four works by Harihara contain first-person narratives: the *Piṇḍōtpatti Ragaḷe* (aka the *Saṃsāravyāmōhanirasana Ragaḷe*), the *Puṣpa Ragaḷe*, the *Rakṣā Śataka*, and the *Pampā Śataka*. However, the personal character that these texts present—steeped in poverty and depravity—does not correspond well with the erudition that is reflected in the writings of Harihara, and most scholars consider these works not as genuinely autobiographical but rather as an authorial strategy meant to communicate devotional intimacy, a postulation that seems cogent in light of Harihara's overall effort in his works to popularize devotion to Śiva (Nāyaka, Veṅkaṭācala Śāstrī, and Sundaram 1977, 1275–77).

19. In some sources this guru's name is Mādarasa and in others it is Māyidēva. We are not told about the guru's specific sectarian affiliation. In the *Rāghavāṅka Carite*, the initiation is termed a *sujñānadīkṣe*, which is a general attribution that can be translated as "initiation of deep understanding."

signals later recognition of Harihara's unique metrical choice, to which I return below.

Even the thematic framing of the story in Kailāsa itself mirrors the *Ragaḷegaḷu*: almost all of the *Ragaḷegaḷu* stories about the Kannada saints also begin in Kailāsa, and these framing stories, exactly as we find here, provide a clear telos to the saints' earthly incarnations. Like his protagonists, Harihara is remembered as uniting with Śiva's image and then ascending back to Kailāsa after completing his earthly task of composing the saints' stories.

The use of heavenly framing is not new but was already popular in the Sanskritic Purāṇas from the middle of the first millennium CE onward. There, this frame connects the pan-Indian god with his specific locale in the South Asian peninsula. What we find in the vernacular south-Indian devotional literature is, however, a distinct offshoot of this narrative technique, with the descent to earth not of the god but of his attendants, manifested on earth in the form of saintly devotees. This shift marks an important transition in the hagiographic literary culture of south India, a shift of narrative focus from the god himself to his human Bhaktas. The narrative technique of placing the pre-born Śaiva saint in heaven next to his or her god had been introduced by the twelfth-century Tamil *Periya Purāṇam*,[20] but it appeared to gain its own force in the *Ragaḷegaḷu* with repeated invoking of the Kailāsa framing strategy and even a specific technical term to describe the Kannada saints as "born to a divine cause (*kāraṇika*)," a term that links them to their prenatal existence in Śiva's heavenly abode.[21]

The biographical details about Harihara being born in Hampi, initiated into the Śaiva faith, and worshiping Śiva Virūpākṣa correspond as well with benediction verses that bookend each of the saints' stories in the *Ragaḷegaḷu* and are dedicated to Śiva Virūpākṣa, "the king of Hampi (*hampeyarasa*)."[22] When Harihara grows up, he follows his god's order and

20. See the Kailāsa frame story about the Tamil saint Cuntaramūrtti in Peterson (1994, 201–2) and the identification of six Tamil Nāyaṉmār as *avatārapuruṣas* ("human incarnations") in Cutler (1987, 49).

21. The *Saṅkṣipta Kannaḍa Nighaṇṭu* (the *Concise Kannada Dictionary*) by the Kannaḍa Sāhitya Pariṣattu plainly defines *kāraṇika* as "a divine being, a human incarnation" (Prasād 2001, 258 s.v. *kāraṇika* 2). My tranlsation of the term as "born to a divine cause" foregrounds its semantic link to the word *karaṇa* in the sense of "cause, instrument."

22. Harihara's *Girijākalyāṇa* also celebrates Hampi. Similar claims for Śiva's divine sovereignty over a specific locale also govern the city of Banāras (Eck 1999, 95).

moves to Dvārasamudra to become the chief accountant (*karaṇika*) of the Hoysaḷa king Narasiṃha Ballāḷa.[23] Here, Harihara establishes good ties with Kereya Padmarasa, the king's chief minister (*mukhyamantrin*), who is himself a Śaiva poet. But despite this friendship, Harihara has a rift with the king, which leads to his quitting his position at the court and beginning his journey back to Hampi. This falling out has a crucial impact on Harihara's life since, the traditions claim, his parting from the court leads Harihara to start composing poetry, a change semantically communicated by his transformation from a *karaṇika* ("an accountant") to a *kāraṇika* ("a saintly person born to a divine cause").[24]

The rift with the king starts when some antagonistic courtiers complain to the king that Harihara signs every account page in the state budget book with the name of his personal god, Śiva Virūpākṣa. The king interprets this as an indication of embezzlement, and immediately calls for a public audit of Harihara's book. During the audit, however, Harihara starts waving his hands in the air and shouting "Virūpākṣa!" The courtiers whisper to each other: "The insanity of his devotion has finally gone to his head!" and they all start laughing, but Harihara retorts: "Crazy is the worldling (*bhavi*) who wallows in this world's sickness, forgetful of contemplation (*dhyāna*) of Śiva." Harihara explains to the king that he is waving his hands because, at that very moment, the curtain that covers Śiva's image in Hampi (Śiva Virūpākṣa) has caught fire in a *dhūpārati* (waving of incense and lamp) ceremony. Put differently, Harihara has held out his hands in Dvārasamudra to extinguish the fire in Hampi, located hundreds of miles to the north.

When Harihara shows the king his sooty palms, the king decides to send a messenger to Hampi in order to check if indeed such an incident has occurred. After arriving in Hampi, the messenger enters the Virūpākṣa temple and learns from the local priests that the curtain had indeed caught fire during the *dhūpārati* ceremony, and that Harihara had come rushing in and extinguished the fire with his bare hands. When the messenger returns with this information, the Hoysaḷa king is so thrilled that the hair on his body stands on end. He prostrates himself in front of Harihara and says: "Please go up north in order to stay near Śiva, king of Hampi. I shall provide you with all that you may need." The king then orders that gold

---

23. Dvārasamudra is oftentimes written in Kannada as Dōrasamudra and is more famously known today as Haḷeyabīḍu or Halebid in English transcription.

24. This wordplay is discussed in Liṅgaṇṇa (1979, 391).

be showered on Harihara (*kanakābhiṣēka*). Harihara, however, refuses the offer and says: "From this moment onward I will follow only god. If I desire in my mind the support of a human, I shall go to hell (*naraka*)." With this resolution in his heart, Harihara leaves King Narasiṃha and sets out for Hampi.

As noted earlier, the recognition of Harihara's affinity with Hampi in his life story, here communicated through Harihara's telekinetic transportation to Hampi to save the image of his god, corresponds with the frequent attributions to Śiva as the lord of Hampi in his own writing. But this incident contains other features that echo Harihara's stories in meaningful ways. For example, temple worship is strongly affirmed by this story in a manner that is utterly commensurate with Harihara's narratives about the Kannada saints.[25] Also, in addition to the evident connection between Harihara and the religious center of Hampi, the story conveys a deeper insight regarding Harihara's religious commitment: according to this story, it is clear that Harihara's existential commitment to Śiva has a worldly, contingent context outside the realm of personal devotion and well within his professional and public life. The episode opens with the appeal by Harihara's rival accountants to the king regarding Harihara's use of Śiva Virūpākṣa's name in signing the state accounts book. This writing practice would seem to go beyond the realm of personal faith, or at least to extend it to the fiscal and/or political arenas. The fact is that Harihara signs his god's name—strangely enough—in the state's financial records and not in some religious or literary composition. As the story tells us, this eccentric practice naturally causes the king to become suspicious, and this suspicion leads to Harihara's performing, not without affront, an open and public audit of his records. It is safe to assume that what disturbs the king in Harihara's conduct is not only the latter's religious predilections but also questions regarding his accounting practices and perhaps even his political fidelity.

In Chapter 5, I discuss the Śaraṇas' stories, composed by Harihara himself, in which the relationship between Śivaśaraṇas and royal financial resources are—as in Harihara's life story—fraught with tension and sharp edges. We find in these narratives fruitful cooperation with the king, but also tension, suspicion, caprice, and conspiracy. Significantly, several central figures in this tradition's early phases were said to have occupied central

25. See Ben-Herut (2016).

roles in courts. These roles included accountants (*karaṇikas*),[26] treasurers (*bhaṇḍāris*), and chief ministers (*daṇṇāyakas*), and the list of persons includes Harihara, his associate Kereya Padmarasa, Harihara's nephew Rāghavāṅka, the famous Basavaṇṇa, Kembāvi Bhōgaṇṇa, Koṇḍaguḷi Kēśirāja, and Teluga Jommayya. In each of these figures' stories, tension between the religious and the political is a central theme. Like Harihara, Padmarasa, Rāghavāṅka, Basavaṇṇa, Bhōgaṇṇa, Kēśirāja, and Jommayya try to combine the two modes of living (the religious and the political) with varying degrees of success and end up turning their backs on court life in order to devote themselves to religious life.

As the story about Harihara at the king's court unfolds, we see that Harihara's religious devotion openly clashes with his political environment. Moreover, throughout this story, Harihara himself is evidently aware of the political implications of his religious leanings. For example, during his confrontation with the king, we read that Harihara openly refers to his god as the "king of Hampi," a title that has direct and clear political connotations when uttered in front of the Hoysaḷa king, whose kingdom extends to Hampi.[27] In this and in other revealing phrases that betray Harihara's intense devotional commitment, the ideological friction with his political surroundings becomes tangible.[28] This friction reaches its climax during the audit, when Harihara enters into a religious trance and, in the resolution that follows, when Harihara completely turns his back on worldly matters. He refuses the admiring

---

26. The plethora of references regarding the historiographical role of *karaṇikas* in medieval south India invites further study. The fact that Narayana Rao, Shulman, and Subrahmanyam (2003) focus on indigenous forms of historiography by Karanams of sixteenth- to eighteenth-century Andhra Pradesh, who are also accountants at the king's court, suggests a continuum between these cultural spheres. It also suggests the centrality of the *karaṇikas* for medieval south-Indian historicity dating from at least the thirteenth century.

27. Hampi was located at that time at the periphery of Hoysaḷa territory, after having been made part of the regional empire during the reign of Ballāḷa II (Narasimhacharya 1988 [1934], 53).

28. On the complicated religious terrain of the Hoysaḷas, see Singh (1975, 6). Ec. Dēvīrappa describes the multi-religious and multi-linguistic culture at King Narasiṃha's court (1979, 3–4). Emic traditions claim that the Hoysaḷa dynasty after the time of King Viṣṇuvardhana (twelfth century) was affiliated with Vaiṣṇavism, and that King Viṣṇuvardhana also had a personal relationship with the famous promulgator of Śrīvaiṣṇavism, Rāmānuja (Nilakanta Sastri 1976, 388). Conversely, a recent dissertation by Katherine Kasdorf points to a more complicated history with regard to the religious affiliation of specific Hoysaḷa kings (Kasdorf 2013, 128–38). In any case, the assumption that the Hoysaḷa kings had to politically navigate their court between different sects seems cogent, even if we do not read the story about Harihara in a historical mode.

king's benevolent offer to be his patron. Instead, Harihara proclaims his preference for a voluntary retirement to a complete devotional life in Hampi, committing himself never again to rely on human backing or support.

This story reveals a sociopolitical tension that is one of the key features in Harihara's own writings and that, according to all the stories, can have only one possible resolution: a strong and explicit rejection of courtly life in favor of uncompromising devotional life. The normative prescription in these stories explicitly sets up the two modes of living against one another, without allowing any space for compromise. But this supposedly straightforward message is obfuscated by a completely inverted underlying leitmotif, which is the glaring political career of the Śaraṇas. As we just saw in the incident with Harihara and the king, we will find that the need to reject the court and its political, religious, and metaphysical compromises occurs many times *within* the court and after a limited period of fruitful cooperation between the religious leader and the political leader.[29]

Harihara's story continues with his arrival in Hampi and his taking up residence next to the Virūpākṣa temple. Harihara starts composing the Śaraṇas' stories inside the temple, sitting next to the god. As Śiva narrates the Śivabhaktas' stories, Harihara writes them down. But Śiva's accounts are so terse that one ascetic (*tāpasa*), unable to bear their brevity, approaches Harihara and protests: "Why are you abridging the Śivabhaktas' stories in such a way?" Harihara drops his pen, goes to Śiva Virūpākṣa and says: "Why have you brought upon me a deriding Bhakta?" Śiva, always attuned to his Bhaktas (*bhaktādhīna*), replies: "From now on I shall only narrate lengthily, and you too shall write it in this way." Now the stories come out infinitely long, with no end in sight. Again, a revered Śivabhakta approaches Harihara and complains: "In the manner in which you have started writing, these stories will never reach their conclusion!" Harihara retorts: "It is Śiva Virūpākṣa, by making these stories either too short or too long, who is the cause of this problem!" He then goes to Śiva's inner chamber (*garbhaguḍi*) and shouts at the god: "You arch traitor! You are again and again failing me, making me look like a nobody in the eyes

29. For the hagiographical tradition of south India, the basic structural tensions between the Bhakta poet and the king are not unusual. Such an example is the dramatic story of the seventeenth-century Sanskrit poet Nīlakaṇṭha Dīkṣita, who quits his position as the chief minister of King Tirumala Nāyaka after the latter blinds him. See Ben-Herut (2011, 74–77). This leitmotif is connected to the one about the frustrated poet at the king's court (Granoff 1995).

of the Śivabhaktas!" Harihara decides to cut off his own head.[30] Śiva immediately appears before Harihara, stops him, and says: "Each one of these life stories is so elaborate that it would take years to narrate. It was for this reason that I told you the stories in an abridged manner. Do not hurt yourself so recklessly. You will please me only by paying no heed to the Bhaktas' complaints! Even if they abuse you, you must not be saddened!" Then Śiva orders Harihara to worship him daily with fresh flowers, an order Harihara follows faithfully.

At this point we depart from Harihara's life story in order to more closely examine this traditional account of how the *Ragaḷegaḷu* was composed. It is revealing in several aspects. The most immediately obvious is the reference to the uniquely active participation of Śiva in the crafting of the *Ragaḷegaḷu*.[31] None of the stories about Harihara composing his other works is similar to what we are told here. The creative process of composing the *Ragaḷegaḷu* is utterly reciprocal, equally involving Harihara and Śiva. In fact, the joint venture is hardly symmetrical: Śiva is the actual composer of the stories, to the level of deciding the style and length of the narration, while Harihara is on the passive, receiving end of the creative dyad, as we learn from his frustration, from his dramatic reproaches of Śiva, and from Śiva's responses to those reproaches. In fact, the theme of co-authoring the *Ragaḷegaḷu* was already hinted at in the framing story, in which Śiva actively sends his attendant from Kailāsa down to earth so that he may serve as the god's earthly voice for the Śaraṇas' stories.

This account of the composing of the *Ragaḷegaḷu* also portrays the intimate relationship between Harihara and his god, an intimacy that allows Harihara to complain to Śiva, to chastise him, and all this to his face. In the relationship between them, the Bhakta's sense of intimacy with Śiva grants him direct, undisturbed access to the god. But perhaps what is more striking is the fact that this intimacy also removes any sense of reverence: Harihara has no doubt that his troubles originate in the god's failures and does not hesitate to say this to the god. Harihara's complaints

30. This is a recurring devotional trope in South Asia. Harihara himself writes about another famous Bhakta, Ēkānta Rāmayya, who cut off his own head and succeeded in retrieving it. See Ben-Herut (2012).

31. A similar claim regarding Śiva's active involvement in hagiographical composition appears in a traditional account about the Tamil *Periya Purāṇam* (Peterson 1994, 192–93), but can be linked back to the commemorated history of the Tamil *caṅkam* poets, with the story about Śiva and Nakkirar (Zvelebil 1986).

are evidently pertinent, for Śiva takes the trouble to amend his poetic ways and, when this strategy again fails, to explain his own contested artistic choices to Harihara. The god, then, is not immune to criticism. He can make mistakes, correct himself, and politely ask his devotee to bear this divine imperfection. The intimate and direct relationship between Harihara and Śiva is emblematic of the *Ragaḷegaḷu* stories, and we shall observe in many incidents discussed throughout the book how Harihara's figuration of the relationship between the devotee and the god implies, together with the expected appreciation of divine presence in the life of the saint, also a clear tone of intimate irreverence that is one of the hallmarks of the Kannada Śivabhakti tradition.

Textual Experimentation in the Ragaḷegaḷu

From an artistic point of view, the account of the dialectical creativity between the poet and his god during the composition of the *Ragaḷegaḷu* conveys a sense of dissatisfaction with this text on the part of the immediate audience of Śivabhaktas. It also describes the creative literary process as fraught with difficulties. This rather brief anecdote is, after all, a kind of creation myth for a new and unique literary style and, as the story tells us, the process of creating this new poetry involves experimentation, revisions, repeated criticism and resistance, frustrations, and even passing failures. All these reflect the tradition coming to terms with the highly unusual style of the *Ragaḷegaḷu.*

At the heart of the stylistic difficulties attested to in this story lies the problem of plotting the length of the narratives. At first, Harihara's Ragaḷes are criticized for being too short; then for being too long; finally, after being made to explain to Harihara the reason for the lengthiness of the Ragaḷes, Śiva urges his devotee to disregard the devotees' criticism. In this process it becomes clear that Śiva does not know how to please Harihara's audience in terms of their expectations for a good story, but still urges his devotee to carry on with this literary project. From a literary perspective, the narrative describes the labor and toil involved in artistic exploration—the literary experimentation that is required in order to discover the right balance that will faithfully present the Śaraṇas' stories in the new literary style of the *Ragaḷegaḷu*, against the aesthetic expectations of its intended, immediate audience.

As much as labor and toil are at the heart of any creative writing, they become painfully acute when one experiments with new genres and expressional modes. It is for this reason that any discussion about Harihara's poetic innovation cannot be complete without a consideration of his stylistic choices. Beyond the thematic introduction of a new set of religious, social, cultural, and political value systems into the literary arena, at the linguistic level Harihara's *Ragaḷegaḷu* introduced into the history of written literature in Kannada the direct and demotic register of Middle Kannada (*naḍugannaḍa*), displacing archaic forms of Old Kannada (*haḷegannaḍa*).[32] Moreover, Harihara's eponymous meter choice for the *Ragaḷegaḷu* is equally groundbreaking. In most cases, classical Kannada literary works were written in *campū*, a highly ornate style that involved interchangeable Sanskrit, Prakrit, and *dēśi* (local) meters. Harihara's choice of a single meter called *ragaḷe*, which had been sporadically used in earlier works, as the central meter used throughout the *Ragaḷegaḷu* was unorthodox, perhaps even exotic.

Unlike other meters, *ragaḷe* entails not bounded verses but brief lines that continue from one to the next, with no structural or thematic break other than an internal line structure of four *gaṇas* (beat-based metrical subunits) and a basic rhyming technique (*prāsa*) that connects one verse to the following one, as in couplets.[33] In fact, the only definite, structured break in a *ragaḷe* passage appears at its very end, before the beginning of the following chapter or as a conclusion to the entire poem, in this case oftentimes after a continuous reading of hundreds of verses. In addition, even-numbered chapters in the *Ragaḷegaḷu* are written in prose, again dictating—as in the case of the odd-numbered chapters written in *ragaḷe*—a continuous reading.

Thus, at the most basic level, reading or listening to a Ragaḷe text involves a sense of indetermination that is caused by the absence of

32. The linguistic transition of the period is neatly described in Nilakanta Sastri (1976, 361). The linguistic turn evinced in Harihara's *Ragaḷegaḷu* reflects a broader change in literary style and expression that had started earlier. The twelfth-century *vacana* poets exercised daily language and unconventional literary practices in their compositions a century before Harihara. However, the linguistic register that is employed in the early *vacanas* is difficult to historicize, since they were transmitted orally for the first several centuries. Furthermore, the *vacanas* did not receive any attention from medieval literati, in contrast to Harihara, who was a recognized, influencing, and accomplished author (Nagaraj 2003, 359–68).

33. This rhyming technique is a defining feature in pre-modern Kannada poetry, usually applied in two modi: *ādiprāsa* (rhyming at the beginning of a line) and *antyaprāsa* (rhyming at the end of a line). Sheldon Pollock, building on Nāgavarma's discussion in the *Chandōmbudhi*, writes about *prāsa*: "[I]t is something essential for Kannada, without which poetry in the language is said to be unable to achieve beauty" (2004, 395).

bounded verses. The uninterrupted style of composition of the *Ragaḷegaḷu* differs from other Kannada literary styles, which embed structural pauses between each verse.[34] The distinctiveness of the *ragaḷe* meter's unbounded flow stands out not only against the relief of Sanskrit-based meters but also against local (*dēśi*) ones. For example, *ṣaṭpadi*, a local six-foot meter popularized by Harihara's nephew Rāghavāṅka, is described as "a self-contained, densely packed, patterned verse that typically presents a complete image, thought, or picture connected by a syntactic thread that creates a conceptual whole."[35] This verse-level monad, which as a literary practice is pervasive in South Asian compositions, is missing from the *ragaḷe* as it is used by Harihara for full-length compositions. The audience of a Ragaḷe poem, instead of apprehending the composition in a "per-verse" manner and pace or switching between changing meters and short prose sections as is the case in the *campū* compositions, is confronted with a continual and even forcefully monotonous reading without strict structural boundaries or arrests.

To demonstrate the effect of the *ragaḷe* meter on narrative transmission in the *Ragaḷegaḷu*, I provide here the opening lines of the *Guṇḍayyana Ragaḷe*, in which the protagonist Guṇḍayya is introduced. Although it is not possible to replicate the experience of reading or listening to the Kannada text in written English form, I nevertheless hope that reading the following passage might provide a sense, albeit an indirect one, of the gripping flow of narration that this text communicates to its audience in its original form. In the following passage, I have deliberately kept the translation as literal as possible and the punctuation to a minimum in an attempt to convey the original, continuous flow of the text:

> In the northern region there was
> An eternal city called Balluke
> Where a Śaraṇa of Śiva the moon bearer resided
> Graceful and free from illusion
> And his craft of making pots
> Gave delight to the dance of Śiva of forehead endowed with an eye.
> His name was Kumbara ["Potter"] Guṇḍa ["Servant"]
> And it was sweet to the ears of Śiva the moon bearer.

---

34. Kurtakoṭi (1995, 167–68).

35. Vanamala Viswanatha in Rāghavāṅka and Viswanatha (2017, xxix).

Every little observance, my god![36]
The greatest devotee on earth, my god!
What can I say of the work he did?
Even as I see it, still it is difficult to describe:
Guṇḍayya's energy-base became the base for his potter's machine
His effort became its revolving axis
The six energy-centers became the potter's wheel
His shining navel was the very center of the instrument
His illusionary body became the clay
And remembrance of Śiva became the thread with which he fettled the clay.
His dedication to Śiva became the turning rod
While his revolving fists were his life force
And his devotion was the burning furnace
In concentrated effort he pounded
And the heat of his inner parching dried everything up
Burning with consuming fire
With a flood made of blissful tears
And a boiler made of various forms of devotion
He was sated with Śiva's fluids of compassion
And full of bliss gave the pots to Śivabhaktas

entenaluttarabhāgadoḷ irpudu
santata ballukepuravenisirpudu
allirpam śaśimauḷiya śaraṇam
sallalitam māyāniruharaṇam
ghaṭakāyakavāyatavāgirpudu
niṭilākṣana naṭan ege nalivappudu
nāmam kumbara guṇḍan enippudu
sōmadharana kiviginidāgirpudu
nēmasthaṃ nēmastham śivaśiva
bhūmiyoḷ uttamabhatkaṃ śivaśiva
māḍuva kāyakavadan ēn embeṃ
nōḍuvaḍenagaridinnentembeṃ
ādhāraveyādhāraṃ adāgire
vedheye cakrada moḷe tānāgire

36. The literal expression here is "*śivaśiva,*" an exclamation that denotes great concern or awe.

mige ṣaṭcakrame cakraṃ adāgire
sogayipa nābhiye nābhiyadāgire
kanasina kāyaṃ mṛttikeyāgire
nenahaṃ cāṭedāraṅgaḷavāgire
niṣṭheye piḍivurudaṇḍaṃ adāgire
muṭṭi tiruguvudu jīvanaṃ āgire
māḍuva bhakti kaṭāhaṃ adāgalu
kūḍida karaṇade mardisutāgalu
mige śōṣāṇadātapadindārisi
bage migal udarāgnigaḷiṃ dāhisi
ānandajalaplāvanaṃ āgire
nānā bhakti kaṭāham adāgire
śivakāruṇyāmbugaḷiṃ tīvute
śivabhaktargānandadoḷ īvute[37]

This passage continues without any formulaic break until the end of the poem. No formal markers divide the narrative into subsections. Rather, the unfolding of this story continues, moving seamlessly from its exposition through the ensuing events until it reaches its denouement. The original Kannada dictates a continuous and gripping reading or listening experience, in which the reader or listener barely has time to stop for a breath. Kīrtinātha Kurtakōṭi, a literary critic, describes the *ragaḷe* meter as generating the effect of a gushing river with a potentially endless emanation of ordered and balanced waves. These, in turn, carry an uninterrupted, rhythmic flow that Kurtakōṭi compares to that of the body's blood circulation and of life-breath.[38]

The flow of the *ragaḷe* meter creates a space for other devices that communicate the unique emotive quality of the *Ragaḷegaḷu*. Verses nine to twelve in the above passage demonstrate the clear, emotional expressivity that generates a sense of Harihara's direct and immediate presence:

---

37. *Guṇḍayyana Ragaḷe* vv. 1–28 in Harihara and Suṅkāpura (1976b, 211–12).

38. Kurtakoṭi (1995, 168). Veṅkaṭācala Śāstrī uses a comparable metaphor of a river cycling between ebbs and tides (1978, 302). Along similar lines, Narasiṃhācār (2008, 154–55) also mentions the stylistic oscillation found in the *Ragaḷegaḷu*, though he uses the metaphor of a kite whose flight is controlled by Śiva Virūpākṣa. Harihara's entry in the *Encyclopaedia of Indian Literature* contains the following statement: "Rhymes, rhythms and alliterations were naturally best suited to this metric form due to its running nature without being bound by any rules or regulations of the old traditions" (Datta 1987, 1549 s.v. *Harihara [Kannada]*).

Every little observance, my god!
The greatest devotee on earth, my god!
What can I say of the work he did?
Even as I see it, still it is difficult to describe.

The first two of these lines end with the exclamation "*śivaśiva,*" translated here as "my god!" This is a colloquial expression, still prevalent in common parlance, but its seamless incorporation into a thirteenth-century literary text was innovative. Similarly, the lines that follow, expressing the author's limited ability in describing the devotee's work, are deliberate devices to communicate to the reader or listener of this text a deeper sentiment of astonishment at the saint's piety as figured by the text.

The poetic devices I mention here, and others that permeate the *Ragaḷegaḷu,* stand apart from the pan-Indian, Sanskritic plethora of embellishment and belong instead to a less erudite and more local and performative tradition. In a deeper sense, too, the *Ragaḷegaḷu* does not share the condensed intellectual idiomaticity that is the hallmark of Sanskrit literature but utilizes a more straightforward and linear way of presenting its content. The informed listener is rarely required to suspend his or her absorption in the text in order to reflect on hidden meanings or suggestions, or to relish a specifically rich embellishment; these are infrequent in the *Ragaḷegaḷu.* Harihara was the first to break away from the heavily Sanskritized *mārga* style and to compose in a manner that was influenced by the poetics and themes of oral literature and the emerging cultural world of *bhakti* (including, of course, the *vacana*s themselves) while at the same time also sporadically using the embellished, poetic mode of expression that was typical of the classics-oriented literary culture of his time. Harihara's unique blend of oral, non-elite traditions and courtly literary traditions created something new that was to impact the world of Kannada literature for the next several centuries, practically to the end of its pre-modern phase.

Another salient feature of the *Ragaḷegaḷu* poetic form is the fragmented nature of the text. Often throughout this book I refer to the *Ragaḷegaḷu* as a "corpus" in the sense of a collection of separate poems. And indeed, Harihara composed a series of independent poems, each dedicated to a different saint or a particular theme related to devotion (usually liturgical). There is no organizational trajectory to this sporadic structure; other than the shared texture between the separate Ragaḷes, the text has no formal mechanism to unify them.[39] This means that there are no textual boundaries that mark the beginning or ending of the *Ragaḷegaḷu*, a fact that implies some uncertainty regarding which poems are included in the collection. As Eṃ. Eṃ. Kalaburgi explains in his introduction to the popular edition of Harihara's Ragaḷes, the "bundles" (*kaṭṭugaḷu*) of manuscripts of Ragaḷes found in religious institutions and archives throughout Karnataka, all titled "Harihara's Ragaḷes," contain different poems.[40] Expansive counts of Ragaḷes considered to have been written by Harihara, such as that by Kalaburgi, go beyond a hundred, while the most restrictive count by Ec. Dēvīrappa comes to a total of sixty-one Ragaḷes, out of which eighteen were written about Śaivas from the Kannada-speaking region.[41] In this study, I follow Dēvīrappa's critical and widely accepted count, focusing on the eighteen Ragaḷes written by Harihara about the Kannada saints. My readings in the *Ragaḷegaḷu* in this book are from two critical editions by Eṃ. Es. Suṅkāpura.[42]

Beyond the textual problem of determining how many Ragaḷes were authentically written by Harihara, the open-bounded structure and the fragmented nature of the *Ragaḷegaḷu* have commendable implications, one of which is the straightforward and clear narration of each saint's life. Harihara's sporadic narratives can be contrasted with Cēkkiḻār's in the Tamil *Periya Purāṇam* and Pālkuriki Sōmanātha's in the Telugu *Basava Purāṇamu*. All three narrate the stories of Śaiva saints from south India and were written during the twelfth and thirteenth centuries.[43] Although the three texts share a similar (though obviously not identical)

---

39. Conceptually, the fragmented nature of the *Ragaḷegaḷu* bears similarities to the definitive north-Indian hagiographical composition, the *Bhaktamāla* ("Garland of Bhaktas") (Hawley 2005, 189).

40. Harihara and Kalaburgi (2011 [1999], xix–xx).

41. Harihara and Dēvīrappa (1995 [1968], xxvi–xxvii). The eighteen Ragaḷes are: *Ādayyana Ragaḷe, Ēkāntarāmitandeya Ragaḷe, Kēśirāja Daṇṇāyakara Ragaḷe, Kōvūra Bommatandeya Ragaḷe, Guṇḍayyana Ragaḷe, Teluga Jommayyana Ragaḷe, Nimbiyakkana Ragaḷe, Prabhudēvara Ragaḷe, Basavēśvaradēvara Ragaḷe, Bāhūra Bommatandeya Ragaḷe, Bhōgaṇṇana Ragaḷe, Mahādēviyakkana Ragaḷe, Musuṭeya Cauḍayyana Ragaḷe, Śaṅkaradāsimayyana Ragaḷe, Surigeya Cauḍayyana Ragaḷe, Rēvaṇasiddhēśvarana Ragaḷe, Vaijakavveya Ragaḷe, Hāvinahāḷa Kallayyana Ragaḷe.*

42. Harihara and Suṅkāpura (1976a, 1976b). Other publications of Harihara's Ragaḷes are Harihara and Kalaburgi (2011 [1999]); Harihara and Dēvīrappa (1995 [1968]); Harihara and Haḷakaṭṭi (1968).

43. Ben-Herut (2015).

Śaiva imaginaire, the Tamil and the Telugu texts differ from the Kannada text in that they embody, as their titles suggest, a Purāṇic narration style, one that attempts to encompass an encyclopedic set of themes and stories under one thematic frame.[44] While the central thematic thread of the Tamil *Periya Purāṇam* is the life of Cuntarar and that of the Telugu *Basava Purāṇamu* is the life of Basavaṇṇa, Harihara's *Ragaḷegaḷu* has no such overarching thematic frame; each Ragaḷe about the Kannada saints opens with either the saint's prenatal career in Kailāsa, as discussed above, or with his or her birth on earth, and culminates with the saint's departure from the human realm and ascension back to Kailāsa to reunite with the god Śiva.[45] As mentioned, the result of this bounded narrative strategy in the *Ragaḷegaḷu* is a certain neatness in the saints' lives. The narrative in each *Ragaḷegaḷu* poem is linear and clear, generally devoid of complicated or disorienting digressions or subplots, while the narrative structure and leitmotifs shared among the stories (a prenatal incident in Śiva's heavenly abode, life on earth, devotional experiences and miracles with a climactic denouement, and a reunion with Śiva) provide a sense of narrative cohesion to the text as a whole. One area in which this neatness is easily demonstrable, and also has profound implications regarding the devotional world this text projects, is that the saints are not "forced" to associate with each other by a framing narrative.[46] As I noted in the introduction, the deeper implications of the fragmented structure of the *Ragaḷegaḷu* pertain to the text's literary image of the community of devotees. This community, in consequence of the separated stories, is extremely varied—a topic I address in the following chapters.

The Doyen of a New Literary Era

Kuppaḷḷi Veṅkaṭappa Puṭṭappa, popularly known as Kuvempu, who was the first Kannada author to receive the Jnanpith Award (a prestigious,

---

44. This is not the only distinct poetical feature of the genre (or multiple genres?) of regional Purāṇas, clearly distinguishable from its (or their) Sanskrit textual ancestor (Shulman 1980, 29). A comprehensive study of what regional Purāṇas entail in poetic terms has yet to appear, although the article by Anne Monius (2009) about mythical time in regional Purāṇas is a substantial step toward such a study.

45. Cuntarar's life as a narrative frame in the *Periya Purāṇam* is discussed in Peterson (1994, 197). See Ebeling (2010, 456, 472) for a discussion about individual stories with the *Periya Purāṇam* and its overall structure.

46. Ben-Herut (2012, 156–60).

national award for outstanding literary contribution) commented once that "the same great revolution done by Basavaṇṇa in the religious realm was done by Harihara in the literary realm."[47] Kuvempu's magnum opus, the *Rāmāyaṇa Darśana*, was influenced by Harihara's metrical style in the *Ragaḷegaḷu*. Similarly, many contemporary literary scholars in Kannada acknowledge Harihara's contribution to the development of Kannada literature. Ti. Es. Śāmarāya points to Harihara as the single most important poet among the Śaiva poets in Kannada, including the *vacana* composers.[48] K. S. Radhakrishna, a prolific translator of Kannada poetry, terms Harihara "the first revolutionary poet of Kannada."[49] Under the entry "Harihara" in the *Encyclopaedia of Indian Literature* one finds the following statement: "Harihara is known as a revolutionary poet in the sense that he completely changed the mode of poetic expression . . . He heralded a new era in the field of literature and was widely appreciated as the poet who changed the technique and theme of poetry."[50] S. D. Saudattimath, a prolific philologist, attests that "Harihara is recognized as one of the 'four great poets' in the history of Kannada literature, spread over a period of two thousand years."[51] Ec. Dēvīrappa, a leading philologist who did considerable research on the *Ragaḷegaḷu* during the second half of the twentieth century, writes that the whole body of Śivabhakti literature in Kannada in the medieval era is considered the "Harihara Tradition" (*harihara sampradāya*), and adds that there was no other poet quite like Harihara in the Kannada-speaking regions.[52] Ṭi. Vi. Veṅkaṭācala Śāstrī, one of the most acclaimed philologists of Kannada literature living today, in his monumental monograph on Kannada prosody, the *Kannaḍa Chandaḥsvarūpa*, writes that it was a great event in the history of Kannada literature that Harihara paid notice to the distinct ability of the metrical features of *ragaḷe* to

47. Quoted by Eṃ. Eṃ. Kalaburgi in Harihara and Kalaburgi (2012, xxii).

48. Śāmarāya (*c.*1964, 9).

49. Shivaprakash and Radhakrishna (1990, 58).

50. Datta (1987, 1549 s.v. *Harihara [Kannada]*).

51. Saudattimath (1988, 1). The other three being Pampa (eleventh century), Kumāravyāsa (fifteenth century), and Ratnākaravarni (sixteenth century). This scheme might be a response to the famous Ratnatraya ("triple gems") of classic Kannada poetry, who are Pampa, Ranna, and Pōnna.

52. Dēvīrappa (1979, 30).

beautify narrative poetry.[53] Another eminent literary historian, Ḍi. El. Narasiṃhācār, perhaps the leading figure in the field during the first half of the twentieth century, brings to the fore Harihara's innovative style (which he describes as perfect), his sophisticated usage and maturity of language, and his unparalleled influence on the medieval poets, both those of *mārga* and those of *dēśi*, by developing existing and inventing new poetic and metrical tools.[54] Narasiṃhācār concludes his discussion of Harihara by stating that this poet is one of the greatest (*atiśrēṣṭha*) among the Kannada poets. There are other scholars too who echo these claims in their appreciation of Harihara's importance for the world of Kannada literature.[55]

Beyond Harihara's formal innovations in the *Ragaḷegaḷu*, his contribution is significant in that he used these formal textual features in order to generate in the text's intended audiences what South Asian literary theorists call *bhaktirasa*, an emotive and devotional response. Chandra Shobhi makes an explicit connection between the uniquely flowing, simple, and emotional course of the *Ragaḷegaḷu* and the ecstatic religious sentiment of devotion to Śiva,[56] and it is clear from reading the original that the stylistic choices made by Harihara in the *Ragaḷegaḷu* all enhance the emotional effect on the reader or listener. All the Śaraṇas' stories told by Harihara in the *Ragaḷegaḷu* have dramatic weight and abound in life-risking and normative-defiant moments, and it is at these narrative moments that Harihara expresses his inability to communicate his overflowing devotional sentiments by employing syntactical repetitions, onomatopoeic words,[57] and bursts of descriptive passages.

---

53. Veṅkaṭācala Śāstrī (1978, 302–3).

54. Narasiṃhācār (2008, 154–55). Together with few other Kannada scholars, Veṅkaṭācala Śāstrī and Narasiṃhācār are described by Sheldon Pollock as "scholars endowed with authentic philological sensibilities, deep historical understanding, and keen critical intelligence" (2004, 389).

55. These include Si. Nāgabhūṣaṇa (2005, 221–22); Saṇṇayya (2002, 143–53); Es. Ḍi. Savadattimaṭha in his Kannada writings (1999, 321); and Kīrtinātha Kurtakōṭi (1995, 151–73).

56. Chandra Shobhi (2005, 212): "Unlike the *campu* [*sic*], the *ragaḷe* form . . . enabled Harihara to describe the free flowing mood of *bhakti*. While each line has a fixed number of *mātra* [*sic*] *gaṇas*, *ragaḷe* does not have fixed number of lines and hence can conceivably extend limitlessly. This quality suits Harihara's objective of celebrating the excessive devotion of *śaiva* devotees and their actions."

57. For lists of onomatopoeia used by Harihara in the *Ragaḷegaḷu*, mostly exclamational, see Gonāla (2010, 52); Saudattimath (1988, 102–3).

The Complexities Within Harihara's Legacy

Different facets of Harihara's life and work portray an uncompromising, perhaps even eccentric, persona. The narrative traditions about Harihara dramatically describe how he blatantly rejected the comforts of courtly life in favor of an abstemious religious life. From the perspective of literary criticism, Harihara refused to continue following in the footsteps of his poetic predecessors in Kannada and instead chose to pave a new literary way. It is because of these traits that Dēvīrappa describes Harihara as "revolutionary" (*krāntipuruṣa*).[58] Of course, this term should not be read literally. Harihara, in contrast to some of the leading Śivabhaktas he wrote about in his *Ragaḷegaḷu*, was not a leader of the masses and did not directly change the society of his times. His revolution was literary rather than social, and it inaugurated a new era in Kannada literature, an era that would continue for several centuries.

Despite Harihara's traceable influence on Kannada literature from the thirteenth century onward, the relation of literary and religious successors to his work was complicated. On the one hand, Harihara is frequently eulogized by later Kannada authors and anthologizers, all of whom recognized his literary acumen and its significance. On the other hand, there are very few who adopted Harihara's style of composition in the *Ragaḷegaḷu*. A similar complexity exists with regard to Harihara's religious vision in the *Ragaḷegaḷu*. On the one hand, Harihara is repeatedly referred to as the first written source for learning about the remembered history of the twelfth-century Bhaktas. But on the other hand, his understanding of their sainthood, devotional practices, and devotional life in general was rejected by later narrative traditions. In this sense, this book is not only an attempt to uncover a lost link in the Kannada Śaiva imaginaire but also to understand *why* it was lost (or rather—why it lost the appreciation of the later tradition).

Although Harihara's innovative work inaugurated the era of medieval Kannada literature, different from the previous classical era in terms of language, style, narrative strategies, and themes, it did not become a new classic or role model to be copied. In spite of the revolutionary nature of Harihara's work, or perhaps *because* of it, what might be ostensibly termed "Harihara's literary and religious legacies" were to be contested by the same tradition that commemorated his personal audacity and literary

58. Dēvīrappa (1979, 29).

ingenuity and acknowledged his historical significance in the development of its own religious poetry. Only few directly followed Harihara's style of Ragaḷes.[59] No meaningful medieval Kannada poet, with the exception of Harihara's contemporary and *bhakti* comrade Kereya Padmarasa, utilized the *ragaḷe* meter in a manner similar to that of Harihara. Since the 1920s, the only pre-modern Ragaḷes to be printed in Karnataka aside from Harihara's have been a handful by a minor poet who lived in the seventeenth century.[60]

This state of affairs might seem surprising when we consider the high regard in which Harihara—and his *Ragaḷegaḷu*—have been held by pre-modern Kannada poets.[61] Moreover, the technical simplicity of the *ragaḷe* meter might be thought to have produced numerous followers. Considering these factors, how can we explain the fact that the literary style created by Harihara in the *Ragaḷegaḷu* did not prevail?

From the perspective of literary style, the nub of the problem may actually be found precisely in the inherent formulaic simplicity of *ragaḷe*. The form's metrical traits generate a text that is very simple in its structure, and in mediocre hands this simplicity can easily deteriorate into technical monotony. Kurtakōṭi remarks:

> The rhythm of versification can become technical as it stretches, as if endlessly, in the uniformity of the syllabic arrangement (*mātregaṇa*) [of the *ragaḷe* meter]. Nevertheless, despite this monotony, the rhythmic diversity that Harihara creates is surprising.[62]

---

59. An exception to this is Pālkuriki Sōmanātha, who experimented with the *ragaḷe* meter in his Kannada, Telugu, and Sanskrit compositions, but in a limited fashion. Sōmanātha's *Basava Purāṇamu* and *Paṇḍitārādhya Caritre* are both written in *dvipada*, which is a meter that is related but not identical to *ragaḷe* (Somanātha, Narayana Rao, and Roghair 1990, 5–6). Tribhuvana Tāta, a minor poet of few Ragaḷes, is also worthy of mention. There were, in addition, those who continued the limited use of *ragaḷe* within a metrically diversified text, in continuance with the classic tradition of *campū* (Veṅkaṭācala Śāstrī 1978, 308–15). Some modern poets have actually picked up Harihara's *ragaḷe* style in a robust manner (Shivaprakash and Radhakrishna 1990, 58). One possible explanation for the renewed interest in *ragaḷe* in the twentieth century could be its inherent structural simplicity that corresponds well with modern literary trends.

60. A single Ragaḷe attributed to Bhīmakavi is also said to have been published in 1970. See the survey compiled by Saṇṇayya (2002, 143–53) of Ragaḷe publications in Kannada during the twentieth century.

61. See quotations from later texts about Harihara's greatness in Īśvaran (1971, 12–15).

62. Kurtakoṭi (1995, 161).

Veṅkaṭācala Śāstrī also praises Harihara's ingenuity in his effort to break the inherent monotony of the *ragaḷe* meter[63] and later explains:

> In none among the *ragaḷe* poets subsequent to Harihara can his devotional frenzy, divine inspiration, lofty voice, and the like, be traced, and their works appear like pale imitations when compared against his. This is the case not only with regard to verse construction, but also to dialog construction, word repetitions, various alliterations, tonal modulations, and so on. However, with regard to metrical composition, not only is Harihara's accomplishment not visible in others' works, but also many weaknesses stand out.[64]

According to Veṅkaṭācala Śāstrī, the case is not so much that later poets did not try to follow in Harihara's giant footsteps, but that they simply did not possess his poetic virtuosity.[65] Harihara's work was thus inimitable, and this was the reason that no work by the other *ragaḷe* poets made it into the literary pantheon of Kannada as Harihara's *Ragaḷegaḷu* did.[66]

Something of Harihara's unique quality is reflected in the following critique by K. S. Radhakrishna, which simultaneously praises and scolds Harihara's style:

> [Harihara's] chief weakness is his unrestrained poetic fluency that fails to register the consistency which is the hallmark of the creation of any great poet. Strangely enough, his strength appears to lie in his weakness: he writes always in ecstatic joy which not even the greatest of poets can sustain for any length of time for his poetry to be consistent. In his intense moments of joy Harihara's brilliance is incomparable and it takes us to the world of mystics; its sparkling poetic sheen leaves the reader dazzled. But suddenly from the heights of ecstasy, he falls into the abyss of mundane prosaic statements.[67]

---

63. Veṅkaṭācala Śāstrī (1978, 305).

64. Ibid., 309.

65. This opinion is also echoed by Saṇṇayya (2002, 143).

66. Paradoxically, there were attempts to compose Ragaḷes under Harihara's name, which led to questions regarding the authorship of those composed by him.

67. Shivaprakash and Radhakrishna (1990, 59).

The point to be made with regard to the failure of later traditions to continue producing Ragaḷes is that, despite this failure, Harihara's *Ragaḷegaḷu* had a substantial impact on the medieval literary tradition in Kannada. Although we do not find any other significant *ragaḷe* narrative work in pre-modern Kannada poetry, the impact of Harihara's *Ragaḷegaḷu* on medieval Kannada literature can be easily traced: it is Rāghavāṅka, Harihara's nephew and protégé, who adopts the literary strategies developed by Harihara in his Ragaḷes in order to put forth the less chaotic and more contained meter of *ṣaṭpadi* (six-foot verse structure), and it is this meter, and not the *ragaḷe,* that becomes the standard medium for Kannada narrative compositions in the medieval period to follow.

Rāghavāṅka's composition style for his narrative works, based on the single meter of *ṣaṭpadi,* embodies many of the innovations that Harihara introduces in his *Ragaḷegaḷu,* such as the central theme of Śivabhakti and the lives of Śivabhaktas, the linguistic shift to Middle Kannada, and an expressivity based on oral traditions.[68] At the same time, the foot-based verse structure of the *ṣaṭpadi* has a much wider appeal than the uncontrolled flow of the *ragaḷe*—for the composer as well as for the audience—and this is the basis for the *ṣaṭpadi*'s success among later authors.[69] Thus, from the perspective of literary history, it is not that Harihara's literary revolution went unnoticed or failed, but rather that, as is the case with most revolutions, it was translated into less extreme and more formulaic practices that soon became the norm.[70]

There are also ideological issues with Harihara's *Ragaḷegaḷu* that contributed to what can be termed as an alienation of this text by later Vīraśaiva authors. As we advance in the history of Vīraśaiva literature from the thirteenth to the sixteenth century, we find references to Harihara's work increasingly accompanied by testimonies to a growing

68. Rāghavāṅka and Viswanatha (2017, xiv).

69. See Kurtakoṭi (1995, 171–73). The Telugu meter of *dvipada* with which Pālkuriki Sōmanātha wrote his *Basava Purāṇamu* had a similar (though less totalistic) fate to that of Harihara's *ragaḷe* (Narayana Rao and Shulman 2002, 19).

70. Vanamala Viswanatha, who translated Rāghavāṅka's masterpiece *Hariścandra Carite* to English, writes that in contrast to Harihara, Rāghavāṅka "valorizes classical courtly poetry and Shaiva institutional practices" (Rāghavāṅka and Viswanatha, xvii). This statement does not account for Harihara's own compositions in courtly styles or for the historical complications involved in associating Harihara with a ubiquitous rejection of traditional Śaivism, but it does acknowledge Rāghavāṅka's more familiar and acceptable style of composition in comparison with that of his radical uncle.

discomfort with Harihara's portrayal of the Śivaśaraṇas, a discomfort that is further demonstrated by the repeated need to rewrite their remembered history. This trend can be explained by Harihara's unique religious vision, a vision that becomes less and less suitable for the specific needs of the institutionalized tradition as it develops over subsequent centuries.

Again the text's unusual structure merits our attention. While later encyclopedic hagiographies weave many stories about different Śaraṇas around one central figure (Basavaṇṇa, Allama Prabhu, Mahādēviyakka, and others), Harihara's *Ragaḷegaḷu* has no such enveloping thematic framework. Instead, each of his Ragaḷes is dedicated to the life of a particular Śivaśaraṇa, be it a famous Sanskrit poet from the pan-Indian imaginaire like Bāṇa (temporally situated before the turn of the first millennium), a Śaiva of the Tamil Nāyaṉmār tradition like Kaṇṇappa (from the turn of the first millennium), or a more recent saintly person from the Kannada-speaking region like Basavaṇṇa. As I discuss in detail in the following chapter, the only criterion for entering Harihara's hall of fame is having a life story that exhibits a clear and unwavering devotion to Śiva, while issues of specific actions, creeds, or traditions are not foregrounded. This nonhierarchical inclusiveness, in which different Bhaktas from different locales and eras are grouped together without any organizing principle—be it chronological, religious, thematic, or other—invites doctrinal obscurities and ambiguities, especially when dealing with a religious phenomenon that oscillates between Brahminical orthodoxy and radical iconoclasm.[71]

The fragmented structure of the *Ragaḷegaḷu* can be juxtaposed with the integrative plotting of the *Basava Purāṇamu*. In contrast to Harihara's neat arrangement of distinct Śaiva saints, each of which is treated in a separate poem within the corpus, the *Basava Purāṇamu* presents the saints' stories within concentric narrative frames. The latter text's convoluted plotting indicates that Pālkuriki Sōmanātha is invested in establishing Basavaṇṇa as the absolute political and religious leader of the Vīraśaiva movement for generations to come. To this end, Sōmanātha literally (as well as literarily) weaves into his narrative about Basavaṇṇa a bewildering number of stories about other Śaraṇas and, in this way, subjugates their historical significance to that of Basavaṇṇa. Sōmanātha is by no means the first to exercise

71. I allude here to Richard Davis's *Ritual in an Oscillating Universe: Worshiping Śiva in Medieval India* (1991).

this narrative strategy. We find a similar structure used in the Tamil *Periya Purāṇam*, composed more than a century earlier. Notwithstanding textual and literary differences, both these texts nominally belong to the genre of vernacular Purāṇa and participate in the broad south-Indian Śaiva narrative tradition.[72]

What is important for our discussion here is the fact that the *Ragaḷegaḷu* lacks the political agenda regarding Basavaṇṇa that the *Basava Purāṇamu* has. It appears that this political agenda contributed to the immense popularity of the Kannada version of the *Basava Purāṇa* among the medieval Vīraśaiva community, a popularity that with time clearly exceeded that of Harihara's *Ragaḷegaḷu*.[73] Put differently, we can say that—in a manner that is perhaps paradoxical to modern dispositions—the clear plotting style of the *Ragaḷegaḷu* contributed to its marginalization by more grandiose and convoluted accounts, such as that of the *Basava Purāṇamu*.

The presentation of piety in the *Ragaḷegaḷu* was problematic for the later tradition for other reasons as well. Harihara's enhanced focus on devotionalism as the sole criterion for his writing about saintly characters allows him some leeway with regard to the saints' infallibility, and as consequence the protagonists in the *Ragaḷegaḷu* are imperfect from a doctrinal point of view or that of the religious community. For example, Harihara tells us that Basavaṇṇa, in his prenatal existence an attendant of the god Śiva in the god's heavenly abode in Kailāsa, was given the task of distributing flowers to those present. But Basavaṇṇa accidently neglected Śiva's son Skanda, lied about it, and was consequently sent by Śiva to live as a human being on earth and atone for his misdeed by equally serving all of Śiva's devotees.[74] This episode, woven around Basavaṇṇa's ethical failure, was never retold by the later medieval hagiographers. Instead, they picked up a different story about the

72. We do not have any concrete proof or claims by the authors regarding direct appropriations of the *Periya Purāṇam* either by Harihara or by Pālkuriki Sōmanātha. However, the structural similarities between the Tamil *Periya Purāṇam* and the Telugu *Basava Purāṇamu* suggest direct textual appropriation by Sōmanātha. A support for this postulation can be found in the fact that Sōmanātha knew Tamil and composed a few verses in this language.

73. Desai (1968, 244–53). One could make in this case a broader claim about the correlation between historical progression and the growing fantastic hyperbolism in South Asian hagiographies. For such a study about a modern, twentieth-century tradition, see Rinehart (1999).

74. This is a summary of the first chapter of the *Basavēśvaradēvara Ragaḷe* (Harihara and Suṅkāpura 1976a, 23–28). See also Desai (1968, 250).

circumstances for Basavaṇṇa's human birth, in which Basava committed no sin or mistake.[75]

Another problem with the reception of the *Ragaḷegaḷu* by the later Kannada Vīraśaiva community began to develop a few centuries after the time of Harihara. As Chandra Shobhi cogently argues, the religio-political climate of the Vijayanagara court from the fifteenth century onward required coherent communal religious narratives from participating sects.[76] Harihara's text—despite its acknowledged contribution to the Vīraśaiva tradition—could not provide such a collective narrative. Particular features of the *Ragaḷegaḷu,* namely the inclusion of different Śaiva sects and the uncensored manner of describing some Śaraṇas, seem to have become its weak points when encountered by new, puritanical demands of the Viraktas, the fifteenth- and sixteenth-century reformers at the Vijayanagara court. Chandra Shobhi writes:

> They [the fifteenth-century *virakta* poets] find Harihara to be a problematic figure, whose account of *śaiva* devotees had to be challenged . . . He does not write about a collective in any of his *ragaḷes* nor does he or [do] other poets of the pre-*virakta* era write about Lingayat theology and practice, as Cāmarasa and the various editors of *Śūnyasampādane* do.[77]

Chandra Shobhi shows how doctrinal anxieties regarding contemporaneous communal identity and the manner in which the Vīraśaiva past was projected reshaped the fifteenth- and sixteenth-century narratives about the Śaraṇas. He presents an example of this by focusing on the changing nature of the important mystical figure of Allama Prabhu, contrasting the depiction of young Allama's romance with a voluptuous dancer in Harihara's *Prabhudēvara Ragaḷe* and his abstemious piety in Cāmarasa's *Prabhuliṅgalīle.*[78] Harihara starts his story about Allama in Kailāsa, where Allama (as a Śivagaṇa called Nirmāya) is infatuated with a divine damsel (Surasati). The distracted couple is sent to earth by Śiva in order to

---

75. The purged version makes its first textual appearance in the Telugu *Basava Purāṇamu* several decades after the *Ragaḷegaḷu.* See Somanātha, Narayana Rao, and Roghair (1990, 41–55).

76. Chandra Shobhi (2005, 195–225).

77. Ibid., 212–13. See also Kalaburgi in Harihara and Kalaburgi (2012, xxii).

78. Chandra Shobhi (2005, 195–207).

culminate their earthly desires outside of Kailāsa. The narrative goes on to tell the sensuous love story between the two heavenly beings as worldly youngsters, a love affair that ends tragically with the unexpected death of the young woman. The death throws Allama into an abysmal dejection, followed by a religious epiphany that alters his life and sends him on a spiritual mission. Allama's journey finally culminates in his union with Śiva at Śrīśailam. Within the logic of this narrative framework, Allama's humanness (including his vices) plays a crucial dramatic role, since Harihara's narrative logic dictates that the more earthly the young Allama's affair is, the darker his post-affair depression and the more effective the drama of his spiritual awakening will be. Indeed, Harihara seems to celebrate young Allama's earthly (and theologically faulty) desires with erotic descriptions of Allama's sexual union with his lover.

Matters are very different in Cāmarasa's version. Cāmarasa, who labors in his text to reconstruct Allama as the utmost spiritual authority of the Virakta movement (a role that is almost alien to Harihara's Allama), cannot allow the perfect mystic Allama to be stirred by earthly desires. Accordingly, Cāmarasa completely drops the Kailāsa story about the erring Nirmāya and transforms the earthly union between Allama and his lover into a broken metaphor for an asymmetrical and passionless encounter. In fact, in Cāmarasa's text, Allama's lover dies precisely because of her failure to seduce Allama.[79] Other Virakta authors create less extreme reconfigurations of Harihara's Allama than that drawn by Cāmarasa, though they still reconstitute the saint's figure according to theological restraints that are completely absent in Harihara's work. For example, in Lakkaṇṇa Daṇḍēśa's *Śivatattvacintāmaṇi*, a voluminous fifteenth-century work, Allama's heavenly persona Nirmāya desires a female beauty only after Śiva has chastised him over another issue. This narrative shift is intended to ameliorate Allama's "original sin," as his arousal is reframed and explained away by Lakkaṇṇa Daṇḍēśa, in contrast to Allama's quite straightforward heavenly infatuation in Harihara's version.[80]

I would like to support Chandra Shobhi's claims regarding the reconfiguration of Allama by the later Viraktas. Beyond the issue of earthly lust, a more general discrepancy between Harihara's depiction of Allama and all the later depictions pertains to his volubility. Here, again, we sense

79. Ibid., 204–6.

80. This incident appears in the *Śivatattvacintāmaṇi* 29.34–31. See L. Basavarāju (2001 [1960], 44–45).

a chasm between Harihara and the later writers. While in Harihara Allama appears to be a laconic person who, despite some sporadic spiritual encounters, shuns human contact and verbal exchanges, in the later accounts Allama is a provocative and confident debater, an orator. Somewhat paradoxically, it is the former depiction of Allama that better fits his philosophically suspicious attitude toward language as conveyed by many of the *vacanas* attributed to him.[81] Conversely, Allama's latter depiction better fits the huge corpus of *vacanas* attributed to him by the medieval tradition.

As stated earlier, these specific examples point to a larger trend by the later authors to replace Harihara's narratives about the Śaraṇas with more doctrinally aligned accounts. Chandra Shobhi even presents an emic reflection from a later seventeenth-century account of Harihara's problematic status in the view of the Viraktas at the Vijayanagara court. The text describes a Vaiṣṇava minister who comments while debating with a Virakta about the latter's intent to retell the stories about Śivaśaraṇas: "[You] characterized the verses of Hampe Harihara as *abaddha* (incoherent) . . . "[82] Clearly, Harihara became something of a doctrinal problem for the later Vīraśaivas, and it appears that this state of affairs contributed to the marginalization of Harihara's *Ragaḷegaḷu* in the history of Vīraśaiva literature.

A Devotional Literary Turn

Harihara wrote the *Ragaḷegaḷu* soon after Śaiva devotional culture had started to make inroads into the northern regions of the Kannada-speaking region, and his stories about the recent Kannada devotees reflect a conscious effort by this accomplished poet to reconfigure traditional and conventional literary expression so it could accommodate this new culture.

In accordance with the inclusive devotional message of the saints' own poetry in the *vacanas*, the *Ragaḷegaḷu* appealed to new audiences. But the Ragaḷes are not similar to the *vacanas*: the former are much lengthier, composed in strict meter (albeit simple) and in written form (rather than oral), and they convey a devotional message through life narratives rather than through lyricism (although the first-person voice so characteristic of the

81. Chandra Shobhi quotes a line from a famous *vacana* attributed to Allama: "See, *lipi* (script) that should not be erased ought not to be written" (2005, 180). On Allama's antilingual metaphysical stance, see Nāgarāj (1999, 45–84).

82. Chandra Shobhi (2005, 198).

vacanas does find its way into the *Ragaḷegaḷu* on occasion). Furthermore, Harihara is not remembered in tradition as a *vacana*-composer but is associated with a separate group, that of accomplished Śaiva *kavis* (poets), a title that none of the *vacana* composers could (or would) own.

The literary acumen of Harihara and the recognition he received for his literary achievements, even from non-Śaiva poets, place the *Ragaḷegaḷu* in a unique moment in the history of Kannada literature, marked by the turning away from elitist and intricate forms of literary expression modeled on the convention of the pan-Indian Sanskrit tradition and toward simplified and local forms that involved contemporary figures and themes taken from the familiar and quotidian cultural world of the Kannada-speaking region. The following chapters deal with the content of the *Ragaḷegaḷu* stories dedicated to the local Kannada saints, and with how the social and religious world in which they operated, the nascent world of Kannada Śivabhakti, is imagined in this text.

2

Who Is a Bhakta?

HAVING SET THE stage in the introduction with strategies for reading the *Ragaḷegaḷu* and in Chapter 1 with basic details about the text's literary context, I turn now to an analysis of central themes in the *Ragaḷegaḷu* stories about the Kannada saints, an analysis that will take up the rest of this book in a movement from the center to the boundaries. This chapter begins that analysis by focusing on the innermost aspect of the devotees in the *Ragaḷegaḷu*, their sentiment of devotion. In addition to being central to their lives, the devotees' interiority is the element that is most clearly shared among the text's bewildering variety of Śaiva characters with their different religious behaviors. The question of what connects an educated, rich, and learned Brahmin Śaiva at a king's court and a poor, uneducated pot-maker is emblematic for South Asian devotional religion in general, because the appeal to wide audiences that is shared across all *bhakti* traditions immediately raises specific questions about how each *bhakti* tradition accommodates social differences under the very general umbrella of "devotion."

By focusing primarily on the variety of traditions, communities, religious practices, and literatures that use the term *bhakti*, scholarship in recent decades has problematized a simple meaning of this term, approaching it as a polysemous label that embraces many levels of religious devotion.[1] The term *bhakti* is derived from the Sanskrit verb root *bhaj* ("to share, to participate," "to be devoted to, to resort to," among other meanings) and is mentioned in relation to religious attitudes as early as the middle of the

---

1. Hawley (2015); Cort (2013).

first millennium BCE in Pāṇini's Sanskrit grammar.[2] *Bhakti* is commonly translated as "devotion," a complicated term in itself that carries a set of cultural biases.[3] But even beyond translational issues, the various historical and literary contexts in which the term *bhakti* has been used over the past two and half millennia makes it difficult to narrow it down to a coherent set of theological tenets, religious practices, or social attitudes.[4]

Following John Cort's assertion that "*bhakti* is not one single thing,"[5] the goal of this chapter is limited and specific: to unravel Harihara's understanding of *bhakti* and its agentive derivation *bhakta*, or "devotee," by analyzing his use of these terms in the *Ragaḷegaḷu*.[6] Harihara himself, by including among those he calls Śivabhaktas figures from outside the Kannada-speaking region, assumes a *bhakti* discourse that takes place in a setting that is larger than the local one. Like Harihara, I relate throughout this book to a *bhakti* discourse that extends beyond a narrow geographic area. However, my conversation with other traditions does not in any sense assume the existence of a unified, agreed-upon, or coherent historical or social phenomenon. In this sense, the *bhakti* discourse resembles in its diversity the Indian highway as once described to me by Joyce Flueckiger: a thoroughfare hosting a bewildering variety of means of conveyance, from the feet of the village man and the ox cart, through the motorcycle and the bus, to the lavish executive car. All of these make use of the same route of transportation but do so in radically different ways.

---

2. Hawley (2015, 5) and footnoted references. See also the extensive discussion in Novetzke (2008, 7–23), Pechilis (1999, 3–8), Sharma (1979, 62) on the etymology and early appearances of the term.

3. Cort (2002); Hallisey (1988, 1–57).

4. Various scholarly efforts have been made to enhance our analytical awareness of the historical diversity covered by the term *bhakti*. An early critique of an essentialized understanding of *bhakti* was made by Krishna Sharma (1987, 1979). Jack Hawley's recent monograph *A Storm of Songs* (2015) focuses on the historical construction of *bhakti* in the sense of a historical religious movement that swept the subcontinent. According to Hawley, the narrative of the "*bhakti* movement" is relatively recent and particularly north-Indian and Vaiṣṇava-oriented. Some scholars approach *bhakti* from historical and social perspectives (Novetzke 2008; Pechilis 1999; Lorenzen 1995). See also Burchett (2011); Cort (2002).

5. Cort (2002, 62).

6. Patton Burchett writes: "[W]e should *not* approach the theory/ideology of *bhakti* as some unitary presence inherent in *bhakti* songs, poetry, and hagiographical stories, but rather as a *range* constructed variously by different readers and listeners in their encounters with *bhakti* art forms" (2009, 117, italics in the original).

Harihara's *Ragaḷegaḷu* makes a good case for the plethora of religious behaviors that are included under the terminological canopy called *bhakti*. The variety of religious behaviors, forms of verbal expression, and social formations that this text includes and validates as *bhakti*—even when we limit ourselves to the *Ragaḷegaḷu* stories from the Kannada-speaking region—do not constitute a unified religious world. The one thing that they do have in common is that they all prescribe a mode of religious devotion: a sense of extreme veneration and dedication to the god Śiva.

The term *bhakti* is usually invoked by Harihara to describe a saint's piety and emotional state. This is made evident by the fact that he oftentimes couples *bhakti* with other words that denote emotion, such as *bhaya*, in the grammatical structure of a compound made of coordinative nouns (*dvandva*). *Bhaya*, literally "fear, trembling," is used in the *Ragaḷegaḷu* as an auspicious religious sentiment attributed to a devotee, and can be translated as "awe." In a similar vein, *bhakti* can be translated in the context of the *Ragaḷegaḷu* as a sentiment of devotion. Accordingly, Bhaktas can be translated as "devotees" in the sense that they are people endowed with a sentiment of devotion toward the god Śiva.

Who are the Bhaktas of the Kannada-speaking region according to the *Ragaḷegaḷu*, and is there a discernible set of practices or attitudes that could characterize them? This question gains historical significance when considered against the more congealed notion of the Vīraśaiva tradition that was to take shape in the centuries to follow, apparently with particular reformative force around the fifteenth and sixteenth centuries of the Vijayanagara era. It is difficult to think of Śivabhakti in the Kannada-speaking region today without associating it with several principles. These include a conscious (and at times protestive) discounting of a devotee's social status (with particular antagonism toward the Brahminical class), celebrating the ideal renunciatory vocation of the roaming Jaṅgama, nurturing a passionate and exclusive commitment to faith in the god Śiva (*ēkaniṣṭhe*), carrying and worshiping a personal emblem of the god (the *iṣṭaliṅgadhāraṇe*) while rejecting (at least rhetorically) temple worship, developing an original theological system (that eclectically draws on extrinsic Śaiva doctrines), and treasuring a canon of devotional songs (known today as *vacanas*) as well as a developed remembered history woven around a cadre of saints from the twelfth century.

Despite the fact that all of the above characteristics of this devotional tradition as it is currently known appear in the *Ragaḷegaḷu* stories, the corpus does not share the cohesive and institutionalized sense the tradition was to gain in later centuries. Most of the Śaiva saints that populate the *Ragaḷegaḷu* are from earlier periods and from places other than the Kannada-speaking region. The majority of them belong to the Nāyaṉmār, the sixty-three Śaiva saints associated with the Tamil region, and by the time of the *Ragaḷegaḷu* the stories of their lives had already been written down for about a century in the Tamil *Periya Purāṇam*. The centrality of Harihara's retelling of the lives of the Tamil saints in his Kannada corpus raises a host of questions, such as how these retellings compare with the stories in the *Periya Purāṇam*, how they compare with the stories about the Kannada saints, and why the Tamil saints' lives are even included in the *Ragaḷegaḷu* at all.[7] These are questions that I do not address in this book.

It could be expected that the diversity of Śaiva protagonists in the *Ragaḷegaḷu* in terms of their locale and period (the corpus also includes stories about Sanskrit poets of the first millennium and from various areas in the subcontinent) would find expression in the diversity of their devotional practices and lives. But—and this is a crucial point in terms of this book's concerns—the discernible group of *Ragaḷegaḷu* saints who are specifically associated with the Kannada-speaking region in the text itself presents a panoply of worship practices and of styles of exemplary religious life. While in general the Kannada saints adhere to some of the above principles associated with the Vīraśaiva tradition, they do so only sporadically and side by side with other practices, and there is no overarching dogmatic scheme nor are there "canons of faith" that could set boundaries for their devotional world. Put differently, practices that are not usually identified with the Kannada devotional tradition or even rejected by some proponents of the later tradition find their way into the stories and sometimes even take center stage.

The clearest example of this is in regard to temple worship. In the *Ragaḷegaḷu*, as many as seventeen out of the eighteen stories about saints in the Kannada-speaking region feature a Śiva temple as a valid and integral arena for devotional worship.[8] While in many South Asian devotional

7. See Ben-Herut (2015).

8. Ben-Herut (2016).

traditions there is nothing deviant in the affirmation of temple worship, some strands in the later Vīraśaiva tradition developed an unambiguous antipathy toward temple worship, to the extent that the entry for "Śaivism: Vīraśaivas" in the *Encyclopedia of Religion* contains the following statement: "Vīraśaivism may have appeared as a reaction of Dravidians against Brahmanic (and therefore Aryan) domination. Temple worship, sacrifice, and pilgrimages are condemned as useless."[9] Harihara's inclusion of temple worship (side by side with worship of the personal *liṅga*) clearly does not cohere with such an understanding.

The difference between the well-known "condemnation" of temple worship and what is told in the *Ragaḷegaḷu* stories about the Kannada saints is not the only case of dissonance. Under the entry "Liṅgāyat" in *The Oxford Dictionary of World Religions*, it is stated that "Liṅgāyats" adopted, among other things, the "denial of caste distinctions . . . denial of brahmanical superiority and authority, rites, and rituals. Women and men came to be regarded as equal."[10] Although these descriptions authentically represent the tradition's understanding of its collective self,[11] they do not correspond well with Harihara's earlier vision of Kannada Śivabhakti, which was far more diverse and less "doctrinal." Harihara's stories do contain frequent rejections of Brahminical superiority, yet at specific points they also affirm some Brahminical practices, rites, and values.[12] While they exhibit an avid rejection of caste-based exclusion from the ritualistic arena, this rejection does not imply a "denial of caste distinctions" in terms of labor divisions, group customs, and social roles. Although some of the stories in the *Ragaḷegaḷu* support women's relative independence, this is usually limited to the religious arena, and the relation between men and women in this saints' corpus is far from anything that could be regarded as one of "equals." My point here is not to scrutinize dictionary entries; their limited ability in describing complex social and historical phenomena is well accounted for. Rather, my intention in examining the common claims expressed above about Kannada Śivabhakti is to highlight instead of to gloss over the complexities and subtleties that are central in these early narratives.

---

9. Padoux (2005, 8043).

10. Bowker (1997, 581).

11. See, for example, Nandimath (1979 [1942]).

12. I examine this more closely in Chapter 4.

Single-Minded Dedication

While religious practices, caste and social affiliations, and even Śiva's own personality vary from story to story, from place to place, and from one character to another, all of the Śaraṇas from the Kannada-speaking region in the *Ragaḷegaḷu* share a basic and unyielding spiritual dedication that underlies their various devotional acts.[13] The strongest and most identifiable thread that runs through all the *Ragaḷegaḷu* stories and, more broadly, the early Śaiva imaginaire of the Kannada-speaking region is a total and exclusive sentiment of devotion to Śiva. This sentiment is manifested in the stories in a multitude of ways, but all of them betray strong determination and preclude reflection or doubt.

Devotional dispositions and intimate relationship with the god are articulated in this corpus in their most intense forms. The Bhakta's internal space—one's attitudes and responses toward oneself, society, and the god—is uniquely configured toward the absolute and the extreme, and narrative action in the *Ragaḷegaḷu* is primarily shaped by this uncompromising disposition. The literary figurations of the Kannada saints' lives in the *Ragaḷegaḷu* are characterized by an extreme vision and resistance to compromise. David Shulman, while comparing the devotional dispositions of Tamil and Kannada Śaivism as articulated in the early narratives, recognizes the uniquely acerbic voice of Kannada Śivabhakti, which conveys "a horror of compromise and paradox, a drive toward absolutization, hence toward straightening out the zigzag patterns so characteristic of the Tamil Śaiva universe."[14]

Shulman's diagnosis of Kannada Śaiva devotionalism is based on the Telugu *Basava Purāṇamu*, but it is equally applicable to the *Ragaḷegaḷu*.[15] Emotionally and cognitively, the Śaraṇa in almost all of these narratives remains impervious to contingencies, nomic compromises, and oppositional resistance. Oftentimes, the internal penchant for absolute theology does not remain enclosed in the devotee's interiority in the *Ragaḷegaḷu*

13. From a pan-Indian perspective, the devotional stress on interiority presents a certain challenge to the overarching analytical observation that Hinduism is orthopraxic. Compare with Alf Hiltebeitel in Hawley (1991, 27).

14. Shulman (1993b, 50).

15. In the introduction, I pointed to significant differences between the Telugu *Basava Purāṇamu* and Harihara's *Ragaḷegaḷu*, but the two texts clearly belong to the same literary and devotional tradition grounded in the Kannada-speaking region, where this Telugu text had more impact than in the Telugu literary milieu.

stories but erupts in impatient, protestive gestures against members of other religious communities, fellow devotees, oneself, and even against the god. Some of the protagonists are violent, others irascible; all of them are intractable. This tradition, in short, is hot-tempered and obstinate, constantly defining itself against the mundane, often in a volatile manner. We shall observe below how, in some cases, the burning impatience and absolutized disposition that characterize this tradition are also projected onto the relationship between the Bhakta and Śiva, giving license to the Bhakta to exercise control over his or her god.

The term in the *Ragaḷegaḷu* for the sentiment I describe here is *ēkaniṣṭhe* (literally, "a single dedication"). Kittel's *Kannada-English Dictionary* translates *niṣṭhe* in a general and somewhat vague fashion: "devotion or attachment to, devotedness, ordinary and uniform practice; religious duty; believing in, faith, reliance."[16] The particular sense of *niṣṭhe* for the Kannada devotional tradition and specifically for Harihara, however, warrants a more specific unpacking. The *Vīraśaiva Lexicon for Technical Terms* (*Vīraśaiva Pāribhāṣika Padakōśa*) provides a more particular sense by defining *niṣṭhe* as "devotion endowed with unwavering belief . . . Firm belief is *niṣṭhe.*"[17] This definition foregrounds the uniquely intense quality of *niṣṭhe* by echoing the Sanskrit verbal root from which it is derived, *(ni) sthā*, in the sense of "to be grounded." It is a complete and single-minded determination, dedication, commitment, and adherence to Śivabhakti.[18] Harihara's use of the word "*niṣṭhe,*" which appears frequently in the text during particularly emotionally-laden moments, points to the author's understanding of the saint's interiority as a single-minded devotional commitment that pays no heed to costs or implications.

Harihara's understanding of "single-minded dedication" in its uncompromising, even consuming, sense is demonstrated in a short Ragaḷe dedicated to a devotee called Cauḍayya.[19] The Bhakta Cauḍayya performs his

---

16. Kittel (1982, 886 s.v. *niṣṭhe* 2).

17. Vidyāśaṅkara (2000, 296–97 s.v. *niṣṭhābhakti*). In the doctrinal world of Vīraśaivism, *niṣṭhe* signifies one of the six sub-stages of the first of the six spiritual phases (*ṣaṭsthala*) taken by the devotee on his path to Śiva realization. The presentation of *niṣṭhābhakti* as a fixed stage within the philosophical scheme of *ṣaṭsthaḷa* appears in the *Siddhāntaśikhāmaṇi*. See Śivayogiśivācārya (2004 [1966], 267–73) and the English translation Śivayogiśivācārya and Maritoṇṭadārya (2007).

18. Sascha Ebeling identifies "single-minded devotion" with the broader category of sainthood (2010, 436).

19. *Surigeya Cauḍayyana Ragaḷe* in Harihara and Suṅkāpura (1976, 435–41).

daily vows and ritual observances (*nēmas*) without fail. Every morning, he goes to the pond to purify himself and pick flowers for worship (*pūje*) at the local Śiva temple. But every time Cauḍayya enters the temple, it is so crowded with people that he cannot even get a glimpse of Śiva before the afternoon arrives. By then, the fresh flowers in his hands have wilted and Cauḍayya is filled with frustration. One day, with tears in his eyes, Cauḍayya makes a vow (*āṇe*) to Śiva: if on the following day, or any other day, a person comes between him and Śiva, he will do away with that person, and the responsibility for preventing this is Śiva's. From this time forth, and with great dedication (*niṣṭhe*), Cauḍayya starts carrying a dagger (*suragi*) whenever he visits Śiva's temple. And indeed, on every subsequent visit, Śiva makes sure that no one stands in the way between him and the devotee.

One night, Śiva appears in Cauḍayya's dream and says he is hungry. Cauḍayya immediately gets up and orders his wife and her assistants to prepare, in the middle of the night, auspicious food for Śiva. Cauḍayya takes the prepared food and heads to the temple. After arriving there, he approaches Śiva's image, places the food in proper plates and waits, with folded hands, for the god to eat. But despite Cauḍayya's pleadings, the image does not respond. Finally, Cauḍayya pulls out his dagger and places it on his own neck. At that moment, a hand comes out of the *liṅga,* takes the food, and starts to feed Śiva's five mouths, as well as all the other gods, goddesses, and attendants (Gaṇas) in the hall. Although Śiva is full, some food still remains, so Śiva, afraid (*añji*) that Cauḍayya will use his dagger, continues to eat until the food is finished. Cauḍayya, now satisfied, decides to make the practice of feeding the *liṅga* a daily observance (*nēma*).

Many days pass in this way, until one morning, as Cauḍayya enters the temple with the dagger ready in his hand, two visitors to the town—unaware of Cauḍayya and his vow—stand in his way to see Śiva. Cauḍayya immediately stabs them to death and throws their bodies aside. He then turns toward Śiva and asks: "Is it proper that you are blocked from my view?" The Bhakta continues to perform his rituals while people gather outside the temple around the two dead bodies and ask: "Is this proper?" They call Cauḍayya to step outside, and when he sees the commotion, he turns to the two dead bodies and shouts: "Get up, you two!" Both immediately stand up and fold their hands in reverence to Cauḍayya. Then flowers rain from the sky, and a heavenly chariot (*puṣpaka*) descends, picks up Cauḍayya and the two Bhaktas, and takes them to Kailāsa. When Cauḍayya enters Kailāsa, Śiva turns to his attendants and says: "This is Cauḍayya, a great devotee who will not allow anything to come in the way between me and him. He kept his observance, killed those who stood between us, and then brought them up here. Have you ever seen such a wonderful devotee?"

The Ragaḷe about Cauḍayya thematizes the intensity that characterizes the interior world of the *Ragaḷegaḷu* saints. In this story the saint, engaged in his daily service to Śiva's temple image, will do anything—including murder—to make sure nothing (and no one) hinders his worship. The story focuses on Cauḍayya's daily actions as a worshiper, but the plot is shaped by Cauḍayya's internal state, which is that of *niṣṭhe,* or single-minded dedication. This term is used by Harihara at crucial moments of the story, such as when Cauḍayya, faithful to his vow, starts carrying a dagger with him to the temple.

But Cauḍayya's unwavering dedication is manifested most strongly through his momentary bursts of impatient and even violent behavior. Two such moments are connected to Cauḍayya's readiness to use his dagger. In the first, he places his dagger on his own neck and threatens to kill himself if Śiva does not eat the food he has brought him.[20] Śiva yields to Cauḍayya's threat and starts eating against his own will. Cauḍayya (in contrast to his god) operates in an intense and hermetic mode that dictates a complete dedication to express—in fact, externalize—his devotion at any given moment. In the second scene of violence, Cauḍayya uses the dagger to do away with two Bhaktas who stand in the way between him and his god's temple image. Here, Cauḍayya's vow not to have his view of Śiva obstructed is kept even at the price of murdering two fellow Śiva devotees.

While this level of violence is exceptional for the *Ragaḷegaḷu* saints, all of them share the same determination as that of Cauḍayya, a determination that is impervious to deliberation and that is easily expressed through extreme actions. A Bhakta in the *Ragaḷegaḷu* can be a Brahmin or an Untouchable, a man or a woman, can worship alone or in a group, at the temple or in his or her backyard, through composing poetry, offering flowers and other objects to a temple image or to a personal *liṅga,* making religious vows, or simply consecrating a day's work to the god. Still, the trait shared among all of the Kannada saints in this corpus is their complete unfamiliarity with any sense of reflection or hesitation when it comes to

20. The literary trope of self-sacrifice is found in several Ragaḷes. See below and Chapter 6.

their disposition toward the god.[21] They are continually prepared to demonstrate devotion or perform their devotional duties with a mechanical and absolutized dedication, oblivious to any earthly consequences.

The uncompromising aspect of the Bhakta's dedication has another signifier in Harihara's devotional lexicon, which is *vīra* (valor).[22] In later periods, it would become synonymous with all the devotional strands of Śaivism in the Kannada-speaking region (as in "Vīraśaiva"), but Harihara uses the term *vīra* sporadically and in very specific way to describe a particular aggressive mood. Perhaps unsurprisingly, the term *vīra* appears in the *Ragaḷegaḷu* almost exclusively in sectarian settings where the Bhakta is required to challenge a member of another sect in public. During these interactions, the term *vīra* signifies the Bhakta's tenacity in expressing his or her devotion by opposing the religious other, at times in violent ways.[23] I discuss in detail this operative mode against the religious other in the final chapter of this book.

The Divine Devotee

In addition to serving as an illustration of an intense devotional attitude, the story about Cauḍayya is useful for describing how the relationship between the devotee and the god is configured in the *Ragaḷegaḷu*. This relationship, first and foremost, relies on the god's accessibility to the devotee, an accessibility that does not end with the god's physical presence made available to the devotee but extends more deeply into the nature of their relationship. All South Asian devotional traditions share a recognition of some measure of intimacy between the devotee and the god. The deep connection between the devotee and the god is already central

---

21. The neighboring and related hagiographic tradition of the Tamil Nāyaṉmār emphasizes a similar effort to communicate this intense devotion through action. Indira V. Peterson writes: "[T]he core of the Tamil Śaiva ideal of devotion, and therefore of sainthood, is the capacity to love Śiva with intense emotion, and to express this love in equally intense and spontaneous acts of devotion" (1994, 205; see also p. 212).

22. Eṃ. Cidānandamūrti draws a direct connection between the concepts of *ēkaniṣṭhe* and *vīra* (1989, 432).

23. The term *vīrabhakti* as denoting this belligerent mode in Harihara's stories is briefly mentioned by M. Chidananda Murthy (1983, 203–4, 205n3). A similar association is provided by David Shulman, when he writes about the Vīraśaiva movement as depicted in the thirteenth-century Telugu *Basava Purāṇamu*: "It is an impatient movement, in love with an exclusive and absolutized truth, and prepared to fight for it; it is not by chance that its exemplary figures are classed as *vīras*, 'heroes'" (1993b, 50).

in the earliest canonical text that foregrounds *bhakti*, the *Bhagavad Gītā*. There, the dialog between Arjuna and Kṛṣṇa is framed by the narrative of their earthly connection (their familial ties and Kṛṣṇa's role in combat as Arjuna's charioteer) but is configured by the much more profound theme of the god made available, in person, to the devotee.

This basic theological frame of a concrete, direct, and genuine connection between the devotee and the god controls regional devotional traditions in South Asia, and some of them, including the Kannada tradition, also recognize and articulate the devotee's power over the god that is implied by this intimate connection.[24] Sometimes, as is the case with the Kannada tradition, the reciprocity that imbues this intimate relationship is pushed to its ultimate conclusion, endowing the Bhakta with considerable control over the god, to a point of transgressing the assumed boundaries of the hierarchical relationship.[25] The Kannada tradition projects a stark sense of the devotee's mastery over the god, a mastery that can at times even imply irreverence and that situates Kannada Śivabhakti at a rather extreme end in terms of the nature and temperature of the religious sentiment it expresses.

As to the god's role in the text, it is evident that despite his repeated appearances his role is limited. Throughout the *Ragaḷegaḷu*, Śiva takes on limited roles at specific moments; rather than a lead role, he has only guest appearances. Moreover, in his sporadic appearances, Śiva usually takes on a servile approach toward his devotees, the protagonists. Against the rhetorical backdrop of the godhead's greatness, which is repeatedly reaffirmed, the dramatic role of Śiva in the stories is modest and moderate. The devotee, in contrast, is anything but moderate, even in his or her direct interaction with the divine. We already had a glimpse of the "irreverent devotee" in the previous chapter, with the portrayal of Harihara's relationship with Śiva according to later literature. When Harihara's anger and frustration at the Bhaktas' complaints about his flawed composition peak, he erupts, accusing Śiva of being an "arch traitor" and blaming him for making Harihara look like a nobody in the eyes of the Śivabhaktas.[26]

---

24. See Novetzke (2008, 186); Shulman (1992, 97).

25. It is possible to tie together the intense and personal relationship between the devotee and the god that is characteristic of the Kannada Śaiva tradition with the practice of *liṅgadhāraṇe*, carrying a personal *liṅga* (*iṣṭaliṅga*) on the devotee's body. See Leslie (1998, 229); Zydenbos (1997, 525); McCormack (1973, 175).

26. Śivarudrappa (1976, 239–40).

Harihara's indignation is apparently normative, at least according to the author of the passage, who immediately comments on the true relation between Śiva and his devotees as being one in which the former is dependent upon the latter (*bhaktādhīna*). Even Śiva himself, in his response to Harihara, is not concerned with the devotee's indignation toward him; his only interest is in satisfying and placating Harihara.

This incident conveys the broader recognition of the early Kannada hagiographic tradition that the god depends upon the devotee. This recognition has implications regarding the devotee's liberties in his or her relationship with the god, as will be discussed below. Some *vacanas* convey a similar understanding of the god–Bhakta dyad, but Harihara is the first to communicate it in narrative form. Not long after Harihara, the Telugu author Pālkuriki Sōmanātha expresses a similar understanding in his *Basava Purāṇamu*.[27]

The Śaraṇa in the *Ragaḷegaḷu*, like any other saintly character, is a man of god, a person whose earthly presence conveys divine qualities.[28] In this sense, the saint is truly a Janus-faced figure: facing god but at the same time facing the humans around him or her.[29] Divine empowerment of the human protagonist is usually grounded in the *Ragaḷegaḷu* stories by a framing narrative about the saint's prenatal career as one of Śiva's attendants in the heavenly abode of Kailāsa. In all these framing stories, the Śaraṇa serves Śiva or his wife Pārvati and then does something that displeases them. The transgression always results in the god or the goddess punishing the Śaraṇa by sending him or her to earth, the imperfect world of human beings.

At the most basic level, the narrative strategy of surrounding the Bhakta's earthly life with a heavenly existence, both before and after the earthly incarnation, supports the text's premise regarding the saint's divine aspect. In the case of the *Ragaḷegaḷu* stories—and of other related texts as well—this strategy also provides a divine telos to the Śaraṇa's earthly biography. In other words, the theological significance of the saint's actions

---

27. See, for example, the story of Nimmavva (Somanātha, Narayana Rao, and Roghair 1990, 144–49) and the discussion in Shulman (1993b, 57–62).

28. See examples from medieval texts of the Abrahamic religions in Cornell (1998); Brown (2015 [1981]).

29. A. K. Ramanujan describes the Kannada devotees in an advanced spiritual state as "living in two worlds, half-mad, half in a coma, 'a fool of god'" (1973, 174). Sascha Ebeling describes the Tamil saints of the *Periya Purāṇam* as "slaves to Śiva, but lords and masters to the ordinary devotee" (2010, 472).

on earth is revealed or hinted at by the heavenly framing narrative. For example, as mentioned in the previous chapter, Basavaṇṇa is said to have been sent to earth by Śiva because, while distributing flowers for worship at the heavenly hall in Kailāsa, he mistakenly skipped Śiva's son Skanda.[30] Śiva, in response, sends him to earth to learn how not to be partial in dealing with the god's devotees. Using this expository scene, Harihara highlights what he perceives as the most profound aspect of Basavaṇṇa's presence on earth, which is taking care of all Śivabhaktas regardless of their family origin, social affiliation, trade, caste, and so on. Equal service to all Bhaktas is indeed recognized as one of the hallmarks of Basavaṇṇa's leadership by the subsequent tradition.

Since contradiction, friction, and disharmony are antithetical to the benign, utopian atmosphere of Śiva's heaven, the Śaraṇa's impropriety propels his or her exile to the earthly realm.[31] In this manner, the *Ragaḷegaḷu* stories present a reverse symmetry between the saint's flawed behavior in heaven and his or her piety on earth, where the Śaraṇa embodies a divine perfection that builds the way back to heaven. Thus, the literary device of the Kailāsa framing story plays an important role in establishing the saint's divine authority on earth.

God's Ungracious Wife

The intimate relationship between the saint and the god in the *Ragaḷegaḷu* is epitomized in the *Ragaḷegaḷu* by the term *śaraṇasati liṅgapati* ("Śaraṇa is wife, *liṅga* is husband"). The metaphor of husband and wife, resting on the cultural standard of a stable, reciprocal, and harmonious relationship, leans in the *Ragaḷegaḷu* stories toward the Brahminical, *śāstra*-based subjugation of the wife to her husband.[32] This is demonstrated, for example, in the term's definition in the *Vīraśaiva Lexicon for Technical Terms* (*Vīraśaiva Pāribhāṣika Padakōśa*): "Thinking himself as wife and the *liṅga* as husband, the one who is in the existence of devotion (*bhaktibhāva*) surrenders

30. Chapter 1 in the *Basavēśvaradēvara Ragaḷe* in Harihara and Suṅkāpura (1976, 23–28).

31. Śiva's heavenly domain in Kailāsa is indeed constructed in utopian terms, and thus cannot bear imperfections. Michel Foucault writes: "*Utopias* afford consolation: although they have no real locality there is nevertheless a fantastic, untroubled region in which they are able to unfold; they open up cities with vast avenues, superbly planted gardens, countries where life is easy, even though the road to them is chimerical" (1973, xviii).

32. Leslie (1989).

one's complete being (*sarvasva*) to Śiva."[33] At the same time, the idealized notion of an intimate and peaceful relationship between husband and wife is subverted or at least complicated in the *Ragaḷegaḷu* by deeper and somewhat turbulent currents.

The expression *śaraṇasati liṅgapati* is used several times in the Ragaḷe about Basavaṇṇa in order to describe his intimate and intense relationship with the god Śiva. The basic contours of the principle also shape Basavaṇṇa's initiation into the Śaiva faith in this text.[34] The initiation takes place at Śiva's temple at Kappaḍi, with Śiva's chief attendant Nandi serving as the priest. Basavaṇṇa is about to leave for the Kalacūri capital Maṅgaḷavāḍa to embark on a public career, as Śiva has ordered him in dream and against his own will. Therefore, the initiation is orchestrated by Śiva as a wedding between him and his devotee in order to affirm the close connection between Basavaṇṇa and Śiva, despite the nearing physical separation. The incident is described in poignant language. After Nandi presents Basavaṇṇa with a personal *liṅga* and the five-syllable mantra (*pañcākṣari*), they both sit down on the floor in the temple's inner chamber, which looks like a wedding hall. Deities escort the groom, and the objects of the senses escort the bride. Harihara writes that the senses themselves circulate the burning lamp around the bride and groom, and the fluid of devotion (*bhaktirasa*) is poured over their hands.[35] At the most auspicious moment for the wedding, life and death hold the partition screen of worldly life (*saṃsāra*) between husband and wife. When it is removed, Basavaṇṇa gently looks at Nandi's face and then embraces him, while they are showered with cumin seeds and pieces of jaggery. Harihara concludes by stating that Śiva (in his local manifestation as Kūḍalasaṅgamadēva) is husband and Basavaṇṇa is wife.[36]

Harihara constructs the *mise en scène* of Basavaṇṇa's initiation as a wedding between Basavaṇṇa (as wife) and Śiva (as husband),[37] and

33. Vidyāśaṅkara (2000, 497).

34. Chapter 4 in the *Basavēśvaradēvara Ragaḷe* in Harihara and Suṅkāpura (1976, 38–41).

35. Here Harihara plays on the deeper meaning of *bhaktirasa* as an aesthetic experience (*rasa*) of devotion.

36. *Basavēśvaradēvara Ragaḷe* 4.prose in Harihara and Suṅkāpura (1976, 41): *saṅgaṁ patiyāgi basava satiyāgi*.

37. Chidananda Murthy reads the marital overtones of this temple initiation in a literary fashion when he comments: "One is really reminded of the dēvadāsi system of marriage where the bride goes to the temple and marries the deity there without the mediation of

he explicitly alludes to *śaraṇasati liṅgapati* at the end of the passage. The nuptial metaphor is made explicit throughout by the use of technical terms: wedding hall (*vivāhamaṇṭapa*), bridesmaid and groom (*nibbaṇigar, suvāsiniyar*), ritual washing of the bride's and the groom's hands (*kaidhāre*), an astrologically auspicious moment for conducting the wedding (*muhūrtam*), and so on.[38] Later, with Basavaṇṇa's public success as an administrator and as a Śaiva leader, he will marry a human (in fact, two). However, the nuptial metaphor does not dissipate in the later part of Basavaṇṇa's life story. For example, in the seventh chapter of the Ragaḷe about Basavaṇṇa, a communal Śiva worship takes place at Basavaṇṇa's house, and toward the end of the passage Harihara describes the event using wedding-related terms.

In this episode and in others in the *Ragaḷegaḷu* stories, the active role given to the Śaraṇa-as-wife in the intimate marital relationship affirms the essential supremacy of the god-as-husband implied by the concept of *pativratā*—the traditional South Asian standard for the ideal wife. At the same time, it also expands the emotional and relational spectrum between this "married couple" to allow the human-as-feminine to complain and chastise "her" divine-as-male partner. In the third and last chapter of the Ragaḷe about Kēśirāja Daṇṇāyaka, this Kalyāṇa administrator who decides to leave the court and live as a roaming Śaiva renouncer reaches the banks of a river and prepares to worship the *liṅga*, when accidently the *liṅga* is thrown into the river and cannot be found.[39] Kēśirāja, praised by Harihara at this point for his dedication (*niṣṭhe*), sails a boat to the middle of the river, where he calls out to his *liṅga*: "Śiva Sōmanātha! If I was always faithful to you, then come back to me. Otherwise, I shall perish and disappear from this earth!"[40] To the joy of the Bhaktas standing on the

a priest" (Chidananda Murthy 1983, 205n2). The term *dēvadāsi* does not appear in the *Ragaḷegaḷu*. On dēvadāsis, see Soneji (2012).

38. In several episodes in the stories about the Kannada saints, Harihara employs temple ritual as a metaphor for internal worship, with similar allusions to bodily and mental parts as homologous to ritualistic instruments. Here, however, temple worship and internal worship are fused together through the wedding ritual.

39. Chapter 3 in the *Kēśirāja Daṇṇāyakara Ragaḷe* in Harihara and Suṅkāpura (1976, 194–201). M. Chidananda Murthy comments, with specific regard to this episode, that historically a Śaiva who lost his personal *liṅga* was expected to immediately commit suicide (1983, 204).

40. Summary of *Kēśirāja Daṇṇāyakara Ragaḷe* 3.115–24 in (Harihara and Suṅkāpura 1976, 198). Kēśirāja's sentimental appeal is reminiscent to that of Sītā, the *Rāmāyaṇa* heroine and paragon for *pativratā* in the classical South Asian imaginaire, when her faithfulness to her husband is put to a public test on two occasions (Shulman 1991; Kinsley 1988, 74, 76).

riverbank, the *liṅga* leaps out of the water. Kēśirāja, however, is not satisfied. Angry, the Śaraṇa-as-wife (*śaraṇasati*) addresses the wet *liṅga*: "Why have you come out like this? Where are all the ritual decorations I adorned you with?" Śiva, with love toward his Bhakta, returns to the water, decorates himself with flowers, sandalwood, and other things, then comes out of the water again and sits in the palm of Kēśirāja, looking fresh and shining.

Kēśirāja's tone and behavior in this vignette, in his apparent role as the devotee-wife of Śiva, are shaped by the wide range of emotions of a wife who has just managed to reunite with her missing husband. The devotee is devoted and attached to his "husband," but also has been worried that his "husband" is lost in the river. When the *liṅga* suddenly appears, the worries are replaced with anger and scolding, as the devotee asks the *liṅga: Why did you return without the decorations I put on you?* At this point, Harihara fittingly refers to Kēśirāja using the term *śaraṇasati* in order to consciously evoke stock themes from the world of love poetry. *Śaraṇasati*—Śaraṇa as wife—is taken in this scene in its fullest sense: the absolute attachment, the fidelity that characterizes the Śaraṇa, also involves emotions such as frustration, anger, and a need to reprimand. Further, it implies a corresponding submissiveness on the part of the husband, here enacted when the *liṅga* silently obeys Kēśirāja's demands and returns to the river to decorate itself before reuniting with the Bhakta. Thus, the concept of *śaraṇasati liṅgapati*, as it is used in the *Ragaḷegaḷu*, stretches beyond a simple notion of complete submissiveness to the god, expanding the range of possible emotional and relational structures to include more demotic—but no less intensive—interpersonal modes.

Later traditions about Harihara tell the story of a rich prostitute from Andhra who falls in love with Harihara after reading or hearing his Ragaḷes. She decides to come to Hampi and marry Harihara, but when she arrives and confesses her wish to the poet, he refuses her on the grounds that he is already married to Śiva, as the god's wife.[41] The later tradition, then, recognizes and reaffirms Harihara's understanding of *śaraṇasati liṅgapati* as a tool for empowering the devotee's spiritual commitment by providing him or her with a specific type of agency that can protect against worldly compromises and interactions.

---

41. Śivarudrappa (1976, 239).

Anthropocentric Devotion

The analysis in this chapter of the figuration of the saint in the *Ragaḷegaḷu* points to the centrality of human agency. The saint's journey from the divine realm in Kailāsa to the earthly position of a Śaraṇa involves not only an obvious movement in the stories from fantastic imaginaire and cosmic themes to a more earthly, familiar, and locale-sensitive environment and demotic themes but also a deeper shift from god-centric plotting to a new narrative focus on human action and agency. Indira V. Peterson notes with regard to the Tamil *Periya Purāṇam* the "hagiographer's shifting focus from Śiva to the saint and the hymn in the miracle narratives,"[42] and this observation naturally applies to any narrative tradition that focuses on saintly, but ultimately also human, figures. In the case of the *Ragaḷegaḷu* stories, however, the anthropocentric move involves, in addition to the empowerment of the human devotee, a diminishing of the god's role and influence in the human world.[43] At times the saint in the *Ragaḷegaḷu* does not only enjoy divine agency within a human setting but also exercises this divine agency over his own deity during the latter's guest appearances on earth.

An initial step in Harihara's realignment of the god/human power relationship can be located in his identification of the human Śaraṇa with Śiva, an identification that might surface through passing comments. For example, Harihara notes that King Bijjaḷa sees Basavaṇṇa as Śiva himself and, a bit later in the story, that Basavaṇṇa recognizes the Śaraṇas who come to visit him as Śiva.[44] Śaṅkaradāsimayya, a devotee who receives from Śiva the god's third and fiery eye, literally embodies on earth one of Śiva's most conspicuous external markers. Śaṅkaradāsimayya's identification with Śiva is made explicit in the text by King Jayasiṃharāya, who shouts while begging the Śaraṇa to stop emitting fire from his third eye: "O Lord! You are an incarnation of Rudra!"[45]

In itself, the embodiment of the god through his devotees on earth does not necessarily imply a subversion of his totality. On the contrary, it

---

42. Peterson (1994, 209). See also Monius (2004b); Cutler (1987, 48–49).

43. Laurie Patton discusses an older paradigm of the human's subversion of the gods in the *Bṛhaddēvatā* (1996, 215–53). This thematic correspondence points to a deeply ingrained tension in classical South Asian narrative thought between human and divine agents.

44. *Basavēśvaradēvara Ragaḷe* 6.prose in Harihara and Suṅkāpura (1976, 49–52).

45. *Śaṅkaradāsimayyana Ragaḷe* 2.prose in Harihara and Suṅkāpura (1976, 258): *dēvā rudrāvatāran.*

corresponds well with the metonymic understanding of the divine through earthly manifestations, an understanding that is foundational for South Asian religious thought in all of its diversity.[46] The subversive aspect of the identification between the god and his devotee emerges when this metonymy is placed on its head, with the appearance of the god bringing to the mind of the spectator his human devotees. In the Ragaḷe dedicated to Bommatande, when the Śaraṇa sees the statue of his god Śiva Rāmanātha brought into town carried on a bull, he bows down and declares: "Now I see in front of me Dāsimayya's ritual plate, Nambiyaṇṇa's thoughts, Bhōgayya's wealth, and Guṇḍayya's dance."[47] This exclamation reverses the metonymic understanding of the god, suggesting a vision of Śiva that is larger than Śiva himself, a Śiva who is a part of a larger network of his saints. By interjecting statements such as the above, Harihara subverts or at least complicates the assumed superiority of the god.

There are also episodes in which the Śaraṇa's empowerment directly exceeds Śiva's omniscience and omnipotence. In the Ragaḷe about Basavaṇṇa, the charismatic protagonist is challenged by another Śivabhakta to provide him with stupendous amounts of riches, since Basavaṇṇa promised to always satisfy his Śaraṇas' desires (a promise made public through one of his poems).[48] On the night before the imperious Bhakta arrives at Basavaṇṇa's house to challenge him, Śiva appears before Basavaṇṇa to warn him of the impossible demand that the Bhakta is about to make. The brief conversation that ensues between Śiva and Basavaṇṇa is surprising and even comic in terms of the parts played by each side: it is Śiva who expresses his worry that Basavaṇṇa will not be able to come through, while Basavaṇṇa is completely calm, expressing his confidence in Śiva that the

46. There are numerous instances of this metonymic theology. The most obvious is the concept of *avatāra*, the deity's descent to earth and taking on an earthly form (of a human or animal). But there are other, less pronounced metonymic embodiments of the divine on earth. For example, Gaṅgā as goddess is potentially present in every drop of water. Diana Eck (1996) writes: "In fact, in every temple and home the Gaṅgā is called to be present in the waters used in ritual, either by mixing those waters with a few drops of Gaṅgā water or by uttering the name and mantras of the Gaṅgā to invoke her presence" (p. 138). See also White (2003, 32); Feldhaus (1995).

47. *Kōvūra Bommatandeya Ragaḷe* 2.prose in Harihara and Suṅkāpura (1976, 368): *dāsimayyana tavanidhi bhāsuravādide, nambiya bembaḷiyinmbugoṇḍude, bhōgayyana bhāgyaṃ baḷisandude, kumbaraguṇḍayyana nṛtyadaphalaṃ naḍetandude.*

48. *Basavēśvaradēvara Ragaḷe* 12.prose in Harihara and Suṅkāpura (1976, 87). In a rare reference to Basavaṇṇa's poems, Harihara quotes a verse in which Basavaṇṇa vows to decapitate himself if he fails to fulfill his promise. Notably, Harihara refers to Basavaṇṇa's poem using the word *gīte* ("song") and not *vacana*.

god will prevail and provide. Basavaṇṇa's serenity is contrasted with Śiva's own worry, and this adds a comical tone to the scene. Basavaṇṇa's trust in Śiva is so complete that it becomes the latter's concern to fulfill whatever Basavaṇṇa has promised to other devotees. This episode demonstrates the theological ellipsis implied by the devotee's exhaustive empowerment in this tradition: Basavaṇṇa is dependent on Śiva to fulfill his promise, but Śiva's commitment to deliver on Basavaṇṇa's promises inherently subjugates him to his human devotee. In simple terms, the god is diminished here to an instrument in the hands of his Bhakta.

David Shulman identifies in the Telugu *Basava Purāṇamu* the same paradigmatic asymmetry between the human's complete dedication and the god's inhibitions:

> The ultimate is . . . an entirely familiar and domesticated being, so close and real as to preclude any thought of compromising one's commitment to him. Only *he*, when embodied in his play, is in danger of introducing forms of compromise, from which his servants must now save him.[49]

The context for Shulman's statement is the poignant story of Siriyāḷa as it appears in the Telugu *Basava Purāṇamu*, but it is equally pertinent to the Śaraṇas' stories in the *Ragaḷegaḷu*, as both texts share the same Śivabhakti world particular to the south Deccan regions.[50]

Earlier I noted that Cauḍayya was exceptional in terms of his readiness to kill himself or others in order to fulfill his religious vows, but the array of stories presented above points to the fact that the other saints who populate this corpus have an equal level of conviction and dedication. Cauḍayya simply embodies the same devotional principle in the most acute of narrative settings, that involving death. Recall that Cauḍayya places his dagger on his own neck and threatens Śiva, announcing that he will kill himself if Śiva does not eat the food prepared for him. The morbid quality of this scene is not the most striking feature here; many South Asian *bhakti* traditions celebrate such intense, life-staking moments in which the Bhakta extracts something from the god by threating to do away with his own life. What is exceptional—and perhaps also disturbing—in

49. Shulman (1993b, 62).

50. Shulman (1993b, 48–67); Somanātha, Narayana Rao, and Roghair (1990, 144–47).

Cauḍayya's threat is Śiva's docile response to it: the god does not dare to stop eating—even though he is more than satiated—simply to satisfy his volatile devotee. Śiva in this scene brings to mind the lead character in Stephen King's *Misery*, Paul Sheldon, fixed to a bed and nursed by his fervid and twisted admirer Annie Wilkes.[51] The episode of Cauḍayya force-feeding Śiva is a portrayal of a god violated by his devotee, and the author Harihara does not condemn the saint's aggressive treatment of the god but instead celebrates it, stating: "Śiva was fed, fearing Cauḍayya. Coerced by the steadfast dagger, he ate."[52]

Another moment in which the asymmetry between the devotee and the god is evident occurs toward the end of Basavaṇṇa's Ragaḷe, in its concluding chapter.[53] Śiva, disguised as a Jaṅgama, visits Basavaṇṇa and invites him to climb onto the heavenly chariot (*puṣpaka*) and fly with him to Kailāsa, Śiva's abode. Basavaṇṇa refuses, answering: "Does Kailāsa have Śiva assemblies (*gōṣṭhis*) like the one we have here? If not, I would rather stay!" Śiva, realizing that Basavaṇṇa prefers to stay on earth, returns to Kailāsa alone. Basavaṇṇa's refusal is grounded in the communal experience that permeates the assemblies of devotees. In previous chapters of this Ragaḷe, Basavaṇṇa has hosted several such assemblies, which are described by Harihara as mystical and enthralling. Basavaṇṇa's choice to stay on earth and celebrate the Śaiva faith rather than joining Śiva himself in Kailāsa marks, as in the tableau of Cauḍayya force-feeding Śiva, a narrative *reductio ad absurdum* of the Bhakta's intense devotional dedication, in this case postponing the *summum bonum* of reuniting with Śiva by entering the heavenly realm in Kailāsa. As in the case of Cauḍayya, Basavaṇṇa's celebration of the deity—in this case in the setting of the assembly—so enthralls him that he arrives at a point of paradox and contradiction beyond the assumed boundaries of the god's devotee. The fact that the text can sustain Basavaṇṇa's direct refusal to join Śiva attests to the particularly extreme type of anthropocentrism that, according to the *Ragaḷegaḷu*, characterizes Kannada Śivabhakti.

---

51. King (1987).

52. *Surigeya Cauḍayyana Ragaḷe* vv. 109–110 (Harihara and Suṅkāpura 1976, 438): *ārōgisida śivaṃ cavuḍarāyaṅgañji | dhīran alagaṁ kitaḍārōgisidan añji.*

53. *Basavēśvaradēvara Ragaḷe* 13.25–56 in Harihara and Suṅkāpura (1976, 93–94). Harihara dedicated twenty-four chapters to the Ragaḷe about Basavaṇṇa's life, of which only the first twelve chapters and the concluding chapter are extant.

3

The Society of Devotees

THE ANALYSIS OF the *Ragaḷegaḷu* saints' internal devotion in the previous chapter provides a foundation for moving outward to examine their social relations.[1] Practically all the *Ragaḷegaḷu* narratives about the Kannada saints emphasize the tension and struggle involved in the protagonist's interactions with society. The uncompromising interior attitude of the devotee in the *Ragaḷegaḷu* implies almost inevitable friction, dissonance, and difficulty when the devotee is confronted with the flawed human world that surrounds him or her. This chapter begins the thematic exploration of how perfect devotion is played out in an imperfect world by confronting the ideal of unmediated connection between the devotee and the god with the complex social realities of differentiation, exclusion, and hierarchy.

The Kannada Śivabhakti tradition is famed for its uncompromising resistance to the Brahminical ideology of ritualistic and social supremacy. The *Ragaḷegaḷu* stories exhibit different aspects of this resistance, one of which is the social diversity of the Śaiva protagonists. The collective of Bhaktas, as it is imagined by Harihara, consists of poor people as well as rich, young and old, male and female, people hailing from the margins of society as well as from its center, people whose trades include professions considered base and polluting as well as those considered prestigious and lucrative. This stunning variety is not glossed over in the stories but highlighted, sometimes in surprising ways, such as through conflicts and disagreements among members of the same devotional community who hail from different backgrounds. In the *Ragaḷegaḷu*, a devotee's social traits—his or her social class, gender, religious and sectarian affiliation,

1. A shortened version of this chapter appears in the forthcoming edited volume by John S. Hawley, Christian L. Novezkte, and Swapna Sharma, entitled *Bhakti and Power*.

familial heritage and customs, economic background, profession, and so on—can play a substantial role in his or her engagement with other members of the devotional community (as well as with people outside the community). Rather than eschewing narrative moments of potential friction, Harihara uses them to offer possible ways of reconciliation and accommodation of a plethora of practices and attitudes that are at times in contradiction with each other. In this chapter, I focus on the complexities involved in Harihara's attempt to gather up social differences under the canopy of devotion to Śiva. The result, I argue—in comparison to the ideal of a society composed of equals—is knotty, one that forces us to think about the imagined community of Śaiva devotees in the *Ragaḷegaḷu* not as a coherent social entity but as a dialectical, multi-headed creature.

Kannada Śivabhakti is surely among the more vociferous *bhakti* traditions to argue against Brahminical discrimination in the ritual arena, and one consequence of this clear message is contemporary scholarship's highlighting of the tradition's nondiscriminatory aspect over any other, referring to tradition as a whole using terms such as *egalitarian, democratic,* and *gender-equal.* As I mentioned in the introduction, the trend toward identifying in early pre-modern Kannada Śivabhakti a voice that is "egalitarian" is problematic, because the significations implied by this term and similar ones are steeped in Western and modern value systems. Robert Zydenbos recognized this problem when he made the memorable comment that "to write that Vīraśaivism has been 'democratic,' 'feminist,' or 'egalitarian' from the beginning, as some modern writers do, is somewhat like writing that nuclear weapons were used in the *Rāmāyaṇa*, as some other authors do."[2] Prithvi Datta Chandra Shobhi made a similar observation by probing the historical underpinnings for the terminological anachronisms that plague the discourse about Kannada Śivabhakti, both by the Indian public and by scholars.[3] John S. Hawley, in his recent monograph about the *bhakti* movement, describes Chandra Shobhi's work as a—

> critique of the manner in which contemporary Lingayat organizations in their anti-Brahmin rhetoric have sought to portray Basavaṇṇa and his contemporaries as apostles of egalitarianism

2. Zydenbos (1997, 535).

3. Chandra Shobhi (2005). See also Champakalakshmi (2011a, 273–74)

> pure and simple—fully modern Enlightenment beings who long ago inveighed against caste society but were suppressed, unheard.[4]

But there are complications beyond the pervasive anachronistic use of etic categories, as we find when we examine the manner in which resistance to Brahminical discrimination is expressed in the early literature of this tradition. The vision of nondiscrimination in the *Ragaḷegaḷu* is, in fact, doubly bounded: first by the sectarian filter of exclusive belief in Śiva (Harihara's social sensibilities apply only within this fold, and the stories do not convey any interest in social equality outside it); and second by the *Ragaḷegaḷu*'s qualification that limits social nondiscrimination solely to the realm of devotional agency. Put succinctly, while Harihara's stories argue forcefully for ritualistic freedom, total liberty in the realm of personal devotion, and open interpersonal communication among fellow devotees, the devotees' social landscapes as charted in his stories sometimes remain conservative and hierarchical.[5]

Qualifying Bhakti's *Egalitarian Voice*

Before attending to the Kannada narrative, it may be helpful to elucidate in more general terms the tension in devotional discourses between the promise of unhindered worship and access to the divine, and on-the-ground social and sectarian barriers within the arena of worship as well as outside it. The principle of allowing for uninhibited and unmediated access to the god for people of any social background is assumed to be foundational in many *bhakti* traditions, but its translation from a vague and abstract principle to canonical literary expression and into networks of social relationships, arrangements, and institutions can involve ambiguities and conflicting messages, as well as a reactionary conservatism.[6]

The tension within South Asian devotional rhetoric between complete devotional agency at the personal level and its curbing in various social

4. Hawley (2015, 323).

5. Scholarship relating to other South Asian devotional traditions is also becoming more aware of this discrepancy. Patton Burchett writes: "[I]t is not simply that there has been a failure to put the egalitarian *bhakti* theory of these 'untouchable' hagiographies into actual practice, but rather that the messages in these hagiographies are themselves far less democratizing and socially progressive than they might at first appear" (2009, 116).

6. See Philip Lutgendorf's discussion regarding the "cracks in the mirror" of the *Rāmcaritmānas* (1991, 392–409).

arenas (ritualistic and others) can be found in the earliest canonical text associated with South Asian devotionalism, the *Bhagavad Gītā*.[7] It is a notoriously multilayered text, one that lends itself to different interpretations, especially with regard to such complicated topics as social and religious status. Therefore, the reading I suggest below of one verse is not so much for the sake of locating or arguing for a single "core" meaning or attitude in the *Bhagavad Gītā* toward the *bhakti* license for everyone to worship the god, but rather to demonstrate how the complexities associated with social equity in the discourse of South Asian devotionalism have ancient roots. The following words, spoken by Kṛṣṇa to Arjuna, demonstrate some of the complexities involved:

> The wise see the same
> in a Brahmin accomplished in knowledge and training,
> in a cow, in an elephant, and in a dog,
> as well as in a dog-cooker.[8]

According to this verse, the wise should see as the same or perceive as equal (*samadarśināḥ*) all sentient beings, represented here by a list of five examples (a learned Brahmin, a cow, an elephant, a dog, and a dog-cooker). We can immediately note that this verse does not promote an equal *treatment* of different beings by society but rather their *perception* as equal by those endowed with right knowledge.[9] More than prescribing social inclusivism, then, this verse rhetorically champions in a vague and general manner an egalitarian *view* of all sentient beings, and nothing in these words actively confronts the traditional social hierarchy repeatedly prescribed in the Brahminical Sanskrit canon, the *varṇavyavasthā* ("system of social classes").[10]

---

7. Richard Davis writes: "The path of devotion [in the *Bhagavad Gita*] is something new within Sanskrit literature . . . The *Bhagavad Gita* provides the earliest treatment in Indic literature of a religious orientation that would be of enormous significance for the subsequent development of Hinduism and other Indian religious traditions as well" (2015, 22–23).

8. *Bhagavad Gītā* 5.18: *vidyāvinayasampanne brāhmaṇe gavi hastini śuni caiva śvapāke ca paṇḍitāḥ samadarśināḥ.*

9. It is possible to read *darśina*, the "seeing" by the wise, in its deepest theological denotation, as it semantically relates to the term *darśana*. On this term and its religious significances, see the classic monograph by Diana Eck (1998).

10. An oft-quoted prescription for class hierarchy in the *Ṛg Veda* is found in verse no. 12 of hymn 10.90, which deals with the creation of the world from dismembering the body of

But even the limited "egalitarian" view offered by the verse appears tenuous when the list of equals is considered closely. For example, the first "equal" example is the Brahmin, uniquely described here as being endowed with the gifts of knowledge and training, a description that renders him inherently superior to the others that follow. Likewise, the order of the subsequent examples is suggestively hierarchical, starting with the cow (the most auspicious animal in Brahminical circles), followed by the elephant (a highly revered animal), and the dog (a detested animal in the classic Brahminical imaginaire). The last example, "dog-cooker," a common signifier for a low-caste person or an outcaste,[11] is listed after the most defiled animal and is separated by an additional co-ordinating conjunction.[12] In contrast, various *bhakti* poets in the second millennia, including Harihara, invoke canine imagery and the symbolically related "dog-cooker" in different ways to challenge such schemes of social ordering.[13] This list, again, imparts a sort of underlying, prescriptive ordering of social entities.

In the case of the above verse, it is difficult to overlook the *Bhagavad-Gītā* author's adoption of the traditionally derogatory sense attached to the term "dog-cooker" as signifying lowly social status. If the list is organized in order of importance as suggested by the supremacy of the Brahmin at the top, the position of the dog-cooker is recognized as being on the very lowest level of sentient beings, lower than the food that signals the person's social baseness, the dog. This reading, of course, runs against the verse's declared egalitarianism; it generates an acute sense of internal disjunction or contradiction, or at least a bitter tension between

---

the primordial man. Here we find for the first time the claim for four distinct social classes (called *varṇas*), with the Brahmins, or priests, associated with the primordial man's mouth and the Śūdras, or servants, with his feet.

11. There are various social classifications for "dog-cooker" in the classical texts (Patton 2008, 222n4). The general signification, however, is derogative. David Gordon White writes: "Scavenging their food like dogs, living like dogs, even eating dogs . . . low-caste and 'outcaste' Indians are marginal, dangerous, and polluting to the persons belonging to the upper levels of society" (1995, 290).

12. The enclitic copulative conjunction *ca* ("and") appears twice in the list: first after the dog (stressed by the word *eva*), and then again after the dog-cooker. This duplication syntactically emphasizes the separateness of the "dog-cooker" from the rest of list. Intriguingly, the list's order is not kept in all translations of this verse. See, for example, Easwaran (2007, 31).

13. See discussions on dog-cookers in the *Bhāgavata Purāṇa* in Hopkins (1968, 19–20) and on dogs in Marathi *bhakti* poetry in Tulpule (1991). See also Keune (Forthcoming, 8–9); Fisher (2017, 36–37). On the brief episode in the Tamil Buddhist text, the *Maṇimēkalai*, in which Viśvāmitra decides to eat a dog because of extreme hunger, see Ulrich (2007, 234–35).

the proclaimed ideal of equality and the manner in which it is prescribed or argued for. The sense of hierarchy (and specifically, the low ontological status of the dog-cooker) is embedded in the explicit and opposite argument the verse is making, with no mention of how the knot could be untangled.

Religious-Based Nondiscrimination

Such complications persist also in the vernacular devotional texts that proclaim the promise of "seeing equally."[14] This is true even in the case of *vacanas*, which are generally regarded as expressing the nondiscriminatory stance of the Kannada tradition in the most lucid and uncompromising manner.[15] In one of the *vacanas* popularly attributed to Mahādēviyakka, the famous twelfth-century female Bhakta and *vacana* composer, there appears a curse according to which one who does not worship properly "shall go through a hundred births in a dog's womb and will then end up in the house of an outcaste."[16] This statement clearly runs against any simplistic understanding of "anti-caste" attitudes attributed to the Kannada Śivabhakti tradition: in a manner that echoes the use of the canine references in the *Bhagavad Gītā* above, both a dog's birth (*śvānayōni*) and an outcaste (*cāṇḍāla* in the original) are invoked here in conformity with

---

14. A few examples: The rich literary tradition of the last three hundred and fifty years about Eknāth, the saint who is the one mostly associated with caste sensibilities in the Marathi Vārkarī tradition, is multivocal and fluid with regard to his on-the-ground engagement with the socially unprivileged (Keune 2011; Novetzke 2011; Burchett 2009, 122–24). The early Tamil *bhakti* literary works, both Vaiṣṇava and Śaiva, make claims for social equality but also strengthen the social supremacy of Brahmins, mainly through their temple-based ritualistic culture (Champakalakshmi 2011b; Peterson 1994, 195–96; Veluthat 1993). See also Burchett (2009, 117). A case in point of a model vernacular text in which the ambivalence toward social hierarchy reaches a state of perpetual paradox or dialetheism is the *Rāmcaritmānas* (Hess 1988, 244–48; Lutgendorf 1991, 352–60). See also discussions in Hawley (2015, 328–30); Pechilis (1999, 27–30).

15. Robert Zydenbos (1997, 529) points to the overt discrimination implied in specific verses of another core text in the Vīraśaiva canon, the *Siddhāntaśikhāmaṇi*, and Vanamala Viswanatha (Rāghavāṅka and Viswanatha 2017, xix–xxiv) points to the complexities of Rāghavāṅka's treatment of outcastes in the *Hariścandra Carite*.

16. Taken from Mahādēviyakka's *vacana* no. 417 (Rājūra 1993, 125). The *vacana* quotes the said verse from the *Śivadharma Purāṇa* in Sanskrit: *iṣṭaliṅgam aviśvasya tīrthaliṅgasya pūjakaḥ / śvānayōniśatam gatvā cāṇḍālagṛham ācarēt*. A similar statement is made two verses earlier in Kannada: *iṣṭaliṅgaviddante sthāvaraliṅgakke śaraṇenden ādaḍe / taḍeyade huṭṭisuvanu śvānana garbhadalli*.

the traditional social prejudice associated with them.[17] The fact that such a straightforwardly Brahminical stance is associated with Mahādēviyakka, regardless of the historical question of whether it can be authenticated as originally written by her, calls for some degree of alertness, sensibility, and nuance when making claims about "social equality," even in the case of the *vacanas*.

To those less familiar with the Kannada devotional tradition, it might be useful to point out that several stories in the *Ragaḷegaḷu* directly deal with the need to respect Śaiva devotees who are profoundly different from each other, hailing from different social, occupational, and economic backgrounds. The Śaiva protagonists in these stories are men and women, Brahmins and non-Brahmins, affluent as well as poor people, artisans and wandering ascetics; some are public figures who lead communities and perform miracles, while others are laymen who worship Śiva privately in their backyards. The wide range of the characters that populate the *Ragaḷegaḷu* corresponds well with the social diversity attributed to the *vacana* composers themselves and is astounding when considered in the context of traditional Kannada literary themes, which are generally elitist. As recognized by Kannada scholars, the *Ragaḷegaḷu* is the first narrative work in the history of Kannada literature to favorably engage with the lives of people from the margins of society, their occupations, behaviors, and language.[18] In addition to introducing and giving voice to the subaltern in the *Ragaḷegaḷu*, Harihara's stories forcefully argue for nondiscrimination in the religious arena of Śaiva devotees. In one particular story, Harihara repeatedly invokes the term *samaśīla* ("equal conduct") to explicitly argue for nondiscrimination among the Bhaktas in the religious context of worshiping Śiva.[19] This term is also significant in the *vacanas*' parlance and, in its simplest sense, implies complete equality among the society of

---

17. I anachronistically translate here "*cāṇḍāla*" as "outcaste," which is a modern term but is nevertheless apt for signifying a low social status.

18. On the pioneering aspect of the subaltern discourse in the *Ragaḷegaḷu*, see Saudattimath (1988, 1–2). See also Gonāla (2010); Mariguddi (2008); Candraśēkhara Naṅgali (2003); Mīrā (2003); Śrīmati (2003); Liṅgaṇṇa (1979).

19. The particular Ragaḷe is *Teluga Jommayyana Ragaḷe*, discussed in detail in the following two chapters. "*Samaśīla*" is glossed in the *Vacana Nighaṇṭu*, a lexicon of technical terms used in *vacanas*, as "equal virtuous conduct" (*samāna sadācāra*, Rumāle 2003, 363 *s.v. samaśīla*). A slightly more general definition, "having the same customs or character," is provided in Monier-Williams et al. (1986, 1152 s.v. *samaśīla*) with references to the *Mahābhārata* and the *Bhāgavata Purāṇa*.

devotees—although, as Mahādēviyakka's *vacana* discussed above shows, this ideal is not ubiquitous.

In the *Ragaḷegaḷu,* the figure of Basavaṇṇa is identified, perhaps more than any other Śaraṇa, with the value of nondiscrimination. Although Harihara composed the *Ragaḷegaḷu* not many decades after the purported events associated with Basavaṇṇa, the author evidently recognized the historical significance of Basavaṇṇa to Kannada Śivabhakti. Harihara dedicated twenty-four chapters (of which only thirteen are extant) to Basavaṇṇa's life. The Ragaḷe about Basavaṇṇa is by far the longest of all the Ragaḷes, and it is uniquely decorated with a rich array of opening verses for each chapter.[20] This Ragaḷe is the earliest written account of Basavaṇṇa's life and consequently also of the emergence of the Kannada Śivabhakti movement. It has therefore been repeatedly revisited by Kannada writers both in pre-modernity and in recent times. The first four chapters of the Ragaḷe describe Basavaṇṇa's heavenly career, his birth on earth in a town called Bāgevāḍi, his youth, and his early adulthood in Kappaḍi. It is only in the fifth chapter of the text that Basavaṇṇa's life takes a public turn at the court of King Bijjaḷa at Maṅgaḷavāḍa. The account of this period in Basavaṇṇa's life makes up the bulk of the Ragaḷe as we have it today, up till the penultimate chapter, the twelfth. Chapters 5 to 12 switch between the setting in the court and the setting in Basavaṇṇa's home. The thirteenth chapter (the last that is extant) concludes Basavaṇṇa's life.

From the very beginning of this Ragaḷe, Harihara foregrounds nondiscrimination. The opening passage describes how Vṛṣabhamukha ("Bull's Face"), one of Śiva's attendants in his heavenly abode Kailāsa, came to be born on earth as Basavaṇṇa ("Bull").[21] In this scene—as mentioned previously—Śiva asks Vṛṣabhamukha to distribute flowers to all those present in the god's hall. Vṛṣabhamukha proudly follows the command but unintentionally skips Śiva's son Skanda, and Skanda complains to his father. Vṛṣabhamukha, in response, denies the allegation, although his face

---

20. The second longest Ragaḷe, with nineteen chapters, is dedicated to the Tamil saint Nambiyaṇṇa (Cuntarar). The *Mahādēviyakkana Ragaḷe* also has an irregular set of opening verses.

21. The Kannada derivation for "*vṛṣabha*" is "*basava,*" hence the association of Basavaṇṇa with bulls in general and with Śiva's bull Nandi in particular. Basavaṇṇa's common title "Basavēśvara," therefore, has three meanings: the first is "Lord Basavaṇṇa" and the second and third are "Lord of the Bull/of Basavaṇṇa," who is Śiva. The temple dedicated to Basavēśvara in Basavaṇṇa's birth town Bāgevāḍi celebrates under the appellation "Basavēśvara" both Basavaṇṇa and Śiva.

turns white with shame. At this point, Śiva turns to Vṛṣabhamukha and says: "How could you lie and not distribute to my son? . . . Because of this, you shall take a human birth."[22] Vṛṣabhamukha does not want to leave Kailāsa and asks for Śiva's forgiveness, but Śiva insists that Vṛṣabhamukha shall first help on earth all of Śiva's devotees without exception and only then return to Kailāsa. Basavaṇṇa's subsequent life on earth is indeed dedicated to equal care for all the members of the Śivabhakti community, and this leitmotif pervades and at certain points is made explicit in several episodes of this Ragaḷe.[23] Other Śaraṇas in the *Ragaḷegaḷu*, such as Kēśirāja and Bommayya, also exhibit in their stories non-partiality to other Bhaktas.[24]

However, despite the *Ragaḷegaḷu*'s stress on nondiscrimination, it is presented in the stories not as a stand-alone social value but as related to the exclusive worship of Śiva and mostly invoked in the context of ritual. While attributes such as the devotee's occupation, social class, or gender do play a part in the *Ragaḷegaḷu* stories, the individual's relative autonomy is directly derived from exclusive belief in Śiva and from his or her commitment to serve the god. In the *Ragaḷegaḷu*, a Bhakta, regardless of social background, cannot be treated as a lesser person but only as a Bhakta. Anyone who falls outside the category of Śivabhakta is utterly rejected as a religious other, regardless of social background. Put plainly, the category of social empowerment in the *Ragaḷegaḷu* is strictly religious.

Even within the fold of Śiva devotees, the nondiscriminatory prescription in the *Ragaḷegaḷu* is not monolithic but multilayered and dialectic. By "multilayered," I wish to indicate that different Ragaḷes highlight different aspects of the social world, such as gender, occupation, and class, and that these continue to play a significant role in the identity of the specific devotee. In other words, although the *Ragaḷegaḷu* devotee is entitled to complete autonomy in the arena of ritual and in the fellowship of Bhaktas, that devotee's biographical markers such as gender, familial condition, or

---

22. *Basavavēśvara Dēvara Ragaḷe* 1.59, 63 in Harihara and Suṅkāpura (1976a, 25): *husinuḍivarē koḍade ennaya kumārage / idaṟindavondu jananam ninage dorakitu.*

23. One case in point is when Basavaṇṇa arranges a devotional gathering for the community of Śivabhaktas. In response, the enthralled crowd of devotees starts to eulogize Basavaṇṇa, testifying that Basavaṇṇa, among other things, does not discriminate according to a Jaṅgama's *jāti* and does not recognize impurity in consecrated food (*prasāda*). *Basavēśvaradēvara Ragaḷe* 8.prose in Harihara and Suṅkāpura (1976a, 62): *jaṅgamadalli jātiyan arase, prasādadally apavitrateyan ariye.*

24. Kēśirāja is discussed in the following two chapters.

occupation continue to shape (and limit) his or her social roles outside the arena of ritual. The idea of social mobility or volitional choice of occupation is completely alien to the text.

By characterizing nondiscrimination in the *Ragaḷegaḷu* as "dialectic," I mean that the stories convey at times social dynamics, processes, and interpersonal negotiations that reflect the *difficulties* in practicing nondiscrimination in the complex and rich social contexts of south-Indian medieval society.[25] For example, in one incident in which two Śaraṇas confront each other about "equal conduct," Harihara comments that Śiva desires, as part of the restlessness of his divine playfulness (*līlālōla*), to ignite quarrels between his beloved Bhaktas, a comment that attests to the difficulties of maintaining harmonious relationships between different members of the Śivabhakti community.[26]

The following three sections discuss specific stories in the *Ragaḷegaḷu* in which the religious identity of the Bhakta affects in complicated ways the nonreligious aspects of his or her of life, namely occupation, financial background, and gender. In each of these areas the Bhakta, perhaps surprisingly when examined through an egalitarian lens, remains bounded in his or her external social roles. The discussions in the sections that follow show that the social world of the Bhaktas of the *Ragaḷegaḷu* can at times remain quite conservative, and even when it does transgress traditional norms regarding given social roles (perhaps most strongly in the realm of female agency and autonomy), the transgression is never absolute but carefully negotiated and contained.

Work and Its Felicities

A hallmark of Kannada Śivabhakti, one that has undoubtedly contributed to the high regard in which this tradition is held, is its rejection of social

---

25. There is also a modern recognition of the complications inherent in the nondiscriminatory ideal associated with the early Kannada Śivabhakti myths. For example, a modern Kannada play by Girish Karnad (2005, 48) exemplifies well the inner tensions present among different members of the varied community of Śivabhaktas. Julia Leslie identifies in a scene from Karnad's play "the potential conflict between the notion of *kāyaka* [the significance of one's occupation] and the Vīraśaiva insistence on the abandonment of caste" (1998, 256).

26. *Śaṅkaradāsimayyana Ragaḷe* 2.prose in Harihara and Suṅkāpura (1976a, 252): *nijabha ktapraṇayakalahalīlālōlacitta*. I discuss this episode in detail below. Śiva's *līlā* is a central component in Śivabhakti theology as well as more broadly in Hindu thought. Many devotional narratives convey the inexplicability of the god's intervention in the human world (Monius 2004).

ranking according to occupational background. Rejection of this type of social ranking is central in the *Ragaḷegaḷu* stories about the Kannada Śaraṇas, but it does not imply free choice of occupation or a promise of release from the constraining matrix of hereditary or familial occupations (unless the devotee chooses to completely renounce society and become an itinerant renouncer). Rather, the social critique of the *Ragaḷegaḷu* with regard to traditional attitudes toward familial occupations is narrower, aiming to purify occupations that, according to Brahminical-centered social ideology, are considered ritualistically polluting. In some stories, work ethics and the Bhakta's profession are not always central to the saints' lives, and some of the protagonists are renouncers who have no particular occupation. But some stories in this corpus actually elaborate on the devotee's occupation. Further—and here lies an important nuance regarding Harihara's rendering of work and devotional life for some of his figures—in most of the stories in which the devotee is identified with a specific line of work, Harihara draws a direct theological link between the devotee's occupation and his or her religious experience.[27]

The Ragaḷe that prescribes the devotional value of work in the most pronounced manner is dedicated to Kumbara ("the potter") Guṇḍayya. Harihara makes the connection between the devotee's work and devotion explicit right at the beginning of this Ragaḷe by stating that when Guṇḍayya taps on his pots, he makes Śiva happy. Harihara comments that each pot Guṇḍayya makes is like a different form of *bhakti*. Guṇḍayya goes to Śiva's temple one day and, seeing the god, his eyes fill with tears of excitement. Upon returning to his home and work, Guṇḍayya starts to make pots without stopping for food or sleep, seeing constantly in his mind the ritual he attended. The continual drumming music of his pots reaches the Himalayas and delights Śiva. In Harihara's words, what is seen as work on the outside is music on the inside; what is seen as tapping on the outside is worship on the inside. Śiva rests inside Guṇḍayya, and this celebration goes on for many days. Then, Śiva takes Pārvati to earth to meet the enthralled Bhakta. When Śiva reaches Guṇḍayya's house, he and Guṇḍayya start dancing together. Seeing this, other gods want to join in by playing their music, but Śiva refuses their offer, saying he desires to

27. This is true both for prestigious occupations held by Bhaktas who are also Brahmins and serve as the king's advisors and for traditionally polluting occupations at the margins of society. See the *Kēśirāja Daṇṇāyakara Ragaḷe*, the *Basavēśvaradēvara Ragaḷe*, the *Guṇḍayyana Ragaḷe*, the *Nimbiyakkana Ragaḷe*, and the *Teluga Jommayyana Ragaḷe*.

hear only the sound of the pots. All the world's inhabitants start to dance with Śiva and Guṇḍayya until Pārvati, fearing that the earth will not be able to hold this dance, asks Śiva to cease. Śiva yields, stops dancing, and embraces Guṇḍayya. A heavenly chariot (*puṣpaka*) comes down from the sky and takes Guṇḍayya to Kailāsa. There, Śiva introduces Guṇḍayya to all his attendants and declares: "Is there anyone who can make me, the one loved by the whole world, dance to beautiful drumming sounds?"[28] Then, he officially declares Guṇḍayya one of his attendants.

The storyline in this Ragaḷe is linear and straightforward, centering on the devotee's profession and its soteriological effect: Guṇḍayya the potter, after visiting the local Śiva temple, enters into a frenzy of pot-making. The banging sounds on his pots reach Kailāsa, and Śiva in his joy begins to dance. Next, Śiva comes down to earth and dances with Guṇḍayya. Finally, both the Bhakta and his god rise to Kailāsa, where Guṇḍayya is consecrated as Śiva's attendant.

While pot-making is central to the story, Guṇḍayya's mystical experience rests on a general devotional principle that is not limited to his occupation: the devotee's concentration during his work, which is completely given to the god.[29] A phrase found in several of the later tradition's canonical texts and one of its most famous slogans till today is *kāyakavē kailāsa*, "work itself is Śiva's heaven." The expression is glossed in the *Vīraśaiva Pāribhāṣika Padakōśa* ("The Vīraśaiva Lexicon for Technical Terms") as "doing work out of a feeling of complete surrender to Śiva."[30] This slogan attests to the tradition's general premise that work is, in fact, a devotional vocation.[31] It is significant that the sounds of Guṇḍayya's pot-making reach heaven after

---

28. *Guṇḍayyana Ragaḷe* vv. 263–65 in Harihara and Suṅkāpura (1976b, 221): *jagavellavan olidāḍisuvennaṃ / sogayipa tanna sunādakkennaṃ / maḍakeya danigāḍisidavar uṇṭe.*

29. Pot-making does have ritualistic value. In contemporary Vīraśaiva society this occupation is prominent enough to provide the name for a whole sub-caste ("Kumbara Lingayat") (Singh 2003, 925–27). The classical Kannada poet Ranna celebrates the pleasing sounds of pot-drumming in the *Gadāyuddha* 3.49 (Ranna and Subrāya Bhaṭ 1975, 113). Pot-making has distinctive ritual and even mystical qualities, not only in Karnataka but elsewhere in South Asia as well. See, for example, Killius (2003); Clarke (2002). The Tamil hagiographical tradition of the Nāyaṉmār also celebrates the vocation of pot-making through the devotional figure Tirunīlakaṇṭhapāṇa (or Tirunīḷakaṇṭa Yāḻppāṇa), a potter by profession, who plays the lute in Śaiva temples and wins the god's praises. In that story, however, Śiva does not come down to earth (Cēkkiḻār and McGlashan 2006, 363–64).

30. Vidyāśaṅkara (2000, 123 s.v. *kāyaka* 1).

31. The textual history of the term is quite complicated (Michael 1982, 617n2). See discussions of the meaning of this term in Ishwaran (1992); Ramanujan (1973, 34–35). Harihara uses the term *kāyaka* several times to describe Guṇḍayya, starting at verse no. 5, although it is difficult

his return from the temple, when Guṇḍayya's mind is totally captivated by the image of Śiva and he is steeped in a working trance of sorts. By stressing Guṇḍayya's visit to the temple and its aftereffect in his work, Harihara sends a vital message about the importance of the Bhakta's internal state during his or her work, which, when tuned toward the god, can bring about spiritual liberation.

In an article dealing with what he terms "Vīraśaiva work ethics," based on his readings in the sixteenth-century *Śūnyasampādane*, R. Blake Michael critiques the identification made by Weber and other scholars between the Vīraśaiva work ethic and that of Protestantism, particularly with regard to the validation of wealth accumulation in the latter tradition. He writes: "Nowhere [in the *Śūnyasampādane*] is there a notion comparable to Calvinist predestination, nor does the notion develop that social and economic status reflect (but do not cause) one's condition of election."[32] Michael acknowledges the centrality of the concept of work in the saints' stories of the *Śūnyasampādane*, but—perhaps propelled by his wish to distinguish between this *bhakti* tradition and Calvinist notions of predestination and economic success—he sets aside the arena of the devotee's work and does not see it as having a religious value of its own.[33] In the paragraph concluding this article, Michael writes:

> According to the Vīraśaivas . . . worldly occupation is to be performed cheerfully and conscientiously, but only until more important soteriological events occur. For them, work in one's given occupation remains a mere pastime, not a genuinely holy calling.[34]

In contrast to Michael's conclusion, I argue that there is room in this devotional narrative tradition for regarding work itself as a form of worship, in a mode that is detached and parallel to the tradition's general appreciation of renunciatory forms of living. While the layperson does not formally dedicate his or her life to Śiva worship,

---

to deduce that he is consciously alluding to "*kāyakavē kailāsa*" as an already-established theological concept.

32. Michael (1982, 616).

33. Some of the *Śūnyasampādane* stories that Michael discusses also deal with the religious efficacy of work. See the story about a devotee called Nuliya Candayya (ibid., 613–15).

34. Ibid., 617.

that person's mundane work can become a form of devotional self-dedication.[35] Judging from Guṇḍayya's Ragaḷe, if one is intensely focused on Śiva during his or her work activity, the god will reveal himself to the devotee and carry him or her with him to the heaven of Kailāsa. In this way, by shifting the tradition's soteriology inward toward the devotee's interiority, even mundane work can become a *sādhana*, a spiritual quest.

Moving from the story's theological to its social level, it is evident that Harihara's avid theological affirmation of work in the story about Guṇḍayya and in others runs against the traditional Brahminical ranking of one's occupation according to a scale of purity, and it is difficult not to appreciate the pre-modern radical exoneration of all types of work implied by this underlying vocational theology. But such sanctifying of one's occupation also carries an inevitable conservative effect of upholding existing and traditional labor divisions. No stories in the *Ragaḷegaḷu* tell about a devotee who pursues an occupation different from that to which he or she was born or which he or she was trained to profess, and it appears that Harihara has little interest in the external social conditions of one's work beyond the basic argument for its given spiritual legitimacy and value.[36] The social revolution offered by this tradition, according to these stories, is in the spiritual capital of one's work and not in its social capital.[37] The *Ragaḷegaḷu* stories do not convey any sense of rejection of hereditary, guild-like labor structures. A poor potter, such as Guṇḍayya, even as an ardent Bhakta, remains a poor potter, but such contingent, material, and social circumstances are simply rendered irrelevant in light of his absolute spiritual liberation.

Furthermore, there are moments in the *Ragaḷegaḷu* stories in which the devotee's occupation and social class bear social significance. During the early career of Basavaṇṇa as King Bijjaḷa's accountant, the king's chief accountant Siddhadaṇḍa learns that the new, junior accountant Basavaṇṇa belongs to the same community of Brahmins called *kamme* to which he

35. The title of Michael's article, "Work as Worship in Vīraśaiva Tradition," itself conveys this theological sense as well.

36. In another article, Michael writes: "What existed was not a fully egalitarian society but a community of religious equals who continued to fulfill the tasks assigned [to] them by their occupations" (1983, 368). His claim that "the Vīraśaivas permit a certain voluntary choice of occupation based not on birth but on preference" (1982, 616) is not supported by the *Ragaḷegaḷu* stories.

37. I borrow the term "spiritual capital" from Verter (2003).

belongs.[38] This affiliation quickly translates in the story into nepotism, as it facilitates Basavaṇṇa's meteoric ascendance to a top administrative position. Harihara's style in this episode is not cynical nor does it contain even a trace of social criticism regarding the "nature" of Basavaṇṇa's promotion being due to his Brahminical background. Rather, it celebrates his public and professional successes, as they serve the betterment of the Śaivas.

Even after the discriminatory baggage of one's work has been jettisoned, work remains a significant component of the identity of the saint. The naming pattern of saints from the broader cadre of Kannada Śivabhakti supports this claim.[39] Some of the most famous composers of *vacanas* and saintly figures in the tradition are remembered in relation to their profession. This is the case not only with Kumbara ("potter") Guṇḍayya, but also with Jēḍara ("weaver") Dāsimayya, Taḷavāra ("night watcher") Kāmidēva, and many others.[40] Like the saints' places of origin, their occupations can operate as an important identity marker for their biography and persona. Therefore, the celebration of any occupation's legitimacy is paradoxical in terms of personal freedom in the social realm, since the total rejection of Brahminical prejudice against certain occupations, followed by the proud endorsement of them as vocational callings, also precludes or minimizes the potential for endorsing social mobility.

Wealth Matters

Like Harihara's treatment of the value of work, his rendering of material wealth and fiscal affluence in the *Ragaḷegaḷu* contains two central messages that are in tension with each other. The first of these is the admonishment against social privileging derived from monetary success. In accord with the stories' celebration of all types of work, including work traditionally considered low-income and ritually unclean, there is a persistent claim in the stories that a rich devotee's affluence cannot justify either haughtiness over other devotees or self-indulgence: in the *Ragaḷegaḷu*, an excess of money should be used only to better less-fortunate devotees.[41]

38. The episode is told in the *Basavēśvaradēvara Ragaḷe* 5.69–150. Siddhadaṇḍa is said to be a leader of the *kammekula* in verse 5.71. See also verses 107–9.

39. Vijaya Ramaswamy makes a similar claim based on *vacanas* (1996, 52–55).

40. See lists in Devadevan (2016, 40–41); Nandimath (1979 [1942], 109–17).

41. Michael, based on his studies of the sixteenth-century *Śūnyasampādane*, writes: "The acquisition of wealth or the frivolous enjoyment of mammon is strongly prohibited. Excess

An episode from the life story of Śaṅkaradāsimayya, a poor, itinerant devotee, expresses this message very clearly by confronting a rich devotee with a poor one and stressing the latter's superiority over the former.[42] At the beginning of the episode Harihara contrasts Śaṅkaradāsimayya's saintly persona with the consequent material success he achieves when his fame spreads to all regions and people start flocking to see him, bringing him expensive clothes and other gifts. Śaṅkaradāsimayya refuses to take any gifts and prays to Śiva for advice about what to do with them. Śiva orders him to bring them to him as offerings. At this point in the story, Harihara switches to another Bhakta named Jēḍara Dāsimayya, who lives in Mudanūru.[43] He is a proud Bhakta, who gets whatever he wants from Śiva, and the god, wishing to teach Jēḍara some modesty and restraint, decides to have him meet Śaṅkaradāsimayya. Śiva appears to Śaṅkaradāsimayya in a dream and commands him to go on pilgrimage to various Śaiva sites. Finally, Śaṅkaradāsimayya reaches Mudanūru. Many people live there, receiving material supplies and financial support from the affluent Jēḍara, who has an endless treasure (*tavanidhi*)[44] supplied by Śiva. When Jēḍara hears that the eminent Śaṅkaradāsimayya is in town, he goes out to meet him, and together they start a Śiva assembly (*śivagōṣṭhi*). But when Śaṅkaradāsimayya's wife Śivadāsi asks for some grains of rice, Jēḍara's heart is filled with pride. Like needlessly giving coolness to the moon and light to the sun, Jēḍara offers them a huge quantity of his rice. Śaṅkaradāsimayya, sensing Jēḍara's pride, says: "It is true that we are just poor beggars who eat whatever you put in our begging bowl. But you can go to the garbage pile at the front of your house, and inside it you will find a

---

gain, beyond what one needs for a pure and simple life, is either forbidden or strictly controlled. Furthermore, the appropriate place to put one's excess is not into productive capacity . . . but into the hands of others who are less fortunate," (Michael 1982, 616).

42. What follows is a summary of the first part of the second chapter of the *Śaṅkaradāsimayyana Ragaḷe* in Harihara and Suṅkāpura (1976a, 250–53).

43. Jēḍara Dāsimayya is renowned for composing *vacanas* (Ramanujan 1973, 91–110). Ramanujan follows the persistent conflation in Kannada scholarship between the tenth-century Dēvara Dāsimayya ("Lord-Servant of the God") and the twelfth-century Jēḍara Dāsimayya ("Weaver Lord-Servant") (Nāgabhūṣaṇa 2000).

44. Kittel glosses *tavanidhi* as a Sanskrit derivation of *tapōnidhi* (Kittel 1982, 701 s.v. *tavanidhi*), a term that denotes "an eminently pious man" (Monier-Williams et al. 1986, 437 s.v. *tapōnidhi*). However, in this story the term has a literal meaning of a never-ending treasure, as glossed in the Kannada Dictionary of the *Kannaḍa Sāhitya Pariṣattu* (Veṅkaṭasubbayya 2010 [1977], 3366 s.v. *tavanidhi*). The unfolding of this story clearly indicates that this gloss is more fitting.

treasure of gold worth more than your rice. Your endless treasure was given by the god, and it is only he who provides. Now scram!"[45] Jēḍara, feeling like a dried-up vine, departs and goes back to his house. He returns with his wife Duggaḷavve, and both of them fall humbly at Śaṅkaradāsimayya's feet, begging for his forgiveness. Śaṅkaradāsimayya's anger subsides and he blesses Jēḍara: "May Śiva Rāmanātha give you endless treasure that grows infinitely." Then, he sends the couple back to their home, where they find a huge treasure, ten times larger than what they had before and continually growing in front of their eyes, and they rejoice.

In this story we see how wealth and prosperity can generate arrogance even in the heart of a great devotee such as Jēḍara. Wealth, according to Harihara, has a corrupting quality, and it is utterly ephemeral, as is demonstrated by the ease with which Śaṅkaradāsimayya threatens and restores Jēḍara's fantastic wealth. Śaṅkaradāsimayya's assertion in his admonishment to Jēḍara that he (Śaṅkaradāsimayya) is just a simple beggar is ironic, for, as the story shows, a beggar of Śiva can have infinite access to earthly resources if he so wishes; the real beggar is the one who is misled by falsities such as material wealth.[46] This story, then, ridicules the false superiority of rich people who donate money and food to the poor, and it champions material abstinence as conducive to devotional integrity and spiritual superiority.[47]

Within such a value system, the significance of social status can be thought of as debilitated or even inversed, but parallel to arguing against the significance of wealth, the episode also acknowledges that wealth is necessary for sustaining the community of Bhaktas. Whether through the gifts imparted on Śaṅkaradāsimayya or the public feedings funded by Jēḍara, the text recognizes the importance and even indispensability of transference of tangibles among the members of the devotional community as part of a spiritual encounter. In this way, while undermining the social superiority of a rich person, the episode implicitly endorses or renders natural the giving by the rich to the needy (as long as everyone involved

45. This is a summary of Śaṅkaradāsimayya's speech in *Śaṅkaradāsimayyana Ragaḷe* 3.prose in Harihara and Suṅkāpura (1976a, 254).

46. The premise about the axiomatic access the devotional saint has to material wealth can also be found in other South Asian traditions (Mallison 2013).

47. On a note similar to the premise in the previous footnote, the contrast between devotion and wealth can be located in texts of other devotional traditions. Thomas H. Hopkins writes with regard to the *Bhāgavata Purāṇa*: "It is implied that the conflict between wealth and devotion is so great that only a poor person can be a true follower of *bhakti*" (1968, 15).

in this transaction falls inside the fold of the Śaiva devotional community, of course).

The assertion regarding wealth's beneficial use for the betterment of the devotional community sometimes resurfaces in the *Ragaḷegaḷu* stories. One of the central themes in the Ragaḷe about Basavaṇṇa is his lavish giving to devotees. Early on in his story, when Basavaṇṇa is instructed by Śiva to go to the capital city of King Bijjaḷa and take care of the city's devotees, he decides to accomplish this task by becoming an accountant (*gaṇaka*) at the king's court, and this choice makes evident the inherent connection in this tradition between monetary affairs and the improvement of the devotional community.[48] After Basavaṇṇa becomes the king's treasurer, the material care he gives to the local community of devotees becomes a leitmotif of his life, as Basavaṇṇa's service to the Bhaktas expands to include responsibility for their material well-being. Indeed, the text at times celebrates this material aspect with long descriptions of valuables such as gold bracelets and silk clothes given by Basavaṇṇa to the Bhaktas, who do not conceal their enjoyment in wearing these items.

Beyond a general concern for the livelihood of devotees who are poor or who are wandering ascetics (Jaṅgamas), the *Ragaḷegaḷu* describes the Śiva assemblies and festivals (*śivagōṣṭhis* and *gaṇaparvans*) as requiring financial support that depends on the generosity of the rich. In several saints' stories we find descriptions of events in which a large number of devotees gather to worship and praise Śiva for an extended period (over several days and weeks sometimes). The events usually take place on property belonging to an affluent devotee who sponsors the occasion and, more specifically, provides for the costly mass feeding. Basavaṇṇa, for example, hosts several such assemblies in his private palace at Maṅgaḷavāḍa, and in the Ragaḷe about Kōvūra Bommatande, Harihara goes into great detail in his description of the huge amount of rice required and the considerable labor involved in its preparation (husking the rice, cooking it, and then serving it).[49]

In sum, money evidently plays an important role in the lives of Bhaktas as figured by Harihara, but only in terms of its facilitating religious activities and supporting less-fortunate devotees. Harihara's rhetoric conveys

---

48. *Basavēśvaradēvara Ragaḷe* 5.7–16 in Harihara and Suṅkāpura (1976a, 42).

49. Mass feedings of devotees are described in the *Basavēśvaradēvara Ragaḷe, Kōvūra Bommatandeya Ragaḷe, Śaṅkaradāsimayyana Ragaḷe*, and *Kēśirāja Daṇṇāyakara Ragaḷe*.

a concern to prevent wealthy devotees from being patronizing and developing a sense of superiority or haughtiness, and this concern speaks volumes about the economic heterogeneity of the Bhaktas' communities and the challenges this heterogeneity entailed, at least in Harihara's mind.

Female Roles and Female Transgressions

In South Asia, devotional attitudes regarding the status of women are closely tied to those regarding social discrimination based on occupation and wealth, as discriminating practices against low classes and women are both entrenched in society by orthodoxy and are grounded in considerations having to do with impurity. In recent decades, there has been growing scholarly interest in women's roles and voices within devotional discourses in an attempt to develop ways of understanding female agency, in terms not just of the ideal of gender-based equity but also of the complex social configurations of women devotees in history and literature.[50] A memorable essay by A. K. Ramanujan, "Talking to God in the Mother Tongue," published in the Indian feminist journal *Manushi* in a volume dedicated to women and *bhakti,* brings to the fore the centrality of the female voice in devotional literatures, along with the recognition that in many cases this voice is enunciated by male authors.[51] Ramanujan's discussion of female voicing by male authors is illustrative of how female agency within the devotional discourse is rarely straightforward and comprehensive but rather involves multiple concentric circles of appropriation, caveats, and containment. These sensibilities apply also in the case of the early Kannada saintly imaginaire.

The cadre of Kannada Śivabhaktas and *vacana* poets is, in fact, heavily populated by many female figures, and the exceptional conspicuousness of female figures who express their subjective inner worlds and act with relative independence and freedom speaks volumes about the somewhat progressive stance this tradition holds with regard to the status of women in society, their agency, and their own voice.[52] Harihara himself dedicates several stories in the *Ragaḷegaḷu* to women saints, carving a new literary

50. See, for example, Hawley (2015, 335–36); Pechilis (2012, passim; 2008); Craddock (2011); Simmons (2011, 151); Pande (2010); Lutgendorf (1991, 392–409).

51. Ramanujan (1989).

52. R. Champakalakshmi writes: "The Vīra Śaiva rejection and criticism of the idea of pollution which was applied to women illogically in several contexts, especially in the menstrual period, directly question the patriarchal, gender subordination of women in various ways" (2011a, 275). See monographs by Ramaswamy (1996) and Michael (1983, 361–62).

space for female figures who have their own agency in connection with their devotion to Śiva. These stories present a liberating vision of an active and resolute female voice of devotion that also has a say in the social arena, especially with regard to marriage. In a nutshell, it is a vision that deviates considerably from the traditional restricting representation of the "virtuous wife" (*pativratā*) sanctioned by male Brahminical authority.[53]

The Kannada female saint Mahādēviyakka, through her life story and poems, has transcended the sphere of regional culture and belongs to the celebrated group of female devotees commemorated across the subcontinent.[54] She is remembered in particular for her stark rejection, in the lyrical *vacana*s attributed to her, of gender difference in respect to complete devotion to the god. Mahādēviyakka, whose life story in the *Ragaḷegaḷu* was followed by numerous accounts over the eight centuries that followed, is a woman who decides to leave her powerful landlord husband against his will and to live instead as a wandering renouncer devoted to the worship of Śiva, a radical change that is further dramatized by a marked change in her external appearance: she gives away her clothes and uses her long locks of hair to cover her naked body.[55] This story, as well as the *Ragaḷegaḷu* stories of three additional female devotees I discuss at the end of this section, namely Vaijakavve, Nimbavve, and Māyidēvi, directly problematize the woman devotee's intimate relationship with the male partner.[56] In all four cases, the female devotee deviates from or transgresses the limits of the

---

Leela Mullatti estimates that there were about fifty female saint-leaders in the early period of the tradition (Mullatti 1989, 7, 39–42). See list in Ramaswamy (2007, 156–60). See also Champakalakshmi (2011a, 276); Yaravintelimath (2006).

53. On conservative articulations of the "virtuous wife," see Leslie (1989); Kinsley (1988, 70–78).

54. John S. Hawley points to a list by the intellectual activist Madhu Kishwar of four central figures, including Mahādēviyakka (2015, 335). Mahādēviyakka is highly venerated and commemorated by many communities in Karnataka today, and there are numerous publications, both in English and in Kannada, of her *vacanas*. See Akkamahādevi and Basavarāju (1966). For English translations, see Ramanujan (1973, 111–42).

55. The contours of Mahādēviyakka's life resonate with the stories about the Tamil saint Āṇṭāḷ and the Rajasthani and Gujarati saint Mīrābāī regarding the basic challenging, based on devotional grounds, of arranged marriage (Āṇṭāḷ and Venkatesan 2010; Hawley 2005, 89–178, respectively).

56. Three additional female Śaraṇas discussed in the *Ragaḷegaḷu*—Kōḷūru Koḍagūsu, Ammavve, and Hērūra Heṇṇu—are not considered here, since the Ragaḷes about them might be later additions to the corpus. Koḍagūsu is an extremely popular figure in the Kannada traditions, referred to in some other Ragaḷes and throughout the later Vīraśaiva literary tradition.

traditional role of virtuous wife as expected in conservative society, and this recurring theme attests to the defiant potential of the *Ragaḷegaḷu* and its endorsement of female empowerment—empowerment that is tied, of course, to unbounded devotion to Śiva.[57]

Despite this female empowerment, it would be incorrect to interpret the representation of women in this corpus as anticipating contemporary claims for gender equity.[58] Women devotees, celebrated as protagonists who exercise their spiritual will in the *Ragaḷegaḷu*, are nevertheless tied to and limited by their traditional roles and duties as daughters, mothers, and especially wives. Mahādēviyakka, whose rebellion against patriarchal oppression is perhaps the most pronounced, is not an exception to this rule, and in the Ragaḷe dedicated to her story, Mahādēviyakka's success in maintaining her spiritual as well as her social independence—even at the price of walking out on her marriage—is never fully accepted by the people surrounding her.[59] Her parents and husband repeatedly try to dissuade her and she, in response, is pushed to reclusion and finally to abandoning her life as a human. The only trajectory of Mahādēviyakka's abdication of her social role as a married woman in the Ragaḷe is renunciation, which is quickly followed by her passing away and ascension to Śiva's heaven.

Before discussing the price Mahādēviyakka is required to pay in the Ragaḷe as a woman who wants to dedicate her life to the god, it might make sense to first throw light on the text's gender-based sensitivity,

---

57. Vijaya Ramaswamy has produced a gender-based critique of female devotion to the male god based on readings of various *vacanas* (1996, 28–33). Compare with Glushkova (2005), especially p. 181.

58. My discussion in this section, which considers the asymmetry between man and woman in the *Ragaḷegaḷu* stories, can be contrasted with the discussion on women's status according to *vacanas* in Mullatti (1989, 34–36), which concludes with a statement about "the perfect equality given by Virasaivism [*sic*] to man and woman in their marital life." R. Blake Michael's analysis of women's stories in the early sixteenth-century *Śūnyasampādane* points to an asymmetrical treatment of women as that I am identifying in the *Ragaḷegaḷu* (1983), as does Zydenbos (1997, 534). See Laurie Patton (2002, 5) on the necessity of developing multiple approaches to the question of gender in the context of South Asia. On p. 203, Patton writes: "Whatever the strategies, and whatever the individual scholar's opinions about the role of activism within the academic field of Indology, a new era is opening up for textual practices by and about women."

59. Vijaya Ramaswamy notes that Mahādēviyakka is suspiciously absent from lists of fellow devotees referred to by other female *vacana* composers, which Ramaswamy understands as an indication of their rejection of her and her unruly behavior (1996, 43). R. Champakalakshmi also makes a similar claim regarding the negative reaction to Mahādēviyakka by the people surrounding her, apparently based on readings in the *Śūnyasampādane* (2011a, 275–76).

which controls Mahādēviyakka's story right from the beginning. For example, the usual framing story of the saint's heavenly career as an attendant of Śiva is replaced here (as in all the Ragaḷes about female saints) with the saint serving as a female attendant of Pārvati, who is presented in this Ragaḷe as the goddess in charge of the saint's earthly incarnation. Likewise, just before Mahādēviyakka's incarnation on earth, her parents specifically ask Śiva for a daughter, which can be read as an indication of the legitimate space for female progeny in this text. Later, when Mahādēviyakka turns ten, she is formally initiated into the Śaiva faith by a guru and receives her *iṣṭaliṅga,* the devotee's personal emblem of Śiva. This girl's initiation is remarkable in light of traditional Brahminical attitudes based on Vedic exegetics regarding female exclusion from the ritual, where women's religious practices are relegated away from the formal and public ritual sphere.[60] As demonstrated by Mahādēviyakka's story, the Kannada Śivabhakti tradition offers women personal access to the god, in the form of the *liṅga,* in the same manner allowed for men.[61]

The different versions of Mahādēviyakka's story generally agree with these details about her life, but the Ragaḷe about Mahādēviyakka differs from later retellings in a crucial narrative point. While in the Ragaḷe Mahādēviyakka's failed marriage to a non-Śaiva serves as the story's central theme, later retellings, in an attempt to completely purge the saint from worldly ties, deny the occurrence of the marriage by claiming that Mahādēviyakka retired from society before the wedding.[62] Of seven chapters

60. McGee (2002).

61. Eva-Maria Glasbrenner articulates the religiously bound equality foundational for Vīraśaiva mystical thought in the following passage: "[I]t is believed in Vīraśaivism that both male and female bodies house a soul (*aṅga* or *jīva*) that is capable of mystical knowledge. Men are neither theoretically more suitable for the religious path, nor do they have an easier or broader access to religious practices or religious knowledge, while women play an equally prominent role as producers of authoritative religious literature (e.g., Akka Mahādēvi . . .). Also the theoretical conception of cosmic principles as 'male' Śiva and 'female' Śakti and their further subdivisions, as well as the parallel micro-(*aṅga*) and macro-(*liṅga*) cosmic principles of soul and God support the notion of different forms of existence that, however, are of equal worth, of one primeval entity (*śiva*)" (2015, 196n3).

62. As R. Blake Michael shows, the later retellings of Mahādēviyakka's story claim that she refused the marriage altogether and, instead, renounced society until becoming a member of the Kalyāṇa community of devotees. See synopsis and further primary sources in Michael (1983, 362–63). A. K. Ramanujan uses the *Śūnyasampādane* as the source for his presentation of Mahādēviyakka's life (1973, 112nI). The author of the fourth version of the *Śūnyasampādane* dedicates a whole chapter (no. 16) to Mahādēviyakka and to her *vacanas.* See Siddhavīraṇāryaru et al. (2007 [1965], 279–396); Michael (1992, 50–52).

in the Ragaḷe, four (chapters 3 to 6) are dedicated to Mahādēviyakka's wedding and consequent marriage, and the seventh to her experiences in Śrīśailam and her uniting with Śiva immediately after having walked away from the marriage (without joining the Kalyāṇa community of devotees as later versions claim). The plot of the Ragaḷe, then, marks Mahādēviyakka's marriage as the most significant episode in her biography, albeit one that is detrimental to her devotional cause: it is a tragic event in the Mahādēviyakka biography, one that will determine the course of her future life, setting it on a path of renunciation. The centrality of the marriage for Mahādēviyakka's earthly life is signaled early on, in the opening sequence at Pārvatī's palace in heavenly Kailāsa. There, Mahādēviyakka, as Pārvatī's attendant, is sentenced by her mistress to be born on earth and marry a non-Śaiva worldling (*bhavi*) as punishment for having called a Śiva attendant who entered the hall "*bhavi*."[63] Mahādēviyakka's punishment of marriage to a non-Śaiva is mentioned by Harihara at this early stage of the story and, indeed, the young maiden, who is devoted to the god from early childhood, disdains the idea of marriage to a human—even more so to a non-Śaiva.

This particular non-Śaiva, named Kauśika, is also a powerful local king, and he repeatedly threatens Mahādēviyakka's parents until they finally coerce her to agree to marriage. Despite the tying of Mahādēviyakka to a worldly husband, or perhaps because of it, the Ragaḷe highlights the female protagonist as a woman who is strong-willed, uncompromising, and determined to live her devotional life to the full, even as the wife of a non-Śaiva who is utterly unsympathetic to her religious sentiments. To begin with, she presents two conditions for her consent to be married to a nonbeliever, and both conditions are concerned with assuring her the freedom to worship Śiva. The first condition is that she will be free, as Kauśika's wife, to worship Śiva, to participate in Śiva assemblies, to serve her guru, and to choose when she will spend time with the king. The second stipulates that if the king prevents her from doing any of the above-mentioned activities three times, she will be permitted to terminate the marriage and walk away. Mahādēviyakka's conditions for the marriage, which Kauśika immediately accepts, convey the female devotee's sense of self-empowerment. At the same time, this self-empowerment is completely derived from Mahādēviyakka's interest

---

63. *Mahādēviyakkana Ragaḷe* 1.105 in Harihara and Suṅkāpura (1976a, 103): *ele bhaviye nōḍi poḍavaḍu poḍavaḍendenalu.*

in worshiping Śiva. In other words, it is only Mahādēviyakka's devotion that gives her the ability to impose on her husband valid conditions for the marriage.

From a literary perspective, the agreement anticipates its breaching later in the story. When Kauśika breaks the terms three times, Mahādēviyakka indeed leaves him. With the prenuptial agreement, Harihara formally sanctions Mahādēviyakka's divorce, as if arguing for the legitimacy of Śiva devotion from a legal or quasi-legal stance. Thus, while Mahādēviyakka's walking away is figured by Harihara as spurred by a spontaneous moment of frustration, the prenuptial agreement renders Mahādēviyakka's abandoning of married life as premeditated and ethical. According to this story, not allowing a woman to practice her Śaiva belief justifies cancellation of the marriage. Harihara apparently was not alone in this remarkable assertion of female and religious-based agency. Velcheru Narayana Rao, in the introduction to the English translation of the Telugu *Basava Purāṇamu*, comments:

> In brahminic religion, women are placed in the same category as the low castes . . . In Vīraśaivism, every person, without regard to caste or sex, receives a liṅga. Paṇḍitārādhya even sanctions a woman to disobey her husband if he does not share her Vīraśaiva devotion. The *Basava Purāṇamu* repeats Paṇḍitārādhya's instruction, and illustrates it by the story of Vaijakavva in the sixth chapter.[64]

Narayana Rao refers in the above quote to the *Basava Purāṇamu* story of Vaijakavva, in which we find the following statement:

> If a husband deviates from the devotion to Śiva, it is completely appropriate for the wife to disobey him. If a wife worships Bharga [Śiva], she can never go wrong by leaving her husband.[65]

In the first quote, Narayana Rao points to the overt clash between the social values of traditional Brahminical society and those of the emerging *bhakti* movement. In the second quote, Pālkuriki Sōmanātha, the author of the Telugu *Basava Purāṇamu*, legitimizes *bhakti* resistance to

64. Somanātha, Narayana Rao, and Roghair (1990, 12).

65. Somanātha, Narayana Rao, and Roghair (1990, 216). See also p. 300n45.

continuing a marriage with a husband who is not faithful to Śiva.[66] Despite these clear affirmations of the devotee wife's agency and the possibility for dismantling a marriage based on religious incongruence, it is difficult to read them as normalizing the possibility of divorcing one's husband. In Mahādēviyakka's case, divorcing is only the outcome of her husband's incompatibility with and antipathy for the Śaiva faith as it is expressed in his breaching of the prenuptial agreement. Consonant with orthodoxy, the text does not recognize an institution or even a formalized ceremony for divorce.[67] It should not come as a surprise that divorce within contemporary Vīraśaiva communities is not encouraged.[68]

With her departure from married life, Mahādēviyakka also turns her back on society as a whole. Casting aside her clothes, refusing to engage with fellow devotees or return to her parents' home, she chooses to seclude herself in a cave in Śrīśailam and, finally, to join Śiva's heavenly world. It is at this point in the story, perhaps, that the religious impulse of Mahādēviyakka's divorce comes to the fore in its most extreme trajectory: Mahādēviyakka is not reintegrated into society but completes her life outside society as a renouncer. A similar pattern characterizes the Tamil Vaiṣṇava Āṇṭāḷ and the north-Indian Mīrābāī, and is brought to an even more extreme denouement in the story of the early Tamil Śaiva devotee Kāraikkāl Ammaiyār, about which Karen Pechilis writes: "Even as the text turns toward describing the devoted woman's culminating trajectory to sainthood, it suggests that there is no place for such a woman in the social world, for she becomes a *pēy* or ghoul, a socially constituted antisocial being."[69] Like Ammaiyār's external appearance as a ghoul, Mahādēviyakka's nakedness marks, together with the totality of her devotion, also her ultimate departure from normative social life.

---

66. Leela Mullatti identifies in Basavaṇṇa's *vacanas* a broader concern for the welfare of the married female devotee when her husband is enraged. Mullatti's claim is supported by her translation of a *vacana* verse as: "Should a husband rage, the wife must leave . . . " (1989, 37). The verse in the original does not explicitly mention the wife: *gaṇḍa munidaḍe maneyolage irabāradayyā*, from *vacana* no. 825 in Basavaṇṇa (2001 [1993], 212).

67. See Nicholas (1995).

68. Mullatti writes: "Easy divorce is possible for either party only for misconduct" (1989, 33). Lindsey Harlan (1995), writing about attitudes toward Mīrābāī among married women in contemporary Rajasthan, describes a felt resistance among Mīrābāī's female admirers regarding her violation of the normative code of a married, and then widowed, woman.

69. Pechilis (2008, 25–26).

The devotee named Vaijakavva in the Telugu *Basava Purāṇamu* has a separate Ragaḷe dedicated to her in the *Ragaḷegaḷu*, in which she is named Vaijakavve.[70] Her life story starts out in a manner similar to that of Mahādēviyakka: a Śaiva female devotee is forced by her family to marry a non-Śaiva. But in contrast to Mahādēviyakka's husband, Vaijakavve's is explicitly recognized as a Jain.[71] Generally, Vaijakavve is described in this Ragaḷe as a servile wife, until she defies her husband's religious conventions by handing over food made for Jain sages to a Śaiva mendicant. This transgression leads to a harsh argument between Vaijakavve and her Jain husband, an argument that culminates in the husband beating his wife. The next morning, however, when confronted with his wrongdoings by fellow Jains at the town's Jain temple, the husband repents. At this point Vaijakavve appears in front of the local Jain community, opens the locked door of the Jain temple, reveals the Śiva *liṅga* mysteriously placed inside the temple the previous night, and proceeds to initiate her husband and the rest of the local Jain community into the Śaiva faith. As with Mahādēviyakka's autonomy in the religious field, the initiation by the wife of her husband and the Jain community is dramatic, spontaneous, and highly emotional. It also challenges traditional gender boundaries regarding public ritual spaces and presents an antinomian role model for female religious autonomy, agency, and self-empowerment.[72] In light of the overt challenge of gender boundaries in this story, it is unsurprising that Vaijakavve is referred to as a role model by other female characters in the *Ragaḷegaḷu*.[73]

A much more complicated representation of female sainthood in the *Ragaḷegaḷu*, compared with those of Mahādēviyakka and Vaijakavve, is the provocative story about Nimbavve (also Nimbiyakka). In her earthly life, Nimbavve is a poor female devotee who works as a servant for a non-Śaiva and sleeps with Śiva's male devotees out of a sense of

70. The *Vaijakavveya Ragaḷe* in Harihara and Suṅkāpura (1976a, 225–38).

71. I discuss the sectarian implications of this story in Chapter 6.

72. On Brahminical conservatism regarding women's role in the ritual, see Banks Findly (2002); McGee (2002). On female gurus in later devotional traditions, see Pechilis (2008, 25). See also Laurie Patton (2002, 5–7). Patton writes: "The universalism of bhakti has raised the question of women's participation in what were traditionally male, brahmin roles" (p. 7).

73. Vaijakavve is mentioned in the *Mahādēviyakkana Ragaḷe* 1.84 as one of Pārvatī's consorts in Kailāsa and is again mentioned in verse 3.181 when Mahādēviyakka's parents refer to famous cases of female devotees who married non-Śaivas (Harihara and Suṅkāpura 1976a, 103, 119 respectively).

service to the devotional community. Despite her lowly economic and social status, Nimbavve is rendered by Harihara as an independent and strong-minded figure who insists on practicing her religion in whatever way she finds fit. For example, late in story, when Nimbavve's father dies, Harihara describes Nimbavve herself performing her father's funeral rites, which, as in the case of Vaijakavve initiating her own husband, is a radical deviation from traditional and Brahminical gender-exclusion from the arena of ritual.[74] In this Ragaḷe, as in the Ragaḷe about Mahādēviyakka, Harihara signals female centrality by presenting Pārvati, rather than Śiva, as the deity in charge of the saint. At the beginning of the Ragaḷe, in the customary framing backstory of the saints' pre-human life as attendants in heavenly Kailāsa, one of Pārvati's attendants angrily refers to another attendant as "servant," and Pārvati, in response to the indignity implied by this term as used by the first attendant, orders that she be born in the world of humans as a poor servant named "Acid Lime" (*nimbi*) to indicate the absence of dignity in her fate as a human. And indeed, human life is not sweet for Nimbavve. While she is still young, all of her family perishes accept for her ill father, and Harihara movingly describes their economic hardships and deterioration, which culminate with Nimbavve taking on the position of a servant in the house of a non-Śaiva Brahmin.

By now, Nimbavve is a beautiful maiden who has started to associate with other Śaivas. At one point, a Jaṅgama follows her home and expresses his desire to have her. Nimbavve first prays to Śiva and then has sexual relations with the Jaṅgama. From this moment on, Harihara writes, she sleeps with devotees with complete dedication, serving each in an equal manner as if his body is made of gold, whether he be a handsome person or disheveled, whether he can walk or not, whether he can speak or not.[75] In itself, Nimbavve's impartiality with regard to her partners can be linked to Harihara's general concern with nondiscrimination among the devotees' fellowship, although in the case of Nimbavve's sexual conduct this nondiscrimination takes a provocative turn, touching on the transgressive subject of unsanctioned sex.

---

74. *Nimbiyakkana Ragaḷe* vv. 158–59 in Harihara and Suṅkāpura (1976a, 220): *taruṇi nimbavve maṟuguttalli maranāgi / entakke eccattu tandeyaṃ saṃskarisi.*

75. *Nimbiyakkana Ragaḷe* vv. 145–48 in ibid.: *cannuḷḷa cadurigaru bandaḍondē teṟaṃ / honna maiyāgi bandavaroḷ ondē teṟaṃ / naḍeyadaru naḍevavaru bandaḍondē teṟaṃ / nuḍiyadaru nuḍivavaru bandaḍondē teṟaṃ.*

Harihara does not overlook the provocative nature of Nimbavve's activities but rather legitimizes Nimbavve's choices. While raising possible caveats, he also responds to them and in this way asserts her agency. For example, right after highlighting Nimbavve's impartiality in equally serving devotees of all kinds, Harihara adds: "Without scarring her mind, she unites with Jaṅgamas, acting with full awareness until they are satisfied."[76] The potential for self-affliction caused by Nimbavve's practice is clearly acknowledged in this quote, but it is also rejected. The ethical tensions and conflicts surrounding Nimbavve's behavior are addressed in the strongest way when Nimbavve consents to have sex with a suitor who comes up behind her while she is preparing to worship the *śivaliṅga* in the temple. Harihara attends to the problematic aspects of Nimbavve's behavior via a dramatic conversation between Pārvati, Śiva, and the devotee as the sexual act ensues on the temple floor. First, Pārvati, objecting to Nimbavve's behavior and appalled by Śiva's disregard, confronts the god by asking him: "Is this proper behavior for men? Is this a good example for women?"[77] Śiva, prompted by his wife's rebuke, pops his head out of the temple *liṅga* under which Nimbavve is having sex with the devotee and chastises Nimbavve for engaging in such an action in a holy place, a place in which he, the god, resides. Nimbavve replies plainly to this criticism by asking the god: "O Lord! Is there a place on earth in which you do not reside?"[78] Śiva, once again dumbfounded by a female interlocutor, cannot offer a retort or contradict the metaphysical truth expressed in Nimbavve's rhetorical question. Convinced by Nimbavve's basic argument, Śiva promptly tells her that she may ask him for a boon.[79] Nimbavve requests that the god allow her to join him in Kailāsa, thus bringing to completion her desire to unite with him, a desire only partially fulfilled on earth by means of her sexual servitude to Bhaktas.[80] Through this tripartite conversation,

76. *Nimbiyakkana Ragaḷe* vv. 149–50 in ibid.: *manadalli kaleyilladaitandu kūḍuvaḷu / nenahinali nelasi taṇivannegaṃ māḍuvaḷu.*

77. *Nimbiyakkana Ragaḷe* v. 183 in ibid., 221: *puruṣarige nītiyē strīyarige lakṣaṇave.*

78. *Nimbiyakkana Ragaḷe* v. 191 in ibid.: *dēvā jagadbharita nīn illadeḍey uṇṭe.*

79. *Nimbiyakkana Ragaḷe* vv. 193–94 in ibid., 222: *enda mātiṅguttaraṃgāṇadīśvaraṃ / sandaṇisi meccidem̱ bēḍikoḷḷene . . .*

80. The sexual cum epiphanic context in this *mise en scène* suggests a quasi-Tantric understanding of sexual union as a means for attaining godhood, but there is no explicit allusion to a Tantric worldview in the text. Compare with Glasbrenner (2015). See Biernacki (2006) for a reading of female agency in north-Indian Tantric manuals of sexual rites.

and especially through Nimbavve's victory in this argument and her subsequent ascension to heaven, Harihara argues against conceivable ethical censure of Nimbavve's acts, placing enthralled devotion over normative behavioral and ethical boundaries, and traditional configurations of gender roles. The story of Nimbavve is conspicuously absent from any of the later Śaiva texts about this region, a possible indication of a certain level of discomfort on the part of later traditions with regard to Harihara's presentation of the provocative and problematic acts of Nimbavve.[81]

A modern reader's attempt to ethically frame Nimbavve's Ragaḷe is fraught with difficulties. On the one hand, Harihara avidly creates for the female devotee in this story an independent, willful role. Throughout the story, Nimbavve makes choices and takes action to better her life and that of her father, and she openly expresses personal freedom in her worship of the god as well as in the postmortem rituals for the father. The unique agency Harihara reserves for Nimbavve is made evident not only in the character's actions but also in her speeches to and arguments with those who try to stop her. But here, of course, lies the difficulty with Nimbavve's conduct, since her sexual activity with random devotees implies the legitimization of taking advantage of Nimbavve's body, of using it for the gratification of male urges. Harihara directly deals with the social impropriety and the implied exploitation in this situation, and he rejects both on devotional grounds, but his radical coupling of holiness and casual sex in the name of devotion remains ethically troubling. It is difficult to interpret the story within a narrow ethical frame of either the empowerment of women in their struggle for increased agency or the subjugation of women to a male-centered and religiously sanctioned sexuality, and the fact that the author of the *Ragaḷegaḷu* is himself a male only furthers the difficulty beyond the issues signaled by Ramanujan in his above-mentioned article. In this sense, Nimbavve's Ragaḷe can be read as an extreme case of interpretive open-endedness, at least by the modern reader.[82]

The type of sexual provocation found in Nimbavve's Ragaḷe can also be found in a short episode from the twelfth chapter of the Ragaḷe about

81. There is a different and popular character in the cadre of Śaraṇas called Nimmavve or Nimbiyakka. See Somanātha, Narayana Rao, and Roghair (1990, passim); Shulman (1993b, 48–67); Śāmarāya (2009 [1967], 224–25).

82. The issue of female sexuality in contemporary social struggles in Karnataka and their public reception is discussed in Epp (1992).

Basavaṇṇa's life. In this episode Śiva orders his attendants to occupy all of Maṅgaḷavāḍa's prostitutes, while he appears in Basavaṇṇa's palace disguised as a sixteen-year-old, described by Harihara as a *viṭa* (libertine) and a *sukhijaṅgama* (pleasure-seeking Jaṅgama).[83] Basavaṇṇa receives the young Śaiva with upmost respect, and the guest asks Basavaṇṇa to supply him with a woman, since there is none available in the whole city. Basavaṇṇa, agonizing over not being able to satisfy the holy man himself, offers to him his own wife, Māyidēvi. Māyidēvi readily agrees, but when she disrobes in front of the young libertine, he immediately restores his heavenly form. Harihara concludes the episode by praising Māyidēvi, who managed to see the god in his true and complete appearance.

This episode continues the leitmotif of Basavaṇṇa's life, his endless giving to Śaiva devotees, which in this case is brought to the extreme by his agreeing to share his own wife with another person. The wife Māyidēvi (literally "Goddess of Illusion") is also a devotee of Śiva and is happy to cooperate, which only accentuates the story's ethical crisis for the modern interpreter, similar to that discussed above with regard to Nimbavve.

At the same time, the story implicitly mirrors a conservative stance according to which the wife is obligated to fulfill her husband's wishes, however whimsical or transgressive. In fact, the skeletal theme of a guest who demands to sleep with a married wife and gets the husband's consent for the act is entrenched in the broader narrative imaginaire of South Asia. There is a story in the *Mahābhārata* about a young married couple called Sudarśana and Oghavatī who are visited by a licentious Brahmin. This story is referred to in a later Brahminical manual for the chaste wife called *Strīdharmapaddhati* as a tale that illustrates the ideal wife's determination to carry out her husband's commands.[84] Closer to home is the story appearing in the twelfth-century Tamil text the *Periya Purāṇam* about a devotee who gives his wife to Śiva, disguised as a Brahmin but also a Śiva devotee.[85] As in the Tamil story, Harihara reframes the core of his story about a husband sharing his wife with a guest by turning the guest into the incarnation of the god on earth. The result is a shift in the story's ethical prescription, from one revolving around marital relations and hospitality customs into consuming devotionalism with erotic overtones.

---

83. *Basavēśvaradēvara Ragaḷe* 12.prose in Harihara and Suṅkāpura (1976a, 89–90).

84. See synopsis and discussion in Leslie (1989, 310–12).

85. Peterson (1994, 213).

Narrowing in on the gender relations implied by Basavaṇṇa's order to his wife Māyidēvi, however, puts the story in a rather conservative light.

In conclusion, an analysis of the *Ragaḷegaḷu* stories involving social interaction reveals a complex picture in terms of how nondiscrimination—essential for ideal devotional life in this religious literature—is translated in the social realm. Nondiscrimination is manifested in its fullest in this text only in the context of ritual encounters; when two or more devotees meet to worship the god, all social markers fade and the devotee's pious sentiments can manifest and get the appreciation of fellow devotees without hindrance. Outside ritualistic contexts, however—in more mundane social arenas—nondiscrimination is played out in a limited fashion. Here, hereditary occupation remains a central ingredient of the devotee's identity, wealth and social status decrees social power, and one's gender dictates one's prescribed roles, in the private domain as well as outside it. In Harihara's literary vision, the charter of nondiscrimination is unapologetically heralded in the religious arena, but elsewhere it is implicated by conservative forces that keep their sway in spite of the overall devotional message.

4

A Bhakti *Guide for the Perplexed Brahmin*

THE PREVIOUS CHAPTER initiated the thematic movement outward and away from the devotee's uncompromising devotional interiority toward his or her social interactions by exploring the social identity of the devotee. Here, I continue the exploration of the social roles and behaviors prescribed for the devotee in the *Ragaḷegaḷu* stories about the Kannada saints by considering Harihara's treatment of Brahmins.[1]

The literary character of the Brahmin takes a central role in the *Ragaḷegaḷu*. Brahmins appear frequently in the stories, both as protagonists and as antagonists (often in the same story). In addition, Harihara at times refers to Brahminical values and notions, usually from a critical stance, though not always.

There is no simple way of understanding Harihara's rendering of Brahmins in the *Ragaḷegaḷu*. This chapter and the next deal with separate components that together contribute to the general cultural notion of "Brahminism" and what constitutes the literary character of the "Brahmin." As we shall see, some of these "Brahminical" components are treated favorably by Harihara, while others are treated negatively, thus suggesting that Harihara is offering in his narratives ways for Brahmins to participate in the devotional community while maintaining at least some of their Brahminical lifestyle. Brahminism, in the sense of a purity-based ideology of exclusivism, is overtly opposed, but some Brahminical

1. Brahmins are usually referred to in Harihara's text as "*vipras*," a generic term for Brahmin priests. See Philip Lutgendorf's discussion of a creative etymology for this term (1991, 398). Compare with Ramanujan (1981, 120).

practices are allowed to remain. Further, Brahmins themselves, as we shall see in the stories, are perceived as integral and prominent members of the devotional community. The plots present alleviating prescriptions to help the conflicted Brahmin who wishes to become a Śivabhakta but who, due to traditional Brahminical values or practices to which he or she is accustomed, faces obvious, real-life difficulties in adjusting to the new social world of *bhakti*.[2]

In general, the Kannada Śivabhakti tradition is renowned for its overt opposition to some Brahminical attitudes and practices that interfere with this tradition's vision of unmediated worship of the deity available to one and all. Staunch opposition to Brahminism as an epitome of ritual pedantry and social divisiveness can be found in many kinds of articulations, from early *vacanas* to the rhetoric of some strands of modern Vīraśaivism, and in scholarship that presents the Kannada tradition as "anti-Brahminical." Robert Zydenbos argues against this trend, attributing "anti-Brahminism" to a specifically modern context of Vīraśaivism: "Only in most recent times have certain Vīraśaivas, who are active in the cultural and political sphere and who wish to project themselves as 'progressive,' hopped onto the anti-brahmin bandwagon in search of socio-political profits. . . ."[3] While this book focuses on a single—and very early—moment in the tradition's self-projection, it does find support in Harihara's stories for Zydenbos's principal argument against essentializing the tradition's relation to Brahminism through a negative lens. The *Ragaḷegaḷu*'s complex rendering of Brahmins in its stories places this tradition much closer to other *bhakti* traditions than has usually been assumed.

Devotional traditions in South Asia are not exceptional for paying considerable attention in their literatures to Brahminism. Brahminical attitudes, values, practices, priestly and scriptural authority, social stature, and so on occupy the center stage of South Asian thought and culture for thousands of years, and nascent and non-hegemonic traditions are naturally inclined to posit themselves against the self-proclaimed epitome of cultural hegemony known as "Brahminism." Moreover, some basic

2. Different *bhakti* traditions develop different strategies for coping with this challenge. The Telugu Ārādhyas, who are historically and ideologically connected with the Kannada Śivabhakti tradition, present a syncretic vision (one that has been woefully understudied) to affirm both Brahminical values and practices and social openness based on devotional principles.

3. Zydenbos (1997, 531).

concerns shared among many South Asian devotional traditions run against the social, cultural, and intellectual elitism that is characteristic of mainstream Brahminism, pitting the former traditions against those of the latter. Traits found in many *bhakti* traditions—such as the appeal to broad and popular audiences, enhanced usage of vernacular languages instead of Sanskrit, a general preference for lyrical and emotional over more cerebral and erudite modes of expression, and allowance for unmediated access to the god (at least at the cognitive, personal level)—do not cohere outwardly with formulized Brahminical practices and a Brahminical worldview, even if these have evolved in creative ways over time in response to new social contexts.

At the same time, as has been noted by scholars, *bhakti* traditions are far removed from being antithetical to Brahminism.[4] In many *bhakti* traditions Brahmins figure prominently as leaders and role models. Historically, Brahminical values and practices have left their mark on social structures, thought systems, and the imaginaire associated with *bhakti*. As several scholars have pointed out, Brahminism at different times and places was an integral part of the development of *bhakti* culture as well as an active force in shaping it, not only at the social or practical level but also at the ideal and contemplative level, even if the dynamics involved are at times opaque and difficult to discern.[5] Rather than opposing it, then, *bhakti* traditions respond to the social prestige of Brahminism in an endeavor to supersede it, to "out-Brahminize" Brahmins as cultural leaders and spiritual virtuosos, and this general motivation involves several levels—implicit as well as explicit—of appropriation and borrowing. In his exploration of dissent and transgression in early Tamil religion, David Shulman identifies in *bhakti* "the urge to . . . realize the vision implicit in Brahminical values,"[6] a statement that resonates well with W. L. Smith's comment regarding later *bhakti* traditions in north India that "the Bhakta is the true Brahmin of the Kali Yuga."[7] In a similar vein, Brahminical influence on the Kannada devotional tradition can be traced in terms of the

4. Recent work on the complex ways in which Brahminism and *bhakti* relate to each other can be found in *Regional Communities of Devotion in South Asia: Insiders, Outsiders, and Interlopers* (Ben-Herut, Keune, and Monius), forthcoming.

5. This was most recently argued by John Stratton Hawley (2015, 332–33). See also Novetzke (2016, 132–58; 2011); Keune (2014, 2011); Burchett (2009).

6. Shulman (1984, 44).

7. Smith (2000, 162).

latter's self-proclaimed ethos, which is—like Brahminism—based on religious elitism.[8]

At the most basic level, the *bhakti* discourse in the *Ragaḷegaḷu* stories (as in other texts in different *bhakti* traditions) privileges devotion over ritual purity and formalism, and Harihara displays vehement impatience with pedantic insistence on ritualistic regulations, of which untouchability is the epitome.[9] Other socially restricting Brahminical practices, such as limiting Vedic and scriptural study to the upper classes, are also argued against by the stories. Despite this clear agenda, however, some narrative developments point to more complex and multilayered negotiations between people at opposite poles of society even if all, as Śiva devotees, are considered equal. Such differences are not always overlooked or effaced in the stories; sometimes they serve as a starting point for the author to concoct some form of social negotiation. The treatment in the *Ragaḷegaḷu* stories of the innate tension between Brahminness, the quality of being a Brahmin, and the socially inclusive *bhakti* is, thus, nuanced. For this reason we shall be attentive to Harihara's literary strategies in relation to solving conflicts that arise between two devotees who are equal in their unwavering faith to Śiva (and, therefore, in their spiritual status) but are also very different from each other in their social practices and backgrounds.

In most cases, the episodes that focus on a meeting between two Śaivas—one a Brahmin and the other a low-caste person (*antyaja*)—are told from the point of view of the former and not the latter, and it is the Brahmin who is required to recalibrate his set of stringent traditional behaviors and values in order to accommodate the inclusive ways of devotional life.[10] According to the stories, a traditional Brahmin who wishes to

---

8. Robert Zydenbos writes: "Rather than abandoning high-caste (i.e., high-*varṇa*) norms, the Vīraśaivas cultivated them, and they encouraged others to do the same" (1997, 531).

9. The story of Kaṇṇappa the hunter, first appearing in writing in the Tamil *Periya Purāṇam* and then retold in the *Ragaḷegaḷu* and the *Basava Purāṇamu*, is a good example of a narrative arguing for favoring personal devotion over Brahminical ritual purity. See discussions of this story in Cox (2005); Monius (2004, 148–50). Along with this devotional claim, however, the *Periya Purāṇam* presents an unabashed conservative social view, especially with regard to temple access. See the Tamil hagiographical treatment of an Untouchable devotee, in which his Brahminical prenatal background has to be revealed first through a trial by fire before he can enter the Śaiva temple (Ebeling 2010; Vincentnathan 2005; Pechilis 1999, 128–33).

10. The only exception to the narrative's one-sided adherence to the Brahminical point of view is the case of the meeting between Kēśirāja the Brahmin and Jommayya the hunter, with the meeting described twice (in the *Kēśirāja Daṇṇāyakara Ragaḷe* and in the *Teluga Jommayyana Ragaḷe*). I discuss this episode below.

follow Śivabhakti is faced with complex challenges, and the text's answers to these challenges are sometimes just as complex. The focus on matters pertaining specifically to a Brahminical way of life suggests that Harihara, himself a Brahmin, has in mind a Brahminical audience, and I propose that we think of these specific stories as a guidebook for the perplexed Brahmin.[11]

Inverting Untouchability

The stories discussed here, as well as the corpus more generally, demonstrate how untouchability and Brahminism are interlinked in this devotional world: it is impossible to think of Untouchables apart from the background of Brahminical ideology that is identified most closely with the conceptualization and exercise of untouchability in social life. Untouchability (*aspr̥śyate*) and more generally the idea of low social status (conveyed by the denigrating Kannada designation *poleya*, generally used in these stories by vile Vaiṣṇava Brahmins to describe others) are derived from Brahminical attention to ritual purity and the tenacious efforts required to maintain it.[12] The term *poleya* itself connotes the absence of purity, as it derived from *pole*, which means "impurity" and is associated with sin.[13]

The following quote from the opening section of the *Bhōgaṇṇana Ragaḷe* demonstrates the Brahminical point of view of the *Ragaḷegaḷu* narrator.[14] The protagonist of the story, a Brahmin Bhakta, is described as follows:

---

11. There are other literary strategies for recalibrating Brahminical identity according to devotional worldviews. Christian Novetzke, writing on the symbiotic relationship of Brahminism and *bhakti* in his work on Marathi *bhakti*, offers a dialectical model for the Brahmin's central role in composing *bhakti* materials, with the Brahmin author and performer of *bhakti* materials, whose intended audiences are mostly non-Brahmin, ridiculing the character of the Brahmin as a form of ventriloquizing prevalent criticism about Brahminism while preserving the Brahmins' social position and legitimacy within changing social configurations, thus "separat[ing] Brahminism and Brahmins discursively in public culture" (2011, 235).

12. See an analysis of Brahminical ritual purity in the pre-modern Tamil Śaiva imaginaire in Shulman (1980).

13. In the *Kannada-English Etymological Dictionary*, the word *poleya* is defined as: "man belonging to the 5th *varṇa*, Untouchable" (Učida and Rajapurohit 2013, 664 *s.v. poleya*). *Poleya* is derived from *pol* ("meanness, vileness, badness, noxiousness") and from *pole* ("1. impurity from childbirth, death, etc. 2. menstruation, menses defilement, meanness, sin 3. bad thing 4. sin").

14. See also discussion in Ben-Herut (2016, 141–45).

[He was—]
never inquiring about Śivabhaktas' origin (*jāti*),
never distinguishing between Śivabhaktas,
never appreciating Harabhaktas according to their lofty language,
never appraising Harabhaktas for their superior knowledge.[15]

This introductory passage directly puts forth what Harihara considers the ideal treatment by a Brahmin of his fellow Bhaktas: avoidance of discrimination by social markers, namely one's caste (*jāti*),[16] one's class as conveyed by manner of speech, and one's formal education.[17] The behaviors negated in this passage are traditionally ascribed to Brahmins and, indeed, Bhōgaṇṇa is himself a Brahmin. His story commences when he invites to his house an old, poor Śivabhakta. Bhōgaṇṇa washes the old Bhakta's feet and offers him food. Other Brahmins, appalled by Bhōgaṇṇa's behavior, go to the king and complain that a Brahmin has allowed an Untouchable to enter his home. The king, always attentive to his Brahmin advisors, calls Bhōgaṇṇa and demands an explanation for his disorderly behavior. Bhōgaṇṇa says: "Listen, king. I never invite Untouchable non-Śaivas, such as your Brahmins, into my house, and how can it be wrong to take in a Śivabhakta?" Hearing this, the king retorts: "Are you calling my Brahmins Untouchables? You had better leave this place at once!" As the story unfolds, Bhōgaṇṇa's banishment from the town causes a crisis, and the king and his Brahmin attendants are forced to recognize Śiva's greatness. They finally apologize to Bhōgaṇṇa and beg him to return to the town, a request to which he benevolently accedes.[18]

In the introductory passage quoted above, Harihara overtly argues against Brahminical discrimination and social exclusion. The series of negations in the passage makes clear that those who consider themselves Śivabhaktas have only one criterion by which a person should be judged, and that is one's faith. If one is wholeheartedly devoted to Śiva, if one

15. *Bhōgaṇṇana Ragaḷe* vv. 11–15 in Harihara and Suṅkāpura (1976b, 225): *śivabhaktaroḷage jātiya vicāripudilla / śivabhaktarolage bhēdava kalpisuvudilla / harabhaktarolage jāṇnuḍiyanarasuvudilla / harabhaktaroḷagadhikavidyavarasuvudilla.*

16. On the multiple meanings of *jāti* in the context of Kannada Śivabhakti, see Zydenbos (1997, 529). See also Ramesh Bairy (2009) on caste and Brahmins in Karnataka today.

17. These nondiscriminatory ideals operate in this universe only within the religious fellowship of Śivabhaktas. See previous chapter.

18. This is a summary of the opening episode of the *Bhōgaṇṇana Ragaḷe*. I discuss this Ragaḷe in some detail in Ben-Herut (2016).

is a true Śivabhakta, one is entitled to be treated as an equal, since any marker that might be judged as negative (one's family origin, manner of speech, or formal education) is irrelevant. This claim, made in the opening passage of the Ragaḷe, is put to the test a few verses later when Bhōgaṇṇa takes into his home an old, poor Untouchable and treats him with the honor due to any Śivabhakta.

As previously noted, the imagined equality prescribed in the *Ragaḷegaḷu* is not democratic or catholic, since it applies to Śiva's devotees only. According to this text and to early Kannada Śivabhakti more broadly, resistance to social discrimination is tightly linked to religious devotion and is meaningless outside it.[19] The social ideal of a tightly knit Śaiva community undergirds the denouement of Bhōgaṇṇa's story, with the one-sided recognition by the non-Śaivas that they have been utterly wrong not to recognize the superiority of *bhakti*. In this regard, Bhōgaṇṇa's *lèse-majesté* is instructive, since Bhōgaṇṇa inverts the agencies of Brahminism, re-ascribed now to Śivabhaktas, and of untouchability, re-ascribed now to non-Śaiva Brahmins. In other words, the story does not argue for the abolition of the *idea* of untouchability, just as it does not argue against elitism, which the Brahmins claim for themselves. Rather, it inverts the designations of the two social groups and, as it does so, it appropriates for Untouchables the elitism traditionally associated with Brahminism. According to this inversion, the real Untouchables are the non-Śaivas (even if considered Brahmins by birth), while all Śaivas are the true Brahmins.[20]

A similar reversal is found in chapter 10 of the Ragaḷe about Basavaṇṇa, in an episode that is duplicated in many later Vīraśaiva Purāṇas. One day, Basavaṇṇa, accompanied by a large procession of Bhaktas, goes to visit elder Śaivas living outside the city limits. As he is arriving, he hears the sound of bells inviting Śivabhaktas to consume the food consecrated to Śiva (*ārōgaṇe*). Basavaṇṇa decides to eat with the local Śivabhaktas. He enters the house of Nāgidēva and joins him in eating the communal sacred food (*saṅghaprasāda*). A Vaiṣṇava spy sees this and immediately rushes back to the city to inform the Brahmin community. The result is

19. We can note the difference in this regard from at least some of the modern forms of social activism in India, such as in the case of the Marathi reformers of the twentieth century, led by B. R. Ambedkar, who did not consider *bhakti* a relevant arena for their social struggles (Keune 2011, 365–67; Zelliot 1995, 217–18).

20. See Burchett (2009, 126–30). The redescribing of Brahminism in South Asian imaginaire is at least as old as the early Upaniṣads. See, for example, the conversation between Hāridrumata Gautama and Satyakāma Jābāla in *Chāndōgya Upaniṣad* 4.4.

that a group of Brahmins is sent to King Bijjaḷa. On entering his presence they declare: "Great Lord! Basava's rule grows contrary (*viparīta*) to custom by the day! He mixes with people he considers noble followers of Śiva, and—moreover!—if we call a person in the streets of the Untouchables 'Untouchable,' he would kill us right then and there. Furthermore, he eats at the house of a staunch devotee and then comes into your court and pollutes it! If this continues, we cannot remain here."[21]

King Bijjaḷa asks Basavaṇṇa to meet him outside the palace, in an open field. There, Bijjaḷa says to Basavaṇṇa: "Listen! It is improper for you to call Untouchables great, eat in their homes, and then come here without purifying yourself." Basavaṇṇa answers: "It is insane that you listen to just anyone. It is not true that I went to homes of Vaiṣṇavas, or touched or even smelled those Untouchables!" Hearing this, the king responds: "How can you call people who learn the Vedas, Purāṇas, Śāstras, and Āgamas Untouchables? And how can you call an Untouchable a Śaiva noble? If we cut a Brahmin's body, will blood flow out of it? And if we cut that of an Untouchable, will milk flow? Be sensible!" Basavaṇṇa laughs at Bijjaḷa's words and says: "If blood does not flow out of a Brahmin's body, and milk from a devotee, then I shall dissociate myself from the Bhaktas' community!"

Basavaṇṇa quickly goes and finds the Bhakta Nāgidēva and brings him to the field. He prays to Śiva and then says to Bijjaḷa: "Summon here those who are dull-minded by the notion of *karma* (*karmajaḍas*)." When they arrive, Basavaṇṇa, standing in front of everyone, makes a cut on the body of one Brahmin. Not only does blood flow out, but some ugly insects crawl out as well! Then Basavaṇṇa cuts Nāgidēva's toe and squeezes it gently. Rivers of milk gush out! All the Śaraṇas cheer him, and the people of other religions (*parasamayis*) quietly leave the field. Basavaṇṇa turns to Bijjaḷa and says: "Dear King, how can divine nectar (*amṛta*) turn bitter? You do not know the greatness of the Śaraṇas. Those stupefied by the Vedas (*vēdajaḍas*) have spoiled your thought." Then Basavaṇṇa places Nāgidēva on an elephant and leads him to his house, where he has him sit on an honorable seat and showers him with gifts.[22]

Like the story of Bhōgaṇṇa discussed above, this episode presents an ethical inversion of untouchability. When asked by Bijjaḷa to explain why

21. *Basavēśvaradēvara Ragaḷe* 10.prose in Harihara and Suṅkāpura (1976a, 75).

22. This is a summary of the remainder of the tenth chapter of the *Basavēśvaradēvara Ragaḷe*, excluding the concluding section.

he has shared sacred food with a Śaiva who is considered by the Brahmins to be an Untouchable, Basavaṇṇa does not deny his action but, rather, demonstrates to Bijjaḷa—through a miracle—a spiritual hierarchy that is opposite to that professed by the Brahmins.[23] The miracle is a graphic illustration of the inversion of untouchability: the blood and the maggots that issue from the body of the Brahmin are cultural marks of extreme pollution; the milk that flows from the toe of the so-called Untouchable is a symbol of purity. The subversive reversal of the dyad "lowly person" (*poleya*) and "eminent person" (*hiriya*) is presented here in a particularly provocative manner. The inversion is invoked by the narrator and by the character of Basavaṇṇa in the story in order to do away with any notion of Brahminical superiority and to replace it with the superiority of the Śivabhaktas.

But there is significant Brahminical logic behind Basavaṇṇa's miracles. Milk and blood, the substances that mark purity and impurity in this scene, are taken from the Brahminical ritualistic grammar and can be read as a token for a religious grammar that Basavaṇṇa and, by extension, Harihara and at least some of his audience share with other Brahmins. Furthermore, the malevolent Brahmins' ethical defect in this episode is more specific than general Brahminical discrimination. All the antagonist Brahmins here are people of the court; they are privileged. They have access to the king and exercise influence over him. Most important, their names give evidence of the fact that they are overwhelmingly Vaiṣṇavas.[24] Therefore, the courtiers are charged by the author with a very specific wrongdoing: a Brahminical but also non-Śaiva—specifically Vaiṣṇava—discrimination, one to which we shall pay attention separately in Chapter 5.

Appropriating Vedic Knowledge

In his critique of the ubiquitous egalitarianism sometimes associated with Vīraśaivism, Robert Zydenbos makes the following observation: "While

23. One of the inversions in this story is articulated by Basavaṇṇa himself, who denies having eaten in houses of the "real" Untouchables, i.e., *bhavis*.

24. Harihara provides a long list of Vaiṣṇava names in the *Basavēśvaradēvara Ragaḷe* 10.prose (Harihara and Suṅkāpura 1976a, 75): *nārāṇakramitaṃ kṛṣṇapeddi viṣṇubhaṭṭaṃ kēśavabhaṭṭaṃ viṣvaksēnabhaṭṭaṃ murārikramitaṃ sauripeddi mukundabhaṭṭaṃ padumanābhaktramitaṃ gōvindapaṇḍitam dharaṇīdharabhaṭṭaṃ vaikuṇṭapeddi jalaśayanakramitaṃ daśāvatārabhaṭṭam janārdanapeddi vāsudēvaghayisam acyutakramitaṃ dāmōdarabhaṭṭaṃ.*

on the one hand the Vīraśaivas use the vocabulary of egalitarianism, they have also used the classical Indian vocabulary of hierarchic inequality throughout their entire history . . . the Vīraśaivas have always seen themselves as hierarchically superior to the rest of society."[25] But Brahminical influence on Kannada Śivabhakti goes beyond an apparent inversion of social superiority. In a story about a goldsmith named Kallayya,[26] the challenging of Brahminical authority involves, in addition to the inversion of Brahmin values and themes, their acceptance into, influence on, and fusion with the Śaraṇa's cultural system. For most of the story, Kallayya has little contact with people of other sects. The text tells us that as a child Kallayya hated non-Śaiva worldlings (*bhavis*), whom he considered unworthy (*aprastuta*), but that he was not bold enough to face them directly. Soon after, we are told about an incident in which Kallayya refuses to work for a wealthy Vaiṣṇava.[27] Sectarian interactions, however, remain indirect.

It is only after mastering the Śāstras that Kallayya starts confronting non-Śaivas face to face and in public. In only a few verses, Harihara tells us that Kallayya, a non-Brahmin artisan, masters Brahminical scripture and wins theological debates, not only against the paradigmatic, traditional, non-Brahmin "others"—atheists (Lōkāyatas), Buddhists (Bauddhas), and materialists (Cārvākas)—but also against Brahmins.[28] In this offhand manner, Harihara redefines Brahminical knowledge: not only is its learning open to artisans, traditionally placed at the bottom of the Brahminical social scheme, but, in addition, the theological superiority provided by this kind of knowledge is used by the non-Brahmin Śaiva to outperform non-Śaiva Brahmins, right in their own scripture-based territory.

This mirror-like appropriation of Brahminical knowledge reemerges in a specific encounter Kallayya has with antagonistic Brahmins toward the end of this Ragaḷe, after Kallayya has become a parent and householder.[29]

---

25. Zydenbos (1997, 531).

26. *Hāvinahāḷa Kallayyana Ragaḷe* v. 8 in Harihara and Suṅkāpura (1976a, 446): . . . *honnakāyakavalli toḷatoḷage.*

27. *Hāvinahāḷa Kallayyana Ragaḷe* vv. 83–104 in Harihara and Suṅkāpura (1976a, 448–49).

28. *Hāvinahāḷa Kallayyana Ragaḷe* vv. 191–94 in Harihara and Suṅkāpura (1976a, 452): *vēdidiṃ śāstradiṃ gītamaṃ pāḍutaṃ / vādadiṃ vipraraṃ geldu nalidāḍutaṃ / lōkāyataranalli bauddharaṃ sōlisute / lōkadoḷ cārvākaraṃ geldu rañjisute.* A similar hagiographical account of a Bhakta winning in philosophical debates is provided for Harirām Vyās (Pauwels 2002, 239–40).

29. The following is a summary of *Hāvinahāḷa Kallayyana Ragaḷe* vv. 355–438 in Harihara and Suṅkāpura (1976a, 457–58).

Kallayya sends his daughter to fetch water to be used for the worship of Śiva.[30] While returning from the water tank to the temple, carrying on her head the mud pot full of water, Kallayya's daughter sees a Brahmin named Sōmāji coming toward her on the opposite side of the road. Suddenly, a raging elephant appears and blocks the road. In all the commotion, the Brahmin accidentally touches the young girl. Startled, she starts screaming: "Śiva, rescue me! I have been tainted with sin and the water is now polluted and cannot be used for the ritual!" She quickly takes the mud pot from her head and throws it on the ground, where it shatters.

The Brahmin cannot believe his eyes. He runs to his fellow Brahmins and tells them what has just happened. They go to the girl's father to complain about her, telling him that no one in the world avoids the touch of Brahmins, and that his daughter's reaction implies that Brahmins are polluting. Kallayya responds to them by saying: "Even the dog of a Śivabhakta will not touch you!" The Brahmins reply with a question: "Can your dog recite the Vedas? If so, then we accept that our position is as low as that of a dog." Kallayya immediately goes and gets a black dog from a fellow Śivabhakta. He asks the Brahmins: "Which Veda do you want the dog to chant?" They reply: "The Yajurvēda!" Kallayya prays to Śiva and Pārvati, and the dog instantly starts chanting the Yajurvēda "with the correct tone, sweetly and pleasantly."[31] Kallayya praises the dog, calling him "the King of Vedic Recitation (*vēdakadhipati*)," and concludes: "All Brahmins are equal to Śaivas' dogs!"[32] The Brahmins admit defeat and praise Kallayya, who retires in order to worship Śiva.

As in the stories discussed in the previous section, here too we find a carefully laid out symmetrical inversion of the social order. Once more it is the Brahmins who are the polluting social factor and are therefore rendered as the real Untouchables, while even a lowly animal such as a dog masters Brahminical knowledge or, in fact, its pinnacle—the Vedic hymns.[33] In a way, we have come full circle from the ambivalence

30. There is a hagiographical story about Kabīr's daughter giving water to a Brahmin that has some parallels to this story (Smith 2000, 205 and footnoted reference).

31. *Hāvinahāḷa Kallayyana Ragaḷe* v. 415 in Harihara and Suṅkāpura (1976a, 459): *mādhuryamadhurarasavāda susvaragaḷaṃ*.

32. *Hāvinahāḷa Kallayyana Ragaḷe* vv. 427–28 in Harihara and Suṅkāpura (1976a, 460): . . . *viprarellaruṃ / bhāḷāmbakana bhaktaraliha jāyilake sari*.

33. This story is echoed in a famous episode from the remembered history of the Marathi saint Jnandev (Jñāndēv), although in the Marathi story it is a buffalo rather than a dog that recites the Vedas (Novetzke 2016, 290, 355n10).

of the *Bhagavad Gītā* verse discussed in Chapter 3, in which a knowledgeable Brahmin, a dog, and a dog-eater are seen as equal. The ambiguity expressed in that *Bhagavad Gītā* verse, an ambiguity that at once claims and subverts the devotional thrust for egalitarianism, is replaced in Harihara's episode with flat cynicism. Yes, Harihara seems to say, literalizing the rhetoric of the *Bhagavad Gītā* by asserting that Brahminical knowledge can in fact be owned by anyone, even by a lowly animal, a dog. A more direct intertextual conversation between Harihara and Brahminical scripture might be seen in the equivalence between Brahmins and lowly dogs, made explicit by Kallayya at the end of the passage. This equivalence might rest on an ancient passage from the *Chāndōgya Upaniṣad,* in which a pack of stray dogs were "sliding stealthily in just the same way as priests slide stealthily in a file holding on to each other's back to sing the hymn of praise called *bahiṣpavamāna*. They sat down together and made the sound '*huṃ*.' They sang: 'OṂ! Let's eat! OṂ! Let's drink! . . . "[34] Whether the Kannada story consciously appropriates this Upaniṣadic passage or not, its message is clear: Brahmins are as rapacious as a pack of street dogs and equally robotic, especially in the context of performing Vedic chanting.[35]

While the dripping sarcasm and uninhibited scorn at the climax of the episode—with a Śaraṇa's dog reciting the Vedas "with the correct tone, sweetly and pleasantly"—is exceptionally effective, actual knowledge and mastery of the Vedas is not necessarily regarded as a lowly matter by the author of this text. In fact, the text's approach to the Vedas implies appropriation and even acceptance of some Brahminical values and practices related to Vedic knowledge. Harihara aims at ridiculing the Brahmins' haughtiness by turning the trope of exclusive Vedic knowledge and general untouchability on its head: a Brahmin's touch contaminates ritual water, and the Vedas are mastered by a dog. The inverted trope dictates appropriating the social capital traditionally claimed by Brahmins and, by so doing, also appropriating their social status. This is why the inversion of untouchability and Vedic knowledge and—more to the point—its

34. *Chāndōgya Upaniṣad* 1.12.4–5 in Olivelle (1996, 107).

35. Debiprasad Chattopadhyaya (1978 [1959]) argues for a non-satirical reading of this passage from the Upaniṣads, explaining the label "dog" as referring to the (non-derogatory) epithet of a certain clan of Brahmins (pp. 76–122). Even if we accept this reading, it is evident that later *bhakti* poets use the dog–Brahmin trope in its derogatory sense. For example, comparisons between dogs and Brahmins can be found in some of the Bharuds (theatrical poem-songs) attributed to the Marathi saint Eknāth (Novetzke 2011, 241–42).

performance in public is so central in this story, for it plainly imparts to Śivabhaktas the social supremacy that is usually claimed by Brahmins. Consequently, exhibiting mastery of Vedic knowledge denotes in this story social acceptability, legitimacy, and prestige. When we consider the earlier episode in Kallayya's life story, the one in which he wins in theological debates with Brahmins and others using Vedic and Śāstric knowledge that he acquired through learning, it is clear that our protagonist is already familiar with the value of mastering the Vedas when challenging or being challenged by Brahmins. In view of the fact that Kallayya himself is not a Brahmin but a goldsmith, the access he gets to Vedic knowledge implies a democratization of esoteric knowledge as well as social upscaling in the Bhakta's personal biography.

Significantly, Harihara does not view the Vedas in themselves as being directly efficacious or meaningful on a theological or cosmological plane. That he lacks such an appreciation of Vedic literature is evident when he tenaciously repeats the designation "those stupefied by the Vedas" (*vēdajaḍas*). On the other hand, the narrative development admits the very earthly and social advantage one gets from mastering the Vedas, especially during disputes and arguments, since an instrumental or rhetorical approach to the Vedas permeates the narrative tradition of the early Kannada Śivabhakti tradition. Velcheru Narayana Rao identifies a similar thrust in Pālkuriki Sōmanātha's writing:

> Even though Somanātha [the author of the Telugu *Basava Purāṇamu*] vehemently rejected brahminism and brahminic literary styles, he accepted the Vedas, the *purāṇas,* and the *śāstras* . . . Although in every detail the BP [*Basava Purāṇamu*] was antibrahminic, Somanātha insisted that the religious practices advocated therein closely adhere to the vedic texts. He took care, however, not to extend the respect given the texts to their chanters, the Brahmins.[36]

Narayana Rao turns our attention to the possibility that Sōmanātha's tributes to the Vedic scriptures are empty in light of the anti-Brahminical voice of the *Basava Purāṇamu.* This insight, considered together with the above episode from the Ragaḷe about Kallayya, suggests that the Vedas are accepted by this Śivabhakti tradition, if only in the most utilitarian sense, which is for the sake of social interaction with people of other sects. We

36. Somanātha, Narayana Rao, and Roghair (1990, 7).

might contrast this appraisal of Vedic knowledge as secondary and utilitarian with actually effective verbal knowledge—the knowledge about Śiva, formally reserved to Āgamas and, more genuinely and intimately perhaps, to the new literary culture of this tradition, most notably the poems by and stories of famous Bhaktas. In any case, the theological chasm between Vedic knowledge and the Bhakta's intimate knowledge of Śiva is repeatedly asserted throughout Harihara's text, and a particular antipathy is reserved for traditional followers of the Vedas. Thus, when a Śaraṇa named Musuṭeya Cauḍayya meets Śiva in Kailāsa, Harihara writes: "Cauḍayya prostrates to Śiva's twin feet . . . the feet which cannot be visualized by seekers of Vedic knowledge."[37]

While the affirmation of the Vedas found in the *Ragaḷegaḷu* may be strictly instrumental, it also attests to a certain degree to a familiarity and even intimacy with Brahminism, giving a lukewarm embrace if you will to this basically antagonized world. The complexity involved is conveyed by mechanical endorsements of the Vedas, similar to what Narayana Rao describes in his discussion of the Telugu *Basava Purāṇamu* quoted above. An example of such perfunctory acknowledgment of the Vedas can be found in a heated argument between the high-class female Śivabhakta Vaijakavve and her Jain husband, when she exclaims with regard to the doyen of his heterodox faith: "The Jina is not even mentioned in the Vedas and the Śāstras."[38] Here, the instrumental appropriation of the Vedas that generally governs the corpus is replaced with a reliance—a half-hearted one—on the actual theological pertinence of Brahminical scripture. In this case, the declarative embrace of Brahminical knowledge demarcates a boundary, clearly placing the Jains outside it. And, indeed, on the whole Harihara's contentious disposition against the Jains is very different from his treatment of Brahmins, as we will see in the following two chapters, which deal with this bipartite typology of the religious other in the *Ragaḷegaḷu* stories.

Despite the ubiquitous anti-Brahminical rhetoric in the *Ragaḷegaḷu*, the relevant stories are informed with a real undercurrent of familiarity and shared ground with Brahmins. In this corpus, Brahminness is not imagined as an ultimate enemy to be wiped out but rather as something

37. *Musuṭeya Cauḍayyana Ragaḷe* vv. 159, 161 in Harihara and Suṅkāpura (1976a, 430): *musuteya cavuṇḍarāyaṃ harana caraṇakke . . . vēdaṅgaḷ arasi kāṇada pādayugaḷakke.*

38. *Vaijakavveya Ragaḷe* v. 213 in Harihara and Suṅkāpura (1976a, 234): *vēdadoḷage śāstradoḷage nōḍal illa nuḍiyal illa.*

to be appropriated. It is not surprising that, in history, the Vīraśaiva tradition indeed adopted quasi-Brahminical features such as a relatively strict set of rituals (albeit highly simplified), a set of unique social practices (including a distinct form of vegetarianism), denominational institutions, an original canon, a theology of its own, and even a rigid and hierarchical social structure unique to Vīraśaiva society, in which, again mirroring Brahminism, the priestly class is superior to the others. Several scholars describe Vīraśaiva society as a carefully structured super-caste.[39]

Commensality Practices and Dietary Rules

Discord among fellow Śaivas in the *Ragaḷegaḷu* often revolves around food practices set against a background of Brahminical ideology regarding purity and pollution. In addressing the topic of ritualistic food consumption, stories in the *Ragaḷegaḷu* present the qualms and complexities that emerge out of real-life situations when Śaivas from different social backgrounds come together for a shared meal. Significantly, Harihara weaves these stories in a manner that not only presents these difficulties but also offers ways to negotiate and alleviate them, usually with the active participation of a Bhakta Brahmin.

In South Asian societies in general, commensality (the public event of consuming food as a group) is a highly charged arena for social exclusion based on class and purity.[40] Traditional Brahminical ethics forbid Brahmins from joining with people of lower classes for the sharing of food. The basic logic for this prohibition is that the higher one's social class, the more restrictive one's diet.[41] Therefore, sitting to eat with a person of a

39. Lise Vail (1985) demonstrates this well in her analysis of contemporary Liṅgāyatism, although this is not the central focus of her argument. See also McCormack (1973, 169); Zydenbos (1997, 530).

40. For more on the Gordian knot of commensality and caste in South Asia and how it has changed in contemporary society due to market forces, see Madsen and Gardella (2012, 92) and further citations there.

41. One outcome of this principle is that food cooked by Brahmins can be consumed by all strata of society; an example of this type of food is the strict vegetarian cuisine served today in the Udupi Hotels chain of restaurants, which is based in coastal Karnataka (Madsen and Gardella 2012, 96). Lived traditions and history obviously render more complex schemes than this general rule, as carefully stated by Katherine E. Ulrich: "That vegetarianism steadily increased in prestige over the course of centuries in South Asia is uncontested; the precise regional, sectarian, and caste patterns in which this shift occurred are little documented" (Ulrich 2007, 242–43). See also Srinivasan (2000). In addition to social mobility and caste, life-cycle rituals can also place strictures on one's diet. See the example in Banerji (2003, 86).

lower social class can expose a Brahmin to inadvertent consumption of forbidden, polluted food, and the act of sharing food potentially involves a dangerous exchange of bodily fluids that might jeopardize the Brahmin's purity.[42]

Devotional traditions sometimes share with Brahminism a concern for eating-related behaviors, placing particular emphasis on commensality. As a few scholars have noted, *bhakti* in the literal sense of "sharing" can refer to the sharing of consecrated food, or *prasāda*, among ritual participants.[43] We can see how, whether in Brahminical or *bhakti* circles, diet clearly plays a critical role. In the words of Katherine E. Ulrich, "[f]ood passes through the boundaries of the body and becomes part of you, and in situations where social and religious groups are marked by distinctive diets you become part of a community as a result."[44] Devotional emphasis on the communal and ritualized consummation of consecrated food can result in the formation of boundaries similar to those of Brahmins regarding who is within the circle of sharing food and who is outside it.

The shared interest of the Brahminical and *bhakti* traditions in food practices is expressed in paradigmatic South Asian devotional stories.[45] In many of them, commensality, usually regarded as a contentious, volatile, and provocative issue, is deliberately presented against the background of Brahminical purity-based restrictions. In the case of early Kannada Śivabhakti, the social prescription for commensality can be evinced in a passage from the *Dīkṣābōdhe*, a Kannada Śivabhakti doctrinal text roughly contemporaneous with the *Ragaḷegaḷu* that was composed by Harihara's close associate Kereya Padmarasa. In the *Dīkṣābōdhe*, the author prohibits eating inside the house of a non-Śaiva and commands that meals be eaten in Śaivas' houses.[46]

---

42. See the episode on p. 96 in Bismillah and Ratan (1987). For a contemporary practice demonstrating the other end of this principle, in which low-caste devotees participate in a ritual involving the use of food left over from that consumed by Brahmins in order to absorb their purifying saliva, see Karanth (2012).

43. See Novetzke (2008, 18–19); Pechilis (1999, 66).

44. Ulrich (2007, 229).

45. See case examples in the Marathi tradition (Keune 2014, 7; 2011, throughout; Novetzke 2011, 241–42), the northern Sants (Pauwels 2010; Burchett 2009, 120–22; Smith 2000, 205–9), and the Tamil traditions (Ulrich 2007).

46. *Dīkṣābōdhe* 1.413–18. The probably later *Siddhāntaśikhāmaṇi* makes similar claims, though couched in a more sectarian and specifically Vīraśaiva discourse, in vv. 9.29–33.

Like Padmarasa, Harihara pays special attention to the theme of commensality among the fellowship of devotees in the *Ragaḷegaḷu*. In several stories in the corpus we come across elaborate descriptions of specific types of dishes, complex preparations, and public feedings of crowds of devotees—descriptions that detail the considerable logistical, monetary, and labor investments such meals require.[47] Commensality is portrayed in these stories as a central arena for publicly asserting the collective religious identity of the community of devotees.

But Harihara's treatment of food issues throughout his narrative has a deeper level, which concerns the internal dynamics among Śaivas from different backgrounds when it comes to sitting down and eating together. Here, the set of Brahminical dietary requirements and practices emerges as something that needs to come to terms with the redrawing of identity boundaries by the devotional community. We approach this gastronomic arena, then, with a specific set of questions in mind: What, according to these stories, can a Brahmin Śivabhakta and an Untouchable Śivabhakta eat when they join together to worship Śiva? Should they follow strict, Brahminical vegetarianism despite the *bhakti* tradition's disavowal of this excluding culture? Should they follow a less restrictive diet that has greater popular appeal? Can dishes containing meat and other kinds of food—popular and favored among lower strata of society but morally abhorred by Brahmins and others—be included? And a question that is perhaps more fundamental than all the others: What is the metaphysical paradigm Śivabhaktas should follow with regard to their food ethics?

As we shall see, the *Ragaḷegaḷu* provides complex answers to these questions, treating commensality as a social event for creatively negotiating the ideal of sameness against the complexities involved in bringing to the dining table people from different backgrounds.

---

47. In the opening of the second chapter of the *Kōvūra Bommatandeya Ragaḷe*, the protagonist saint organizes a public feeding with enormous amounts of rice. The second chapter of the *Śaṅkaradāsimayyana Ragaḷe* contains an argument between two devotees (Jēḍara Dāsimayya and Śaṅkaradāsimayya) about feeding Bhaktas, and the third chapter describes another huge public feeding. In the opening of the seventh chapter of the *Basavēśvaradēvara Ragaḷe* Basavaṇṇa feeds a large crowd of devotees. The feeding of Śaiva mendicants is seen in the *Ragaḷegaḷu* as having special significance and plays a major role in two stories about sectarian conflicts with Jains, the *Vaijakavveya Ragaḷe* and the *Ādayyana Ragaḷe*, which I discuss in Chapter 6 of this book.

Cooking with Onion

In light of the centrality of food matters in communal religious life, it is not surprising that in the eighth chapter of the Ragaḷe about Basavaṇṇa, when Śaraṇas praise Basavaṇṇa for his support of the community of Śaiva devotees in a series of rhetorical questions, they proclaim: "Does he inquire after a Jaṅgama's caste (*jāti*)? Does he recognize impurity (*apavitrate*) in consecrated food (*prasāda*)?"[48] Like Bhōgaṇṇa in the passage quoted earlier, Basavaṇṇa is a Brahmin hailed for his refusal to differentiate among Bhaktas on the basis of their social position. In this case, Basavaṇṇa's impartiality is immediately linked to food through the claim that, for him, no food offered during worship of Śiva can be impure, even if it does not conform to Brahminical (or other) dietary restrictions. The text's overt ethical prescription is formulated here against an invisible—but very present—Brahminical exclusivism, but this totalistic claim regarding food practices does not serve as the end point of the discussion in the *Ragaḷegaḷu* stories about the Kannada saints. Rather, it is only the beginning. In what might be intentionally (and ironically?) structured by Harihara, three chapters later Basavaṇṇa does in fact breach the rhetorical commitment to accept any food consecrated to Śiva.

The incident itself is elaborate, as if to deliberately problematize Basavaṇṇa's supposedly long-forsaken Brahminical origins, or at least to confront him with them.[49] A Bhakta called Kinnara Bommatande hears about Basavaṇṇa's generosity and decides that he wants to meet him. Bommatande sets out on his journey and, as he is entering the city, the hair on Basavaṇṇa's body suddenly bristles and he thinks to himself: "This is a sign that a great Śaraṇa will soon come to visit me!" When Bommatande arrives at Basavaṇṇa's house, the latter receives him with great honor. Despite the fact that Basavaṇṇa is surrounded by twelve thousand Śaraṇas, he himself takes care of Bommatande and performs an elaborate Śiva ritual together with him. Bommatande is very pleased by this welcoming reception, and the affection between the two grows from day to day.

One day, Bommatande thinks to himself, "Whatever I bring for Śiva, Śiva shall take," and he decides to cook for the god an onion curry. Other

48. *Basavēśvaradēvara Ragaḷe* 8.prose in Harihara and Suṅkāpura (1976a, 62): *jaṅgamadalli jātiyan aṟase, prasādadalli apavitrateyan aṟiye.*

49. *Basavēśvaradēvara Ragaḷe* 11 in Harihara and Suṅkāpura (1976a, 79–86).

Śaraṇas join Bommatande in the preparations, and soon the odor of onions cooking reaches Basavaṇṇa. When he smells this odor, Basavaṇṇa exclaims: "Who brought this uneatable (*abhōjya*) food here?" Bommatande hears what Basavaṇṇa has said and starts to seethe inwardly, thinking: "I should not have come here. I have made a heavenly dish (*amṛta*) for Śiva Mallayya to enjoy, and Basavaṇṇa is complaining! I cannot stay here!" Filled with anger, Bommatande leaves Basavaṇṇa's house and departs the city, stopping for the night at a nearby village.

When Basavaṇṇa joins the other Śaraṇas for worship and notices Bommatande's absence, the Śaraṇas tell him what has happened. Basavaṇṇa, deeply disturbed, says to the group of Bhaktas: "I have made a grave mistake. I have sinned against the whole community of Bhaktas and I should be punished. Tell me how to correct this situation!" The Śaraṇas respond by saying, "What caused this mess is onion, so let onion fix the problem!" Basavaṇṇa agrees. He immediately orders a large quantity of the best onions. These are placed on carts that set out in procession surrounded by musical instruments and decorations. When the procession reaches Basavaṇṇa, he orders that the animals be decorated with onions and that the people wear onions as ornaments. Onions are distributed to the populace until the whole city is filled with them. Then the procession resumes, this time with Basavaṇṇa leading it. He sits on an onion seat, with onions in his hands and decorating his clothes and his hair as they all proceed toward the house in the nearby village where Bommatande is staying. When Bommatande sees the spectacle, he is amazed and immediately understands that Basavaṇṇa wishes to appease him. Bommatande thinks: "What a great person is Basavaṇṇa. He has understood his mistake and turned anger into love."

When the two meet, Basavaṇṇa prostrates himself at Bommatande's feet. Without saying a word they embrace, and both shed tears of joy. Bommatande returns to Basavaṇṇa's house and, on entering, he finds huge piles of onions all over. He hears Śaraṇas singing to the onions, and he sees many varieties of onion dishes spread out everywhere; they have the color of jasmine and the taste of moonlight. All the Śaraṇas offer the dishes to Śiva and consume them afterward. They praise Bommatande and Basavaṇṇa, and Basavaṇṇa vows that this onion festival is to be a yearly celebration and that, from now on, eating onions will become one of his own religious observances (*nēma*). Harihara concludes the story by telling us that Basavaṇṇa is the moon for Śivabhaktas, and the scorching sun for the stupid people of all other religions (*parasamaya timira*).

Basavaṇṇa's initial revulsion at Bommatande's cooking with onion serves as the story's peripeteia after the honeymoon-like beginning. The sudden, unintended crisis between the two devotees propels the plot toward its main thematic thread: legitimizing non-Brahminical food practices. Although Basavaṇṇa's dislike of onions might be a personal preference, this dislike rests on a broader Brahminical practice of avoiding the eating of onions, as suggested by his complaining to his fellow devotees: "Who brought this uneatable food here?"[50] When Basavaṇṇa recognizes that his own gustatory prejudice, rooted in his Brahminical background, has implied social condescension and maybe even exclusion, he reverses his stance, replacing a deeply ingrained habit with a celebration of onion consumption. In the story, communality based on Śiva-devotion clearly trumps Brahmins' predilections. Thus the story can be read as Basavaṇṇa's temporary relapse into Brahminism and his immediate reawakening from that elitist "old world" into the current reality of establishing an inclusive devotional communion. By legitimizing the use of onion, Basavaṇṇa publicly reaffirms the allowance for any kind of consecrated food not just as an idealized principle but also as a lived practice.

The story also makes a makes a broader communal comment by redrawing food-related boundaries for the community of Kannada Śivabhaktas, prescribing cooking practices that lean toward non-Brahmins. While Karnataka Vīraśaivas (or at least most of them) are known to this day as vegetarian, they are also known to favor onion dishes.[51] Although it is difficult to directly connect this story with how Vīraśaiva cooking patterns were shaped in actual history, it can be read as an attempt to mythologize this unique communal marker, to naturalize through sacred narrative the

50. Onion is proscribed in classical texts. It is stated in *Mānava Dharmaśāstra* 5.19: "By eating mushrooms, a village hog, garlic, a village fowl, onion, or leek intentionally, a twice-born falls from his caste" (Manu and Olivelle 2004, 139). Changing practices regarding cooking with onion and garlic in relation to Brahminical restrictions during the last century and a half are discussed in Srinivasan (2000, 188–89, 201–202). In Jainism there is a similar proscription against using onion (Ulrich 2007, 241). See also Guha (1985, 147); Singh (1975, 87–89).

51. On vegetarianism in the Vīraśaiva tradition, see Ripepi (2007, 71n16); McCormack (1973, 179); Desai (1968, 323). The following is an anecdote about the cultural hold of Vīraśaiva cooking: While on a visit to Kannada University in Hampi, north Karnataka, one of my language teachers from the American Institute of Indian Studies (AIIS) program, who is a Brahmin, commented to me as we ate that the food served to us had been cooked by a Vīraśaiva. When I asked how she could tell, she said it was because of the particular spices used and the onion. Later she went to the kitchen and confirmed that her assumption had been correct.

consumption of onion while weaving into the myth active resistance to Brahminical customs, regardless of how deeply rooted they are.

Animal Killing and Meat Consumption

While the above story neatly rewrites the dietary boundaries of the Śivabhaktas' community to include onion, the following story deals with a food ingredient which, from an ethical perspective, is much more problematic: meat. A famous *vacana* attributed to Basavaṇṇa endorses the ethical rejection of animal killing:

> The sacrificial lamb brought for the festival
> ate up the green leaf brought for the decorations.
>
> Not knowing a thing about the kill,
> it wants only to fill its belly:
> born that day, to die that day.
> But tell me:
> did the killers survive,
> O lord of the meeting rivers?
>
> (*vacana* no. 129)[52]

Some scholars read this *vacana* and similar ones as signifying a Vīraśaiva prohibition of animal killing, although, as Robert Zydenbos notes, *vacana*s that express a more tolerant approach to animal killing and meat consumption are also attributed to Basavaṇṇa.[53] This multivalence is also visible in the following story by Harihara, in which proscriptions of meat consumption and animal killing under the aegis of Śiva devotion receive a complex interpretation. As in the story discussed in the previous section, this story revolves around the relationship between two Śivabhaktas, one a Brahmin and the other not, although here the occupation of the non-Brahmin Bhakta is placed in the foreground. He is a Bhakta who hunts animals and eats their meat, and these practices link him with society's lower castes, perhaps even placing him at society's periphery.[54]

---

52. Translated by Ramanujan (1973, 76).

53. Zydenbos (1997, 529n22).

54. The Kannada term for a hunter is Bēḍa, and Harihara uses the verb associated with this occupation "to hunt" (*bēṇṭeyāḍu*). See, for example, *Teluga Jommayyana Ragaḷe* 3.45 in Harihara and Suṅkāpura (1976a, 392).

The Bhakta, called Teluga (or Telugu) Jommayya, is described in the *Ragaḷegaḷu* as having a volatile temperament and a personal history of violence.[55] At the beginning of the Ragaḷe about him, he kills a Brahmin at the court of King Permāḍirāya for telling a story in which Viṣṇu triumphs over Śiva.[56] This is the only instance in the *Ragaḷegaḷu* stories about Kannada Śivabhaktas in which a Brahmin is killed, and it is important to note that in this story the direct (and justified) reason for murdering him has to do not with his Brahminness but rather with his sectarian Vaiṣṇava affiliation. In any case, the spontaneous murder troubles Jommayya both ethically and judicially, and soon after this incident, following the order given to him by Śiva, he retires to hunt animals.[57] In the opening passage of the section about Jommayya hunting, Harihara carefully addresses the ethical problem of the violence inherent in the killing of animals, and it is immediately obvious that the author is taking pains to exonerate Jommayya from any ethical failing. Harihara writes:

> When Jommayya spots a mob of deer—themselves motivated by a divine wish to reach Śiva's heaven—he says to himself: "This is not a sin but an order from Śiva." He aims his arrow at the animal, chants Śiva's mantra, and then shoots. The animal is startled. The arrow cuts through its head, and it falls to the ground. At that very moment, the animal's soul (*jīva*) is liberated and ascends to Śiva's heaven in Kailāsa. This is proper devotion (*bhakti*) aiming straight to liberation (*mukti*), with arrows that grant the ultimate calm (*nirvāṇa*). The sages (Ṛṣis) bless Jommayya, who never shoots an animal unmarked by Śiva.[58]

This passage reconfigures the violence inherent in hunting animals, recasting Jommayya's deeds as auspicious, devotional, and even beneficial

---

55. Jommayya's epithet "of Telugu" remains unexplained in this Ragaḷe, though *vacanas* attributed to him carry a signature line with dedication to "Telugēśa" (Lord of Telugu) (Śāmarāya 2009 [1967], 182). Harihara's silence regarding the Telugu background of Jommayya might indicate the permeable boundaries between the Kannada and Telugu cultures in this temporal and spatial setting. See Ben-Herut (2015).

56. I discuss this incident in detail in the following chapter.

57. The *Teluga Jommayyana Ragaḷe*, chapters 1 and 2 in Harihara and Suṅkāpura (1976a, 381–90)

58. This is a summary of *Teluga Jommayyana Ragaḷe* 3.1–44 in Harihara and Suṅkāpura (1976a, 391–92).

for the hunted animals, since it releases sages from the curse of incarnating on earth in animal form and actively unites them with the god.[59] The text does not ignore the demerit inherent in killing but, rather, upends its ethical value under the mantle of faith in Śiva.[60] The story develops into a complete episode woven around the ethical question of Jommayya's hunting, with the above snippet serving as a prelude to the conflict that is to follow. It is an ethical conflict between the devotee hunter and a devotee Brahmin who starkly opposes hunting and meat eating.[61]

The meeting between the two Śivabhaktas is, as one would expect, highly charged.[62] It begins when Kēśirāja, the celebrated administrator to King Permāḍirāya and himself a Brahmin, arrives in the forest in order to meet the famous devotee Jommayya. On entering Jommayya's hut Kēśirāja is appalled to find animal carcasses scattered on the floor. Repulsed, Kēśirāja decides he cannot remain in the Bhakta's hut and—against all conventional rules of hospitality among fellow Śivabhaktas—hurries off to stay instead at the local temple of Śiva.

Although Kēśirāja tries to conceal from Jommayya his sense of horror at the latter's way of life, he is unsuccessful, and tension arises between the two because of Kēśirāja's refusal to go to Jommayya's home. At this point, Jommayya performs a miracle that "breaks the ice": he makes the *śivaliṅga* that Kēśirāja is holding in his hand fly up into the air, and this demonstration of supernatural capabilities so impresses Kēśirāja that he relents and agrees to enter Jommayya's blood-stained hut in order to join him in a shared ritual of worship of Śiva.

---

59. Narrative claims for animals' salvation after they are sacrificed appear already in the Vedas (Das 2017, 10–11; Patton 2007, 16).

60. A similar theological rationale guides the Tamil story about the hunter called Kaṇṇappa, who is also a Śiva devotee. As in this case, that text celebrates the auspiciousness of offering game meat to Śiva (Ulrich 2007: 249–50; Cox 2005; Monius 2004; Peterson 1994).

61. See Ulrich (2007, 233–34) for the reversed claim about Brahmins identified as cow eaters in the *Maṇimēkalai*, an early Tamil Buddhist text. Meat consumption and deer hunting are problematized in several episodes in the classical epics (*Mahābhārata* 1.109.5–9, 3.139, 16.5.18–20; *Rāmāyana* 1.2.1–16, 2.57–58, 3.41–47), and the ethical conundrums associated with these activities are echoed in modern religious discourses (Hess 2001, 38–41). See also Doniger (2009, 321–25, 437–38).

62. This episode is narrated twice by Harihara, once in the *Teluga Jommayyana Ragaḷe* and once in the *Kēśirāja Daṇṇāyakara Ragaḷe*. Since the two versions of the story are similar, I summarize and discuss here the one appearing in the third chapter of *Teluga Jommayyana Ragaḷe*, which is more elaborate.

The theological crisis between the two Śivabhaktas, however, quickly resurfaces when consecrated food (*prasāda*) is brought to the table by Jommayya's wife, for the curries she offers to the Brahmin devotee are made of game meat. Kēśirāja is overwhelmed with disgust. Jommayya, seeing this, laughs and addresses Śiva Sōmanātha, Kēśirāja's personal deity, saying: "Please defer to Kēśirāja's inner wish and turn these (meat curries) into rice dishes."[63] At once, the meat curries are transformed into sweets made of rice and jaggery, boiled milk porridge, rice cakes, and fruit dishes. Then Kēśirāja, ecstatic with joy, consumes the sacred food, and both Bhaktas celebrate the whole night through. At the end of the story, Kēśirāja calls out: "Śiva! If you desire it, one's demerit (*pāpa*) is merit (*puṇya*), immorality (*anīti*) is morality (*nīti*), unfit deeds (*aḥkārya*) are proper deeds (*kārya*), confusion (*akrama*) is coherence (*krama*), bad familial origins (*duḥkula*) are good familial origins (*satkula*), unrighteousness (*adharma*) is righteousness (*dharma*)."[64]

Jommayya's self-confidence, evident throughout the story, rests on his uncompromising devotion, and this story demonstrates how devotion wins over purity whenever the two come up against one another. Śiva clearly prefers the former: It is the hunter—and not the Brahmin—whose requests—or perhaps orders?—addressed to the god are fulfilled by the *liṅga*, even in the setting of a temple, a physical embodiment of bounded purity.[65]

The gap in social class and traditional upbringing between Kēśirāja and Jommayya is not ignored but made concrete in the story by the particular manifestations of Śiva that each of the devotees worships: Kēśirāja's personal deity (*iṣṭadēvate*), Śiva Sōmanātha, is markedly a mainstream embodiment of Śiva, worshiped in many Brahminical temples throughout India. In sharp contrast, Jommayya's deity Bhīmanātha (literally, "Lord of Fear") is an obscure, marginalized, and terrible form of Śiva. The tangible difference between the two manifestations of Śiva points to the variations in Śaiva devotional worlds that Harihara is interested in connecting. Rather

63. *Teluga Jommayyana Ragaḷe* 3.177–78 in Harihara and Suṅkāpura (1976a, 397): *ele sōmanātha daṇṇāyakara manadante | palalavam pakvānnatatigaḷam māḍinte.*

64. *Teluga Jommayyana Ragaḷe* 3.215–18 in Harihara and Suṅkāpura (1976a, 398): *asamākṣa nī oliye pāpavē puṇyavadu | usedu nīn olidaṅganītiyē nītiyadu | aḥkāryavē kāryav akramam kramaveyadu | duḥkulam satkulav adharmavē dharmavadu.*

65. See Shulman (1980) for a thorough analysis of the temple as a physical embodiment of purity and the inherent tensions in the medieval Tamil Śaiva imaginaire.

than dismissing one of the two devotees, Harihara untangles the knot using a tolerant approach, with two Bhaktas from different backgrounds (and with different eating restrictions) negotiating and finally managing to bridge their differences in opinion and in customs.

The exculpation of killing is in some ways similar to the discourse about violence in the *Bhagavad Gītā*. In that text Kṛṣṇa insists that Arjuna fulfill his vocational duty as a warrior and start a cataclysmic war against his own family members and close associates, since this killing is in line with the divine design. In fact, the ideological correspondence between the two texts runs even deeper, as both texts openly legitimize violence based on devotional theology.[66] The prescribed social configuration in the Ragaḷe story, however, is the reversal of that in the *Gītā*: while the *Gītā* affirms one's traditional occupation in order to bolster social hierarchy, the Ragaḷe about Jommayya affirms one's occupation while jettisoning any sense of social hierarchy, along with any suggestion of social backwardness—as long as the person is a Śivabhakta, of course.

The activities of hunting, of offering meat to Śiva, and of consuming it afterward, when framed as devotional acts, are utterly purified and legitimized by Harihara in this story.[67] For Harihara, Brahminical-based food restrictions are completely insignificant in comparison with religious devotion. The only exception with regard to meat offerings is when they are served to Kēśirāja the Brahmin. Because of his guest's vegetarianism, Jommayya—in a markedly light-hearted and unapologetic manner—has Śiva convert the meat curries into vegetarian food, not as an acknowledgment of Kēśirāja's ethical grievance but as a generous gesture for an oddball. Here, Brahminical vegetarianism is stripped of any sense of ethical or social superiority and transformed into an empty peculiarity, perhaps even an eccentric one when contrasted with Jommayya's devotional zeal. Harihara prescribes an ad hoc solution to the social crisis, a solution that enables the Brahmin to continue complying with the traditional dietary code while abrogating the Brahminical, purity-based sense of superiority attached to it.

---

66. The ethical case of the *Bhagavad Gītā* is more complex in this regard, being couched in a extended discourse about *dharma*. Nevertheless, devotion to and ethical reliance on the god are central in the *Bhagavad Gītā* for upholding the prescribed *dharma* (Davis 2015, 43–72).

67. Chidananda Murthy writes with regard to Jommayya's eating habits: "There were meat-eaters among the devotees (Ex. Telugu Jommaṇṇa) and they were not looked down upon for this" (1983, 204).

Meat consumption by the hunter-devotee is, in itself, not the central problem for Harihara; far more significant is the breaching of the principle of equal treatment by the Brahmin, and although meat was miraculously converted in order resolve the dietary conflict, the recovery of the Brahmin's understanding of the principle of equal treatment (*samaśīla*) is far more significant for Harihara. This is made obvious in the way Harihara invokes the term *samaśīla* twice in the passage. The first is when Kēśirāja refuses Jommayya's offer to stay at his home because of his disgust at the carcasses. Kēśirāja's refusal is suggestive of the Brahminical exclusion of and separation from low-caste people, and Harihara notes that at this moment Kēśirāja's speech lacked *samaśīla*.[68] The second appearance of the term *samaśīla* in this episode is near the end of the story, when Kēśirāja departs from Jommayya. Here, *samaśīla* is invoked to indicate of Kēśirāja's recovery of a proper understanding that all of Śiva's devotees are equal.[69] Before leaving Jommayya's house, Kēśirāja proclaims that there are no boundaries in the eyes of Śiva, and thus the communal crisis is resolved. Clearly, the problem around which this story is woven is not meat or hunting animals, but the mechanical and markedly Brahminical aversion to (and, implicitly, the consequential social exclusion of) non-Brahmins and their non-Brahminical ways. The story's denouement marks the removal of these Brahminical notions from the Brahmin-Bhakta's mind.[70]

Kēśirāja's bewildered assertion at the end of the episode that Śiva can transform unrighteousness (*adharma*) into righteousness (*dharma*) brings to mind a Tantric reversal of social norms, although the breaching of boundaries implied here seems to emerge more out of intense emotional outpouring than out of the technologically informed world of Tantra.[71] Kēśirāja's expression of bewilderment exhibits his astonishment not only at the considerable gap that exists between his deeply ingrained

68. *Teluga Jommayyana Ragaḷe* 3.98 in Harihara and Suṅkāpura (1976a, 394): . . . *samaśīlallade nuḍidarantalli.*

69. *Teluga Jommayyana Ragaḷe* 3.222 in Harihara and Suṅkāpura (1976a, 398): *kūḍe samaśīlagaṇasantatige pēḷutam.*

70. An almost symmetrically opposite devotional thrust with regard to vegetarianism can be found in Kabīr's poetry (Pauwels 2010, 516–17). Favoring Brahminically based and doctrinal vegetarianism over meat eating is also typical of the early modern hermeneutics of the *Rāmcaritmānas* (Hess 2001, 38–40).

71. Compare with Wedemeyer (2013). Vocabulary and concepts connected to Tantra are rare in the *Ragaḷegaḷu*, in contrast to later Vīraśaiva texts produced from the fifteenth century onward (Glasbrenner 2015).

Brahminical predilections and Jommayya's behavior but also at the ability Śiva-devotion has for collapsing, or at least bridging, this chasm.[72] With Kēśirāja's brief concluding speech, Harihara presents the superiority of devotion over mainstream, formalistic, Brahminically aligned religion, but at the same time he also carves out a space of potential forgiving, a space for accommodating Brahminical predilections without siding with their ideological substratum.

As previously mentioned, Vīraśaivas in Karnataka are traditionally known for maintaining a vegetarian diet and generally oppose the killing of animals in what can be explained as an adoption of Brahminical values and practices or an accommodation to their influence.[73] Jommayya's story appears at first to run against this trend, with its stress on the superiority and precedence of devotional interiority over any prescribed behavior or ritual. However, considering the fact the Kēśirāja did not breach his vegetarianism, one might say that the story remains vague regarding this particular subject. The fact that the ethical conflict between the two Bhaktas is unraveled in a *deus-ex-machina* fashion through a miracle rather than through dialogue or policy-based negotiation suggests that, for this culture, social differences cannot always be resolved in a hermetic manner. In other words, this narrative depicts the limit of prescribing unified shared-food practices, which is the eating of meat.

Reeducating the Educated

The stories considered in this chapter all take pains to argue *against* a cultural parcel of values and practices identified with and championed and nurtured by Brahmins. Hunting and meat consumption, cooking with onion, physical association with Untouchables, and unrestricted access to Vedic knowledge are patently Brahminical anxieties; all come to life and are manifested to the full in the *Ragaḷegaḷu* stories by model devotees. The Brahminical way of life, to which Harihara pays close attention in these stories, is criticized and rewritten in radical ways. Moreover, the Brahminical ethical framework of *karma* in the sense of retribution over multiple rebirths—which oftentimes undergirds Brahminical social exclusivism—is consistently rejected in the stories. This point is explicitly

72. For a phenomenological exploration of the interconnectedness of *adharma* and *dharma* in Hindu thought, see Glucklich (1994).

73. Many *bhakti* traditions take similar stances (Pauwels 2010: 530; Ulrich 2007).

made in the episode discussed above with Basavaṇṇa and Nāgidēva, in which Vaiṣṇava Brahmins are derided by Basavaṇṇa as *karmajaḍas* ("dull-minded by the notion of *karma*").[74]

But despite the fact that ritual virtuosity, social exclusivism, and *karma*-derived ethics, all associated with Brahminism, are utterly rejected, these stories in no way indicate that there is anything inherently wicked or vile in Brahminness. Several leading protagonists, namely Bhōgaṇṇa, Basavaṇṇa, and Kēśirāja, are themselves well-educated Brahmins working as high officials at the court. Although their Brahminical (and worldly) engagements run against the idealistic devotionalism argued for in the stories, their Brahminical "DNA" is not automatically denied by Harihara nor does it preclude them from being "good" Bhaktas. Rather, Harihara charts in these stories a path that Brahmins can follow in order to be considered "good" Bhaktas despite their Brahminical origin—assuming, naturally, that their devotion to Śiva is total. Harihara communicates an acute need to make Brahminness (having Brahminical origins) acceptable while purging it of Brahminism (the ideological championing of Brahminical values). His investment in markedly Brahminical occupations and practices, the room he gives in the stories to Brahmin protagonists who "learn" how to be proper Bhaktas, coupled with his homiletic, almost one-sided resistance to Brahminical stances and consequent legitimization of non-Brahminical practices, all suggest that at least part of the intended audience for these stories is made up of Brahmins.[75]

Considered in this light, some of the *Ragaḷegaḷu* stories can be read as pedagogical tools for teaching Brahmins how to *become* "good" Bhaktas and other, non-Brahmin Bhaktas how to accommodate Brahmins' "special needs" despite their incongruity with spontaneous and open-for-all forms of devotional expression. The following conclusions build upon this theorem, formulating in directly pedagogical terms some principles in the *Ragaḷegaḷu* stories that are aimed for—surprisingly or not—the most educated of all, that is traditional Brahmins. Recently converted Brahmins are

74. Another famous episode from the Ragaḷe about Basavaṇṇa which argues against the principle of *karma* is the one about young Basavaṇṇa removing his *jannivāra*, the sacred thread given ceremoniously to members of the upper classes during childhood. He does so because he understands that "Śivabhakti and *karma* are not the same thing" (*śivabhaktiyum karmavum endum ondāgirade*), *Basavēśvaradēvara Ragaḷe* 2.prose in Harihara and Suṅkāpura (1976a, 30). See discussion about the tension between the principle of *karma* and devotionalism in modern and northern *bhakti* in Hess (2001, 43–45).

75. I wish to thank Jon Keune for his assistance in developing some of these ideas.

required, according to these narratives, to accommodate social difference and recalibrate their social practices according to a more inclusive vision of devotional society. The Brahmin Bhaktas need to learn how to behave toward non-Brahmins, now to be regarded as equals within a shared devotional universe. The stories also redraw the guidelines for proper Brahminical conduct, proposing reconsideration of some Brahminical restrictions (such as refraining from consuming onion) but also allowing adherence to others (such as refraining from eating meat).

From the perspective of clashing social backgrounds, the stories about Kēśirāja and about Basavaṇṇa portray an understanding that personal and social dynamics could become stormy at times, even within the forming community itself, among fellow Bhaktas who come from different backgrounds. Furthermore, the vision of the Śaiva movement as it is portrayed in Harihara's text is an inclusive one: embracing different people from different social backgrounds under a unifying devotional umbrella, with the solutions offered by these stories for accommodating differences varying according to context.

Commensality is a particularly charged arena in which social discrimination is laid bare and contested. The *bhakti* crowd that populates Harihara's stories is highly diverse, consisting of Brahmins and non-Brahmins from different strands of society, and the complex dynamics that are generated by this motley assortment of people become particularly brittle with regard to food practices. The prescriptions that Harihara devises for tackling this problem are diverse: a vegetarian Brahmin can adhere to his nonviolent practices but must not exclude or evade the company of nonvegetarian Bhaktas; onion, though prohibited in the Brahminical diet, becomes for the Śivabhakti community a central ingredient in foods precisely because of Brahminical exclusion.

Thinking about the onion story and the meat story together helps us appreciate the nuance in these prescriptions. The two food stories discussed here delineate communal food ethics that are central to the identity of the Śivabhakti community in the Kannada-speaking region to this day. The ethics are syncretic, both appropriating existing practices (Brahminical and Jain) as well as distinguishing the Śivabhakti from the other sects. One accommodation to differences among Bhaktas can be ad hoc in nature, as in the case of Kēśirāja's meat meal being transformed into a vegetarian meal. Another can be communal and ritualistic, as in the case of Basavaṇṇa's festival of onion. Unlike avoidance of eating onions, avoidance of eating meat is not something that a Brahmin can ultimately be expected to repudiate. But he must understand that meat is potentially holy if offered by another Bhakta, even if the Brahmin himself is not required to eat it. Perhaps more important, the Brahminical sanction against such non-Brahminical, traditionally transgressive practices is revoked in this story.

In this new, complicated world, a Brahmin is allowed to retain some of his traditional behaviors, such as the avoidance of meat, but is also made to recognize and accept that non-Brahmin Bhaktas too can retain their own practices, even if they have been traditionally regarded as impure, since the Brahminical tradition no longer serves as the formal yardstick for piety and proper religious behavior.

5

The King's Fleeting Authority and His Menacing Vaiṣṇava Brahmins

FROM A THEMATIC perspective, this chapter extends the movement outward through the concentric circles that surround the character of the devotee in the *Ragaḷegaḷu*. At this point we cross a border, moving beyond consideration of Harihara's figuring of the saint's interactions with fellow devotees to an examination of his or her interactions with non-Śaivas. The emic term Harihara uses for non-Śaivas, a term that is also used more broadly in the Kannada Śivabhakti devotional nomenclature for religious outsiders, is *bhavis*.[1] *Bhavi* means "worldling," a fitting translation in its most literal sense: by his or her ignorance of Śiva's greatness, the "worldling" is restricted to earthly existence in a quotidian, contingent, limited sense.

Bhavis, or non-Śaivas—with the plural form intended—play a substantial role in the *Ragaḷegaḷu*. Conflicts with non-Śaivas are woven into thirteen of the eighteen stories pertaining to the Kannada saints, an indication of the centrality of "othering" in Harihara's representation of the community.[2] Further, in several of the stories, the conflict between the Śaiva saint and the "other" functions as the main or defining episode in the saint's life, with the "showdown" serving as the plot's crisis. Furthermore, the term

1. A. K. Ramanujan points to the divide in Kannada Śivabhakti thought between "*bhakta* (devotee) and *bhavi* (worldling), men of faith and the infidels" (1973, 29n5).

2. The thirteen Ragaḷes are: *Ādayyana Ragaḷe*, *Ēkāntarāmitandeya Ragaḷe*, *Kēśirāja Daṇṇāyakara Ragaḷe*, *Kōvūra Bommatandeya Ragaḷe*, *Teluga Jommayyana Ragaḷe*, *Basavēśvaradēvara Ragaḷe*, *Bāhūra Bommatandeya Ragaḷe*, *Bhōgaṇṇana Ragaḷe*, *Mahādēviyakkana Ragaḷe*, *Śaṅkaradāsimayyana Ragaḷe*, *Rēvaṇasiddhēśvarana Ragaḷe*, *Vaijakavveya Ragaḷe*, *Hāvinahāḷa Kallayyana Ragaḷe*.

"religious other" is a fairly direct translation of the Kannada expressions *parasamayin* and *paradaivasantāna*, which Harihara frequently uses for referring to people of non-Śaiva religious traditions.[3]

Some Kannada Śivabhakti positions are directed against specific religious groups, which the tradition clearly identifies as separate and inimical, although no one has taken on the task of understanding the typology of this tradition's attitudes toward others. The religious other is figured in multiple ways in the *Ragaḷegaḷu*, not only in a structural sense (ranging from short incidents to major events in the storyline) but also literally, in the form of a variety of individuals presented in the text as outsiders to the tradition. Among the religious others found in Harihara's stories of the Kannada saints is the celebrated Tāntrika Gōrakṣa, or Gorak Nath (whose mention in the *Ragaḷegaḷu* is what appears to be the earliest textual reference to Gōrakṣa in South Asia), as the opponent of a Śivabhakta called Rēvaṇasiddha, to whom Gōrakṣa loses in a battle of magic.[4] Additional religious others mentioned in two verses of one Ragaḷe are atheists (Lōkāyatas), Buddhists (Bauddhas), and materialists (Cārvākas), all of whom are defeated by the Bhakta Kallayya in theological debates.[5]

But apart from these passing references, sectarian conflicts take center stage several times in the *Ragaḷegaḷu* stories with regard to two groups that are clearly marked by the text as religious others: Vaiṣṇava Brahmins and Jains. In this and the following chapter I approach Harihara's othering of Vaiṣṇava Brahmins and Jains using Jacqueline Hirst's twofold distinction between the "opponent other" and the "wholly other" (not to be confused with Rudolf Otto's "wholly other"). In her reading of Śaṅkarācārya's philosophical polemics, Hirst classifies as "opponent others" all those with whom the text argues. "Wholly others," in contrast, are those who

3. *Samaya* has a more specific sense in Kannada than it has in Sanskrit. Among the entries given by Kittel in his Kannada-English dictionary, the most relevant are "congregation" and "dogma"; each sheds light on a different aspect of what we term in contemporary discourse "religion," suspending for the moment the routinized critique of this term (Kittel 1982, 1508 s.v. *samaya* 2 and 10). For similar nomenclature in Tamil Śaiva literature, see Peterson (1998, 179–80).

4. See Ben-Herut (2015, 280); Mallinson (2011, 411).

5. *Hāvinahāḷa Kallayyana Ragaḷe* vv. 191–94 in Harihara and Suṅkāpura (1976a, 452): *vēdidiṃ śāstradiṃ gītamaṃ pāḍutaṃ / vādadiṃ vipraraṃ geldu nalidāḍutaṃ / lōkāyataranalli bauddharaṃ sōlisute / lōkadoḷ cārvākaraṃ geldu rañjisute.* There is a similar hagiographical account of a Bhakta winning philosophical debates in a story about Harirām Vyās (Pauwels 2002, 239–40).

are not explicitly mentioned in it and fall under the text's "silent foil."[6] In this framework the wholly other is mostly absent from the conversation, because it is situated in an area that is beyond the space where intellectual discourse could occur and that is separate from the power structures recognized by the text.[7] My application of Hirst's categories is nominal, in the sense that not only the opponent other but also the wholly other are present and explicitly mentioned in the Kannada context; but while relations with the opponent other lead to argument and negotiation, relations with the wholly other involve an intensified mode of utter rejection. Thus, the heated engagement with the wholly other in what follows is substantially different than its liminal sense in Hirst's work.

The two-tier othering implied by Hirst is nevertheless useful for distinguishing between a religious rival who shares some common ground and can be proven wrong, and a religious rival who is presented by the text as completely alien to the tradition's insiders, one with whom accommodation and/or reconciliation is impossible. In the imaginaire of the *Ragaḷegaḷu*, the opponent other shares with the Śaivas a religious ethos as well as a set of ubiquitous Purāṇic myths (although the sectarian supremacy argued for in Purāṇic stories is contested in some Ragaḷes). Furthermore, the opponent other survives when the stories conclude. Despite heated debates and conflicts, there is a general sense that the opponent other is tolerated in the narrative world of the *Ragaḷegaḷu*. The wholly other, in contrast, is presented by Harihara as completely foreign. Discourse with the wholly other, that is the Jains, is of a much more limited nature, partly in connection with the fact that the two religious parties do not share scriptures (for the Śaivas: Vedic, Śāstric, Purāṇic). The most significant characteristic of the wholly other in the *Ragaḷegaḷu* is that its mere presence is a huge menace. The stories that involve the wholly other have to culminate, it seems, with either its massive conversion into Śaivism or its complete annihilation.

In this part of the book, I deal with the literary figurations of these two groups of others by focusing on the narrative contexts in which a Śivabhakta meets a religious other in the text, how the interaction between the Śivabhakta and the religious other is played out, and the sort of criticism made against the Bhakta's religious other. My goal is to further our

6. Hirst (2008).

7. See Pauwels (2010).

understanding of what the other represented for the Kannada Śivabhakti tradition in its early phases and the ways in which the text's differentiation between two distinct forms of religious others can help shed light on the tradition's concerns and the social context in which these narratives were written.

However, it is important to acknowledge the limits of this inquiry, which are located outside the realm of verifiable history; we simply do not have sufficient historical knowledge or a sustained historical narrative regarding the nature of sectarian exchanges among different religious communities in the Kannada-speaking region of the twelfth and thirteenth centuries.[8] The plethora of unstudied epigraphy and architectural artifacts from this place and time on the one hand, and multiple uncritical and agenda-driven projections of the social, political, and religious past of this place and time on the other, only increase the historical conundrum.[9] A firmer historical contextualization for Harihara's othering is the literary genealogy of a rhetoric of religious othering that permeates south-Indian Śaivism and can also be located in some Jain materials, to which I refer to below. This literary world, of course, should not be read as straightforward history, in whatever way we might think of the term in the context of premodern South Asia.[10]

Another important caveat to Harihara's rhetoric of othering pertains to an added layer of complexity within this literary universe, one that actually might have historical bearing. Despite the neat delineations of Harihara's othering in the *Ragaḷegaḷu*, a close reading of the text's silences and oblique descriptions points to a more complicated literary configuration of the relationship between the Śaiva self and the religious other than that explicitly claimed by Harihara. A consideration of the locations in which Śaivas encounters Jains in the text and the nature of their interactions, for example, reveals that the wholly other in this literature is in many respects close to the Bhakta, perhaps dangerously close. In fact, the Jain wholly others in the stories are closer to the

8. Manu Devadevan, who questions the assumed historical cohesion embedded in the term "religious identity," locates a shift toward a communal sense of religious self among Śaivas in the Kannada-speaking region by the twelfth century (2016, 13–42).

9. See Ben-Herut (2012).

10. Two famous and distinct endeavors to conceptualize South Asian history that is relatively separated from Eurocentric notions of historiography are Narayana Rao, Shulman, and Subrahmanyam (2003) and Nandy (1995).

Śaiva protagonists than the Vaiṣṇava opponent others are. Even when we set aside the historical uncertainties regarding the social conditions in which Śaivas confronted Jains, a close reading of Harihara's stories conveys a sense of acute and even intimate competition between the rising Śivabhakti community and the dominant Jain communities. According to the stories, these competing communities meet each other everywhere: in the forest, in the city, in the markets, in the temple, and—perhaps surprisingly—in the home via intermarriages. The significance here lies in the fact that Harihara's investment in othering the Jains makes very little sense if we do not understand it as grounded in actual social contacts between the two communities, though it is very difficult to determine or essentialize the nature of these contacts, or even to support them with "hard" evidence.

Similarly, in the *Ragaḷegaḷu*, the setting in which the Śaiva meets his opponent other in the form of a Vaiṣṇava Brahmin is meaningful in terms of the nature of the conflict that arises between the two religious agents. Except for one case, all the conflicts between Śivabhaktas and Vaiṣṇava Brahmins unfold at the palace.[11] This location is significant not only because of the implied nearness of Vaiṣṇava Brahmins to the king but also because of the similarly implied nearness of the Śivabhakta to the king. Although the animus toward Brahmins is grounded in a religious and theological debate, it is difficult to overlook the political implications of the religious battle in terms of royal support of religious communities and the political ethic this text prescribes. Continuing the previous chapter's central argument regarding Harihara's effort to accommodate Brahmins inside the *bhakti* fold, this chapter looks at the Śaiva Brahmin-Bhakta who is confronted by antagonistic Vaiṣṇava Brahmins as a political figure and considers the difficulties and contradictions the political vocation entails for a life of a Bhakta.

In the most essential manner, the fact that the Śaiva's opponent other is met at the palace reframes the religious competition with Vaiṣṇava Brahmins as a political contest over the king's patronage and support. To shed light on this political milieu and its implications for a fervently devotional narrative universe, we begin by charting the complicated relationship between the Śivabhakta and the king before attending to the Śivabhakta's relationship with the Vaiṣṇava Brahmins who serve the king.

---

11. The exception is the last chapter of the *Hāvinahāḷa Kallayyana Ragaḷe*, in which the Śaiva protagonist wages a bet with Brahmins over whether his dog can recite the Vedas better than they.

Kings and Hagiography

Kings play an important role in the imaginaire of second-millennium religious literature in South Asia.[12] At the most general level, religious fascination with courtly life and the figure of the king can be explained by the wish to appropriate the power associated with royalty for the various ideological needs of religious traditions. Incorporations of king-related themes in devotional hagiographies are not always positive or straightforward, and they vary greatly between different regions, periods, and factions, ranging from a positive view of the king—and more broadly the institution of human kingship—as benevolent and helpful to the devotional community to the opposite view, one that is negative and evokes an attitude of resistance. But throughout the broad range of possibilities, the king is a central signifier in the sociopolitical field presented in the texts. In a more abstract sense, the king is a conduit of real power with which the specific devotional text wishes to connect in some way or another. The king's power is most concretely expressed in hagiographies in terms of his relationship with the saint-protagonist associated with a devotional tradition and, in connection to that, the king's actual patronage of the devotional community with which the saint-protagonist is associated. The *Ragaḷegaḷu* stories that involve interactions between kings and their courts on the one hand and the Kannada Śaiva saints on the other portray these interactions in a complex but consistent manner across the stories.

The depiction of the king and his court in the *Ragaḷegaḷu* fits into the broader context of south-Indian devotional literature. Starting with the earliest Tamil Bhakta-poets of the final centuries of the first millennium, a new pattern begins to emerge, with the "devotional" god being interjected into the traditional poet-king dyad.[13] This devotional reframing is described by David Shulman as complicating matters, since the king is now faced with a god who is competing with the king "with its own resources for patronage . . . and with a poetic ideology that is largely hostile

12. W. L. Smith comments that the meetings between sages and kings in South Asian hagiographies "seem obligatory" (2000, 159).

13. See discussions in Narayana Rao (1992); Peterson (1992); Shulman (1992). Later north-Indian devotional literature, embedded in different sociopolitical contexts, also presents complications between the royal institution and the authors' devotional worlds. See, for example, the mid sixteenth-century Bundelās from the Braj area (Pauwels 2009). See also Novetzke (2016; 2008, 182–91); Hawley (2005); Smith (2000, 165–71).

to the traditional heroic or courtly panegyric."[14] The resultant tension does not always imply a literary alienation of the king, and south-Indian religious literature uses different strategies for accommodating the king under the supreme sovereignty of the god, such as portraying the king himself as a model Bhakta or as a reliable collaborator and supporter of the devotional community. A different strategy for accommodating the religious and regal visions is the blurring of boundaries between the king and the god.[15]

As an introduction to Harihara's mode of imagining the king, I provide two examples of how other devotional works accommodate the human king. The first, like the *Ragaḷegaḷu*, was composed in Hampi, but more than two centuries later. Vyāsatīrtha, a *mādhva* Brahmin at King Kṛṣṇadēvarāya's Vijayanagara court, is remembered as a religious leader who was politically active in his public work.[16] As Valerie Stoker has pointed out, the narrative account about Vyāsatīrtha, the Sanskrit *Vyāsayōgi Carita*, acknowledges and even celebrates Vyāsatīrtha's political acumen while also carefully purging his political success of any sense of personal interest in worldly power.[17] As we shall see below, Harihara's stories use a similar strategy, but where the *Vyāsayōgi Carita* differs sharply from the *Ragaḷegaḷu* is in its integrative envisioning of the court. The former text celebrates the relationship between the Vijayanagara king and Vyāsatīrtha the saint as intimate, benevolent, and symmetrical: "The Lord of Yogīs [i.e., Vyāsatīrtha], victorious against philosophical opponents, and the Lord of Men, [i.e., the King], victorious against enemies, were each so munificent that they could have changed places, being mutually endowed with increasing compassion, taste, and devotion."[18] We find no reciprocal assessment as sweeping as this one in the *Ragaḷegaḷu*. While there are moments of fruitful cooperation between the king and the saint in the Kannada stories, they are always temporary and sporadic.

The second example belongs to early Tamil Śaivism. In terms of theistic affiliation and theological attitudes, Tamil Śaiva devotionalism is closer to

14. Shulman (1992, 99).

15. Narayana Rao (1992, 150–53); Shulman (1992, 102–5). Few Telugu poets, such as Pālkuriki Sōmanātha and Pōtana, composed devotional literature that is starkly antagonistic toward the king (Narayana Rao and Shulman 2002, 200).

16. Stoker (2016, 2015). On the dating of the *Vyāsayōgi Carita*, see Stoker (2016, 20).

17. Stoker (2015, 138).

18. Translated by Valerie Stoker (ibid.).

the *Ragaḷegaḷu* than are the Vaiṣṇavas of the Vijayanagara court, sharing a theistic affiliation but also a broad set of practices, attitudes, religious texts, and saints. Although a few of the early Tamil poets convey direct hostility toward the human king in their poems,[19] the later hagiographic literature projects a sense of political hegemony grounded in a Śaiva theology.[20] This can be observed, for example, in the first two verses of the fourteenth-century *Tirumuṟaikaṇṭa Purāṇam*:

> [1] In Cōḷanāṭu [the heartland of Tamil south India], where the golden river [Kāvēri] flows from its origin in the mountains that bring joy to the world, a famous king named Rājarāja Apayakulacekaraṉ ruled righteously. The king worshipped the feet of Tiyākēcar, the form of Śiva at Ārūr, a town that is like the crown of the region with its tall and ornate temples. There, servants of the Lord once approached the king, who was delighted to hear them rapturously sing various hymns of the famous three composers. [2] Upon hearing the hymns, the king raised his hands above his head in homage and dissolved into tears of total joy. He meditated upon the Lord's lotus feet, appealing to him to provide guidance so that the hymns might be sung in an organized, rather than an eclectic, manner. Just at that moment, a child as precious as a gem was born to an Ādiśaiva family in Nāraiyūr, a child who would promote the Śaiva path in order to save the entire world.[21]

Regardless of historicity in this idyllic account, it is clear from the passage that the author is invested in figuring the human king as a close and reliable partner of Tamil Śaiva devotionalism. This view of the political system as strongly supportive of Śaivism undergirds the Tamil Śaiva imaginaire as a whole. Although the Tamil kings are not always automatically assumed by the texts to be members of the Śaiva community and at times assume a tangential role in the stories, the Tamil hagiographical texts do not imply any sense of seeking to

19. Shulman (1992, 94–96); Peterson (1992, 123–29). Also, traditional accounts about Māṇikkavācakar portray his relation with a Pāṇṭiya king as fraught with contradiction and tension (Cutler 1987, 148–49).

20. Champakalakshmi (2011a, 108); Peterson (1994, 191–94).

21. Translated by Karen Pechilis Prentiss (2001, 1).

undermine of the kings' status but instead endorse their political hegemony.[22]

Harihara's Kannada hagiographies present a view that is totally different from the warm embrace of royalty portrayed in the above two examples. In all the stories that involve a human king, Harihara depicts him as an unreliable character who lacks genuine loyalty to the Śaiva endeavor. His cooperation with the Śaiva saint in his court rests on dubious, ad hoc, and narrow interests. His political and financial patronage of the Śaraṇa and the community of Śivabhaktas is categorically short-lived, and his support for them is inconsistent. He is usually portrayed by Harihara as personally favoring Vaiṣṇava rather than Śaiva worship, but perhaps his greatest flaw from the perspective of the author is his reliance on Vaiṣṇava advisors, a reliance that always results in his turning against the Śaiva community. It is obvious in these stories that the multi-religious landscape in which courtly politics unfold forces the king to navigate within a complex nexus of at times conflicting loyalties. While this premise could perhaps have served to mitigate the text's critique of the king, such a consideration would be antithetical to the uncompromising fervor that governs Harihara's narratives and that places the king, from Harihara's point of view, on the wrong side of the theological divide, as epitomized by his frequent labeling of the king in the text as a "worldling" (*bhavi*), that is, outside the Śaiva fold. And moreover, according to the Ragaḷes about the Kannada Śaraṇas, courts—like kings—are, thematically speaking, also argued against.

At the same time, despite the courts being antithetical to the idyllic society of Bhaktas, a few stories are clearly invested in placing the Śaraṇa at the center of courtly political action. At times the complex, unholy matrimony between devotional piety and shrewd statecraft is an important theme in the saints' stories. The external tension imposed on the courtly Śaraṇa in the stories discussed below always follows this pattern: on the one hand, the court provides the Śaraṇa with access to the wealth and political support needed to sustain the community of Śivabhaktas, and therefore the Śaraṇa is drawn to spend time at the court and near the king; on the other hand, because of this powerful worldly environment, the Śaraṇa at the court is compelled—in sharp contrast to his piety and devotional ideals—to maintain interpersonal relationships in an atmosphere

22. I thank Anne Monius for this characterization (personal communication, October 2012). See Champakalakshmi (2011b, 70–72); Pechilis (1999, 96–113).

of manipulative dynamics, deceit, and treachery. Though often frustrated by such irreligious obstacles, the Śaraṇa at the court never gives in to them and refuses to compromise his devotional ideals. Again and again, Vaiṣṇava Brahmin antagonists try to implicate him in worldly intrigues, but the Śaraṇa, in response, refuses to employ political connivances and maneuverings and refrains from participating in squalid displays of scheming and worldliness. He will not stray from the devotional path, regardless of the political price it sometimes entails. Instead, the Śaraṇa opts to display his uncompromising religious devotion by means of a public miracle. In this way, not only does the courtly saint overcome malevolent and wily couriers, but he achieves this without having compromised his devotional integrity. The miraculous act, though successfully exonerating the Śaraṇa from courtly and political entanglements, also precipitates the consequential ruin of his intimate relationship with the king. It eventually leads to the Śaraṇa's renunciation of court life in order to dedicate himself completely to Śiva and his Bhaktas.

Harihara's descriptions of Śiva and his saints use royal attributions and insignia. Such descriptions, when coupled with Harihara's negative rendering of the human king and the court, reveal a defiant literary voice that forces us to assume at least some level of sociopolitical autonomy in the cultural context in which this text emerged. Therefore, as a final point for consideration in this chapter dealing with the negative rendering of the king and court in the Ragaḷes about the Kannada saints, I discuss the *Ragaḷegaḷu* using the discourse of the "politics of literature" in order to hypothesize about the sociopolitical conditions that enabled the creation as well as the consumption of such a text and the possible significance it may have had at the time and in the place of its composition.

A key issue in this regard is that of the text's patron: Harihara's undermining of the human king and his formulaic attributions to Śiva as the text's patron are so ubiquitous in the *Ragaḷegaḷu* that we are forced to consider the external conditions that facilitated the composition of this work. In the words of Barbara Stoler Miller and Richard Eaton: "How does a 'style' of patronage define the moral universe of a dynasty or institution and what fact does patronage play in what we term the 'style' of a period or place?"[23] I apply this question to the historical event of producing the

23. Miller and Eaton (1992, 2).

Ragaḷegaḷu in order to think about how the social context of this text and its figuration of the human king in relation to the devotional community reflect the social conditions and cultural premises of the context in which this text was produced.

The Devotee as the King's Administrator

Historically, from the time of the thirteenth-century *Ragaḷegaḷu* onward, Śaiva remembered history of the Kannada-speaking region has shown a particular interest in the city of Kalyāṇa and the two dynasties that ruled it during the twelfth and thirteenth centuries, the Cālukyas and the Kalacūris. Most of the Ragaḷes I will be discussing share this locale and are temporally set in the early and middle parts of the twelfth century. Among the saints associated in the *Ragaḷegaḷu* with the Kalyāṇa courts is Basavaṇṇa, the most important Śaiva leader of the twelfth-century Kannada-speaking region. A gifted poet as well as a political and social figure, Basavaṇṇa is remembered as the person who established a devotional community in Maṅgaḷavāḍa and later in Kalyāṇa that is considered to be the bedrock of all forms of Kannada Śivabhakti.[24]

Basavaṇṇa's political career resonates with that of another saint in the *Ragaḷegaḷu*, Koṇḍaguḷi Kēśirāja, who according to the text served as administrator to the Kalyāṇa king few decades before Basavaṇṇa. The similarity between the lives of two central Śaraṇas in the *Ragaḷegaḷu* indicates that the fascination of the Śaiva literary tradition of the Kannada-speaking region with royalty, financial resources, community formation, and political competition in the thriving city of Kalyāṇa was persistent and deep-rooted. As I discussed in Chapters 1 and 4, the traits shared by Kēśirāja's and Basavaṇṇa's stories reflect a larger narrative paradigm shared across other stories as well, all imagined to have occurred in the courts of Cālukyas and their Kalacūris successors. This paradigm is built upon a set of disharmonic relationships between the Śaraṇa, the king, and representatives of a competing sect, the Vaiṣṇava Brahmins.

The first two chapters of the Ragaḷe about Kēśirāja are especially instructive with regard to Harihara's attitudes toward the institution of

24. Basavaṇṇa's primacy in shaping the Kannada religious and social landscape is incontrovertible, despite the tendency of the *pañcācārya* denomination to harken back to an earlier pan-Indian prehistory (Michael 1983).

the human king, since they focus on Kēśirāja's courtly career.[25] In these chapters, Harihara describes Koṇḍaguḷi Kēśirāja as the chief minister for King Permāḍirāya, likely identified by Harihara with the famous Cālukya king Vikramāditya VI (1076–1127 CE).[26] The story of the saint's brilliant political career commences in Koṇḍaguḷi, the Brahmin quarter of Kalyāṇa, where the faithful Śivabhakta Kēśirāja lives.[27] Śiva Sōmanātha is his lord. Kēśirāja is a capable man who helps everyone around him. Harihara also mentions that he is the composer of eight poems to Sōmanātha, (five of which are extant today).[28] One day, Kalyāṇa's king Permāḍirāya, searching for a qualified man to run his administration, decides on the advice of his courtly Brahmins to appoint Kēśirāja as chief minister (*daṇṇāyaka*) of Kalyāṇa.[29] He summons Kēśirāja, seats him upon a gem-studded chair,

25. The third and last chapter of the *Kēśirāja Daṇṇāyakara Ragaḷe* is dedicated to Kēśirāja's life as a wandering ascetic.

26. There is an elaborate discussion in Kannada scholarship regarding the historical identity of Koṇḍaguḷi Kēśirāja. The most significant inscription about Kēśirāja was found in Koṇḍaguḷi and dated 1107 CE (Archaeological Survey of India 1890). See also verses 9, 11, 12 in Lakshmeshwar inscription C in Barnett (1921–22, 49–50). In 1942, S. C. Nandimath doubted that Koṇḍaguḷi Kēśirāja is the same as Kēśirāja Daṇṇāyaka (the chief minister) (1979 [1942], 110–11). However, according to more recent scholarship, the protagonist of the *Kēśirāja Ragaḷe* was indeed the chief minister of King Vikramāditya VI (Śivānanda 1966–67; Chidananda Murthy 1983, 203; Kalaburgi 2010 [1998]-b, 67–78; Kēśirāja 1978, vi, viii-xvi; Kalaburgi 1970, 40–43). Although Harihara does not explicitly refer by name to King Vikramāditya, there are references to this king as Permāḍirāya in other texts, such as Bilhaṇa's poetic biography of King Vikramāditya (called the *Vikramāṅkadēva Carita*, in Sanskrit) and several inscriptions (Fleet 1988 [1882], 445–46). For a political history of Vikramāditya, see Nilakanta Sastri (1976, 169ff; 1960, 355–70). There is also a less likely possibility that Harihara's Permāḍirāya is the Kalacūri governor Permāḍi, the brother-in-law and son-in-law of Vikramāditya, and the father of King Bijjaḷa (Desai 1968, 13–21). This possibility is less likely, since Permāḍi the Kalacūri was not a king but a provincial governor (Mahāmaṇḍalēśvara) and was residing in the Bijapur area and not in Kalyāṇa.

27. The following is a summary of chapters 1 and 2 of the *Kēśirāja Daṇṇāyakara Ragaḷe* in Harihara and Suṅkāpura (1976a, 183–93).

28. Kēśirāja (1978). The most famous of Kēśirāja's works is the *Ṣaḍakṣara Kanda* (aka *Mantramahatvada Kanda* and *Ṣaḍakṣaramantramahime*). Eṃ. Eṃ. Kalaburgi claims that Kēśirāja is the first to compose Śaiva religious poetry in Kannada (2010 [1998]-a, 144). Kalaburgi also refers to Kēśirāja as one of the Ādyas (literally "the first ones"), a term usually reserved for the Tamil Śaiva Bhaktas that generally signifies precedence (Ben-Herut 2015; Kēśirāja 1978, v; Desai 1968, 329). Both Ḍi. El. Narasiṃhācārya and El. Basavarāju state that Kēśirāja composed *vacanas*, though none are extant today (Basavarāju 2001 [1960], 16).

29. *Daṇṇāyaka* is a Kannada derivative of the Sanskrit *daṇḍanāyaka*. The Kannada term has a wide semantic field and several conventional usages that include army general and chief minister (Desai 1968, 53, 268).

provides him with money and expensive clothes, and orders that a palace be built for him. Kēśirāja assumes all the administrative responsibilities, and the king is greatly pleased with him. In his new position, Kēśirāja also starts caring for the city's Śaraṇas: he builds temples for them, feeds them, and spends time in their company. As mentioned in the introduction to this book, Kēśirāja's administrative commitments soon clash with his predilection for spending time with fellow Śaiva devotees. Kēśirāja is forced to interrupt a Śiva assembly (*śivagōṣṭhi*) in response to the king's summons, although he is uninhibited about his frustration with worldly life. Meanwhile the king, after having been informed of what Kēśirāja has said, becomes angry. The Vaiṣṇava Brahmins who serve as attendants to the king take advantage of the situation and further inflame the king's anger, saying: "That Kēśirāja tells the story of how Śiva, in the form of Śarabha, killed Viṣṇu as Narasiṃha.[30] When he bows down to you and folds his hands, he is actually bowing to the signet ring in his hand, which carries the seal of his guru's foot. He is not bowing down to you at all!"[31] When Kēśirāja finally arrives at the hall, the fuming king, concealing his anger, offers Kēśirāja a seat and starts conversing with him. The king notices that Kēśirāja is not wearing the signet ring on his finger and, when their conversation ends, he also notices that Kēśirāja leaves without prostrating himself. Now the king is really furious, and he orders Kēśirāja to return immediately to the hall. Scowling, with eyes reddened and mustache bristling, the king shouts: "You are disgraceful to me! You were a poor man before you met me, and now you are rich because of me alone! If you cannot appreciate all this wealth, then return it to me at once!" Kēśirāja listens patiently and then responds: "Hear this, Sovereign! I will give you back all your wealth, for no wealth is equal to devotion."[32] Kēśirāja immediately removes all his ornaments, rings, bracelets, and other jewelry. He even gives away the golden box that holds his personal *liṅga* and he strips off all his clothes. Kēśirāja walks away from the king's palace completely

---

30. This is a reference to a story about Śarabha, a magical deer identified with Śiva, who killed Viṣṇu in his form of Narasiṃha, half lion–half man. This story is very popular in south-Indian Śaivism (Geer, Dermitzakis, and Vos 2008, 77–78).

31. Summary of *Kēśirāja Daṇṇāyakara Ragaḷe* 1.129–44 in Harihara and Suṅkāpura (1976a, 187–88).

32. *Kēśirāja Daṇṇāyakara Ragaḷe* 1.173–76 in Harihara and Suṅkāpura (1976a, 189): *kēḷarasa ninna siri ninagikke ninagikke . . . bhakuti sirige sariyillenute.*

naked, having decided to become a renouncer (*virakta*) and never again to serve a human being.[33]

Kēśirāja walks toward his home, holding his personal *liṅga* in his hand and wearing just the locks of his hair as clothes. When his wife sees him in this state, she gives away all her jewelry, dons simple clothes, and joins her husband on the path of renunciation. They leave their house and, after walking a few miles, they reach a hut of a Śivabhakta. The Bhakta seats Kēśirāja under a mango tree, washes him, and hands him white clothes. The host Bhakta praises Kēśirāja for having turned his back on the worldlings (*bhavis*) to become a renouncer. As more Bhaktas arrive, a Śiva assembly commences and continues for seven days. So caught up in devotion are they that no one stops for sleep or food. Many more people flock to the assembly outside the Bhakta's hut, including King Permāḍirāya, who arrives barefoot and dressed in simple clothes. When the king sees Kēśirāja, he prostrates himself before him. Kēśirāja does not recognize him at first, but people tell him: "This is King Permāḍirāya!" Kēśirāja asks the king to stand up, and the king says: "I did such wrong to you! I was full of greed, hatred, and delusion. Return to my palace and I will make it a mansion (*mahāmane*) for Śaraṇas. I shall give my treasure to the Śivabhaktas."[34] The Bhaktas encourage Kēśirāja to accept King Permāḍirāya's offer, and they all return to Kalyāṇa, where Kēśirāja's position as chief administrator is restored. Once again he devotes himself to supporting the city's Bhaktas and helping King Permāḍirāya govern the city. With time, however, Kēśirāja grows weary of serving as chief minister. Once again he decides to leave the palace, this time so that he can visit his fellow Śaraṇas around the country. Finally, he unites with Śiva near the bank of a river.[35]

Kēśirāja's professional career takes up a considerable part of his life story. This career is both impressive and fraught with difficulties, filled with successes and sudden twists. Kēśirāja's refusal to bow down to the king demonstrates this Śaiva literary tradition's commitment to unyielding

33. In fifteenth-century Vijayanagara, "*virakta*" becomes a specific designation for Vīraśaiva reformists (Chandra Shobhi 2005; Desai 1968, 152–54). In the *Ragaḷegaḷu* the term carries a more literal sense for someone who is devoid of attachment to worldly objects and passions.

34. Summary of *Kēśirāja Daṇṇāyakara Ragaḷe* 2.prose in Harihara and Suṅkāpura (1976a, 192–93).

35. Kēśirāja's second iteration as administer and consequent renunciation are told in the third chapter of the *Kēśirāja Daṇṇāyakara Ragaḷe* in Harihara and Suṅkāpura (1976a, 194–201).

devotion and its resistance to honoring the human king. Neither Kēśirāja nor the narrator makes the least attempt to explain or defend Kēśirāja's disrespectful behavior toward the king; it is considered self-evident that a true Śivabhakta does not bow to any worldly being, not even a king. Kēśirāja does not bother to respond to the allegations raised by the Vaiṣṇava Brahmin antagonists, nor to those raised by the king himself, about his anti-Vaiṣṇava propaganda and display of defiance toward the king. Refusing to participate in a petty court exchange, Kēśirāja resigns from his administrative position. The resignation marks a moment of intense inner realization, for this is the point at which Kēśirāja takes on the vocation of a renouncer by casting off his insignia and walking away from the palace, having literally stripped himself of everything and holding his head high.

Kēśirāja's defiant refusal to acknowledge the sovereignty of the human king is axiomatic in the *Ragaḷegaḷu*, and it is also central in Harihara's own life story, as discussed in Chapter 1. When court Brahmins denounce Harihara as insane, Harihara replies to them and to the king: "Crazy is the worldling who wallows in the sickness of worldly existence (*bhava*), forgetting contemplation (*dhyāna*) on Śiva."[36] This statement articulates a foundational disposition that colors all of Harihara's Ragaḷes about the court, a disposition that drives an impatient and uncompromising revulsion to all that is worldly and that sees the court as the epitome of abhorrent worldliness. In the *Ragaḷegaḷu*, the Śaraṇa's rejection of worldliness is portrayed as a reflex. There is no room in the Śivabhakta's subjectivity for reflection, indecision, or doubt regarding the hierarchy of ethics and etiquettes, since the superiority of devotion over mundane, worldly considerations is always a given.

At the same time, Kēśirāja's Ragaḷe conveys a sharp sense of contradiction between Kēśirāja's guileless nature and the connivance required by court life. The narrative portrays King Permāḍirāya's court as fraught with conflicting interests, pressure groups, and ad hoc alliances. The sectarian nature of the accusations made by the king's ministers against Kēśirāja can be read as typical of the usual and brittle workings of a king's court. A trifling bit of gossip or a comment that carries sectarian undertones—such as the allegation that Kēśirāja has told a crowd of faithful the Śarabha

36. *sivadhyānavannu maretu bhavarōgadinda baḷaluva bhaviyu huccu.* This quote is taken from a summary of the *Rāghavāṅka Carite* in Nāyaka, Veṅkaṭācala Śāstrī, and Sundaram (1977, 1266).

story about Viṣṇu's defeat by Śiva—can be used as a sign of political perfidiousness. In perfect opposition to the petty and conniving Vaiṣṇava Brahmin courtiers, Kēśirāja himself is anything but politically savvy, and the political *savoir faire* that is demanded for functioning in such a charged political environment is clearly outside his temperament and sentiment. But what is striking—perhaps even nonsensical—in this binary ethical structure is the narrative claim repeated at central moments in the story that the king desperately needs Kēśirāja for his administrative talent. (Apparently, Kēśirāja's administrative abilities are so rare that the king even comes, barefoot, to beg for Kēśirāja's return to the court). Therefore, there is an irreconcilable tension at the narrative level between Kēśirāja's artless candor and the administrative superiority attributed to him.[37]

Harihara does not make this inherent narrative tension explicit, but it is instructive to dwell on its significance. In light of Kēśirāja's instinctive adherence to a life of devotion, one might ask: Why does he, like other Śaraṇas I will discuss below, agree to take on the demanding public role of serving the king in the first place? And why does he agree to reoccupy his public position against his earlier resolve and despite the worldly engagements and compromises it inevitably entails? This swerving can be explained by the Śaraṇa's commitment to assist the devotional community by supplying them with material resources channeled from his courtly position while sustaining his own spiritual aspirations. In broader terms that also fit the life of Basavaṇṇa, Harihara, and other Śaiva devotees from the Kannada region, the devotee, while demonstrating a mastery of administration and superb management skills, is simultaneously drawn into an absolute subjectivity characterized by an inner experience of intense ecstasy imbued with utopian overtones. In the case of Kēśirāja, this subjectivity is externalized in the ongoing and consuming experience of participation in Śiva assemblies and delighting in the company of Śaiva devotees. At the same time, the Śaraṇa is invested in and drawn by powerful external and worldly forces required for the betterment of the Śaiva community and the world at large. The Śaraṇa's presence at the court and his active involvement in the local ruler's political sphere reflect a frustrating compromise, but this experience—painful as it is for the Śaraṇa—is never peripheral to the saint's life. Not only is the Śaraṇa highly capable in his

---

37. A similar tension is evinced in some hagiographies of Harirām Vyās, as discussed by Heidi Pauwels (2002, 236–37) and with regard to some of the Tamil Śaiva saints (Peterson 1994, 200).

worldly role as an administrator, this role is key for the development of the Bhaktas' community.

But the push-and-pull between worldly commitments and devotional life never reaches a point of equilibrium. It is inherently volatile. In the case of Kēśirāja, although the king's complete surrender and vow to support the Śaiva devotional community does return Kēśirāja to his worldly position as chief minister, this professional comeback is short-lived. Missing a life wholly devoted to Śiva, Kēśirāja again retires from the court and adopts the life of wandering with fellow Śaraṇas, this time for good. This denouement agrees with the patterned telos that also governs other stories in this Śaiva imaginaire, according to which courtly ties are, in the final account, unbearable for the model devotee. For example, in a story by Harihara's nephew Rāghavāṅka about a Śaraṇa called Siddharāma, the Śaraṇa is asked by King Karṇadēva to consecrate him on his throne. When Siddharāma tries to diplomatically refuse, Karṇadēva insists and has Siddharāma brought to him confined inside a sealed chest. But to the king's surprise, when the chest is put before him and opened, he finds that Siddharāma has vanished.[38] A similar rejection of kingly ties can be observed in Harihara's own life story, as he is said to have refused a Hoysaḷa king's generous offer for patronage before quitting his job as a courtly accountant and moving to Hampi to dedicate his life to composing devotional literature.

In conclusion, the ruler's slippery promise to always financially support the Śivabhaktas, which is part and parcel of the narrative tension between unyielding, uninhibited devotion on the one hand and royal patronage and realpolitik on the other, spawns an ill-contrived political utopia in which the Śaraṇa never compromises his devotional etiquette but still wins the king's political and financial support for himself and for his Śivabhakti community. Even as an imagined idea, this state of affairs is brittle and short-lived. In the *Ragaḷegaḷu* and in the Kannada Śivabhakti narrative tradition more broadly, the intimate collaboration between Śaraṇas and the king and his court tends to collapse, together with the Śaraṇa's political career, as a result of an inevitable and terminal embroilment between the two figures. The most extreme case for the paradigmatic termination of the political/financial utopia in the narratives of the *Ragaḷegaḷu* is, as we shall see, the traumatic demise of the Kalyāṇa Bhaktas led by Basavaṇṇa,

---

38. This incident appears in the *Siddharāma Carite* 9.1–20.

which I discuss later in this chapter. But before attending Basavaṇṇa's political biography, I consider the failed courtly career of another Śivabhakta, a career that ends with murder.

Sectarian Violence at the Court

The religious competition that accompanies the Śaraṇa's problematic presence at the king's court can be harsh, and its effects can extend beyond the court to threaten the fate of the whole community of Śivabhaktas that the Śaraṇa nurtures. The following story dramatizes the sectarian tension at the court more strongly than does Kēśirāja's story. In both cases, storytelling plays a role. In the case of Kēśirāja, the story—recounted by Kēśirāja to his congregation, which leads to the Brahmins' complaint to the king about him—has to do with Śiva winning over Viṣṇu. For Teluga Jommayya, who is depicted in the *Ragaḷegaḷu* as an associate of Kēśirāja, it is a Purāṇic Vaiṣṇava story against Śiva that initiates the dramatic action. In Jommayya's case, sectarian storytelling at the king's palace leads to murder.

As with Kēśirāja, Jommayya's story also begins in Kalyāṇa under the reign of King Permāḍirāya.[39] Jommayya is described as an ardent Bhakta of Śiva Bhīmanātha, literally "Lord of Fear." Although Jommayya is said to intensely dislike non-Śaivas, he regularly visits King Permāḍirāya in order to obtain from him gold coins that he later distributes to the Śivabhaktas. The king complies since, according to the text, he is intimidated by Jommayya's fervent temperament and, in addition, wants to please his queen Lakumādēvi, who is a devotee of Śiva and sees Jommayya as her guru.

One day, as Jommayya is waiting for the king to finish his daily worship, he overhears a *purāṇika* (a storyteller of Purāṇic or mythical literature). This *purāṇika* is narrating stories from Vaiṣṇava Purāṇas, lying (*vañcisi*) and denigrating Śiva.[40] Hearing this, Jommayya grows furious. He shouts at the storyteller, saying: "Why are you telling these lies?" Jommayya then draws his dagger and inflicts a mortal wound on the man. Panicked by what he has just done, Jommayya leaves the palace and seeks shelter at a

---

39. The following is a summary of the first two chapters of the *Teluga Jommayyana Ragaḷe* in Harihara and Suṅkāpura (1976a, 381–90).

40. Summary of *Teluga Jommayyana Ragaḷe* 1.107–16 in Harihara and Suṅkāpura (1976a, 384–85).

house of Śivabhaktas. There, crying bitterly, Jommayya confesses to the murder, regretting having ever associated with worldlings. The Bhaktas calm him, assuring him that he has done nothing wrong, since the person he killed was a sinner, a Śiva offender. Consoled by their words, Jommayya collects himself and proceeds with his daily Śaiva rituals.

Meanwhile, at the palace, King Permāḍirāya—whom Harihara calls "the Rāvaṇa of the Kali age" (*kaliyugarāvaṇa*)—finishes his worship and is troubled when he does not hear the storyteller's voice. He also notices that the Viṣṇu statue in the worship room has started to shed tears. On coming out of the worship room, the king discovers the dead body of the storyteller and is both confused and angry. He summons Jommayya to confront him. When Queen Lakumādēvi hears of what is happening, she thinks: "Jommayya never bows to the king because he is a worldling. If I can make Jommayya bow just this one time, it might save his life." And so the queen plans to hold a Siva *liṅga* in her hand when Jommayya appears in front of the king, so that Jommayya will bow down. But when Jommayya spots the *liṅga* in the queen's hand, instead of bowing down, he calls out to it: "Why are you positioned next to a worldling?" As Jommayya stretches out his hand toward the *liṅga*, it leaps out of the queen's hands and into the air. Only then does Jommayya bow down to it. The king, on seeing this miracle, is confounded. A new belief in Śiva is born in him. Without anger, he asks Jommayya why he killed the storyteller. Jommayya answers: "I did not kill the fellow for telling the Purāṇas; I killed him for telling lies about Śiva." The king replies: "Then you must prove to me that the storyteller told lies!" To this challenge Jommayya responds: "How can you imply that a Śivabhakta is wrong? We shall go right now to the dead body, and I will uncover the corpse's shroud. You will find nothing but maggots underneath it!" They go to the place where the dead body has been placed. Jommayya prays to Śiva and declares that he had no hate for the storyteller but only killed a worldling for having told lies. He draws back the shroud and reveals a pile of maggots. Nauseated by the disgusting sight, the king orders that the shroud and the maggots be disposed of and apologizes to Jommayya for having doubted him. Later, the king and his wife shower gold on Jommayya and also grant him a piece of land situated a few miles outside of Kalyāṇa, where Jommayya builds a congregation hall for the Śaraṇas.

Jommayya's story repeats several themes that are found in Kēśirāja's story: a rather loose system for transferring royal money to the Bhaktas' community, facilitated by the charisma of a single Śaraṇa who has exclusive access to political resources; a confrontation between Śaivas and Vaiṣṇavas resulting from public storytelling with specific sectarian claims (Śiva kills Viṣṇu and vice versa); public denial of the king's sovereignty by a refusal to bow down, a denial that is pivotal in both stories as an expression of the Śaraṇa's uncompromising devotion to Śiva; and, finally, a denouement that leads to the Śaraṇa's retirement from court life in favor of Śaiva fellowship away from the city. The parallels between the two stories extend even to their structural framework: both Ragaḷes contain three chapters, of which the first two are dedicated to action at the court and the third to the Śaraṇa's devotional life as a retired devotee. This parallelism culminates with the two devotees actually meeting each other, as discussed in the previous chapter, in the only episode in the *Ragaḷegaḷu* that is narrated twice. All this suggests that Harihara was invested in carving through these stories a specific ethical trajectory for the Śaraṇa's career at the king's court—a trajectory that would bear the Śaraṇa inexorably away from the court.

But what separates Jommayya's story from Kēśirāja's is the extreme level of devotional-based resistance to non-Śaivas in the former. This is demonstrated early on in terms of the sectarian lines drawn in the story. First, there is a clear dividing line between the king's Vaiṣṇava bent (the text describes the king praying to an image of Viṣṇu) and the queen's Śaiva tendencies (her support of and concern for Jommayya). The divergent religious affiliations of the royal couple are depicted in the story as having broad, communal implications. The queen's personal inclination to Śaivism facilitates the king's patronage of the Śaivas, the king's Vaiṣṇava taste allows for public sectarian storytelling at the palace, and the Śaiva faith kindled in the king's heart toward the end of the episode plays an essential role in Jommayya's exoneration at the end. We can see in the queen's resourceful attempt to rescue Jommayya from his own religious stubbornness an indication of the volatile tension at the court between kingly attributions and unyielding devotional commitment.

The atmosphere in which the devotee operates is so weighted that even the act of storytelling can become a cause for sectarian bloodshed. But the volatile connection between religious storytelling and sectarian conflict is not rare, either in the political and social milieus of medieval south India or in modern times.[41] Phyllis Granoff highlights the importance of

41. See, for example, Hawley (2015, 221–23); Bronner (2011); Rao (2011). Even in modern times there is tension between Vīraśaivas and Vaiṣṇava Brahmins around public performances of

storytelling in the contest between Jains and Śaivas in medieval times and writes: "The stories provided the weapons that they [i.e., Jains and Śaivas] wielded; they also became another battleground, each group composing stories to outdo the stories of their rivals."[42] Putting aside for the moment the particular cultural resonances between the Jains and Śaivas in the medieval period, it is evident that this narrative "battleground" was shared by various sects, including the Vaiṣṇava sects. Narration of sectarian stories is understood in this milieu as a public assertion—a sort of a collective speech-act—aimed at strengthening or repositioning one's tradition over the traditions of others. An important ingredient in the flammable potential of storytelling is the flexibility of the oral text.[43] The performative culture of the Purāṇas provides the storyteller ample space to orally recontextualize the Purāṇic text, and this interpretive freedom allows, as is the case of this story, for the inflection and enhancement of sectarian claims. Returning to the *Ragaḷegaḷu* stories, it is evident that in this text the consequences of sectarian storytelling at the court are costly: careers are ruined, communities clash, and people die.

Jommayya's intensity extends beyond sectarianism. While Kēśirāja struggles, at least at the beginning of his political career as the king's minister, to maintain both his devotional commitments and political vocation, Jommayya does not even try to conceal his religious fervor. Stark zeal informs the act of murder at the palace in broad daylight. But can a verbal attack on Śaivism in the form of anti-Śaiva storytelling morally justify killing? The moral stance toward Jommayya's act of killing is developed as the story progresses. Jommayya's immediate response to the killing is fear and regret. Is Jommayya afraid of the political consequences of the act? Or of the personal price he might be required to pay once the king discovers the dead Brahmin? Or is it perhaps that Jommayya's fear is based on an internal moral sense that he has committed the sin of murder? The text gives no clear answer, though it relates Jommayya's general regret when telling his fellow Bhaktas what happened. They, however, are quick to set the moral record straight: Yes, they tell him, the killing of a Vaiṣṇava telling

---

sectarian Purāṇic stories in political settings. See the story about a Vīraśaiva procession at Kolhapur in 1911 (Ripepi 2007, 81–82).

42. Granoff (2009, 14).

43. For discussion about the Purāṇas' oral performative culture, see Prasad (2007); Narayana Rao (2004, 114–15). For the relation of Purāṇic culture and *bhakti* in the Tamil context, see Champakalakshmi (2011b, 71); Shulman (1980).

such a story was justified, and you did the right thing in killing him, since the hellish person offended Śiva.[44] This endorsement calms Jommayya down and completely eases his conscience. When he is later interrogated by the king about the murder, he appears composed and his replies convey nothing of his earlier panic. Harihara's ethical verdict on the killing is thus unequivocal. Self-reflection and ethical doubts do receive brief mention right after the murder, but they are quickly rejected, yet another instance of demonstrating the type of devotional intensity prescribed by Harihara in these stories.

The scene in which the king summons Jommayya to account for the murder starts out as a public trial of Jommayya's act. However, as the scene unfolds, it is radically deflected: from a trial pertaining to a killing at the court, the event as a whole turns into a religious discourse with epiphanic qualities and with Jommayya's miracle-working dictating the plot's progression. First, the *liṅga* held by the queen leaps into the air in response to Jommayya's words and gesture. This miraculous event effectively dissolves the king's hostility toward Jommayya's violent act and induces a change in the Vaiṣṇava king toward an attitude favoring Śiva. At this point, the legal issue of killing a Brahmin at the court is replaced by a sectarian question: How is it possible to claim that Śiva is inferior to Viṣṇu? This question marks the shift in the court proceedings from the ethical to the sectarian, and Jommayya, beckoning the flying *liṅga* with his raised hand, literally has the upper hand. By the time of Jommayya's second miracle, revealing maggots instead of the body of the dead Brahmin, the charge regarding the murder of the Brahmin has completely disappeared.[45]

Richard Davis, discussing miracles in different religious narratives, observes: "Miracles often occur in situations of conflict, where differing systems of belief compete and questions of faith and power are directly at issue. This is when supernatural communications are most needed."[46] Indeed, in Jommayya's case, the miracles he performs before the king not only serve as a display of devotional power but also nullify the sectarian opponent's charges and the general ethical framework on which they rest. Thus, while the text faintly echoes the ethical problems raised by the

44. Summary of *Teluga Jommayyana Ragaḷe* 1.151–54 in Harihara and Suṅkāpura (1976a, 385).

45. A similar incident involving worms infesting a body is recounted in a north-Indian sectarian story and discussed in Smith (2000, 200).

46. Davis (1998, 2).

killing of the storyteller, it celebrates their utter defeat by faith in the god Śiva. In this way, religious competition, political etiquette, and even general and public conduct are superseded in this story by a higher authority, a divine one, controlled by Śiva and his Śaraṇas.

Anti-Court but Pro-Treasury

Whether explicitly stated by Harihara or remaining in the background in the *Ragaḷegaḷu* stories, the motivation behind the Śaraṇa's presence at the king's court lies in his concerns for the Bhaktas' community. The celebrated Kannada literary historian M. Chidananda Murthy remarks with regard to the Śaraṇas of the *Ragaḷegaḷu*: "Many of them were officials who served under a king for the sake of bread: their loyalty was not for the King but for God. God was their real master and not the King" (1983, 204). For this reason, when the Śaraṇa's presence at the court is set against his devotional sentiments and integrity, the latter will always clearly prevail. When issues of faith are on the line, called into question by courtly engagement with sectarian antagonists, the devotee is liable to explode and promptly walk away from his administrative job.

No story in the *Ragaḷegaḷu* collection conveys this foundational tension more strongly than the Ragaḷe about Basavaṇṇa, thematically the most important Ragaḷe in the corpus, as it celebrates the Śaraṇa who is identified more than any other with the ascendance of Śivabhakti in the second-millennium Kannada-speaking region.[47] The dramatic story about Basavaṇṇa and the Kalacūri king Bijjaḷa had a decisive impact on Karnataka's cultural history,[48] although—despite the richness of the literary sources—it is very difficult to connect Basavaṇṇa and Bijjaḷa historically, since the former is utterly absent from contemporaneous epigraphy in which the latter figures prominently. Nevertheless, a profusion of religious texts, mostly Śaiva, describe Basavaṇṇa's central role in the rise to power of the Kalacūri king Bijjaḷa and the latter's extension of his rule

47. The name of the Ragaḷe in Suṅkāpura's edition is the *Basavēśvaradēvara Ragaḷe*.

48. Basavaṇṇa and Bijjaḷa, and more generally the meteoric rise of the Śivabhakti community in Kalyāṇa, have captured the imagination of many writers in Kannada, both in premodernity and modernity. Many stories and plays were and still are written about these events. A stage play that was translated into English and received attention outside of Karnataka is Girish Karnad's *Taledaṇḍa* ("Death by Beheading") (Karnad 2005, 1–102; Leslie 1998). See discussion about modern plays focused on this period in Chandra Shobhi (2005, 295–319).

over Kalyāṇa, which had been a Cālukya capital for centuries. In turn, these sources mention Bijjaḷa's contribution to the establishment of the Śivabhakti movement in twelfth-century north Karnataka. Although differing in details, all these religious accounts conclude with a cataclysm in the form of a bitter falling out between the Śaiva administrator and the powerful king. The quarrel, the nature and details of which vary from one literary source to another, is nevertheless presented in all of the sources as having led to the violent expulsion of the Śaiva community from Kalyāṇa and to the downfall of this imperial capital. Kalyāṇa would never recover.[49]

It is impossible to historically ground Basavaṇṇa in King Bijjaḷa's court. While there are many epigraphical records connected with Bijjaḷa dating from the twelfth century, the earliest inscriptional reference to Basavaṇṇa is from 1251 CE, roughly a century after his purported date of death.[50] This inscriptional obscurity does not have to destabilize our confidence in the fact that Basavaṇṇa actually existed. In light of the magnitude of the cultural "mark" left by Basavaṇṇa (in poetry, hagiography, and the consequent public memory), it seems improbable and intellectually counterproductive to redescribe him as a mere cultural invention. But it is difficult to make specific historical claims regarding Basavaṇṇa. For example, Harihara's account of Basavaṇṇa differs from all the later accounts regarding the administrative center in which Basavaṇṇa operated as King Bijjaḷa's treasurer. Harihara refers to King Bijjaḷa's first political center at Maṅgaḷavāḍa as the location in which Basavaṇṇa started his public career. In contrast, all later accounts speak of Kalyāṇa, the Cālukya capital to which Bijjaḷa shifted his administration after winning over Taila III in 1157,[51] as the location in which Basavaṇṇa operated and nurtured the local Śivabhakti community. The first half of Harihara's account of Basavaṇṇa's life does not mention Kalyāṇa, though it might have recounted Basavaṇṇa's move to Kalyāṇa in the second half of the text, which is not available.[52] Did Basavaṇṇa meet Bijjaḷa for the first time in Kalyāṇa, as most sources

49. Despite the dearth of concrete historical evidence, the story about the active role of Kannada Śivabhakti in the decline of Kalyāṇa is generally accepted by contemporary historians. See Eaton and Wagoner (2014, 14, 34n42).

50. Desai (1968, 132).

51. Nilakanta Sastri (1976, 179).

52. The extant chapters out of a total of twenty-four composed by Harihara are 1 to 12 and parts of 24. In addition, some manuscripts contain verses from the concluding chapter. See Harihara and Suṅkāpura (1976a, 92–95).

claim, or in Maṅgaḷavāḍa? Which of the two locations was more significant for the development of the Kannada Śivabhakti? The two versions do not necessarily exclude each other—it is probable that Basavaṇṇa started out in Maṅgaḷavāḍa and then moved to Kalyāṇa with Bijjaḷa—but I am less interested in this specific historical detail than in the fact that the individual we think of today as the historical Basavaṇṇa is based solely on literary accounts, which at times are at variance with each other. A critical appraisal of the extant sources about Basavaṇṇa forces us to recognize the quasi-dialetheistic mode of this intellectual endeavor, according to which Basavaṇṇa is a historically concrete figure *and* a reconstruction forged from nonhistorical sources.

Harihara's Ragaḷe about Basavaṇṇa, historically the first account about this important Śaiva saint-poet and leader, directly connects Basavaṇṇa's successful career as a religious leader with his public administrative role at King Bijjaḷa's court. In this sense, the Ragaḷe about Basavaṇṇa is similar to the Ragaḷes about Kēśirāja and Jommayya. Further, all three take place at about the same time and in the same location, during the late reign of the Cālukyas and the Kalacūris (Kēśirāja and Jommayya in the early twelfth century and Basavaṇṇa in the middle of the twelfth century) in the northern regions of Maṅgaḷavāḍa and Kalyāṇa.[53] But the similarities run even deeper in the structure of the stories, for, as we shall see, the Ragaḷe about Basavaṇṇa also allots considerable space to Basavaṇṇa's political career, particularly his rivalry at the court with leaders of other religious sects. In all three Ragaḷes the Śaraṇa's interactions at the king's court, though fruitful at first, quickly deteriorate and lead to the Śaraṇa's retirement from this-worldly engagement at the court in favor of a renunciatory devotional life.

In the Ragaḷe about Basavaṇṇa, the protagonist's political ascendance is anticipated before his actual move to Maṅgaḷavāḍa, during the concluding phase of his adolescence in Kappaḍi. Kappaḍi is described in chapter 4 of the Ragaḷe as a large learning center for the Vedic tradition. Here, Basavaṇṇa also comes to know the local manifestation of Śiva, named Kūḍalasaṅgamadēva or Saṅgamadēva.[54] One night, when Basavaṇṇa is sleeping on the temple floor, Śiva appears in his dream and says: "I

53. For the political history of this place and time see Eaton and Wagoner (2014, 4–15); Nilakanta Sastri (1976, 179–80).

54. Ramanujan famously translates Kūḍalasaṅgamadēva as "Lord of the Meeting Rivers" (1973, 47).

will make you famous. Go to Maṅgaḷavāḍa, where King Bijjaḷa resides."[55] Basavaṇṇa refuses to depart from Kappaḍi and the god Saṅgamadēva, so Śiva returns the following night, appears again in Basavaṇṇa's dream, and promises him that he will be with him also in Maṅgaḷavāḍa. Śiva adds that in Maṅgaḷavāḍa Basavaṇṇa is to worship all the Bhaktas and stop the arrogance of those who follow other observances. The following morning, Basavaṇṇa is given a personal *liṅga* by Śiva's bull Nandi and leaves for Maṅgaḷavāḍa.

Early on in Basavaṇṇa's story this episode highlights the fundamental conflict between public life and a life of devotion. Basavaṇṇa is not interested in going to Maṅgaḷavāḍa and initiating a public career, despite the divine imperative. He acquiesces only when Śiva promises to accompany him. Basavaṇṇa is evidently cognizant of the inherent contradiction that exists between renunciatory devotionalism and earthly engagement—a contradiction that we also saw in Kēśirāja's and Jommayya's stories—and Basavaṇṇa is reluctant to abandon devotionalism for earthly engagement, though he finally yields.[56]

Śiva's conversation with Basavaṇṇa also links the devotee's public leadership with resistance to other religious affiliations. Śiva himself sees Basavaṇṇa's mission as simultaneously supporting the Śaraṇas and fighting the religious others. The connection Harihara makes between the Śaraṇa's support of the Śaivas and his active opposition to religious others becomes a sort of a trope in this Ragaḷe, invoked later in the text by the Bhaktas who surround Basavaṇṇa and praise him, and then again by the narrator himself.[57] It is clear that in Harihara's mind public leadership of the devotional community is tightly connected with sectarianism and active resistance to the religious other.

Significantly, both Basavaṇṇa's public career and his leadership of the Bhaktas begin at the king's court. In the first lines of the fifth chapter of the Ragaḷe about Basavaṇṇa, right before he enters Maṅgaḷavāḍa, Basavaṇṇa weighs how he might help the city's Jaṅgamas and decides to become an accountant (*gaṇaka*) at Bijjaḷa's palace. After arriving in the city,

---

55. *Basavēśvaradēvara Ragaḷe* 4.prose in Harihara and Suṅkāpura (1976a, 38): *ninnam mahītaḷadoḷu meṟedapevu, nīm bijjaḷarāyan ippa maṅgaḷavāḍakke pōgemba* . . .

56. P. B. Desai comments with regard to Basavaṇṇa: "A saint and a politician are paradoxical; and it is a strange phenomenon to see the one play the role of the other" (1968, 301).

57. *Basavēśvaradēvara Ragaḷe* 8.prose in Harihara and Suṅkāpura (1976a, 63) and 11.187–88/214–15 in ibid., p. 86.

he immediately sets out for the palace, where he sees incredible riches, huge armies, crowds of courtiers and courtesans, accountants, and also the chief minister (*daṇḍanātha*) giving out money to people. The chief accountant (*gaṇakādhipa*), named Siddhadaṇḍa, is conducting a routine public book audit at the hall. A few minutes after Basavaṇṇa enters, he suddenly shouts out that there has been an error in the calculations. The accountants double check the numbers and discover that Basavaṇṇa is right. Chief accountant Siddhadaṇḍa praises Basavaṇṇa for his acumen and recruits him as an accountant, giving him a salary of one hundred and one gold coins per year. When he finds out that Basavaṇṇa is from the same *kula* (extended family or tribe) of Brahmins called *kamme* as he, his trust in Basavaṇṇa deepens and he promotes Basavaṇṇa, giving him greater responsibilities as collector of taxes from faraway provinces (such as Cōḻa). However, Basavaṇṇa is concerned that all these resources are going to materialists (Lōkāyatas) and not to the Śivabhaktas. He prays to Śiva to help him find a way to support the Bhaktas. When Siddhadaṇḍa falls sick and dies, King Bijjaḷa appoints Basavaṇṇa to be the new caretaker of the kingdom's treasury of gold (*bhaṇḍāri*) as well as the kingdom's chief minister.

According to Harihara, Basavaṇṇa's public career is propitious from the outset and every development ends up being of benefit to Basavaṇṇa, including the sudden passing of his relative and patron Siddhadaṇḍa. Of greatest interest in this section of our discussion is the insight voiced by Basavaṇṇa early in the episode that the best way to benefit the Śivabhaktas is by working as an accountant at the king's court. This insight is explicit in the texts about Kēśirāja and Jommayya, but Basavaṇṇa's Ragaḷe presents it even more clearly and strongly. In the story mentioned earlier about Siddharāma, another Śaraṇa of this milieu, which was written by Harihara's nephew Rāghavāṅka, the saint is described as maintaining relations with the Kalacūri dynasty. Both authors, Harihara and Rāghavāṅka, are themselves connected in their traditional life stories with the region's kingdoms. It is clear that, in this Śaiva narrative tradition, accounting and state administration are consistently associated with leading and supporting the *bhakti* community. What is peculiar in this trend is that it is always coupled with the Śaraṇa's marked antagonism toward the institution of royalty, which I term the Śaiva authors' "anti-courtly sentiment." Basavaṇṇa's own antagonism is first signaled by his reluctance to serve the human king Bijjaḷa when asked to do so by Śiva, and we see this resistance deepen as Basavaṇṇa's story unfolds.

Sectarianism, the second trope shared by these Ragaḷes and later traditions about Harihara himself, is represented by the menacing presence of antagonistic Brahmins. In chapter 6 of Basavaṇṇa's Ragaḷe, the Brahmins complain to King Bijjaḷa about Basavaṇṇa's unorthodox worship practices, and chapter 8 presents a more elaborate incident that again involves Brahmins. The chapter begins with a long description of Basavaṇṇa's complete servitude to the Śivabhaktas of Maṅgaḷavāḍa. His service consists of honoring the Bhaktas and supporting their ritualistic needs, but also—and the text is very explicit and detailed here—of granting them expensive gifts, such as clothes, jewelry, and gold. Basavaṇṇa is described as "craving for [the Bhaktas'] merit" (*puṇya lōbhi*), and this passion is the engine that propels him to give to the Bhaktas incessantly.[58] But Basavaṇṇa's actions do not go unnoticed by other members of the court. Seeing the endless giving by Basavaṇṇa and the success of the Bhaktas' community in the city inflames the envy of the Vaiṣṇava Brahmins. Unable to tolerate the Śaivas' extravagant wealth, they go to King Bijjaḷa and say: "Dear king, this is insane! The Bhaktas are wearing on their bodies the wealth of the kingdom! Their riches exceed yours! Basavaṇṇa is emptying your treasury, and [the Bhaktas'] well-being has become the empire's first priority. What about the Vaiṣṇavas of the kingdom? The Brahmins who believe in *brahman*? The Jains? The followers of the six doctrines (*ṣaḍdaraśana*)? You are mesmerized by Basavaṇṇa, and if you do not awake from his thrall, we shall leave the kingdom. You must call Basavaṇṇa and order an immediate public audit of the treasury books!"[59]

Bijjaḷa is incensed by the words of these Brahmins (Harihara writes that they are like howling jackals, *narigaḷ antūḷi*), and he summons Basavaṇṇa and the rest of the accountants. When Basavaṇṇa appears at the court, he is smeared with holy ash (*bhasma*) and covered with Śaiva insignia, looking like Śiva himself. The accountants audit the books and declare that 180 million coins are missing from the treasury. Bijjaḷa asks Basavaṇṇa for an explanation, and Basavaṇṇa replies: "O king! Do you think that the ocean needs the river? That the sun craves the glitter of a mirror? The Bhaktas can purchase with their own money whatever they need without using a penny from the kingdom's treasury. Come and check the treasury yourself!" They all go to the treasury, open the countless boxes there, and

---

58. *Basavēśvaradēvara Ragaḷe* 8.prose in Harihara and Suṅkāpura (1976a, 61–62).

59. *Basavēśvaradēvara Ragaḷe* 8.prose in Harihara and Suṅkāpura (1976a, 63–64).

start to count the money, but the amounts are simply beyond measure: ten times, a hundred times, a hundred thousand times and ten million times the recorded amount. There is so much more money than what the audit had indicated that everyone simply gives up counting. The faces of those belonging to other religions—the religious others (*parasamayins*)—turn pale, and those of the Bhaktas shine. Basavaṇṇa says to Bijjaḷa: "Do you think all this property is really yours? Don't you realize that you are enjoying the grace of others? To us Bhaktas, a sesame seed from Śiva Saṅgamadēva is like divine fortune, his smallest glitter is the sun. You are operating under the influence of illusion (*māye*), being in fact nothing more than a mud doll. Who are you compared to the Bhaktas?" Basavaṇṇa speaks these words with great fury, and Bijjaḷa, realizing this, immediately prostrates himself before Basavaṇṇa and apologizes. Then, he pours 180 million coins at the feet of Basavaṇṇa to placate his anger. Basavaṇṇa leaves the court and returns to his home, where the Bhaktas welcome him and praise his generosity.

Sectarianism and money are deeply interwoven in this episode, and the king is required to get involved in the matter in order to protect his treasury from being misused. In an oblique fashion, he is also required to mitigate the sectarian tension that permeates the court. The Vaiṣṇava Brahmins, enemies of the Bhaktas, are envious and suspicious of Basavaṇṇa's special access to the treasury, and they are convinced that he funnels state funds to the Bhaktas' community. The Brahmins in this episode fit well into their paradigmatic role as the Śaraṇa's menace at the court. As was the case in the story of Jommayya, the text does not disprove the Brahmins' allegations regarding Basavaṇṇa's embezzlement. Rather, the plot dissolves the Brahmins' challenge through the Śaraṇa's miracle-working, namely, the fantastic inflation of the royal treasury. The plot development in this episode actually allows for the possibility that Basavaṇṇa had indeed used the treasury for his communal purposes, but this issue becomes completely irrelevant once Basavaṇṇa performs his miracle. As already noted, Harihara's resort to a miracle rather than to a direct refutation of the ethical charge made against a Śaraṇa conveys a Śaiva-based ethical prescription that transcends any intercommunal or political etiquette. In this story as well, Harihara's invocation of a *deus ex machina* solution to the Brahmins' charge about Basavaṇṇa's embezzlement suggests the superiority of devotional ethics over any earthly or theoretical moral jurisdiction.

This episode bears similarities to a later account about Harihara at the court of a Hoysaḷa king, discussed in chapter 1. In that story, rival accountants (non-Śaivas, no doubt) complain to the Hoysaḷa king that Harihara has been signing the accounting books with Śiva's name. The complaint plants suspicions in the king's mind. He questions Harihara's professional integrity and demands an immediate public audit. Harihara, not without taking offense, accedes to the audit only to interrupt it midway by performing a miracle, following which the king comes to recognize Śiva's greatness. Harihara, however, refuses to bury the hatchet and decisively quits the court to become a renouncer and a Śaiva poet.

The similarities between the stories about Harihara and Basavaṇṇa are extensive and meaningful: both start with the Śaraṇa's provocative, public gesture of Śaiva devotion. Next, non-Śaiva courtiers react to this provocation by complaining to the king. On hearing their complaints, the king begins to suspect that the Śaraṇa—who in both cases is the chief accountant and has (at least potentially) access to the empire's treasury—is stealing from him. The king then orders a public audit. The Śaraṇa shows up for the audit and proves his spiritual superiority over the king and his sycophants by means of a miracle, leaving the actual accusations regarding embezzlement unanswered. At this point, neither one of the narratives precludes the possibility that the Śaraṇa actually did use the empire's money to provide for his Śaiva community: Harihara performs his miracle during the audit and in effect prevents it from reaching its completion; Basavaṇṇa does not hinder the audit, but its results indicate that not only has no money disappeared but there is actually a huge excess of money in the treasury.[60] Finally, in both stories we find that, despite the king's consequent recognition and acknowledgement of the Śaraṇa's spiritual dominance, the Śaraṇa is not willing to absolve the king for having doubted him: both stories end with the departure of the Śaraṇa from the king's court, though in Basavaṇṇa's case, the final departure occurs a bit later in the narrative.

And yet, despite the leitmotif of cataclysmic denouement, the Śaraṇa's presence at the court in these stories is anything but coincidental. Not only has he mastered skills specifically associated with courtly culture, but he is also recognized and appreciated as an expert by his non-Śaiva court associates. The Śaraṇas' presence at the court is grounded in their

60. In Basavaṇṇa's case, there is a prior claim that Basavaṇṇa always deposits into the treasury all the regional taxes he collects. See *Basavēśvaradēvara Ragaḷe* 6.prose in Harihara and Suṅkāpura (1976a, 49). Descriptions in other parts of this Ragaḷe suggests otherwise.

talent for counting money and their administrative ability, not in their spiritual merit. Basavaṇṇa, Kēśirāja, a protagonist of another Ragaḷe called Bhōgaṇṇa, and in later texts Harihara as well, are described as capable bookkeepers and administrators.

The detailed level of description in these stories of money- and court-related activities in the *Ragaḷegaḷu*—such as the collection of taxes, bookkeeping and money management, names of provinces, and administrative and legalistic protocols—also suggests some familiarity with or at least keen interest in the court on the part of the early Kannada Śivabhakti tradition. Detailed descriptions of worldly engagements, the recognition and open acknowledgment that earthly resources could better the nascent community, and the related claim about the impossibility of sustaining devotional integrity while engaging with a hostile world were probably of particular interest to at least some of the text's audiences. In terms of social level, Velcheru Narayana Rao and other scholars have associated this hagiographic world with communities of merchants and traders because of their preoccupation with money and interest in maintaining cross-regional commercial ties.[61] It is possible that by highlighting the difficulties and dangers of interactions with worldly powers Harihara is participating in a larger conversation and trying to argue against having close financial ties to the court, a condition that may have been familiar to parts of his audience.

Whether genuinely reflecting a concrete socio-economic historical context or not, the stories discussed here convey an unambiguous message: faithfulness to Śiva and his followers wins over general ethical conduct. Accordingly, the failing of the king in these stories is his spiritual myopia, his inability to recognize the superiority of Śiva as manifest by his agents on earth, the Śaraṇas. All the ideological clashes culminate with a public display of the Śaraṇa's superiority. Thanks to an unexpected miracle—a *Śiva ex machina*, if you will—the Śaraṇa is not only exonerated from the worldlings' accusations but immediately transcends earthly considerations and contingencies.[62] Beyond this point matters can never return to their former state. This paradigmatic crisis marks an innate and irresolvable tension between the Śaraṇa and the king, and between the Śaraṇa's inner passion to be submerged in his devotion to Śiva on the one

61. Somanātha, Narayana Rao, and Roghair (1990, 9–10); Nandi (1975).

62. I am grateful to Prithvi Datta Chandra Shobhi for elucidating this motif (personal communication, March 2011).

hand and his need to publically support and sustain the community of Śaraṇas on the other. The premise in the stories surveyed in this chapter, that political life and devotionalism are inherently opposed, dooms the relationship between the Śaraṇa and the king to failure from the beginning. Thus, in addition to the Śaiva authors' general antipathy toward court life, there is also a foundational suspicion with regard to the character of the king, who, being non-Śaiva but—more to the point—being given to political, earthly power, is inherently unreliable. The king, in other words, is an outsider to the devotional Śaiva world.

On the aesthetic, narrative level, the intense commitment to Śiva and the Śaiva community by the Śaiva leader, coupled with this type of devotion's antagonism toward worldly compromise, as delineated so acutely in these stories, precludes the possibility of long-term and peaceful cooperation with a human king. From the Śaraṇa's perspective, his function and presence at the court always involve inner conflict. The overt motivation for his political activities is to better the Śaiva community by providing them with material resources and securing for them the king's general support. At the same time, the Śaraṇa is drawn to a life of renunciation, a life that is antithetical to worldly affairs and contingencies, such as those in which the Śaraṇa is steeped because of his affiliation with the court and his public position. The Śaraṇa's Janus-faced role causes his presence at the court to always be provisional and reliant upon ad hoc solutions. It is only natural that these stories end with the Śaraṇa's dramatic resignation from public office, a resignation accompanied by a public proclamation that he will henceforth dedicate his life to worshiping the god. This ideal of renunciation as a social project is often dramatized in the *Ragaḷegaḷu* stories in the form of the Śiva assembly, the spatial antonym of the court, where the collective of Śivabhaktas headed by the Śaraṇa can share in ecstatic and mystical devotional experiences. In many stories, it is from the Śiva assembly that the Śaraṇa rises up to Śiva's heavenly abode in Kailāsa to unite with the god.

Vaiṣṇava Brahmins as the Opponent Other

Next to the "outsider" king we find in these stories a major group of religious others who are the Vaiṣṇava Brahmin administrators. In terms of social and professional roles, the Vaiṣṇava Brahmin administrator in the *Ragaḷegaḷu* is not completely disconnected from the character of the Brahmin-Bhakta discussed in chapter 4, since both of them operate at the king's court, embodying the stereotypical elitist social status traditionally attached to Brahminism. In this sense, the *Ragaḷegaḷu* conforms to the traditional, Brahminical-centered worldview so prevalent in the pre-modern South Asian imaginaire. There is, however, a clear sectarian delineation between the "good" Brahmins sanctioned by Bhaktas' social and religious circle and those marked as the text's antagonists, that is, the Vaiṣṇava Brahmin administrators.[63] Whereas the former group of Brahmins are Śaivas and therefore included within the fold of Harihara's insiders, the antagonistic court Brahmins are consistently designated by Harihara with Vaiṣṇava names (such as Kṛṣṇapeddigaḷ and Viṣṇubhaṭṭa) and, in keeping with their non-Śaiva sectarian identity, are always hindering the Śaraṇa's advancement at the court.[64] As discussed in the previous chapter, Harihara's efforts to reconcile and include "good" Brahmins within the collective self of Kannada Śivabhakti operates in his wider narrative frame of resistance to Brahminism. This resistance later becomes a hallmark of the mature forms of Kannada Śivabhakti literature and rhetoric, but it is already clearly evident in the *Ragaḷegaḷu* with regard to Vaiṣṇava Brahmin courtiers.[65] The king is usually portrayed in the *Ragaḷegaḷu* as surrounded by Vaiṣṇava Brahmins. He is attentive to their wishes and concerns, especially regarding what they perceive as the troubling aspects of the Śaraṇa's presence at the court. At the same time, the king himself in the stories exercises a certain amount of impartiality with regard to religious affiliation: the intimate relationship he maintains with the Śaraṇa and his consequent but indirect and fleeting support to the local community of devotees are indicative of this impartiality. The broader consideration of the stories, however, suggests that this impartiality is subsumed by a larger identification of the king with his Vaiṣṇava courtiers.[66] Consequently, the Vaiṣṇava Brahmins, motivated by incessant

---

63. See Smith (2000, 199–228, passim) for stories with Brahmins at the king's court in northern devotional traditions.

64. The two Vaiṣṇava names mentioned here appear in *Bhōgaṇṇana Ragaḷe* vv. 73–74 (Harihara and Suṅkāpura 1976b, 228), but there are other Vaiṣṇava names mentioned throughout the text.

65. Compare with the divide between Vedic Brahmins and Śaiva Brahmins in Champakalakshmi (2011a, 94–95). On later sectarian tensions between Śaivas and Vaiṣṇavas at south-Indian courts, see Fisher (2017); Stoker (2016); Bronner (2011); Rao (2011).

66. Harihara mentions more than once in Basavaṇṇa's story a Vaiṣṇava character named "Nāraṇabhaṭṭa" and "Nāraṇakramita" whom he describes as the "King Bijjaḷa's guru." See *Basavēśvaradēvara Ragaḷe* 6. prose and 8.prose in Harihara and Suṅkāpura (1976a, 50 and 63, respectively). Historically, the royal practice of taking on a personal guru (*rājaguru*) and

antagonism toward the Śaiva community, its religious practices, and its social agendas as personified by the Śaraṇa, effectively interfere with and sabotage the intimate relationship between the Śaraṇa and the king. It is this basically dyadic structuring of the "good" Brahmin versus the "bad" Brahmins that marks the courtly Vaiṣṇava Brahmins as one type of religious other in the text.

We do not have a critical or thorough historical account of sectarian interactions between Śaivas and Vaiṣṇavas and various Brahminical factions at the court during the twelfth and thirteenth centuries to allow us to reflect on the relation between Harihara's depictions of the Kalyāṇa court and the actual historical situation. When discussing twelfth-century Kannada Śivabhaktas, Julia Leslie describes the political-religious landscape in this way: "Religious orthodoxy in twelfth-century Karnataka was represented not by the Jains but by the increasingly dominant Vaiṣṇava Hindus. They insisted on the mediation of a learned priesthood, a religious (and, by extension, social) hierarchy based on distinctions of caste and sex, and the importance of temple worship."[67] Leslie does not provide historical support for this claim, and it might be based more on literary sources than on hard evidence. But whether historically grounded or literarily figured, the dominance of Vaiṣṇava orthodoxy at the court she describes conforms to what Harihara portrays in the relevant *Ragaḷegaḷu* stories. In accord with Leslie's claim, in these stories the Brahmins at the kings' courts are markedly Vaiṣṇava. They are invested in maintaining socio-religious hierarchy and are averse to the interests and ideals of the Śaraṇa and the community whose interests and concerns he represents at the court. Nevertheless, there is a significant difference between Leslie's description and the picture of courtly Brahmins presented in the *Ragaḷegaḷu*. For Harihara, in contrast to a clear-cut Śaiva/Vaiṣṇava divide at the court, temple worship and the institution of the temple more generally are not strictly identified as Vaiṣṇava nor are they utterly rejected by him, as scholarship generally holds with regard to Kannada Śivabhakti.[68]

The association of Vaiṣṇava Brahmins with the court is persistent throughout the *Ragaḷegaḷu* stories about the Kannada saints, but the tension it generates for the Śaivas becomes most pronounced in the Ragaḷe

---

thus making the king's personal devotional sentiments public was prevalent among the Kalacūris (Stoker 2016, 7).

67. Leslie (1998, 233).

68. I have argued this elsewhere (Ben-Herut 2016).

dedicated to a saint called Śaṅkaradāsimayya. This central figure was previously discussed with regard to his receipt of Śiva's fiery eye (chapter 2) and his interactions with other devotees (chapter 3). Here, I would like to draw attention to his encounters in the Ragaḷe about him with the king and his Vaiṣṇava courtiers.

In the first chapter of this Ragaḷe, the protagonist starts out as a Vaiṣṇava named Gōvindadēva. One night he is visited by Śiva in a dream and is told that he is to be initiated (*upadēśa*) into the Śaiva faith.[69] During the initiation, performed at a temple by Śiva himself, the newly converted devotee asks for a fiery third eye in his forehead, and his god gives him, according to Harihara, the eye of the famous Kaṇṇappa.[70] Immediately a jet of fire streams out of the newly added eye, and its first target is Viṣṇu's statue, which burns down completely. Then, the Bhakta turns to face Brahmā's statue, which is split and broken to pieces. He deals in a similar fashion with the remaining statues of the thirty-three gods, as well as with the seven Kṛttikās and the eight Vasus. By the end of the fiery ordeal, all the statues in the temple (except that of Śiva of course) are deformed beyond recognition.[71] Only when Śiva himself approaches the Bhakta and shuts down his fiery eye—does it belong to Śiva or to Śaṅkaradāsimayya at this point?—are the third eye's powerful and destructive powers suppressed. As if to emphasize the completeness of Gōvindadēva's change of heart, the devotee asks Śiva to change his name to a Śaiva one, and Śiva grants him the name "Śaṅkaradāsimayya" ("Śiva's venerable servant").[72]

All this is but a prelude to the second chapter of the Ragaḷe, in which Śaṅkaradāsimayya is confronted with the king's Vaiṣṇava Brahmins. Again, the court discussed in this story is that of the Kalyāṇa Cālukyas, this time under the reign of King Jayasiṃharāya, presumably one of Vikramāditya's predecessors.[73] Nothing could be more different from Śaṅkaradāsimayya's

---

69. *Śaṅkaradāsimayyana Ragaḷe* 1.79 in Harihara and Suṅkāpura (1976a, 244).

70. Harihara creatively interjects the famous south-Indian story about the Tamil Śivabhakta Kaṇṇappa, who gave one of his eyes to Śiva (Ulrich 2007, 249–50; Cox 2005; Monius 2004; Peterson 1994). See *Śaṅkaradāsimayyana Ragaḷe* 1.158 in Harihara and Suṅkāpura (1976a, 247).

71. The invoking of deities' melting images as a trope for their spiritual falsity can be also found in one of the *vacanas* attributed to Basavaṇṇa: "How can I feel right / about a god who eats up lacquer and melts, who wilts when he sees fire?" (from *vacana* no. 558 in Ramanujan 1973, 28).

72. *Śaṅkaradāsimayyana Ragaḷe* 1.199–208 in Harihara and Suṅkāpura (1976a, 248–49).

73. Eaton and Wagoner (2014, 4).

religious piety than the connivance of King Jayasiṃharāya's Brahmins. Harihara's antipathy toward the court Brahmins at this point of the text peaks, as he ridicules their consuming interest in material gain. He cynically describes them as "skillful in getting gifts of cows" (*gōdānada sādhakaru*) and also as "courageous in getting gifts of women" (*mahiṣīdāna sāhasigaru*).[74] These Brahmins, upon hearing about the supernatural deeds Śaṅkaradāsimayya performs, suggest that the king confront the Śaiva devotee by putting him in front of Viṣṇu in his ferocious form of Narasiṃha, half man and half lion. The king decides to collaborate with the Vaiṣṇava Brahmins' scheme and invites Śaṅkaradāsimayya to the city. After a few days, the king and his Brahmins meet Śaṅkaradāsimayya and offer to take him on a tour of the city's Śaiva temples but, as if spontaneously or by mistake, they lead him to a Viṣṇu temple. The Viṣṇu image inside the temple is described by Harihara as being made of gold, though he immediately adds sarcastically that it looks as beautiful as a chicken. The king then asks Śaṅkaradāsimayya to open his third eye and perform an auspicious consecration (*ghanapratiṣṭhā*) for this Narasiṃha statue. Śaṅkaradāsimayya tries to refuse, saying he does not wish to harm the statue or the celebrated people around him, but the king insists, commenting tauntingly (*parihāsa*) that this would be a benevolent consecration.[75] With this, Śaṅkaradāsimayya loses his temper. He removes the cover over his third eye and opens it wide. Fire immediately shoots out of the eye and burns the Narasiṃha statue. Harihara relishes every detail of the conflagration. First, Narasiṃha's beard catches fire. Then, his mouth goes up in flames, resembling a large frying pan. The lion's incisors break off and fall to the ground. The tongue crumbles to pieces. The eyes pop out of the lion's face, which is now covered in flames. Its fingernails twist in the unbearable heat. Finally, the entire statue melts to the ground like wax. King Jayasiṃharāya and the Vaiṣṇavas are greatly frightened. They beg for Śaṅkaradāsimayya's mercy, declaring that they now recognize that he is Śiva's incarnation on earth. Śaṅkaradāsimayya assents. He closes his third eye and replaces its cover, assuring them they have nothing further to fear from him. He then returns to his house to continue the Śiva assembly with his fellow Śaraṇas.

As if the sectarian bent in Śaṅkaradāsimayya's story were not pronounced enough, Harihara refers to Śaṅkaradāsimayya in the verses that

---

74. The expression Harihara uses, "*gōdānada sādhakaru*," is particularly acerbic, since *sādhaka* usually denotes a seeker of higher, spiritual goals. See *Śaṅkaradāsimayyana Ragaḷe* 2.prose in Harihara and Suṅkāpura (1976a, 256).

75. *Śaṅkaradāsimayyana Ragaḷe* 2.prose in Harihara and Suṅkāpura (1976a, 257).

follow as the one who "stopped the arrogance of those faithful to other divinities" (*paradaivakulada garvavan iḷupi*).[76] Further, as in the stories surveyed above, the Purāṇic imaginaire inflames the sectarian tension that saturates the king's court, with Śaṅkaradāsimayya as a quasi-incarnation of Śiva who is challenged by Viṣṇu Narasiṃha and prevails.[77] Although this story, in contrast to the other stories discussed in this chapter, transposes the location of the sectarian showdown from the court to the temple, the conflict still revolves around the king's own religious affiliation and, by extension, that of his political supporters.

Despite the violent imagery of burning Viṣṇu's image at the temple, the sectarian attack on the Vaiṣṇava religious other, as in all the rest of the stories that involve conflicts with Vaiṣṇava Brahmins, is in fact quite limited. To begin with, Śaṅkaradāsimayya's brutal attack on the image is accidental and spontaneous, an immediate response to a well-planned provocation. There is nothing orchestrated in Śaṅkaradāsimayya's searing of the statues of other gods, not even during his earlier initiation episode. In fact, in neither of the attacks is there any sense of premeditation, of a well-thought-out scheme to destroy the competing religious community. As much as the spontaneous attacks are celebrated by the text as moments of victory, these moments are also short-lived and bounded. The text openly celebrates the emotional catharsis involved in the annihilation of any sort of religious other, but at the same time it also recognizes and warns against the dangers that such a reckless and unruly assault poses. Śiva himself warns of this when he appears before the fire-emitting Śaṅkaradāsimayya during the first torching:

> "Oh, dear child, if you look with your third eye
> you shall burn all the other gods,
> and all the worldlings who serve other gods,
> and then—the whole city, and the whole world, and the earth itself!
> Not a single man shall remain, my dear child!
> Enough, please, enough!"[78]

---

76. *Śaṅkaradāsimayyana Ragaḷe* 3.9 in Harihara and Suṅkāpura (1976a, 259).

77. The identification between Śaṅkaradāsimayya and Śiva is explicit throughout this Ragaḷe.

78. *Śaṅkaradāsimayyana Ragaḷe* 1.188–93 in Harihara and Suṅkāpura (1976a, 248): . . . *hō hō magane nīṃ nōḍe / dēvar ire mikkuhoṛagaṃ nōḍuvare matte / bhāvipaḍe paradaivavaṃ nōḍuvare matte / puravuridu jagavuridu dharevuridele magane / narar obbar uḷiyadantappudinnele magane / bēḍayya bēḍendu* . . .

Śiva's brief admonishment makes explicit the underlying sectarian premise in this story, as well as in the *Ragaḷegaḷu* as a whole, according to which co-existence with Vaiṣṇava Brahmins and more broadly with Vaiṣṇavism, despite its being a source of competition, tension, and friction, is also an integral and natural component of the religious landscape. Śiva himself connects the uncontrolled annihilation of other Brahminical gods with the destruction of the whole world. The Brahmin other, then, is an opponent to overcome, but one whose existence, albeit menacing, is assumed by the text as axiomatic. In addition, the texture of the *Ragaḷegaḷu* communicates a sense of ideological relatedness to some aspects of Brahminism through the recognition of shared scriptures (Vedas, Śāstras, Purāṇas) and even shared practices (public and communal storytelling, shared temple worship of multiple Purāṇic gods that include Śiva). Thus, a Śaraṇa's victory over Brahmins often involves a marked appropriation of their ethics and value system, such as the rhetorical untouchability ascribed to non-insiders, as discussed in the previous chapter.

I have already mentioned that Brahmins are lexically marked in the *Ragaḷegaḷu* as a religious other (*parasamayin, paradaivasantāna*), but in spite of this generic denotation, their othering in the stories is of particular kind. They are an other to resist and argue against, an opponent other. Active resistance to Brahmins is always of a contained, limited nature in these stories and does not involve wholesale or premeditated destruction. The court Vaiṣṇava Brahmins in these stories are not destined to die, but rather need to be corrected and to realize Śiva's greatness. More broadly, they are others who need to be proved wrong rather than exterminated. The imagined eradication of the religious other in the *Ragaḷegaḷu* is wholly reserved to a separate religious group, the Jains. It is with regard to Jains, the wholly others, that Harihara's antagonism is unrestricted and relentless, and I discuss this distinct form of othering separately in the following chapter.

Politics, Patronage, and Devotion

Harihara's political resistance to the king and the court is not expressed in the *Ragaḷegaḷu* stories in the form of explicitly political subversion. Harihara does not directly describe or encourage a political coup or usurpation of the existing political structure. In all the stories, the non-devotee kings and their Vaiṣṇava Brahmins remain in power while the Śaivas leave the court and the empire's capital city for a life of renunciation away from the social center. Non-Śaiva and human sovereignty remains, in the most limited sense, intact in these stories.

And yet, Harihara's undermining of the human king in the *Ragaḷegaḷu* is real and inescapable. While the plot and its telos leave the human king in place, other levels of the text vociferously argue for his subversion. To begin with, many dramatic moments in the *Ragaḷegaḷu* depict the saint's outright disregard for normative recognition of the king's stature coupled with the king's willingness to acknowledge the superiority of the saint over him. For example, when Jommayya and Kēśirāja are expected to bow down to the king in public, they adamantly refuse. In the case of Kēśirāja, the bowing is reversed when the king, having gone outside the city dressed as a simple man to meet the saint, is described as prostrating himself on the ground and begging for Kēśirāja's forgiveness and his return to the city.[79] Similarly, when Basavaṇṇa proves King Bijjaḷa wrong for having doubted his integrity in managing the state's treasury, Bijjaḷa falls at Basavaṇṇa's feet and asks for forgiveness. In stark contrast to the harmonious symmetry between the king and the saint in Vyāsatīrtha's life story, to which I referred in the opening part of this chapter, Harihara deliberately breaks this idyllic depiction and forcefully argues for the saint's supremacy over the king. He describes Kēśirāja's and Basavaṇṇa's seats in king's hall as more ornately decorated and raised higher than that of the king, and repeatedly portrays the saints themselves carrying royal insignia, such as a white umbrella. In the *Ragaḷegaḷu,* the saint never genuflects to the human king. If anything, it is the human king who bows down to the saint. Thus, even if Harihara's stories keep the human king in his royal position, he is left there humbled, if not humiliated.

Subversion of human rulership can also be found in other elements of the text. The title of the Ragaḷe dedicated to Basavaṇṇa and his most common sobriquet in the text is the "Godly Lord Basava," (*Basavēśvaradēva*), a title that leaves little room for any human sovereignty over Basavaṇṇa or, for that matter, over any other Śivabhakta.[80] Conversely, the human king in the *Ragaḷegaḷu* stories receives a sobriquet that is derisive, as in

---

79. See a similar reversal in the later, north-Indian hagiographic imaginaire (Pauwels 2002, 234).

80. Basavarāja ("King Basava") and Basavēśvara ("Lord Basava"), as well as Basavaṇṇa ("Elder Brother Basava"), are popular designations for this Śaraṇa to this day. For royal titles of other Śaraṇas in the *Ragaḷegaḷu,* see Savadattimaṭha (1999, 325).

the beginning of the Ragaḷe about Jommayya, where Harihara refers to King Permāḍirāya as the "Rāvaṇa of the Kali age."[81] A similar inversion of literary convention can be located in the formulaic benediction verses (*maṅgaḷaślōkas*) in the *Ragaḷegaḷu*. Traditionally reserved in pre-modern courtly literature to eulogizing the text's patron, usually the ruler of the region, the *maṅgaḷaślōka*s in Harihara's text are dedicated to the "King of the City of Pampā" (*pampāpurada arasa*), who is Śiva Virūpākṣa who resides in pre-Vijayanagara Hampi (originally Pampā).[82] The practice of dedicating Kannada devotional literature to Śiva instead of, as is customary, to a human king-patron is extended by Harihara to other works, such as the *Girijākalyāṇa*, and was also adopted by Harihara's nephew Rāghavāṅka in his own poems.[83] The *Hampeyarasana Ragaḷe* ("Ragaḷe for the King of Hampi") is a Ragaḷe that Harihara dedicates to the king of Hampi, the king being, as one would expect, Śiva Virūpākṣa.

The contrast between the flawed human king and the superior god rests, of course, on a foundational parallelism that permeated the South Asian political imaginaire starting around this period and lasting throughout the second millennium, particularly with regard to the figure of the divine king Rāma.[84] In fact, the Kalyāṇa Cālukya dynasty persistently identified its mythic genealogy with the Īkṣvākus, Rāma's lineage.[85] As evinced in Bilhaṇa's Sanskrit panegyric to King Vikramāditya VI, the *Vikramāṅkadēva Carita*, the trend of comparing Rāma to the human king culminated during the reign of this king. As Lawrence McCrea and Yigal Bronner have effectively shown, Bilhaṇa's eulogy is infused with hinted criticism of this particular king and of the institution of the human king

81. *Teluga Jommayyana Ragaḷe* 2.prose in Harihara and Suṅkāpura (1976a, 388).

82. Harihara's usage of the Dravidian word *arasa* to denote Śiva's reign over Hampi could imply a mundane, political sense of the word rather than the divine sovereignty linked with Sanskritic words for "king" such as *rāja*. I thank Yigal Bronner for noticing this lexical detail (personal communication, June 2014).

83. A traditional story about Harihara knocking out some of his nephew Rāghavāṅka's teeth because he had written about non-Śaiva protagonists conveys this literary commitment (Rāghavāṅka and Viswanatha 2017, viii–ix, xxvii n7; Chandra Shobhi 2005, 199n16; Nagaraj 2003, 364). See a similar trend in Harirām Vyās's poetry and in his hagiographies (Pauwels 2002, 238–39). Although there are literary gestures of perceiving Śiva as "patron-king" in the early Tamil hymns of the Mūvar, Tamil Śivabhakti grew to ideologically embrace and politically collaborate with the institution of the human king, a stance that neutralized the subversive weight of its claims about Śiva's sovereignty (Champakalakshmi 2011b, 70–72).

84. Pollock (1993).

85. For the identification of the Cālukyas with the Īkṣvākus, see Pollock (2006, 155).

more broadly, a criticism that rests on a structural contrast between the human king and the divine king.[86] But what a Sanskrit court-poet can only whisper, a Kannada *bhakti* poet can shout, and in other places. Harihara's writing is so imbued with thematic, linguistic, and stylistic elements generally configured against the human king that, although the *Ragaḷegaḷu* shows no particular interest in the problematic political biography of Vikramāditya, the author's underlying subversion of his and others' royal power is quite clear. And the fact he is writing also for non-elite audiences charges this subversion with new socio-political implications.

Can literature, especially when operating within the format of a tight religious discourse as Harihara's work does, be considered a political act? There are several problems with attributing a concrete political message to the *Ragaḷegaḷu*. An immediate and obvious one is the dearth of verifiable scholarship about the socio-political world in which Harihara operated, as well as about its boundaries, its practices, its exclusions. Although there are some indications that Hampi during the period when Harihara most probably wrote the *Ragaḷegaḷu* did enjoy some level of political and cultural autonomy, it is difficult to assume that Harihara had a concrete political intention to usurp or actively resist the sovereignty of the human king.[87] Still, the voice of the *Ragaḷegaḷu* is political in a discursive sense. Despite the temporal and spatial distance of French modernity from our subject matter, it is useful to consider Jacques Rancière's discussion of the "politics of literature." Rancière writes:

> Politics is first of all a way of framing, among sensory data, a specific sphere of experience. It is a partition of the sensible, of the visible and the sayable, which allows (or does not allow) some specific data to appear; which allows or does not allow some specific subjects to designate them and speak about them. The politics of literature thus means that literature as literature is involved in this

---

86. Bronner (2010); McCrea (2010). Lawrence McCrea notes that "Bilhaṇa develops a dark vision of kingly power" (p. 517).

87. The art historian Phillip Wagoner, writing on the religio-political history of pre-Vijayanagara Hampi, mentions the relative political independence of this area before the establishment of the Vijayanagara empire (Wagoner 1996). The Kannada literary historian Eṃ. Cidānandamūrti points to archeological artifacts of four Śiva temples that surrounded Hampi during Harihara's time as a possible indication of Hampi's religion-based self-governance, despite its inclusion into the far regions of the Hoysaḷa period (Cidānandamūrti 2007).

partition of the visible and the sayable, in this intertwining of being, doing and saying that frames a polemical common world.[88]

The episteme articulated in Harihara's *Ragaḷegaḷu* is political in the sense that, as Rancière writes in the above quote, it "allows or does not allow some specific subjects to designate [some specific data] and speak about them"—data which, in the case of the *Ragaḷegaḷu*, also involved arenas clearly identified with what we term today as political. The cultural milieu of pre-Vijayanagara south-Indian kingdoms is conceptually remote from the modern premises that constitute Rancière's discourse, but despite this, Harihara's stories are so saturated with overwhelmingly anti-courtly sentiment and representations that it is difficult not to read these stories politically in the spirit of Rancière.

The recent and important work of Christian Novetzke about the emergence of Marathi literature in the thirteenth-century points to the significance in reading *bhakti* using a socio-political lens.[89] Novetzke sees the "vernacular turn" of *bhakti* literature as a "the creation of a public discursive field where we find vibrant debates about the social inequities of language, caste, and gender. These debates, articulated in the words of the quotidian world, ostensibly opened up a sphere of ethical engagement across the social spectrum."[90] This postulation about "a public discursive field," also labeled by Novetzke as "a public sphere," can be conceived as a pre-modern subset of Rancière's "polemical common world." Moreover, it resonates well with Harihara's stories, most forcibly, I would argue, with regard to the negative manner with which the court, the king, and his menacing Vaiṣṇava Brahmins are portrayed, since these negative descriptions are contrasted—both in the Marathi materials discussed by Novetzke and in the Kannada materials discussed in this book—with devotional life in the quotidian world.

The text's unflattering descriptions of the court and court life and the acidic rhetoric against the king and his Vaiṣṇava courtiers at specific moments imply at least some degree of cultural leverage that Harihara had when composing these stories. Even if we assume his readership to have consisted only of devotees, they must have enjoyed some sort of relative

88. Rancière (2010, 152).

89. Novetzke (2016).

90. Ibid., 2.

social autonomy to engage in such anti-courtly rhetoric. This points to the existence of a socio-political context that could have allowed such an "anti-courtly" text to be composed, disseminated, and performed—and even be recognized as literature. The fact that the early writers in this tradition, such as Harihara, Pālkuriki Sōmanātha and to some extent also Harihara's nephew Rāghavāṅka, could produce literature that is so clearly antithetical to the idea of human sovereignty indicates a certain amount of relative political freedom. This political freedom could have relied on a network of social and institutional support that existed outside the court, a kind of network that could have sustained the production and transmission of this type of literature.[91] In other words, it is possible that the early Śivabhakti hagiographies were patronized by a collective that was situated away from the court. Novetzke writes that the early Marathi *bhakti* literary world "was produced at the crossroads of towns and cities, among networks of villages linked by trade and roving preachers, under trees, outside temples and monasteries, amid farms and homes,"[92] and Harihara's writing in the *Ragaḷegaḷu* very probably emerged from a similar culture, or at least was considerably influenced by it.

According to Romila Thapar, the significance of a community serving as cultural patron lies in the fact that it "points to a cultural and social innovation for that period. It indicates the emergence of new social groups which, apart from other features, also identify themselves with a particular kind of patronage and with new aesthetic forms."[93] What is additionally striking in Harihara's case is that some of his more conventional work was not confined solely to his devotional community but actually gained recognition in non-religious and elite literary circles not long after his completion of the *Ragaḷegaḷu*.[94]

While Harihara's anti-courtly voice cannot be read as a straightforward history of active social resistance to the twelfth-century rulers of north Karnataka, I suggest we reconsider the historical conditions that enabled the imagining of such stories in publicly recognized written form. In other words, the fact that the literary-imaginary voice of the *Ragaḷegaḷu* was publicly received and historically recognized speaks volumes about

---

91. Jon Keune carefully suggests the same with regard to the Marathi saint Eknāth (2014, 11)

92. Novetzke (2016, 2).

93. Thapar (1992, 32).

94. See introduction and Nagaraj (2003, 363–64).

its historical context. The circumstances that facilitated the new and bold form of religious expression by this *bhakti* literary tradition were no less political than court dynamics even though they probably occurred outside the courts. In fact, these religious texts are politically significant precisely *because* of their anti-court voice. Daud Ali, writing on political interactions in classical Sanskrit literature, criticizes the patronage/legitimacy model by pointing to court interchanges that included multiple agents and more complex interactions than those considered thus far.[95] The impudent voice of Harihara—as well as the voices of other early Bhakta-authors—against the court in this religious literature call for an expansion of Ali's model beyond the court. The political implications embedded in the appearance of a new *bhakti* literary tradition confident enough to figuratively undermine the king's image and that of his court suggest that these authors enjoyed some degree of social and political autonomy. Burton Stein, in his work on patronage and religious institutions in the Vijayanagara Empire, writes of the need to "reach beyond the conventional dyad of a single patron and a single client to encompass the polyadic patronage of most religious benefits and protections in South India"[96] The case of the *Ragaḷegaḷu*, chronologically located between the periods discussed above by Ali and Stein, should be considered along similar lines of complex patronship beyond the strictly royal voice and extending into wider and non-elite social strands that, politically speaking, were situated at some distance from the court.

95. Ali (2004). See also Kaul (2010).

96. Stein (1992, 161).

6

Jains as the Intimate, Wholly Other

THE FINAL MOVEMENT of this book continues the exploration begun in the previous chapter of relations with non-Śaivas who are external to the devotee's religious community, those I have termed "religious others." Here, however, that exploration is extended beyond relations with antagonists who are Vaiṣṇava Brahmins to relations with antagonists who are Jains. In the *Ragaḷegaḷu* stories about the Kannada saints there is a clear dividing line between these two groups of others, and that dividing line is blood red. Vaiṣṇava Brahmins, which I refer to as the text's opponent other, are corrupt, malevolent, averse to the faith, goals, and needs of the emerging Śivabhakti community, and envious of the public successes of the Śaiva Brahmin-Bhakta. At the same time, they can also be redeemed or reckoned with, having the potential to arrive at a proper recognition of Śiva's greatness or at least to be proven wrong. All in all, the Vaiṣṇava Brahmins' menacing presence is tolerated by the Śaiva saints in the *Ragaḷegaḷu* stories. In comparison to the Vaiṣṇava Brahmins, who are portrayed as foolish and corrupt, the Jains suffer a much worse literary fate, being portrayed as vile and disgusting. They are the wholly other, and the Bhakta's response to their presence is violent, impatient, consuming, and total. In the *Ragaḷegaḷu*, the Jains are either exterminated or formally converted to Śaivism, always in large and paradigmatic numbers, and it is safe to claim that religious otherness is most definitively and harshly represented by them.

Texts describing sectarian tensions between Vedic-based religious traditions and Jains were also produced in north India at roughly the same time as the *Ragaḷegaḷu*,[1] but it appears that early south-Indian Śaivism had

1. Smith (2000, 199).

an exceptionally acerbic antipathy toward Jains. This is true not only in the Kannada devotional idiom but also in the Tamil and Telugu.[2] Still, despite Harihara's conscious and exhaustive adoption of the Tamil Śaiva imaginaire in the *Ragaḷegaḷu*,[3] his figuration of the Jain other in the stories about the Kannada saints contains elements that are distinct in comparison with the Tamil canon.[4]

A Wave of Mutilation

We begin our journey into Harihara's narration of conflicts with Jains with the most violent, odious story of Kōvūra Bommatande. No other Ragaḷe provides a similar level of graphic violence coupled with an underlying, uncontrollable urge to annihilate the Jains, in a real, physical sense. The story's culmination has an ironic edge to it, when the same consuming violence inflicted upon the Jains is turned inward toward the Śaivas themselves. The gruesome episode takes place in Kōvūru, which, according to the text, is in the northern region of Kalyāṇa.[5] The local ruler of the town, called Bommatande, is portrayed as an ardent Śaiva devotee. He is a devoted Bhakta of Śiva Rāmanātha, whose temple is located about half a mile away from the town. Harihara describes the town of Kōvūru as swarming with Jain snakes, with eight thousand Jain temples (*basadis*) and eight thousand Jain sages (*ṛṣis*). The Jains, according to Harihara, are eight times worse than the materialists (Cārvākas), and they control the entire administration of the town. In contrast, only three hundred benevolent Śaivas reside in Kōvūru, headed by Bommatande.

---

2. Śaiva antipathy toward Jains in the Tamil tradition was distinct from that toward Buddhists (Monius 2011, 153–60). See also Champakalakshmi (2011a, 440–50; 2011b, 97–98; 2011c, 64–66); Pechilis (1999, 72–74); Peterson (1994, 209–10). In contrast to some texts in the Tamil Śivabhakti literary tradition, the Kannada literature is almost completely mute regarding Buddhists. In the *Ragaḷegaḷu* stories about the Kannada saints, Buddhists are nominally mentioned only once, in the *Hāvinahāḷa Kallayyana Ragaḷe*.

3. On the literary connections between the Tamil and the Kannada Śivabhakti traditions in the first centuries of the second millennium, see Ben-Herut (2015).

4. In this regard, this chapter is a response to Indira V. Peterson's invitation to contrast the contestation between Śaivism and Jainism in Tamil with that of Karnataka, as well as of other regions in South Asia (1998, 165–66).

5. Kōvūru is identified as today's Kōvaḷḷi by Ti. Es. Śāmarāya (2009 [1967], 82n2), though the Ragaḷe describes Kōvūru as situated north of Kalyāṇa, while Kōvaḷḷi is to the south of it and quite remote (almost two hundred miles). See *Kōvūra Bommatandeya Ragaḷe* 1.1 in Harihara and Suṅkāpura (1976, 357).

The story commences with Bommatande and his wife begetting a son with Śiva's blessings.[6] Sixteen years pass, until one day Bommatande hosts a huge festival for the Śivabhaktas (*gaṇaparva*) at the Śiva Rāmanātha temple and orders that he must not be interrupted during the festivities. At that time, a sinful Jain (*pātaki*) goes to Bommatande's palace disguised as a Śivabhakta. Bommatande's son receives him with great respect, but when the two are alone, the Jain takes out a sword, attacks the boy, and cuts him into pieces. Fifteen days later, as Bommatande is returning to the town, the Jains start arguing with him, insisting that there is no merit in Śaiva celebrations. Bommatande performs a miracle by bringing back to life a tree that had been burnt by the Jains, and then he joyfully continues on to his palace. When he arrives, he learns of the murder of his son. Bommatande gathers the three hundred Śaraṇas of the town and, together with his wife Kaḷāvati, they all go to the child's burial space (*samādhi*), where he orders the dead child to get up, and so the child does. Everyone is ecstatic at the miraculous revival.

Bommatande decides to organize another festival, larger than the previous one, but the eight thousand Jain sages demand that this time the celebration be held inside the city, so that they can see Śiva Rāmanātha. Bommatande calls them "malevolent creatures" (*piśācas*) but accepts the challenge of publicly displaying the Śiva statue. Śiva Rāmanātha is brought to the city on a bull, and when the procession passes Jain temples, according to Harihara, the Jinas inside tremble with fear. Bommatande is ecstatic on the occasion and shouts at the Jains: "Burn, burn, you sinner! You are worse than anthills of disgust! You have made three mistakes (referring to the burning of the tree, the boy's murder, and forcing Rāmanātha into the city) and I am finished with you!"[7] Next, Bommatande hears that the Jain sages have organized their own festival. He is furious at this. Swearing to tear down and smash all the Jain naked dolls (*battale bombegaḷu*), he gathers together the three hundred Śaraṇas. They strap on armor and weapons and start killing any Jain they encounter. After slaughtering all the Jains of the town, the Śaraṇas want to go into each house and replace the Jina with a *liṅga*, but Bommatande refuses to even set his foot inside the houses of lowly Untouchables (*holeyas*). Instead, they raze all the Jains' houses, call

6. The following is a summary of the three chapters of the *Kōvūra Bommatandeya Ragaḷe* in Harihara and Suṅkāpura (1976, 359–77).

7. *Kōvūra Bommatandeya Ragaḷe* 2.prose in Harihara and Suṅkāpura (1976, 369): *ele ele pātakarirā suḍu hēsikeya huttugaḷirā mīṟi nuḍida mūṟu pattaṃ sāṟi sairisiden enna pavaṇallaṃ.*

many Śivabhaktas into the town, and reestablish it as a Śaiva settlement (*śivapura*).

The cataclysmic fate of Kōvūra's Jains does not cap the gory violence in this story. In a way, it only anticipates the story's radical culmination. After annihilating the Jains, Bommatande organizes multiple celebrations. One day, during a festive assembly of Śivabhaktas, a scroll falls from the sky, sealed by Nandi, Śiva's attendant. It is a message from Śiva Rāmanātha, who orders Bommatande and his three hundred Śaraṇas to join him the following morning in Kailāsa on the path of bravery (*vīramārga*). Bommatande declares: "The suffering of this worldly existence (*saṃsāra*) is finally over."[8] With excitement and resolve he renounces his reign over the town and, surrounded by the three hundred Śaraṇas, he processes down the main street and then sets out for Śiva Rāmanātha's temple. Harihara writes that inside the temple it is dark as the hair of the village goddess Māriyamma, and that only the glittering of weapons can be seen. Bommatande gathers the heroes, each one glowing with the light of white ash and wearing prayer beads. They all roar in ecstasy over Śiva like lions, like the attendants of Vīrabhadra, Wrathful Śiva. The three hundred Śaraṇas tell Bommatande that they have come of their own free will and are determined to reach Śiva's world by giving up their own bodies. They hold their swords high and, to the sound of trumpets, begin severing parts of their own bodies. The earth itself has never witnessed such a sight. After cutting their toenails, they start to sever their feet and legs. Rivers of blood flow onto the temple's floor and around Śiva's statue. Then they extract their own intestines and cut them into small garlands, which they place on Śiva's head. With swords and axes they hack at each other and shout happily. Fountains of blood gush in all eight directions. They tear out their hearts and rip out their nerves. Now they start chopping up their bones, which break with a sharp splitting sound. Sliding around legless on the bloody floor, they celebrate their devotion without any sense of pain. Bommatande sees this and smiles. Then he takes a sword, cuts off his own legs, and throws them away. The left leg hits some Jains and kills them. The right leg flies into the air and circles all the Śaraṇas. Finally, a heavenly chariot (*puṣpaka*) descends from the sky to take Bommatande to Kailāsa, together with three hundred other chariots, one for each Śaraṇa. When reaching Kailāsa, they all prostrate themselves in front of Śiva, and Śiva

8. *Kōvūra Bommatandeya Ragaḷe* 3.31 in Harihara and Suṅkāpura (1976, 372): *nīgidem saṃsāraduḥkhamam duritamam.*

proudly tells Vīrabhadra and Nandi to observe the heroes who have voluntarily performed a bodily act of worship (*tanupūje*) out of their love for him. Then he grants Bommatande the honor of becoming his attendant.

This story is about a Śaiva ruler of a town controlled by Jains. The ruler has a political-cum-religious problem, having to engage in sectarian competition with Jains in a town he himself rules.[9] But in stark contrast to the stories about Vaiṣṇava Brahmins discussed in the previous chapter, courtly intrigues and the devotee's miraculous deliverances are secondary here. Instead, Harihara accentuates the sectarian conflict and pushes it toward a sweeping and gory denouement. Note how the local Jains are rendered by the author as utterly vile. Motivated only by their sectarian hatred, they barbarically murder the ruler's own son while he is away. Bommatande's retaliation against the Jains' aggression is equally violent: he gathers a small army unit of Śivabhaktas and together they butcher all the Jains of the town. Finally, following Śiva's command from heaven, this army unit headed by Bommatande enters the local Śiva temple and commits a bloody mass suicide.

Advancing from Ragaḷes about courtly Vaiṣṇava Brahmins, it is clear that we are entering *terra nova* in terms of emotional antagonism, internecine implications, verbal hostility, nonrealistic and paradigmatic numbers of victims, and the acerbic nature of public and sectarian confrontation. The last element is most notable. In Harihara's narratives about conflicts with Brahmins, we do not find the high level of resistance to public displays of religious otherness that dominates the *Ragaḷegaḷu* narratives about Jains. Of course, there are some instances of literary claims of violence against Brahmins, including the murdering of a Vaiṣṇava by Jommayya and the burning of a Viṣṇu statue by Śaṅkaradāsimayya, as discussed in previous chapters. But events like these are momentary lapses, exceptions to the general sense of restraint that controls conflicts with antagonistic Brahmins. The Ragaḷes about Jains, in contrast, are suffused with deliberate and orchestrated violence that always results in massive and absolute effects: converting, expelling, or killing the local Jain community.

Harihara's unforgiving treatment of Jains is foundational in other stories in the *Ragaḷegaḷu* too, but the Ragaḷe about Bommatande does stand out, beginning with the moment when the Jain disguised as a Śaiva

---

9. See similar complications, though set in a historical context, that arise from the fusion of saintly and kingly aspirations in Daniel Gold's discussion of Mān Singh, a nineteenth-century ruler of Jodhpur (1995).

draws his sword and kills Bommatande's son. The mechanical, unmitigated viciousness with which the murder is carried out sets in motion the grotesque and hyperbolic violence that takes over the rest of the story. This early moment in the story paves the way for the violence that permeates its unfolding, a violence that progressively intensifies until it reaches a final crescendo: starting with the Jains' unexplained, brutal murder of Bommatande's son, followed by Bommatande's lethal retaliatory attack that annihilates the entire Jain community, and culminating with grisly suicide of the three hundred Śaraṇas orchestrated by Bommatande.[10] Clearly, the gruesome and utterly destructive violence in this story overpowers its narrative progressions. It even transcends the explicit sectarian agenda that controls the first part of the story by giving way to an intense devotional display of public, communal self-sacrifice. The denouement shifts the story from sectarian violence to a more basic use of violence as a religious practice, one that can be directed against the religious self as much as against the religious other.[11]

What was Harihara's purpose in writing this "extreme poetry"?[12] His textual rendering of the climactic mass suicide celebrates the brutal violence of the event by describing in graphic detail and with macabre humor

10. The number eight thousand, specifically attributed to the antagonist Jain community's temples and sages in the first chapter of this *Ragaḷe*, is a literary trope in itself, also used by the Tamil poets with regard to the impaling of Jains at Madurai (Peterson 1998, 181). See also Champakalakshmi (2011c, 65ff); Pechilis (1999, 126–27).

11. The self-massacre by the Śaivas might have some vague resonance in history. There is historical evidence to suggest the possibility of actual practices of religious mass suicide by Śaivas, referred to in this text as *tanupūje*, during medieval times in this region. A mass burial ground containing about six hundred skulls neatly arranged in lines and dating from the fourteenth century (a determination arrived at through the use of carbon-14 testing) was discovered in the city of Aṇṇigere, which is mentioned in the *Ēkāntarāmitandeya Ragaḷe* and in the *Ādayyana Ragaḷe*. Popular media speculated on the origin of this unusual finding, and some have connected it to Śaiva self-sacrifice practices (though other theories were given as well). The claim that this mass burial ground is a Śaiva practice was chiefly made by Eṃ. Eṃ. Kalaburgi, who dubiously uses the *Kōvūra Bommatandeya Ragaḷe* as historical support for such practices. V. Anuradha discusses the practice of severing one's head as an offering to Śiva at Śrīśailam during the fourteenth century (2002: 65). For newspaper reports on the archeological findings, see Nandy (2012); Pattanashetti (2011). For Kalaburgi's claims in popular media, see Srinidhi (2012); Katkar (2012). M. Chidananda Murthy describes an equally lethal practice with regard to the Kannada Śivabhakti tradition: "Among Śaivites, there was a custom that in case a devotee loses his *liṅga* (which is his real master), he should commit suicide immediately" (1983: 204). Further study is required to establish the facticity of these claims.

12. I borrow this term from Bronner (2010), though my use of it is here is very different from that in Bronner's book.

the slashed body parts, blood, and guts. This passage is an authorial *tour de force* in a specific form of literary figuration that aims to generate what Sanskritic poeticians term *bībhatsarasa* ("sentiment of disgust"), one of the eight (or nine according to some enumerations) aesthetic sentiments in classical Sanskritic poetics.[13] As Anne Monius has observed, this representational mode of eliciting disgust can be found in the medieval south-Indian religious imaginaire across languages and traditions, and can be detected in other related Śaiva works, notably the Telugu *Basava Purāṇamu* and the Tamil *Periya Purāṇam*, as well as in earlier south-Indian literature, including Jain texts.[14] It is very possible that Harihara was familiar with this form of south-Indian Śaiva expressivity in general, perhaps even with preexisting and paradigmatic texts such as those mentioned, and that he tried to echo or outshine them in this particular Ragaḷe. However, in contrast to the *Basava Purāṇamu* and the *Periya Purāṇam*, the violent passages in the Ragaḷe about Bommatande are, stylistically, the outlier rather than the norm in the *Ragaḷegaḷu*.[15] While Harihara's antagonism toward Jains in this poem corresponds, as I show below, with what is found in the rest of the *Ragaḷegaḷu* poems that involve Jains, this Ragaḷe is unmatched in its celebration of uninhibited violence, leaving the modern reader (and perhaps the immediate audience as well) aesthetically—if not morally—disgusted. It might be instructive to invoke in this context the term *vīra* and its centrality to this tradition. Literally meaning "heroic," *vīra* becomes one of the most unmistakable signifiers for Kannada Śivabhakti as a whole, but its usage in Harihara's work is much more limited; it is reserved for particularly intense moments, especially those that involve violence and conflict.[16] Since the antagonizing of Jains in the *Ragaḷegaḷu* is of the most extreme nature, stories of conflicts with Jains serve as a culmination of the quality of *vīra* in narrative form.

Despite the intensity of the Jain othering in the *Ragaḷegaḷu*, it is important to recognize the complexity inherent in this representational

13. I borrow the term *tour de force* with regard to this form of expressivity from Narayana Rao et al. (2003, 258), who discuss a compelling passage by the Kashmiri Sanskrit poet Kalhana. See general discussion about *rasa* in Pollock (2016); Gerow (1977). See Chakrabarti (2001) for reflections about *bībhatsarasa*.

14. Monius (2004).

15. See Ben-Herut (2012) for a preliminary stylistic contrasting between the *Ragaḷegaḷu* and the *Basava Purāṇamu*.

16. Chidananda Murthy (1983, 205n3).

strategy. At the most general level, the absolutist othering of the Jains in Harihara's narratives can be explained by the absence of any shared religious repository (such as a shared scripture or temple grounds) between the two religious communities, a repository that could have been used in the stories as a channel for mediation or at least as indexical means for conducting the confrontation between the Śaivas and the Jains. When the Śaivas confront the Vaiṣṇava Brahmins, they can at least argue—as they do in the *Ragaḷegaḷu*—about whose god is championed by the Vedas and the Purāṇas. Such a common ground for discussion, and even for agreeing to disagree, is completely absent in the communication between Śaivas and Jains in the text.

Another force that propels Harihara's antagonism toward Jains, one that is deeper and less visible than the Jains' "exoticism" but that also inherently supplements it and complicates the discussion, is the striking similarity between the Śaivas and the Jains in Harihara's stories, a similarity that is expressed in the domestic, communal, and religious aspects of their lives. While the *Ragaḷegaḷu* stories do not point explicitly to any directly shared religious repository between Śaivas and Jains, the two religious communities are depicted in the *Ragaḷegaḷu* in surprisingly homologous ways. For example, public festivals are a central means for asserting communal identity for both the Śivabhakti and the Jain traditions as they are figured in Harihara's text. This is evinced the life of Kōvūra Bommatande, when the conflict between the two communities intensifies because of fierce competition over whose religious festivals will be conducted on the town's main streets. Apart from the streets, the temple and the home are the two paradigmatic arenas in the *Ragaḷegaḷu* for sectarian conflict between Śaivas and Jains, and they are discussed in the following two sections.

Temple Fights

As I have argued elsewhere, in sharp contrast to the later tradition's stance and also to common scholarly perceptions about Kannada Śivabhakti, the early devotional tradition of the Kannada-speaking region, as depicted in the *Ragaḷegaḷu*, was not averse to the temple or to the normative role it plays in mainstream society, nor to the worship rituals of the *sthāvaraliṅga*, the massive stone emblem of Śiva, that take place on temple grounds.[17] This

17. Ben-Herut (2016).

is not to say that the *Ragaḷegaḷu* stories convey any uniform or simplified notion of the temple. Rather, the temple is figured in the *Ragaḷegaḷu* in a multiplicity of ways and reflects different attitudes and prescriptions. In the sectarian feud with Jains, which is one of the repeated themes in the *Ragaḷegaḷu*, the temple figures prominently.

As a popular setting in the *Ragaḷegaḷu*, the temple—in which saints live, worship, and assert their religiosity—repeatedly serves Harihara as a place to dramatize intense devotional moments, especially those framed by sectarian conflict. In addition, the temple, according to Harihara's narratives, has communal and public significance as a symbol of religious control over a town, a city, or a small kingdom. In other words, the *Ragaḷegaḷu* stories convey a sense that there is a considerable public capital involved in religiously "owning" a town's temple, and the Śaraṇas are after this capital. For Harihara, the Śaraṇas need to dominate the public arena of the temple in a manner that echoes the ancient agonistic framework of battling over the fruits of the Vedic sacrifice, with a single winner in the religious contest over the prize—in this case the temple itself.[18]

The definite moment that signals the conversion of the temple's sectarian identity in Harihara's narratives is captured visually in the triumphant image of the Jina statue smashed to the ground and the *liṅga* erected in its place.[19] In contrast to the considerable investment of the Śaraṇa in winning over the temple, its physical conversion is evidently minimal, simply revolving around the replacement of the image that resides in the temple's inner chamber (*garbhagṛha*) from that of the Jina to that of the *liṅga*.[20] Other than this major symbolic change, the temple remains in the stories as it was before the conversion, both in appearance and in function.[21]

---

18. See Ben-Herut (2012, 138–40) for a discussion about verbal debate as an agon. For a reading of the Vedic ritual as agonistic, see Heesterman (1985).

19. Epigraphical descriptions of conversions of Jain temples to Śaiva ones also highlight the smashing of the Jina statues (Kalaburgi 2010 [1998], 39–43).

20. The literary "technique" for converting a Jain temple by replacing the Jina image with a *liṅga* mirrors Jain stories with the inverted conversion from *liṅgas* to Jina images (Granoff 2009, 7–14).

21. Julia A. B. Hegewald (2015), who studied the archeology/architecture of converted temples in Karnataka and elsewhere, identifies the replacement of the main sacred icon as the most important (though not the only) feature in the temples' conversion (p. 242). Later in the chapter, Hegewald writes that in the conversion of Jain temples to Śaiva hands in the Kannada-speaking region "the temple structures were not normally strongly damaged, and even Jain figural representations were usually not completely destroyed or removed . . . The

There are other indications in the *Ragaḷegaḷu* of the architectural and functional similarities between Jain and Śaiva temples. When Ēkānta Rāmayya, a fervent devotee often mentioned in epigraphical and literary sources, arrives at the outskirts of the city of Abbalūru, he is heartened by the sight of what he thinks are Śaiva temples. Upon entering the city, however, he discovers to his distress that all these temples are, in fact, Jain. His initial joy is immediately replaced with an abysmal dismay, and this dismay provides the moral impetus and narrative logic for the unfolding story, which culminates in the conversation of the city's Jain temples to Śaiva temples.[22] Here, the narrative logic behind Rāmayya's dramatic misidentification of the temples relies on the physical similarities between the temples of the two traditions. It also conveys a deeper recognition of the potential for the Jain temple to "transform" or, more simply, operate as a Śaiva temple. In another story, the Jain temple's doors are closed shut from within by Śiva himself, while the Jain community gathers outside, unable to enter.[23] This scene, with the temple being Jain on the outside and Śaiva on the inside, illustrates the fact that temples have a real and impending potential to quickly switch their sectarian affiliation, to "turn Śaiva."

In the Ragaḷe about Rāmayya, as in the other *Ragaḷegaḷu* stories that involve conflict with Jains, the considerable affinity between the traditions remains in the background and is never made explicit. At the explicit level, the Jains are completely separate. They are the ultimate religious other. As in the case of the Ragaḷe about Bommatande, the Ragaḷe about Rāmayya is imbued with harsh and demeaning language aimed against the Jains. For example, expressions such as "sick dog" (*huḷita kunni*) and "Śiva offender" (*śivadrōhi*) appear frequently. At the same time, despite suggestions of physical violence in the story, such as the powerful image of Rāmayya recovering his detached head and immediately thereafter waving his sword in the air and cursing the Jains, this Ragaḷe does not make

---

preservation of Jain imagery in absorbed religious structures was employed as a sign of victory, as a reminder that the Liṅgāyats had been triumphant and that they had brought to an end the long ruling Jaina elite of the area" (p. 261). Finally, Hegewald claims that the visual image of the standing *liṅga* atop semi-broken but still identifiable Jain residue "underlines and accentuates its [i.e., the edifice's] forcible expropriation and conversion" (p. 262).

22. I have dealt in great detail with the story about Rāmayya, including Harihara's version in the *Ēkāntarāmitandeya Ragaḷe*, in Ben-Herut (2012).

23. The *Dārṛhyatābhaktirasāmṛta*, an Oriya text from the eighteenth century, makes a similar use of the closed-door trope (Smith 2000, 213).

reference to actual direct violence against the Jains. In sum, the Ragaḷe about Rāmayya contains sectarian themes we have already observed in the life of Bommatande, specifically with regard to an absolute and consuming resistance to the Jains, but in the case of Rāmayya the conflict is played out in the more specific setting of the temple and without mention of physical violence.

The Ragaḷe about Ādayya tells the story of the conversion of a Jain temple to a Śaiva one in the city of Puligere.[24] The rich epigraphy and architecture found in this town attest to its historical importance as the religious center of several traditions over many centuries, from before the turn of the first millennium CE and onward.[25] Archeological evidence indicates that during the city's earlier period there was a significant Jain presence which, apparently around the twelfth or thirteenth centuries, was replaced by Śaiva control of the city. It is possible that the historical shift of the city's control from Jains to Śaivas is reflected in the Śaiva literature about Ādayya. In any case, the story of Ādayya's conversion of the temple from Jain to Śaiva is commemorated through inscriptions and carvings found today at the temple grounds. While most of the temple's iconography is markedly Śaiva, one image of a sitting Jina can be found on the temple's outer wall, perhaps a remnant of the site's Jain past.[26]

Harihara's narration of Ādayya's story was followed by later versions written by other Śaiva authors, including Harihara's nephew, the celebrated poet Rāghavāṅka, who further developed Harihara's Ragaḷe about Ādayya into a complete literary work called the *Sōmanātha Cāritra*. Because its theme is useful for the discussion I develop in the remainder of this chapter, I provide here a lengthy summary of the *Ragaḷegaḷu* version of the story.[27]

---

24. Puligere is sometimes referred to as Huligere and today known as Lakṣmēśvara or Lakshmeshwar, located in the Gadag district of north Karnataka.

25. The breadth of cultural artifacts about Puligere is such that these materials merit a comprehensive and independent study. For our purposes, it suffices to refer to the mentioning of Puligere as one of the four centers of Kannada culture in the important ninth-century treatise on poetics, the *Kavirājamārga*, in verse 1.37.

26. The site was visited by the author of this book on June 21, 2014. Kalaburgi's monograph about Śivaśaraṇas of the Kannada-speaking region that are mentioned in epigraphy does not mention Ādayya (Kalaburgi 1970). It is possible that at the time of the monograph's writing the archeological findings on the site had not yet been completed by the Archaeological Survey of India (ASI).

27. The name of this Ragaḷe is *Ādayyana Ragaḷe*.

The narrative commences in Kailāsa, with a chief attendant of Śiva and a divine damsel looking at each other and immediately falling in love. Observing this, Śiva lovingly announces that he has decided to send the two to earth so they can consummate their desires there. In response to their protests, Śiva offers another reason for sending them to earth: on earth there are very haughty Jains, and the attendants must do something to stop them.[28] In accordance with Śiva's wish, the chief attendant is born to a family of faithful Śivabhaktas. He is named Ādayya, and Śiva Sōmanātha is his only guru. At the age of sixteen, Ādayya starts to work with his father, who is a successful merchant. After a brief period of time, the father hands Ādayya sixteen thousand gold coins and sends him to the bustling cities of Puligere and Aṇṇigere in order to become established as a businessman there.[29] Meanwhile, in Puligere, the divine damsel has been born to a Jain family of temple priests. She is named Padmāvati, a common Jain name. When Ādayya enters Puligere and sees the multitude of Jain temples and monasteries (*basadis*), he becomes very angry. Ādayya decides to make the local Śiva temple his home and starts trading and making good profits in that city.

While walking the streets of Puligere, Ādayya sees Padmāvati and is completely captivated by her appearance. Padmāvati gazes back at him, and they fall in love with each other. They marry and live together happily for many days at the house of Padmāvati's family of Jain priests. One day, while taking a stroll near a pond outside the city, the young couple meet three wandering ascetics. They wear the Śaiva prayer beads (*rudrākṣa*) and are smeared with holy ash (*bhasma*), but all three of them look distressed. Ādayya prostrates himself before them and asks the reason for their dejection. The ascetics reply that they arrived in Puligere the previous day and immediately were nauseated by finding in it so many Jain temples and, inside them, naked dolls. Since the three ascetics refuse to take food from filthy Jains, they have eaten nothing since the previous day. On hearing this, Ādayya is overwhelmed with frustration and anger, but Padmāvati immediately offers to cook food for the ascetics.

---

28. One manuscript replaces the injunction "stop them" (*nilisute*) with "educate them" (*śikṣisi*). See *Ādayyana Ragaḷe* 1.26–27 in Harihara and Suṅkāpura (1976, 312).

29. Puligere and Aṇṇigere are mentioned as pilgrimage sites visited by Ēkānta Rāmayya in the Ragaḷe about him. Since Ādayya is considered the one who made Puligere a Śaiva center, it appears that, in this literary world, he preceded Rāmayya.

A short while later and back in the city, Padmāvatī's father invites some Jain monks (described by Harihara as lowly, ignorant, and naked) to his house, where he plans to feed them. But when the Jains arrive, he realizes the food he has made will not be sufficient to feed them all. His wife suggests that they use the food prepared by their daughter for the Śaiva ascetics at the lake. The parents call Padmāvati and ask her to give them the food she has cooked. She refuses, but the father snatches the food from her and gives it to the Jains. As Ādayya approaches his in-laws' house with the three ascetics and sees the Jain monks, he immediately senses that something is wrong. Padmāvati tells him what has happened and offers to cook another meal for the Śaiva ascetics. Ādayya, now fuming, refuses his wife's offer. He thinks to himself: "Killing her, chopping to pieces her father, and hacking the monks to death will not satisfy the ascetics' hunger."[30] He takes the ascetics to the market, where he buys them some fruit and sends them away. Then, upon returning home, he refuses to eat and declares an unbroken fast (*upavāsa*) until he can cut off the heads of the Jains. Facing Padmāvatī's parents, he extends the vow by swearing he will not eat until he brings Śiva Sōmanātha from Saurāṣṭra (in today's Gujarat) to Puligere and places him in the Jain temple run by his wife's family of priests. Padmāvati promptly declares that she will join her husband in making a vow to fast, and Ādayya sets out toward Saurāṣṭra. He walks for many days, indifferent to hunger and to the conditions of the weather, his body bruised and bleeding from the rough road. After twenty-eight days, Ādayya faints at the foot of a wood-apple tree.[31] Śiva Sōmanātha pities Ādayya and appears before him, disguised as an old Śaiva, wearing the sacrificial sacred thread and holding in his hands an umbrella and a begging bowl. After a brief conversation between Ādayya and the old Śaiva, the latter reveals his true form to Ādayya and transports the Bhakta back to Puligere.

When Ādayya opens his eyes, he sees Padmāvati before him. She is ecstatic at his return and orders ritual food (*bōna*) to be prepared for him. But Ādayya refuses to eat until Śiva himself arrives in the city the following day and breaks the Jina statue inside the Jain temple. When the Jain women around Padmāvati hear this, they immediately run to tell

30. *Ādayyana Ragaḷe* 2.prose in Harihara and Suṅkāpura (1976, 322): *ivaḷaṃ kondaḍaṃ paṇḍitanaṃ khaṇḍisidaḍaṃ ruṣiyaraṃ tuṇḍisidaḍaṃ tapōdhanaraṃ taṇipidantāgadenutaṃ.*

31. The wood-apple tree is called *bella* in Kannada and *bilva* in Sanskrit. Its leaves, called *bellavatta* in Kannada and *bilvapattra* in Sanskrit, are used for worshiping Śiva.

Padmāvati's father the disturbing news. Knowing well the character of his son-in-law, the father, accompanied by other Jains, appears the next morning at the entrance of the family's Jain temple. But when Padmāvati's father attempts to open the temple doors, he is surprised to find them sealed shut from within. As mentioned earlier, all the Jains are locked out. After Ādayya and Padmāvati arrive together at the temple and are able to open the doors, everyone is amazed to see that inside the temple stands Śiva Sōmanātha together with his bull Nandi. All the Jina statues inside are broken. Standing inside the temple, Ādayya goes into ecstasy and, incapable of uttering words, he begins to shout incessantly. Śiva approaches Ādayya, embraces him, and brings him back to his senses. Then he orders Ādayya to rescue Śivabhakti by slaying all the lowly (*kṣudra*) Jains.[32] He places in Ādayya's hands thirty-two weapons and orders one of his own attendants to assist Ādayya in the killing. Outside the temple stand one hundred thousand Jains. Ādayya warns them not to go into the temple, but they insist on seeing Śiva Sōmanātha up close and attempt to enter. Those who resist Ādayya are killed by him and those who seek refuge from him are saved. With the assistance of Śiva's attendant, Ādayya kills thirty-two thousand Jains and then returns the weapons to Śiva. According to Harihara, this holy place (*tīrtha*) was later named "Sword" (*khaḍga*) in commemoration of the battle.[33] Meanwhile, a flowered chariot descends from heaven and takes Ādayya and Padmāvati to Kailāsa, to the sounds of the cheering Śivabhaktas and the wailing Jains, and to the general amazement of the city's people. In Kailāsa, Ādayya is happily received by Śiva and regains his status as a Śiva attendant.

The similarities between Ādayya's and Rāmayya's stories as they are told in the *Ragaḷegaḷu* provide a conceptual framework for how Harihara presents the combat with Jains over public spaces. Despite the dramatic twists and turns in the plots of both stories, their telos clearly leads toward one climatic denouement: the public act of transferring the dominance of each city from Jain hands to Śaiva ones. To start with, the physical settings in which these stories take place are similar: like Abbalūru, Puligere is portrayed as a city in its heyday, an important commercial hub, and in both cities the affluence is connected to the dominating presence of Jains and, perhaps more important, to the Jain temples that dominate the urban

---

32. *Ādayyana Ragaḷe* 3.207–210 in Harihara and Suṅkāpura (1976, 332).

33. *Ādayyana Ragaḷe* 260 in Harihara and Suṅkāpura (1976, 334).

landscape. Harihara's choice to have Ādayya begin his retribution against the Jains with a pilgrimage to Śiva Sōmanātha's temple in Saurāṣṭra is probably not incidental. Starting in the eleventh century, this temple figured as a contested site between Jains and Śaivas in Jain literature and also served as a central battleground between various Hindu and Muslim rulers for political and economic control, and it is possible that Harihara, by alluding to this famous location, wished to tap into what was perceived by him and others as another site for Śaiva resistance against a religious other.[34]

I have discussed the agonistic framework for battling over the temple's sectarian identity, but it is instructive also to consider the emotive quality of the conflict, a quality that is an integral and central element in Harihara's narration. In both stories, the mere sight of a Jain temple pains the Śaraṇa, and there are violent implications to this emotional distress. In both cases, the Śaraṇas' basic, almost mechanical ache in response to the sight of Jain temples sets the narrative stage for the clash that will follow, a clash woven around the non-Śaiva identity of the temples and their being claimed by the Śaraṇas. Ādayya is furious when he enters Puligere and sees the Jain temples. After marrying Padmāvati, he is required to share a home with her parents, who are Jain temple priests, a fact that no doubt sharpens his distress. The physically sickening effect of the Jains' control over the city's religious landscape is embodied by the three Śaiva ascetics, who tell Ādayya about their revulsion at the sight of towering Jain temples in Puligere.[35] After this, the eruption of violence against the Jain menace seems inevitable. Likewise, in the Ragaḷe about Rāmayya, the Śaiva protagonist is stricken with grief on realizing that the white temples he saw from afar towering over Abbalūru are not Śaiva as he had initially thought but Jain, and from this moment the plot progresses toward the correction of what is, from the Śaiva author's perspective, an aberration. Thus, in both stories the rivalry regarding the sectarian identity of the temple is associated with a strong emotional tone that undergirds the ensuing conflict.

34. The political history of the Sōmanātha temple is discussed in Thapar (2008, 2005); Davis (1995). The mentioning in Jain literature of Jain–Śaiva contestation in relation to this temple is discussed in Thapar (2005, 109–112). I thank Phyllis Granoff for referring me to relevant Jain literature.

35. In the Ragaḷe about Ādayya, three Śaiva ascetics become physically nauseated upon discovering so many Jain temples in the city of Puligere. Harihara writes that they felt at that moment as if they had entered a forest full of bitter neem trees, a defiled water tank, or the mouth of a tiger. See *Ādayyana Ragaḷe* 2.prose in Harihara and Suṅkāpura (1976, 320).

Furthermore, as in the Ragaḷe about Rāmayya and in other *Ragaḷegaḷu* stories surveyed here, the story about Ādayya is replete with offensive language against the Jinas and against their images, venerated by the Jains at their temples. Complete passages are dedicated to denigrating and abusing both the worshipers and the worshiped. Jina images are referred to throughout the Ragaḷe as "naked dolls" (*battaleya bombegaḷu*), and Jains as "naked on the outside" (*battaleya bāhiryaru*) and as "curs" (*kunnigaḷu*). All of them are repeatedly described as mindless, senseless, and without any control over their senses.

The temple in these stories, then, is an object over which sectarian public conflicts are played out and are also resolved, and it is emblematic of the ubiquitous religious presence of a given community in the city. It is worth recalling here the centrality of the royal court in the Ragaḷes discussed in previous chapters. Schematically, we can say that in the narrative world of the *Ragaḷegaḷu*, antagonistic Brahmins control the court while antagonistic Jains control the temple and, through it, also the city skyline.[36] It is worth recalling at this point that agents from various religious affiliations (including Jains) were most probably present and active in kings' courts at this time and place in a manner far removed from Harihara's neatly fashioned literary presentation.

Jains as Śaivas' Spouses

A central theme of the Ragaḷe about Ādayya, in addition to the communal clash and its culmination at the temple, is the personal relationship between Ādayya, a zealous Śaiva, and his wife Padmāvati, a daughter to a family of Jain priests. This intimate relationship begins, according to Harihara, in the protagonists' prenatal career as Śiva's attendants in the divine world, and is harmoniously extended to their worldly existence, which culminates in their return to Śiva's abode, Kailāsa. The love story between the two heavenly attendants is pivotal to the whole story. The entire first chapter and half of the text celebrates the powerful and erotic love that binds together the two young lovers on earth.[37] The Śaiva sanctity

36. On Jain control over the city skyline in the *Ēkāntarāmitandeya Ragaḷe*, see Ben-Herut (2012, 149, 164–65).

37. This part of the story, including the lovers' infatuation in Kailāsa and the erotic descriptions of their union on earth, is very similar to the Ragaḷe about Allama Prabhu and Kāmalate. In that story, the lovers' erotic union and its abrupt termination with the sudden death of

that underlies Ādayya's and Padmāvatī's human incarnation is, perhaps, more significant in the case of the female, because she is born to a family that is, from the author's perspective, of the ultimate others, the vile Jains, and—even worse—Jain temple priests. Using Padmāvatī's family as pivot, the plot takes a sharp turn from a young couple's intimate love story to a public and communal clash between the Śaivas and Jains of Puligere.

It is difficult to overlook the contrast between Harihara's favoring of the character of Padmāvati and the negative rendering of all the other Jains in the story, including the particularly menacing role given to her own parents, who belong to a family of priests that run a central Jain temple called Surahonne in Puligere.[38] Padmāvatī's parents are the instigators of the violent conflict through their provocative and unfair use of food that was prepared specifically for the Śaiva ascetics. In sharp contrast, Padmāvati is portrayed by Harihara as an intimate companion and faithful supporter of Ādayya's specifically Śaiva agenda. In terms of religious identities, Padmāvati in this Ragaḷe is an anomaly; she does not conform to the otherness attributed to the Jain community as a whole. She is marked by the author as ethically superior even before her birth by virtue of having lived in Kailāsa, and her divine origin colors her entire human life. Throughout the story, the author stresses the categorical difference between Padmāvati and her family. When describing Padmāvatī's birth to a Jain family, he uses the stock metaphor of a lotus growing out of a pond of mud to distinguish Padmāvatī's purity from the "genetic" ignobility of her Jain family.[39] Later in the story, Padmāvati is repeatedly depicted as chaste and faithful to her husband, fully in accord with his dedicated devotion to Śiva, and whenever she is required to choose between allegiance to her Śaiva husband and her own Jain family, she sides with her husband. She always cooperates with the wishes and demands of her fervent husband (by cooking food for the three Śaraṇas, by taking a vow to fast together with Ādayya, and by escorting him to the "showdown" at the Jain temple), and she persistently resists the malevolent intentions of her own family members (she refuses to hand over the food she cooked for the Śaraṇas, and she does not warn her family of her husband's intention to attack and convert the Jain

---

Kāmalate serves as the backdrop for Allama's spiritual recovery as a wandering Śaiva ascetic. See *Prabhudēvara Ragaḷe* in Harihara and Suṅkāpura (1976, 3–20).

38. *Surahonne* is the Kannada name for the Alexandrian laurel flower.

39. *Ādayyana Ragaḷe* 1.136–37 in Harihara and Suṅkāpura (1976, 315): *aruhantada pāpada koggesaroḷu | paṅkajadantire puṭṭidaḷ olaviṃ.*

temple the next day). In accordance with Padmāvatī's benevolent role, it is only fitting that in the story's aftermath she enters Kailāsa together with Ādayya and regains her divine status. This is a clear and final indication of the absolute legitimization of Padmāvati by the author, despite her having been a Jain on earth.

Harihara's rendering of Padmāvatī's character complicates the sectarian picture presented in the *Ragaḷegaḷu* story. Put plainly, we are faced with the challenge of reconciling the text's hostility toward Jain identity in general and the text's favorable treatment of Padmāvati, who is also a Jain. If Jainhood, the quality of being Jain, categorically implies vileness for Harihara, how could it also sanction such a saintly person? Related questions follow: How could romantic intimacy between a Śaiva and a Jain, who is considered totally other, even be imagined by Harihara? And how could such an ideal couple be conceptualized in light of the infinite chasm existing between the two communities, a chasm that is vociferously described by the author as being unbridgeable?

One key to answering these questions is the domestic setting in which the love between Ādayya and Padmāvati is lived out. When he marries Padmāvati, Ādayya shifts his home from Śiva's temple to the house of Ādayya's family, who run a Jain temple. Interactions between the Śaraṇa and the Jain household members other than his wife are evidently volatile: when religious boundaries are crossed, intimate coexistence is instantly replaced by aggressive antagonism.[40] But for the clash to erupt—and here I return to the search for a possible understanding of how to accommodate Padmāvatī's sanctity with Harihara's ideological antipathy toward Jains—the story must assume some sort of coexistence within interreligious marriage. The story's basic structuring depicts a society in which interreligious co-living is not an exotic choice but a daily reality. We are told of the spontaneous and unhindered love story between two youngsters, one an ardent Śaiva who lives in the local Śaiva temple and the other a Jain whose family runs a central Jain temple. Until the cataclysmic conflict around the issue of sacred food, we are not told of any social, familial, or religious discord affecting this complex relationship. Up to the point in which the narrative takes a dramatic turn, the young couple lives at the house of the bride's parents, a Jain house, and Harihara does not report any complications or problems caused either by the bride's parents

40. A similar telos also controls medieval Jain stories about intermarriages with Śaivas (Granoff 2009).

or by her spouse (despite his entrenched antipathy toward the city's Jain temples). Thus, even though Harihara clearly sets up interreligious co-living as a stage for the inevitable religious clash, it is equally clear that the actual practice of interreligious co-living is not considered, in itself, to be anything extraordinary or transgressive in this literary world.

The Ragaḷe dedicated to a female devotee (Bhakte) called Vaijakavve and her Jain husband Nēmiseṭṭi also foregrounds the ubiquitousness of interreligious marriage side by side with conflict over the temple and its ultimate conversion from Jain to Śaiva.[41] This Ragaḷe combines personal and communal aspects into an effective narrative, and the convergence can be seen, from an analytical point of view, as completing Ādayya's story. A girl is born to an auspicious Śaiva family in an auspicious Śaiva town (*śivapura*). Her name is Vaijakavve. She is extremely beautiful and also a faithful follower of Śiva. When her father's sister, who is married to a Jain, comes for a visit and sees her niece's exceptional beauty, she decides she wants the girl to marry her son Nēmiseṭṭi. However, Vaijakavve's father refuses. He says to his sister: "Nēmiseṭṭi might be a fine person, but I will not marry a Bhakte of Śiva to a worldling, a Jain cur."[42] The sister is not deterred by this answer and declares that she will fast unto death if the girl's father will not agree to the marriage. The father's relatives press him to comply with his sister's wish, pointing to the familial relations, their shared origins (same *gōtra*, or tribe), and the horrible alternative of being responsible for his own sister's death of starvation. The father finally yields and wedding arrangements are made, including consulting an astrologer for an auspicious date for the wedding.

Vaijakavve, however, is depressed at the prospect of marrying a Jain and cries out to Śiva, asking how she can continue worshiping him inside a Jain house. Śiva appears to her in a dream and promises not to abandon her in her married life. After four days of wedding celebrations, the young couple moves into the husband's family house. In her new home Vaijakavve is like light within great darkness, like a sandalwood tree among shrubs. She worships Śiva secretly: her heart is the temple, her breath is the ritual lamp. She adjusts to her new Jain environment but at the same time is completely detached from it. She is simultaneously present and absent.

---

41. The name of this Ragaḷe is *Vaijakavveya Ragaḷe*.

42. *Vaijakavveya Ragaḷe* vv. 39–40 in Harihara and Suṅkāpura (1976, 228): . . . *bhavige kuḍenu / mṛḍana bhaktar āvu savaṇagunnigaḷige heṇṇa kuḍenu.*

One day, Nēmiseṭṭi returns home and tells Vaijakavve to cook food for some Jain sages (*ṛṣis*) who will be coming to stay as guests in their house. Vaijakavve obeys her husband and prepares many delicious dishes. While cooking, she suddenly bursts into tears, crying out to Śiva that she would have liked this food to have been consumed by Śivabhaktas or by Śiva himself and not by "Jain curs."[43] Śiva hears her cry and immediately appears in her house disguised as a Bhakta beggar asking for food. Happy to fulfill the Śivabhakta's request, Vaijakavve starts filling the beggar's bowl with the food she has made for the Jain ascetics but, surprisingly, no matter how much food she puts in the Śivabhakta's bowl, it cannot be filled. Vaijakavve continues ladling into the bowl the food prepared for the Jain ascetics until it almost runs out. The Bhakta eats with great appetite, but just before Nēmiseṭṭi returns home with the group of Jains, the Bhakta suddenly disappears. When the Jains discover that their food has been eaten by another, they refuse to eat what is left and instead angrily leave the house.[44] Nēmiseṭṭi is furious that his wife has ruined his Jain vow by spoiling the food with a Śivabhakta's touch. Vaijakavve responds by saying that the whole world is purified by Śiva's touch and that it is madness to worship useless and naked dolls. When Nēmiseṭṭi hears this, he loses all control of himself and beats his wife.

That night, as Vaijakavve lies bruised and aching in her bed, Śiva again appears to her in a dream and promises her that on the following morning he will smash the head of the Jina in the Jain temple. In the morning, as the Jains arrive at their temple to pray, they find its doors locked. They cannot get in, even though they try everything—even an elephant—to try to open the doors. They infer that the Jina inside the temple is refusing to open the doors because of ethical misconduct or some past act of violence committed by a member of the Jain community. At that moment, Nēmiseṭṭi steps forward and admits that he lost his temper the previous night and brutally beat his wife. The whole community goes to Vaijakavve's house to ask her forgiveness. They also ask her to come to the temple with them so that the Jina will agree to open the doors. Vaijakavve respectfully

---

43. This is a summary of *Vaijakavveya Ragaḷe* vv. 159–62 in Harihara and Suṅkāpura (1976, 232). In one manuscript the word *kunni* ("cur") in verse 162 is replaced with *saṅgi* ("a member of a society"), which might be an attempt to neutralize Harihara's offending language.

44. Jain ascetics are supposed to eat only leftovers and food not prepared especially for them. The anomaly here could be read as another criticism of Jains' lax practices, as lay families do cook extra for monks and often feed them the food first before the family eats.

yields to their request but adds that the Jina has nothing to do with this issue; in fact, it is Śiva himself who now resides in the temple after having broken the Jina statue and it is he who is preventing them from entering the temple. Like a kingly goose among crows, Vaijakavve walks with the Jains to the temple and, after she extols the praises of Śiva at the entrance, the doors open. Inside, they all find the Jina shattered and a shining *liṅga* standing in its place. Unable to bear the shame of this, all the Jain leaders (*ṛṣi*s and *paṇḍita*s) leave the temple. Vaijakavve is shivering with ecstatic happiness as her husband Nēmiseṭṭi falls at her feet, begging for her forgiveness. Vaijakavve forgives him, smears holy ashes on his forehead, and initiates him into the Śaiva faith. She orders her husband to make a heap of dirt. He obeys her and a *liṅga* arises from it. This *liṅga* is named *vaijanātha*, "Vaija's Lord." A heavenly chariot descends from the sky and takes Vaijakavve to Kailāsa. Śiva speaks of her greatness to Pārvati and transforms Vaijakavve into one of Pārvati's attendants.

Structurally, the story of Vaijakavve contains elements familiar to us from the story of Ādayya: a Śaiva and a Jain are married and live together at the house of the Jain spouse's parents.[45] Then, a sacred and festive meal is prepared by the woman of the house in order to feed ascetics, but the food is consumed by ascetics of the "competing" religion, leaving the husband frustrated and angry.[46] In both cases, the husband reacts to the provocation with an act of violence that leads to the changeover of a temple from Jain to Śaiva. The stories describe the temple transformation in a similar manner, with the blocking of the entrance to the temple, the smashing of the Jina statues, and the uncanny appearance of *liṅga*s in their stead. Finally, in both stories we find conversions of Jains, though in Ādayya's story this conversion is embedded in a gruesome bloodbath that is absent from Vaijakavve's story.

But despite the structural similarities, a comparison of the two narratives also reveals significant differences. While the Ragaḷe about Ādayya presents a clear distinction between the private realm (a married couple) and the communal realm (a violent sectarian conflict), the story about Vaijakavve interweaves the two realms in a more complex manner: Vaijakavve is forced into the marriage; she tries to uphold her

45. In this story, the newlyweds are also cousins. In many south-Indian communities, the practice of cross-cousin marriage is common.

46. See discussion and additional references regarding the role of the female in hospitality in Pechilis (2008, 23).

married life while practicing her Śaiva faith in secret; the sectarian conflict is ignited by a domestic argument; and finally, the story's denouement highlights the personal sphere of the couple, with the conversion of Nēmiseṭṭi by his own wife. Ādayya's story betrays little interest in verbal exchanges between its characters, while the story about Vaijakavve exhibits a more pliable approach. We find in her story some indications of intercommunal dialogue (such as the theological argument between husband and wife) and the possibility of redemption for the worldly Jain (such as the Jains' repentance, starting on the communal level, moving to Nēmiseṭṭi's personal confession of hitting his wife, and culminating with his conversion to Śaivism). Obviously, things are less violent in this Ragaḷe than in Ādayya's, in which Jains are described as cowering on their knees, begging for their lives to be spared. Vaijakavve's story prescribes a form of resistance to Jainism that is much less violent and more geared toward argumentation, initiation, and redemption, elements that are played down in all the other *Ragaḷegaḷu* stories that involve Jains.

I use the word "resistance" and, indeed, life at the Jain house of her husband is not easy for Vaijakavve and requires resistance. She cannot worship Śiva openly but rather is forced to worship him in secret. The motif of secrecy reminds us of the general shift away from the external and toward the internal that is typical of Kannada Śivabhakti. While external forms of ritual are never discouraged in the *Ragaḷegaḷu,* in this literary world the focus is on the devotees' emotional interiority.[47] The story ends with an ironic twist when Vaijakavve's inability to overtly worship Śiva at the Jain home is transposed in a public celebration of Śaiva worship at the Jain temple grounds.

But resistance to Jainism is played out also on the ethical level, with Harihara's ridiculing of Jain ethics. When the Jains realize that their temple's doors are sealed from within, they begin scrutinizing their recent conduct in search for an ethical violation committed by one of their own, a fault that might explain the Lord Jina's refusal to open the temple to the community. Nēmiseṭṭi promptly comes forward and admits that he has violated *ahiṃsā,* the Jain prohibition of exercising violence, by beating his wife the previous night. The Jain community then assumes that it was this act that caused the Jina to lock them out of the temple. They decide to ask for Vaijakavve's forgiveness in order for her to absolve Nēmiseṭṭi.

---

47. See Chapter 2.

This vignette might be read at first as exhibiting or even promulgating support of Jain ethics, especially nonviolence. A reconsideration of the incident in light of the narrative's setting and its aftermath, however, reveals Harihara's sarcasm, specifically when the Jains' diagnosis and understanding turn out to be utterly wrong. It is not the Jina who refuses to open the temple's door for the Jains but Śiva, after he has entered the Jain temple and smashed the Jina image. Furthermore, what finally leads to the opening of the temple's doors is not the absolving of Nēmiseṭṭi's violence but Vaijakavve's public adulation of Śiva at the gates of the Jain temple. Thus, rather than supporting the Jain ethical framework of nonviolence, Harihara ridicules it.

Food Contestations

As in Ādayya's story, what ignites the conflict in Vaijakavve's story is food, or more specifically, the domestic feeding of ascetics. In Chapter 4 I discussed the fact that commensality and communal feeding can serve as an important area for constructing and asserting religious identity. In the stories discussed there, the sharing of food marked the boundaries of the Śaiva community from within. But the feeding of ascetics can also be an arena for interreligious conflict. This leitmotif is found also in other South Asian devotional traditions.[48] In the affiliated Śaiva tradition in the Tamil area, food practices are invoked in anti-Jain writings a few centuries earlier in the devotional poetry of the Tamil Śaiva saints Appar and Campantar.[49] In those writings, Śaiva food-related criticism of Jains revolves mainly around which food is consumed (and which is forbidden) and the manner in which the food is consumed.[50]

The Śaiva attack on Jain dietary practices in our stories has similarities with that found in the Tamil texts but is not identical to it, for the relevant Ragaḷes focus only on *who* consumes the food.[51] For Ādayya, a Śaiva ritual feeding is thwarted by hungry Jains, and the result, according to Harihara,

48. Keune (2014, 7); Pauwels (2010, 531–34); Glushkova (2005).

49. Monius (2011, 155); Ulrich (2007, 243–52); Peterson (1998, 171).

50. Ulrich (2007, 230). In addition, Tamil Śaivas ridicule the Jain practices of using both hands for eating, naked dining (by certain Jain renouncers), fasting by night, and eating in silence (ibid., pp. 241, 243, 251). Jain dietary practices are highly restrictive (Williams 1963, 39–41, 107–16). See also Singh (1975, 87–89); Dundas (2002, 176–77).

51. None of the restrictions and rules mentioned in the previous footnote with regard to the Tamil culture are described in these Ragaḷes, despite the fact that, as mentioned in

can be nothing short of violent, consuming retaliation. This pattern is inverted in Vaijakavve's case, when food prepared for Jain ascetics is consumed by Śiva, dressed as a Śaiva ascetic. The contrast between the foci of the Tamil and the Kannada Śaiva criticism of Jain food practices brings to the fore Harihara's central concerns in this matter. In the two Ragaḷes we have been discussing, Harihara ignores the type of food prepared for the renouncers of either tradition as well as the religious affiliation of the person who prepares the food to be consumed by the renouncers. In both stories, the wife who prepares the food in response to her husband's request is situated on the "wrong" side of the religious boundary: in Ādayya's story, it is Padmāvati the Jain who prepares food for the Śaiva renouncers, and in Vaijakavve's story, it is Vaijakavve the Śaiva who prepares food for the Jain renouncers. Juxtaposing these scenes from the two Ragaḷes points to an underlying sense of competition between the two communities with regard to ritualistic food. In both stories, the wrong side of the religious barricade is the first to reach the food, and this transgression results in a public conflict.

Alienating an Intimate Rival

The disturbing descriptions of gory violence and more generally the deliberate resistance to ordinary coexistence with the religious other in the *Ragaḷegaḷu* stories raise obvious questions in terms of Harihara's lesson for his intended audience: What is the author's purpose in presenting this violent, outlandish imaginaire? How were these violent stories meant to be understood in their original settings? And how were they understood? Harihara is not exceptional among southern Śivabhakti authors in harboring inimical attitudes toward Jains. A cursory overview of the Tamil Śaiva literary tradition reveals a consistently aggressive tone with regard to Jains. We find anti-Jain polemics in Tamil Śaiva literature as early as the sixth century, and this theme reaches its highest point in the Tamil hagiographies of the twelfth century.[52] In both Śivabhakti traditions we find antagonism toward Jains figured around Jain practices, specifically those pertaining to issues of asceticism, purity, and food consumption, in a variety of settings. The narratives of both traditions contain episodes

---

Chapter 4, other Ragaḷes focus on the centrality of dietary practices to the emerging devotional community.

52. Champakalakshmi (2011a); Monius (2011); Peterson (1998, 164–65, 212–23).

in which Jains are violated and include depictions of rabid acts of violence, at times completely unchecked, accompanied by denigrating and dehumanizing language in reference to Jains.

In the Tamil context, scholars have argued that the orchestrated and ubiquitous antagonism toward Jains found in Śaiva devotional literature can be explained by the need for an emerging religious tradition to define its collective self by alienating the other. Richard Davis writes about the Pallava and Cōḻa periods:

> At this moment of social change, the *bhakti* poets were engaged in constructing a new sense of Tamil identity, incorporating Vedic, Saṅgam, and Śaiva values and practices, and they needed a clearly distinguishable Other to set this forth. Their rhetorical misrepresentation of Jainism gave them what they needed.[53]

The cogent insight regarding the need of a recently formed religious tradition to enhance its sense of collective self by criticizing a "distinguishable other" seems to hold also in the case of the early Kannada Śivabhakti tradition as it is reflected in Harihara's saintly narratives, although Harihara is not invested as are the Tamil Śaiva authors in casting the Jains as foreigners in the local land. The possible reasons for the difference between early medieval Tamil and Kannada perceptions of the Jain other are beyond the scope of this book and involve such issues as the role and hold of Jainism in the early medieval histories of Karnataka and Tamil Nadu and the manner in which the regional languages, literatures, and literary cultures developed in each place (individually and in relation to the pan-Indian Sanskritic literary idiom).[54] Nevertheless, a specific inquiry into Harihara's representation of Jains, while shedding light primarily on the context of the cultural history of Karnataka, can open up possibilities for thinking about religio-social interactions between Śaivas and Jains in neighboring areas as well.

When considering the ways in which the two Śaiva traditions present total opposition to Jain identity, certain differences stand out. In the Tamil *Periya Purāṇam* by Cēkkiḻār, we find competition with the Jains over royal patronage. Jains are portrayed as having access to and influence over

---

53. Davis (1998, 220). See also Peterson (1998, 165).

54. See discussion in Champakalakshmi (1978) on sources used for the historical reconstruction of Jainism in the Tamil land and in Karnataka.

kings, and the Śaivas struggle to assume their position at the court.[55] The Kannada hagiographies do not foreground that connection to polity.[56] Another striking difference between the Kannada and Tamil renderings of Jainism, perhaps related to issues having to do with the court, is the explicit linguistic chauvinism Tamil Śaiva authors express toward the Jains, who are derided for not speaking proper Tamil or Sanskrit.[57] Harihara makes no explicit contrast between Jain identity and local, language-based identity.

The absence in the *Ragaḷegaḷu* narratives of Jain influence at the court does not imply their absence from other public arenas or any sense of subalternity. On the contrary, the stories we have been discussing in this chapter portray powerful and vibrant Jain communities that have a conspicuous public presence as evidenced by economic activity, religious festivals, and large temple edifices. In the Ragaḷe dedicated to the life of Bāhūra Bommatande, a devotee who goes every Monday to visit Śiva's temple in Kalyāṇa, we find an illuminating illustration of this.[58] One Monday, while passing the market on his way to the temple, Bommatande hears a Jain grain-vendor calling out the name of a particular grain called *śaṅkaragaṇḍa*. Bommatande understands the Jain's shouting as offensive to Śiva.[59] Furious, Bommatande calls the Jain a cur and circumambulates the pile of grain as if it were a sacred icon for Śiva. Thereupon, a deep *ōṃ* sound emanates from the pile, confirming Bommatande's faith in the god. When Bommatande finally arrives at the temple, other devotees praise him as the "Terrible Scorcher of the Family of Other Divinities."[60] The market

55. Champakalakshmi (2011a, 439, 444; 2011b, 109–110); Peterson (1998, 177–82); Davis (1998). Karen Pechilis historicizes this arch-narrative by arguing that the early *mūvar*'s hymns, with some similarity to the Kannada texts discussed here, located Jains at centers other than the court (1999, 76).

56. The Ragaḷes that involve Jain figures never mention or imply royal affinities, with the exception of the Ragaḷe about Kōvūra Bommatande, a local ruler of sorts. Compare Harihara's silence regarding the king in the Ragaḷe about Rāmayya with the king's central role in the inscription's version, especially his availability for and close connections with Abbalūru's Jain community (Ben-Herut 2012).

57. Peterson (1998, 172–73).

58. The following is a summary of the first chapter of the *Bāhūra Bommatandeya Ragaḷe* in Harihara and Suṅkāpura (1976, 404–7).

59. "*Śaṅkaragaṇḍa*" literally means "the prowess of Śiva." It is another name for a type of millet called *joḷa*, used in Śaiva rituals (Prasād 2001, 1191 s.v. *śaṅkaragaṇḍa*).

60. *Bāhūra Bommatandeya Ragaḷe* 1.103 in Harihara and Suṅkāpura (1976, 406): *paradaivasantānatimira bhāskaran*.

in this incident, in contrast to the court discussed with regard to Vaiṣṇava Brahmins, is an open space in which members of different communities from different strands of society meet and engage in quotidian, unofficial interactions. In the text there are also other locations—apart from the religiously marked arena of the temple—in which spontaneous encounters between Śaivas and Jains occur, namely forests and domestic spaces.[61] Conversely, the setting of the court is only rarely associated with Jains in the *Ragaḷegaḷu*. It seems that, at least in Harihara's mind, Jains are not directly linked to the palace and the sovereign as the Brahmins are. Rather, Jains are found in more immediate, non-elite, and quotidian places.[62] In a way, the Jains in the *Ragaḷegaḷu* are a more conspicuous and present religious other than the Vaiṣṇava Brahmins, at least from a communal point of view, since the Brahmins are mostly associated with the elites who run the state.

The quotidian nature of the locales in which conflicts with Jains unfold in the *Ragaḷegaḷu* also sheds light on a clearly felt disconnect between the text's overt othering of Jains and its simultaneous oblique portrayal of structured, daily, and intimate social engagements between the two religious groups. The stories portray a socio-religious competition between Jains and Śaivas over festivals, market trading practices, and temple ownership.[63] Within these spaces, each community asserts its presence through a specific set of cultural signifiers, and the competing community strives to replace these with its own. What is perhaps most striking in this tight competition is the considerable parallelism in the text's configuration of the two communities. This parallelism is evident in various areas of social life, including nonreligious areas such as occupations, guilds, and cultural events. Examples that illustrate this include the fact that the suffix "*seṭṭi*," a Kannada derivation of the Sanskrit *śrēṣṭhin* that denotes a rich, high-class merchant, is used in the *Ragaḷegaḷu* to name both Śivabhaktas and Jains;[64] a Śaiva festival is challenged by a Jain festival; and a temple Jina image

61. On marketplaces and their connection to religious communities in late medieval Bengal, see Urban (2001); Sen (1996).

62. Although the palace is a central arena for contestation with Jains in Bommatande's Ragaḷe, it lacks the political configurations that are common to all the Ragaḷes about Brahmins serving at the king's court.

63. See Pechilis (1999, 68–76) on competition over resources between Śaivas and Jains in the Tamil land.

64. Vaijakavve's Jain husband is named Nēmiseṭṭi. An Orissa Śaiva who goes to see Basavaṇṇa in the *Basavēśvaradēvara Ragaḷe* is Mahādēviseṭṭi. In the *Siriyāḷana Ragaḷe*, the

is replaced by an image of *śivaliṅga*.[65] There are also striking similarities in the behaviors of laity in both communities with regard to renouncers, particularly in behaviors that have to do with the centrality and imparted prestige of feeding and, by extension, caring for, "their" renouncers. The renouncers of the two communities behave similarly, roaming in small groups and paying visits to laypeople's houses to receive food. At a deeper level, the leitmotif of the Śaiva administrator-saint that was discussed in the previous chapter is consonant with the ethical code of relinquishing kinghood and retiring to the forest associated with preexisting Jain ethics. The idea that a woman can become a religious teacher for her husband, such as is the case with Vaijakavve, resonates more in south India with the Jain tradition than with the Śaiva tradition.[66] Even nakedness, the specifically Jain signifier that is perhaps most ridiculed by the Śaivas of the south, can also function in the *Ragaḷegaḷu* as a sanctity marker for Śaiva Śaraṇas, as in the cases of Koṇḍaguḷi Kēśirāja and Mahādēviyakka.[67] Dietary restrictions and food rituals of the two communities also appear similar (though not identical).

The narrative tension in the *Ragaḷegaḷu* narratives between the overt othering of the Jain and a daily life of coexistence peaks in domestic realms. All the stories in the corpus about interreligious marriages lead to an inevitable, cataclysmic rupture and the complete Śaiva subjugation of any Jain presence, private or public. Ādayya cannot contain the frustration and

---

Śaiva father of Siriyāḷa's daughter-in-law is named Dhanapālaśeṭṭi. (The /s/ and the /ś/ are interchangeable in some Kannada derivations).

65. See Leslie Orr (2005) for a medieval Tamil goddesses tradition that similarly crosses sectarian categories.

66. Orr (1998).

67. Both of these are described by Harihara as *kēśāmbara*, "clothed with only the hair of the head." Popular posters of Mahādēviyakka depict her long curly hair covering her exposed private parts. It is possible that Mahādēviyakka's naked imagery inspired Alanis Morissette's appearance as a naked-but-not-exposed woman saint who is wandering urban streets in the video clip of her smash hit "Thank U [India]" (2012). Compare with the naked north-Indian figure of Lal Ded, aka Lallā and Lallēśvarī (Ramaswamy 2007; Ahmed 2002) and with Mary of Egypt in saintly traditions of Eastern Christianity and in the *Golden Legend* (Voragine and Ryan 1993, 227–29). An additional and peculiar point of reference to nakedness in Harihara's text appears in the eighth chapter of the *Basavēśvaradēvara Ragaḷe*, when Basavaṇṇa honors Śaiva saints who visit him by placing silk shawls over their shoulders. The saints are described there as *digambarana śaraṇar* ("saints of the naked one") in Harihara and Suṅkāpura (1976, 61, prose). The term *digambara* is famously synonymous with the Jain tradition of the south, although in Kannada it can also mean more generally a naked person, here probably in reference to Śiva himself.

wrath induced in him by his Jain in-laws, and he replaces domestic bliss with his Jain wife with a murderous bloodbath at her family's Jain temple; Vaijakavve cannot worship Śiva freely at her in-laws' Jain house and is ruthlessly beaten by her husband when her Śaiva partiality is exposed. In another Ragaḷe, which I discussed in Chapter 3, about the celebrated Mahādēviyakka, the saint-poetess is caught in a frustrating marriage to a powerful, non-Śaiva king, and the Śaiva wife's last resort for maintaining a pious devotional life is a dramatic and problematic divorce; even in her post-marital, renunciatory stage in the Śaiva haven of Śrīśailam she cannot find shelter from her former husband, who comes chasing after her.[68] Hagiographies are dramatic by their very nature, but it seems that the Ragaḷes that have to do with the domestic other are particularly poignant. It is as if Harihara employs his most pointed narrative arsenal to refute the possibility of even imagining harmonious co-living with the religious other, one who is not a Śaiva and, more specifically, is a Jain. Here, again, a profound resonance with Jain culture emerges, with the latter tradition's own storytelling culture about intermarriages as opportunities for spousal conversions.[69]

In short, Harihara's coherent ideological stance cannot obscure descriptions of a gamut of shared interactions with Jains, not only in public arenas but also in the domestic sphere. The private, domestic space in the *Ragaḷegaḷu* stories is the site of an incredibly deep and real level of shared intimacy between Śaivas as Jains. To begin with, the practice of interreligious marriages between Śaivas and Jains is presented in the *Ragaḷegaḷu* as not uncommon.[70] After all, the stories tell about mixed families living under the same roof. Even in a literary context of hostility toward Jains, these mixed marriages seem well grounded within the boundaries of mainstream acceptability. Mahādēviyakka's parents

---

68. In contrast to later retellings of Mahādēviyakka's life, which usually present her husband as Jain, the *Mahādēviyakkana Ragaḷe* is mute regarding his religious affiliation, although he is portrayed in this text as aloof and insensitive to Mahādēviyakka's Śaiva sentiments and is often referred to by Harihara as *bhavi* ("worldling").

69. Granoff (2011). The parallels between Harihara's stories and the Jain stories discussed by Granoff run even deeper, with monks (and the requirement of the laity to feed them) as the cause for the martial rift and the wife's central role in these interactions.

70. The Śaiva/Jain familial *mélange* also figures in the life of the Tamil saint Appar, as it is told in the *Periya Purāṇam* and in the *Ragaḷegaḷu,* an indication that this practice, even if only as textually imagined, was neither remarkable nor specific to the Kannada-speaking region (Dehejia 1988, 34).

try to convince their daughter to agree to marry a non-Śaiva, saying: "In this world, what is so exceptional or difficult (*utkaṭa*) about living with a non-Śaiva?"[71] They go on to allude to famous past cases of faithful female devotees, including Vaijakavve, marrying non-Śaivas. Ādayya, an ardent Śaiva, falls in love with a Jain and freely moves into her family's house, despite the dissonance between his Śaiva bent and their being Jain priests. Vaijakavve's family already has a mixed marriage in the previous generation, and this does not threaten the family's sense of shared identity; and some relatives even argue with Vaijakavve's father about his exaggerated conservatism in refusing to marry his daughter to a Jain. Again, such conversations are significant exactly because they run completely against the author's own ideology, which strengthens the sense that Harihara writes "against" a prevalent practice of which he utterly disapproves.

Sharing space under the same roof also means sharing food and other domestic practices.[72] Harihara's description in Vaijakavve's story of an astrologer determining an auspicious date for the wedding (*muhūrtam*) suggests that Śaivas and Jains would have been using the same astrological charts.[73] Similarly, there is nothing sectarian in the wedding ceremonies and celebrations. More generally, the weddings, as they are described by Harihara, appear to be celebrated by members of both religious traditions. In other episodes, Jains accommodate Śaivas: a family of Jain temple priests takes into its home the daughter's spouse, who is a zealous Śaiva, and the Jain community of an abusive husband seeks the forgiveness of a Śaiva wife, at the couple's home. The stories allow Jain support of Śaiva interests, as in the case of Ādayya and Padmāvati. They also allow for voluntary Jain conversion into the Śaiva tradition, as with Vaijakavve and her husband Nēmiseṭṭi. There is always a narrative possibility for a Jain's change of heart and, consequently, for

71. *Mahādēviyakkana Ragaḷe* 3.178 in Harihara and Suṅkāpura (1976, 119): *vasudheyoḷu bhaviyoḍane bāḷar ēn utkaṭaṃ*.

72. R. B. P. Singh argues for a continuous Hindu influence on Jain practices and rituals in Karnataka since before the turn of the first millennium (1975, 81–82). Compare with Davis (1998, 217–18).

73. Compare with Leela Mullatti's comment that "there is no necessity to look for 'muhurta,' [*sic*] an auspicious time, for a Virasaiva [*sic*] marriage, because Basavaṇṇa says that at an auspicious act everything inevitably turns out auspicious" (1989, 33). The incongruence between this assertion and Harihara's affirmation of the *muhūrtam* demonstrates difference in understandings of Kannada Śivabhakti and its relation to orthodoxical, Brahminical religion in different historical and social contexts.

his or her acceptance into the Śaiva community. In light of this dense texture of interreligious social interaction, it seems probable to assume that the *Ragaḷegaḷu* is cast in the context of a social reality in which the two communities coexisted with some measure of healthy and ongoing cooperation or at least interaction.

Finally, it is evident that despite Harihara's tenacity in othering Vaiṣṇava Brahmins and Jains, the two groups form distinct groups of religious others in the *Ragaḷegaḷu*. The Brahmins are portrayed as an opponent other, sharing with the Śivabhakti tradition the space of the temple, scripture and canon, and even a set of core values and attitudes. At the same time, Brahmins are usually portrayed as distanced from daily life; they operate mostly at the king's court and in direct relation to his dominion. Accordingly, sectarian competition with Vaiṣṇava Brahmins mostly revolves around royal support and political capital, allocation of financial resources, or social prestige. Śaiva competition with Jains occurs in spaces that are less elitist and more publicly inclusive: in temples, for example, but also in the city's main streets and markets, as well as inside houses and in the intimate unfolding of the fabric of life in interreligious families. While the text does not acknowledge the existence of any shared grammar or system of shared cultural symbols between the Śaiva and the Jain traditions, the social spaces they occupy are intricately interwoven. Locale determines action, and the Śaraṇa is repeatedly motivated by an impulse to displace and supplant Jain control over the public landscape as well as to purge the domestic sphere of the co-presence of Jains. In the narratives that involve Jains, Harihara prescribes sectarian resistance in an interreligious society. By constructing the Jains as a wholly other, Harihara strives to untangle or—better yet, to shear through—the complex web of interreligious connections that serve as the backdrop for these stories.

Conclusion

THE PREVIOUS—AND FINAL—CHAPTER of this book ended with horrifically violent representations of conflicts with Jains, the Śivabhaktas' ultimate and most vilified other in Harihara's stories. Clearly, we have come a long way from the earlier discussions about the devotee's prescribed interiority with which this book began. And yet, the encounter with the devotee's alienated religious other also brings us full circle from the thematic starting point of this book, because the rendering of the Jains in the *Ragaḷegaḷu* involves some of the innermost human constituents: home, spouse, domestic ritual, and familial ties. It is here—in the intimate and familiar spaces of marital life, of shared consumption of food, of living under a common roof, and of other quotidian social interactions—that the competition with Jains is most fiercely expressed.

A deeper connecting thread is also evident in the *Ragaḷegaḷu* between the intensity of the devotee's interiority and the harsh manner with which he or she engages with the farthest other, and this thread is the impatient and uncompromising devotional mode that defines both. In broader terms, the refusal to come to terms with the competing religion of Jainism echoes other forms of resistance in the *Ragaḷegaḷu*: to courtly life, to the institution of the human king, to monetary pursuits and material life, to formal and empty ritualism, to purity-based discrimination, to mundane existence, even to basic morality and a sense of social propriety—anything that might stall or hinder the intense, sweeping experience involved in being immersed in Śiva worship, an experience visually presented so vividly in the image of Guṇḍayya, the passionate potter who dances ecstatically in his own backyard until the god—"in person"—descends from heaven in order to take the enthralled potter with him back to Kailāsa.

Nevertheless, as much as Harihara's characters are unyielding and hot-tempered with regard to their devotion, their life stories as presented by this author unfold in an accommodating and open religious universe. Harihara's envisioning of *bhakti* religion in the Kannada-speaking region is profoundly catholic in the sense of its acceptance of different forms of worship, behaviors, and social realities ranging from the personal to the public, the reformer to the orthodox, the Outcaste to the Brahmin. Harihara's catholicity accommodates—admittedly with some twists and turns—the householder and the renouncer, the traditionalist and the iconoclast, the privileged and the marginalized, the rich and the poor, the government minister and the craftsman, the queen and the prostitute, the priest and the ascetic, the Brahmin and the Untouchable. All are accepted into Harihara's imagined society of devotees, as long as their devotion to the god Śiva holds.

In using the phrase "twists and turns" I am alluding to the discomfort that is sometimes involved in Harihara's broad-minded approach. A close reading of the *Ragaḷegaḷu* stories about the Kannada saints leads me to postulate that Harihara was not interested in portraying a definite or monolithic religious system but instead was looking to appeal to many religious audiences, even when they belonged to different social and cultural spheres. His stories portray a tradition focused totally on worship of Śiva, with little concern for particulars relating to who does the worshiping or how it is conducted. But his stories also recognize the inner and outer conflicts that consequently arise and the social accommodations that have to be made.

In most parts of the text, the inevitable cultural, social, or even religious differences between Śaiva devotees with different backgrounds are left unaddressed, since most stories focus on the life of a single saintly figure. As mentioned, the *Ragaḷegaḷu,* in contrast to later narrative accounts of the Kannada-speaking saints (including the Telugu *Basava Purāṇamu,* which was probably composed not much later), is not constructed around one central figure but, rather, holds together distinct narrative units without any overarching ideological or formalistic organizing principle except for intense faith in Śiva. The structure of disparate stories allows Harihara to include in the *Ragaḷegaḷu* tales of saints from different cultural settings and different social backgrounds, with different practices and different approaches to worshiping Śiva, without forcing on these saints a hermetic ideological, behavioral, or communal coherence.

In specific episodes, however, such as when a poor devotee meets a wealthy devotee (Śaṅkaradāsimayya and Jēḍara Dāsimayya) or when a devotee from a low social strand cooks onion at the house of a Brahmin (Kinnara Bommatande at Basavaṇṇa's home), inevitable cultural gaps that exist between two fellow Śaivas suddenly take center stage. But even at these moments, Harihara appears to refrain from laying down a hard set of normative behaviors and seems content with plotting specific, ad hoc narrative solutions—usually in the form of miracles—to practical crises and conflicts.

In many ways, then, Harihara's catholicity differs from the way in which the essence of Vīraśaivism is perceived by many today: as a puritan sect that revolves around strict moral codes and principles and that is socially distinguishable from orthodox or other cultic forms of Śaiva religiosity. As much as this theoretical or even ideological construct does not factually correspond to the bewildering assortment of communities and individuals in the state of Karnataka and elsewhere today, collectively labeled as "Vīraśaivas" or "Liṅgāyats," it also does not fit the heterogeneous world described in the *Ragaḷegaḷu*. One possible implication of the richness of devotional life depicted in the *Ragaḷegaḷu* is that the multifaceted, real-life messiness that characterizes the Kannada Śivabhakti tradition today—such as whether it accepts or rejects temple worship, what sort of social equity it promotes, or its attitudes toward Vedic scripture and Brahminism—might have been around since a very early stage of the tradition.

Therefore, the heterogeneity of religious life in Harihara's work forces us to reconsider prevalent and oversimplified notions projected back in the form of the tradition's imagined and pristine "myth of origins." One such notion is the idea of a society made up of equals, an idea treated by Harihara with some depth and complexity. The principle of "equal conduct" (*samaśīla*), which is too often and too easily translated today as egalitarianism, is openly heralded by Harihara. But, at the same time, his stories convey a complex message about social realities, a message that runs against a facile understanding of this principle. In the *Ragaḷegaḷu* stories, equal conduct is limited only to those who have full-heartedly committed their devotional sentiment to Śiva, and it is further bounded by the arena of religious activity, namely worship of the god. Any social differentiation, discrimination, or inequity that is not directly connected to worship of this particular deity is ignored in Harihara's stories. While the devotional agency voiced in the *Ragaḷegaḷu*, according to which everyone is entitled to worship Śiva and to gain public recognition for it, is progressive and groundbreaking in comparison to the traditional and conservative Hindu religion of that time and place, it is far from being congruent with modern and Western notions of progressive and liberal social values.

Inherent in the idea of "equal conduct" as Harihara understands it is the centrality of worship in the religious lives of the devotees in the *Ragaḷegaḷu*. The importance of ritual action in the *Ragaḷegaḷu* also calls into question another simplistic notion—usually based on selective readings of the *vacanas*—of Kannada Śivabhakti as an anti-ritual, purely faith-based religion. By calling attention to ritual, I am not denying the intense focus on devotional sentiments or attitudes in Harihara's text, but simply noting that in the stories these sentiments or attitudes are always expressed and visibly affirmed through some kind of action, most often ritual action, whether personal and spontaneous or public and formal.

Therefore, the fact that the sentiment of devotion in the *Ragaḷegaḷu* is tightly linked to visible expression through worship also points to the need to recognize Harihara's open-minded approach to different forms of worship. Put differently, Harihara's celebration of personal, unmediated, and informal worship does not imply a rejection of, resistance to, or even subversion of public, traditional, and formal religious practice conducted at the temple and directed toward the visible, iconic, and traditional image of Śiva. In many of the stories discussed in this book, the temple is naturally presented as a sacred arena in which the devotee undergoes profound devotional experiences, and whenever he or she directly encounters the god, in the temple or outside of it, Śiva is rendered in his iconic Purāṇic image (somewhat against the aniconic, abstract sense of Śiva in the "Puritan" understanding of the tradition).

A complicated message is also found in the *Ragaḷegaḷu* with regard to Brahmins and kings, two of the most prominent characters in the classical South Asian imaginaire. In Harihara's text, Brahmins occupy various narrative roles, and this variety undercuts the assumed essentialized antagonism toward Brahmins so commonly associated with Vīraśaivism. As the custodians of an elitist and conservative religion—which is perhaps the most obvious role Brahmins occupy in many South Asian devotional-based literatures—Brahmins are looked down upon by Harihara. Brahmin characters are depicted in the *Ragaḷegaḷu* as the outdated background for a portrait of the "true Brahmins," who are the Bhaktas. In this role, the Brahmins, who always carry Vaiṣṇava names and with their almost anachronistic insistence on Vedic-based knowledge and purity-based religious exclusion, are vehemently rejected.

On the other hand, however, Brahmins in the *Ragaḷegaḷu* are also acknowledged as uniquely qualified for social and political leadership. They enjoy a privileged position running the king's affairs at the court, a position which Harihara, rather than questioning, accepts as a given. One finds in the *Ragaḷegaḷu* stories Brahmins who fit well into Harihara's imagined world of devotion without having to cast off all of their Brahminical markers. Harihara's strict distinction between Vaiṣṇava Brahmins, who narrowly follow Vedic knowledge and conservative values, and Śaiva Brahmins, who are open to ritual innovation and social differences, opens up rich possibilities for thinking about a specific triangulation of Vaiṣṇava Brahminism that is categorically different from Śaiva religious configurations.

Kings in the *Ragaḷegaḷu* are equally complicated creatures. As a pinnacle of worldly power and political interests, the figure of the king in the *Ragaḷegaḷu* is not highly regarded by Harihara. And yet Harihara persistently weaves the lives of many of his Kannada protagonists with those of the kings, and the Bhaktas enjoy the patronage and support of the latter group for certain periods in the stories. Thus, despite their innate incompatibility with genuine devotion, kings are not to be avoided in the *Ragaḷegaḷu* but are to be engaged with and used, when possible, for their very real potential to better the material conditions of local Śaivas.

Finally, the prevalent idea that Vīraśaivism emerged from a momentous socio-religious rupture that occurred at a specific place and time in history—the city of Kalyāṇa under Bijjaḷa's reign—needs to be revised or at least confronted with the manner in which Harihara depicts the tradition's origins in the Kannada-speaking region, since his descriptions lack the tautological clarity that undergirds the popular narrative about the close-knit community in twelfth-century Kalyāṇa. I am not trying to downplay the cultural significance of Kalyāṇa in the region's history, which in itself is undeniable, as attested in the memorable statement made by one of Karnataka's greatest playwrights, Girish Karnad, that "it becomes inevitable for every Kannadiga to return, like a tongue that returns again and again to a painful tooth, to the victories and agonies of that period."[1] There is also no doubt that for Harihara, Kalyāṇa holds a unique place as a devotional center during the twelfth century, a center in which several prominent figures—including Kēśirāja, Jommayya, Bāhūra Bommatande, Śaṅkaradāsimayya,

1. Leslie (1998, 228).

Rēvaṇasiddha, and of course Basavaṇṇa—operated. Basavaṇṇa's Ragaḷe even conforms to the generally accepted narrative about the role of the Śaiva devotees in the fall of Kalyāṇa, in the form of a short section from the last chapter of the Ragaḷe in one of the extant manuscripts that describes the tragic eruption of violence that led to the dispersal of the devotees and to Bijjaḷa's assassination. But the sections that involve Kalyāṇa in the *Ragaḷegaḷu* should not be confused with Harihara's overall portrayal of early Śivabhakti in the Kannada-speaking region. The devotees mentioned above in relation to Kalyāṇa are described in this text as operating at different periods (presumably from the early twelfth century to its last third), while the city is governed by different rulers (Permāḍirāya, Jayasiṃharāya, Bijjaḷa), and in Harihara's stories these specific devotees rarely meet each other. Furthermore, Harihara is comfortable locating other prominent figures, such as Mahādēviyakka, Rāmayya, and Allama, who in later texts would be identified with the Kalyāṇa fellowship, in other places.[2]

In short, the idea that the origins of Kannada Śivabhakti go back to a single community in the middle of twelfth-century Kalyāṇa led by a rare cohort of exceptional figures who together forged the basic principles of the tradition during spontaneous debates and conversation at the gathering space called the Hall of Experience (Anubhava Maṇṭapa)—a forceful myth that is presented in its fullest form only in the fourth edition of the *Śūnyasampādane* from the sixteenth century—misses the richness of the remembered history presented in Harihara's stories. According to this much earlier remembered history, the tradition emerged out of a plethora of activities conducted by various Śaiva devotees who operated in the Kannada-speaking region at different places and times throughout the twelfth century.

My point in this discussion is not to replace the ubiquitous account about the Anubhava Maṇṭapa fellowship with Harihara's literary account of a more geographically dispersed group of devotees as the correct historical version. Rather, I wish to stress that from a critical perspective, the presence of multiple, incongruent literary accounts regarding the twelfth-century Kannada devotees, a presence that is augmented by the soaring absence of concrete "hard" evidence to support a specific historical-like

---

2. Although Harihara does mention Allama Prabhu's meeting with Basavaṇṇa, he does so in a mere two verses without naming Kalyāṇa. See *Prabhudēvara Ragaḷe* vv. 373–74 in Harihara and Suṅkāpura (1976, 17).

literary claim, leaves us with the minimal requirement to acknowledge the existence of more than one imaginative possibility for how the tradition started in this region.

Understanding a religious tradition from a critical perspective involves the initial recognition of its multiple configurations and reconfigurations in complex and changing sociocultural contexts over long periods of time. Most of all, it requires recognition of the fact that a tradition's own understanding of itself and of greater society has to be complicated and multilayered. Inherent complexity should be assumed in the consideration of *any stage* of a religious tradition, even—and perhaps especially—to its early or "original" or "pristine" stage. In the case of the subject matter discussed in this book, there should be nothing surprising or provocative in the postulation that already in the early stages of the Kannada devotional tradition—as early as the thirteenth century and perhaps already during the dramatic events of the twelfth century—the tradition understood itself in multiple, incongruent, sometimes even contradicting ways along several social and religious axes.

As literature, the *Ragaḷegaḷu* is inherently transitional, reflecting the time of its composition and that era's complications. Therefore, this text represents a worldview that was accepted at that time and perhaps was even canonical, but not necessarily hegemonic or ubiquitous. As tempting as it might be, we must not privilege the *Ragaḷegaḷu* over later accounts as a "truer" depiction of the saints. Harihara's vision of the twelfth-century saints in the *Ragaḷegaḷu* is exactly that, a literary vision. It rests—like other visions in other accounts—on the agendas, interests, and anxieties of his own time and place. The broader point to make is that the pursuit after the "true" history of a religious tradition based on certain textual reports might also involve the inevitable (and perhaps also willful) oversight of different textual claims that would contradict it. The reading of the *Ragaḷegaḷu* in its cultural context offers a case study for dealing with a sacred narrative not as a *historical report* of a tradition's origins, but as a very *real testimony* for the attitudes, dispositions, concerns, and interests of its own time.

Historically, the *Ragaḷegaḷu* is anything but the final word for the commemoration of the early Kannada devotees, yet without question it provided a pivotal literary foundation for the remembered history of the Śaiva saints of the Kannada-speaking region, a remembered history that would be shaped and reshaped over the centuries to come.

Bibliography

PRIMARY SOURCES: TEXTS AND INSCRIPTIONS

Akkamahādēvi. 1966. *Akkana Vacanagaḷu*. Edited by El. Basavarāju. Mysore: Geetha Book House.

Allamaprabhu. 2001 [1960]. *Allamana Vacana Candrike*. Edited by El. Basavarāju. Ballari: Lōhiyā Prakāśana.

Āṇṭāḷ. 2010. *The Secret Garland: Āṇṭāḷ's Tiruppāvai and Nācciyār Tirumoḻi*. Translated by Archana Venkatesan. New York: Oxford University Press.

Archaeological Survey of India and India Dept. of Archaeology. 1890. *South Indian Inscriptions Vol. 20, no. 69*. Madras: Printed by the Superintendent, Govt. Press.

Basavaṇṇa. 2001 [1993]. *Samagra Vacanasāhityada Janapriya Āvṛtti Vol. 1: Basavaṇṇavara Vacanasampuṭa*. Edited by Eṃ Eṃ Kalaburgi. Bangalore: Kannada Pusthaka Pradhikara (Kannada Book Authority).

Brahmaśiva. 1958. *Samayaparīkṣe*. Dharwad: Kannada Research Institute, Karnatak University.

Cēkkiḻār. 2006. *The History of the Holy Servants of the Lord Śiva: A Translation of the Pĕriya Purāṇam of Cekkiḻār*. Translated by Alastair McGlashan. Victoria, BC: Trafford Publishing.

Cuntarar. 1990. *Songs of the Harsh Devotee: The Tēvāram of Cuntaramūrttināyaṉār*. Translated by David Dean Shulman. Philadelphia: Dept. of South Asia Regional Studies, University of Pennsylvania.

Harihara, Hampeya. 1968. *Hariharana Ragaḷegaḷu*. Edited by Pha. Gu. Haḷakaṭṭi. Dharwad: Samāja Pustakālaya.

Harihara, Hampeya. 1969. *Rakṣāśataka mattu Pampāśataka*. Edited by S. S. Basawanal. Dharwad: Liṅgāyata Vidyābhivṛddhi Saṃsthe.

Harihara, Hampeya. 1976a. *Nūtana Purātanara Ragaḷegaḷu*. Edited by Eṃ. Es. Suṅkāpura. Dharwad: Kannaḍa Adhyayanapīṭha, Karnāṭaka Viśvavidyālaya.

Harihara, Hampeya. 1976b. *Śivabhaktimahimā Ragaḷegaḷu*. Edited by Eṃ. Es. Suṅkāpura. Dharwad: Kannaḍa Adhyayanapīṭha, Karnāṭaka Viśvavidyālaya.

Harihara, Hampeya. 1977. *Girijākalyāṇa*. 1st ed. Dharwad: Karnatak University.

Harihara, Hampeya. 1995 [1968]. *Śaraṇa Carita Mānasam*. Edited by Ec. Dēvīrappa. Bangalore: V. R. Kulkarni.

Harihara, Hampeya. 2011 [1999]. *Ragaḷegaḷu*. Edited by Eṃ. Eṃ. Kalaburgi. Hampi: Kannada University Hampi, Vidyaranya.

Harihara, Hampeya. 2012. *Kannaḍa Śaraṇara Kathegaḷu*. Edited by Eṃ. Eṃ. Kalaburgi. Bangalore: Kannaḍa Pustaka Prādhikāra.

Kēśirāja, Koṇḍaguḷi. 1978. *Koṇḍaguḷi Kēśirājana Kṛtigaḷu*. Edited by Eṃ. Eṃ. Kalaburgi. Hubbaḷḷi: Śrī Jagadguru Gaṅgādhara Dharmapracāraka Maṇḍala.

Mallikārjuna. 1972. *Sūktisudhārṇavam*. Edited by En. Anantaraṅgācār. Mysore: University of Mysore.

Manu. 2004. *The Law Code of Manu [Manusmṛti]*. Translated by Patrick Olivelle. Oxford, New York: Oxford University Press.

Padmarasa, Kereya. 1972. *Dīkṣābōdhe*. 1st ed. Mysore: Kannaḍa Adhyayana Saṃsthe, University of Mysore.

Rāghavāṅka. 2004. *Rāghavāṅkana Samagrakāvya*. Edited by Bi. E. Vivēka Rai. Hampi: Prasārāṅga, Kannaḍa Viśvavidyālaya.

Rāghavāṅka. 2017. *The Life of Harishchandra [Hariścandra Carite]*. Translated by Vanamala Viswanatha. Cambridge, MA: Harvard University Press.

Ranna. 1975. *Gadāyuddha Darpaṇaṃ: Kaviranna Viracita Gadāyuddhada (Sāhasabhīma vijayada) Mūlasahita Vivaraṇātmaka Vyākhyāna*. Edited by Pi. Subrāya Bhaṭ. 1st ed. Vidyānagara, Kāsaragōḍu, Kēraḷa: Subrāya Bhaṭ.

Samagra Vacanasāahityada Janapriya Āvṛtti Vol. 5: Śivaśaraṇeyara Vacanasampuṭa. 1993. Edited by Vīraṇṇa Rājūra. Bangalore: Kannada Pusthaka Pradhikara (Kannada Book Authority).

Siddhavīraṇāryaru, Gūḷūra. 2007 [1965]. *Śūnyasaṃpādane: Vol. V*. Translated by S. C. Nandimath, Armando Menezes, and Rudrayya Chandrayya Hiremath. Dharwad: Karnatak University.

Siddhavīraṇāryaru, Gūḷūra. 2007 [1965–1972]. *Śūnyasaṃpādane*. Translated by S. C. Nandimath, Armando Menezes, Rudrayya Chandrayya Hiremath, S. S. Bhoosnurmath, and M. S. Sunkapur. 5 vols. Dharwad: Karnatak University.

Śivayogiśivācārya. 2004 [1966]. *Siddhāntaśikhāmaṇi*. Mysore: Jagadguru Sri Shivarathreeshwara Granthamale.

Śivayogiśivācārya and Maritoṇṭadārya. 2007. *Śrīisiddhāntaśikhāmaṇiḥ with the Tattvapradīpikā*. Translated by M. Sivakumara Swamy. Varanasi: Shaiva Bharati Shodha Pratisthan.

Somanātha, Pālkuriki. 1990. *Śiva's Warriors: The Basava Purāṇa of Pālkuriki Somanātha [Basava Purāṇamu]*. Translated by Velcheru Narayana Rao and Gene H. Roghair. Princeton, NJ: Princeton University Press.

Upaniśads. 1996. Translated by Patrick Olivelle. Oxford, New York: Oxford University Press.

Voragine, Jacobus de, and William Granger Ryan. 1993. *The Golden Legend: Readings on the Saints*. 2 vols. Princeton, NJ: Princeton University Press.

Vyāsa. *Bhagavad Gītā*. (1) 2007. *The Bhagavad Gita*. Translated by Eknath Easwaran. Tomales, CA: Nilgiri Press. (2) 2008a. *The Bhagavad Gita*. Translated by Laurie L. Patton. London, New York: Penguin.

SECONDARY SOURCES

Ahmed, Durre S. 2002. "'Real' Men, Naked Women and the Politics of Paradise: The Archetype of Lal Ded." In *Gendering the Spirit: Women, Religion, and the Post-Colonial Response*, edited by Durre S. Ahmed, 155–83. London, New York: Zed Books.

Ali, Daud. 2004. *Courtly Culture and Political Life in Early Medieval India, Cambridge Studies in Indian History and Society*. Cambridge, UK; New York: Cambridge University Press.

Allchin, Raymond. 1971. "The Attaining of the Void: A Review of Some Recent Contributions in English to the Study of Vīraśaivism." *Religious Studies* no. 7 (4):339–59.

Anonymous. 2017. "Lingayats Resolve to Press for Minority Religion Status." *The Hindu*, August 11, 2017.

Bageshree, S. 2017. "Who Are the Lingayats and What Are Their Demands?" *The Hindu*, July 29, 2017.

Banerji, Chitrita. 2003. "The Propitiatory Meal." *Gastronomica: The Journal of Food and Culture* no. 3 (1):82–89.

Banks Findly, Ellison. 2002. "The Housemistress at the Door: Vedic and Buddhist Perspectives." In *Jewels of Authority: Women and Textual Tradition in Hindu India*, edited by Laurie L. Patton, 13–31. New York: Oxford University Press.

Barnett, Lionel D. 1921–22. "Three Inscriptions of Lakshmeshwar." In *Epigraphia Indica and Record of the Archaeological Survey of India*, edited by H. Krishna Shastri, and F. W. Thomas, 31–52. Calcutta: Government of India Press.

Ben-Herut, Gil. 2011. "Nāyaka Elaborations of Personhood: A Reading of The Descent of Gaṅgā by Nīlakaṇṭha Dīkṣita." In *World Without Borders: Being Tamil, Being Human*, edited by R. Cheran, 72–85. Toronto: TSAR Publications.

Ben-Herut, Gil. 2012. "Literary Genres and Textual Representations of Early Vīraśaiva History: Revisiting Ekānta Rāmayya's Self-Beheading." *International Journal of Hindu Studies* no. 16 (2):129–87.

Ben-Herut, Gil. 2015. "Figuring the South-Indian Śivabhakti Movement: The Broad Narrative Gaze of Early Kannada Hagiographic Literature." *Journal of Hindu Studies* no. 8 (3):274–95.

Ben-Herut, Gil. 2016. "Things Standing Shall Move: Temple Worship in Early Kannada Śivabhakti Hagiographies." *International Journal of Hindu Studies* no. 20 (2):129–58.

Ben-Herut, Gil, Jon Keune, and Anne E. Monius. Forthcoming. *Regional Communities of Devotion in South Asia: Insiders, Outsiders, and Interlopers*. London, New York: Routledge.

Biernacki, Loriliai. 2006. "Sex Talk and Gender Rites: Women and the Tantric Sex Rite." *International Journal of Hindu Studies* no. 10 (2):187–208.

Bismillah, Abdul, and J. A. I. Ratan. 1987. "A Hindi Story: The Guest of Honour." *Indian Literature* no. 30 (3 [119]):88–98.

Bowker, John Westerdale. 1997. *The Oxford Dictionary of World Religions*. Oxford, New York: Oxford University Press.

Bronner, Yigal. 2010a. *Extreme Poetry: The South Asian Movement of Simultaneous Narration, South Asia Across the Disciplines*. New York: Columbia University Press.

Bronner, Yigal. 2010b. "The Poetics of Ambivalence: Imagining and Unimagining the Political in Bilhaṇa's Vikramāṅkadevacarita." *Journal of Indian Philosophy* no. 38 (5):457–83.

Bronner, Yigal. 2011. "A Text with a Thesis: The Rāmāyaṇa from Appayya Dīkṣita's Receptive End." In *South Asian Texts in History: Critical Engagements with Sheldon Pollock*, edited by Yigal Bronner, Whitney Cox, and Lawrence J. McCrea, 45–63. Ann Arbor, MI: Association for Asian Studies.

Bronner, Yigal, David Dean Shulman, and Gary A. Tubb. 2014. *Innovations and Turning Points: Toward a History of Kāvya Literature*. New Delhi: Oxford University Press.

Brown, Peter. 2015 [1981]. *The Cult of the Saints: Its Rise and Function in Latin Christianity*. Enlarged ed. Chicago: University of Chicago Press.

Burchett, Patton. 2009. "Bhakti Rhetoric in the Hagiography of 'Untouchable' Saints: Discerning Bhakti's Ambivalence on Caste and Brahminhood." *International Journal of Hindu Studies* no. 13 (2):115–41.

Burchett, Patton. 2011. "My Miracle Trumps Your Magic: Confrontations with Yogis in Sufi and Bhakti Hagiographical Literature." In *Yoga Powers: Extraordinary Capacities Attained through Meditation and Concentration*, edited by Knut A. Jacobsen, 345–80. Leiden, The Netherlands; Boston: Brill.

Candraśēkhara Naṅgali, Vi. 2003. "Hariharana Ragaḷegaḷu: Sāmājika Darśana." In *Hariharana Ragaḷegaḷu: Sāṃskṛtika Mukhāmukhi*, edited by Vi. Śivānanda, 81–99. Hampi: Kannaḍa Viśvavidyālaya.

Chakrabarti, Arindam. 2001. "Disgust and the Ugly in Indian Aesthetics." In *La pluralità estetica : lasciti e irradiazioni oltre il Novecento*, edited by Grazia Marchianò, 347–63. Torino: Trauben.

Champakalakshmi, R. 1978. "Religious Conflict in the Tamil Country: A Reappraisal of Epigraphic Evidence." *Journal of Epigraphical Society of India* no. V:69–81.

Champakalakshmi, R. 2011a. "Caste and Community: Oscillating Identities in Pre-modern South India." In *Religion, Tradition, and Ideology: Pre-Colonial South India*, edited by R. Champakalakshmi, 235–85. New Delhi: Oxford University Press.

Champakalakshmi, R. 2011b. "Evolution of the Tamil Śaiva Tradition." In *Religion, Tradition, and Ideology: Pre-Colonial South India*, edited by R. Champakalakshmi, 87–120. New Delhi: Oxford University Press.

Champakalakshmi, R. 2011c. "From Devotion and Dissent to Dominance: The *Bhakti* of the Tamil Āḻvārs and Nāyanārs." In *Religion, Tradition, and Ideology: Pre-Colonial South India*, edited by R. Champakalakshmi, 53–86. New Delhi: Oxford University Press.

Chandra Shobhi, Prithvi Datta. 2005. *Pre-modern Communities and Modern Histories: Narrating Vīraśaiva and Lingayat Selves*. PhD diss., University of Chicago.

Chattopadhyaya, Debiprasad. 1978 [1959]. *Lokāyata: A Study in Ancient Indian Materialism*. New Delhi: People's Publishing House.

Chekki, Danesh A. 2003. *The Philosophy and Ethics of the Vīraśaiva Community, Studies in Asian Thought and Religion, 26*. Lewiston, NY: Edwin Mellen Press.

Chekki, Danesh A. 2012. "The Spiritual Path of Devotion: The Vīraśaiva Perspective." *Anthropos* no. 107 (2):555–60.

Chidananda Murthy, M. 1983. "Pre-Basava Vīraśaivism." In *The Chālukhyas of Kalyāṇa: Seminar Papers*, edited by M. S. Nagaraja Rao, 203–5. Bangalore: Mythic Society.

Cidānandamūrti, Eṃ. 1970. "Hariharakṣētra mattu Harihara Kaviya Kāla." In *Saṁśōdhana Taraṅga: Sampuṭa* 2, edited by Eṃ. Cidānandamūrti, 130–34. Bangalore: Bangalore University.

Cidānandamūrti, Eṃ. 1989a. *Liṅgāyata Adhyayanagaḷu*. Mysore: Vāgdēvi Pustakagaḷu.

Cidānandamūrti, Eṃ. 1989b. "'Liṅgāyata' Padada Niṣpatti." In *Liṅgāyata Adhyayanagaḷu*, edited by Em. Cidānandamūrti, 432–34. Mysore: Vāgdēvi Pustakagaḷu.

Cidānandamūrti, Eṃ. 2007. "Indina Bhāratakke Hindina Hampiya Sandēśa." In *Hindūdharma*, edited by Eṃ. Cidānandamūrti, 81–87. Bangalore: Bhārata Vikāsa Pariṣat.

Cidānandamūrti, Eṃ. 2011a. "Basavaṇṇa: Vīraśaivada (Liṅgāyata) Ānvayika Vijñāni." *Vijaya Karnāṭaka*, July 30, 2011.

Cidānandamūrti, Eṃ. 2011b. "'Vīraśaiva' Vivādakke Antime Tere." *Prajāvāṇi*, January 14, 2011.

Clarke, Sathianathan. 2002. "Hindutva, Religious and Ethnocultural Minorities, and Indian-Christian Theology." *The Harvard Theological Review* no. 95 (2):197–226.

Cohn, Robert L. 2005. "Sainthood." In *Encyclopedia of Religion*, edited by Lindsay Jones, Mircea Eliade, and Charles J. Adams, 8033–38. Detroit: Macmillan Reference USA.

Cornell, Vincent J. 1998. *Realm of the Saint: Power and Authority in Moroccan Sufism*. 1st ed. Austin: University of Texas Press.

Cort, John E. 2002. "Bhakti in the Early Jain Tradition: Understanding Devotional Religion in South Asia." *History of Religions* no. 42 (1):59–86.

Cort, John E. 2013. "God Outside and God Inside: The North Indian Digamber Jain Performance of Bhakti." In *Bhakti beyond the Forest: Current Research on Early*

Modern Literatures in North India, 2003–2009, edited by Imre Bangha, 255–86. New Delhi: Manohar Publishers & Distributors.

Cox, Whitney. 2005. "The Transfiguration of Tiṇṇaṉ the Archer." *Indo-Iranian Journal* no. 48 (3):223–52.

Craddock, Elaine. 2011. *Śiva's Demon Devotee: Kāraikkāl Ammaiyār*. Albany: State University of New York Press.

Cutler, Norman. 1987. *Songs of Experience: The Poetics of Tamil Devotion, Religion in Asia and Africa Series*. Bloomington: Indiana University Press.

Das, Veena. 2017. "Violence and Nonviolence at the Heart of Hindu Ethics." In *Violence and the World's Religious Traditions: An Introduction*, edited by Mark Juergensmeyer, Margo Kitts, and Michael K. Jerryson, 7–36. New York: Oxford University Press.

Datta, Amaresh. 1987. *Encyclopaedia of Indian Literature*. 6 vols. Vol. 2. New Delhi: Sahitya Akademi.

Davis, Richard H. 1991. *Ritual in an Oscillating Universe: Worshiping Śiva in Medieval India*. Princeton, NJ: Princeton University Press.

Davis, Richard H. 1995. "The Rebuilding of a Hindu Temple." In *Religions of India in Practice*, edited by Donald S. Lopez, 627–36. Princeton, NJ: Princeton University Press.

Davis, Richard H. 1998. "Introduction: Miracles as Social Acts." In *Images, Miracles, and Authority in Asian Religious Traditions*, edited by Richard H. Davis, 1–22. Boulder, CO: Westview Press.

Davis, Richard H. 2015. *The Bhagavad Gita: A Biography*. Princeton, NJ: Princeton University Press.

Dehejia, Vidya. 1988. *Slaves of the Lord: The Path of the Tamil Saints*. New Delhi: Munshiram Manoharlal.

Desai, Pandurang Bhimarao. 1968. *Basaveśvara and His Times*. Dharwad: Kannada Research Institute, Karnatak University.

Devadevan, Manu V. 2016. *A Prehistory of Hinduism*. Warsaw, Berlin: De Gruyter.

Dēvīrappa, Ec. 1979. "Harihara Kaviya Jīvana Caritre." In *Rasikacakri Hariharadēva*, edited by Bi.Si. Javaḷi, 1–32. Hospet: Sri Jagadguru Kottur Swami Math.

Doniger, Wendy. 2009. *The Hindus: An Alternative History*. New York: Penguin Press.

Dundas, Paul. 2002. *The Jains*. 2nd ed. London, New York: Routledge.

Eaton, Richard M., and Phillip B. Wagoner. 2014. *Power, Memory, Architecture: Contested Sites on India's Deccan Plateau, 1300–1600*. New Delhi: Oxford University Press.

Ebeling, Sascha. 2010. "Another Tomorrow for Nantaṉār: The Continuation and Re-Invention of a Medieval South-Indian Untouchable Saint." In *Geschichten und Geschichte: Historiographie und Hagiographie in der asiatischen Religionsgeschichte*, edited by Peter Schalk and Max Deeg, 433–516. Uppsala: Uppsala Universitet.

Eck, Diana L. 1996. "The Goddess Ganges in Hindu Scared Geography." In *Devī: Goddesses of India*, edited by John S. Hawley and Donna M. Wulff, 132–53. Berkley: University of California Press.

Eck, Diana L. 1998. *Darśan: Seeing the Divine Image in India*. 3rd ed. New York: Columbia University Press.

Eck, Diana L. 1999. *Banaras, City of Light*. New York: Columbia University Press.

Eco, Umberto. 1994. *Six Walks in the Fictional Woods, Charles Eliot Norton lectures*. Cambridge, MA: Harvard University Press.

Epp, Linda J. 1992. "Dalit Struggle, Nude Worship, and the 'Chandragutti Incident'." *Sociological Bulletin* no. 41 (1/2):145–68.

Feldhaus, Anne. 1995. *Water and Womanhood: Religious Meanings of Rivers in Maharashtra*. New York: Oxford University Press.

Fisher, Elaine M. 2017. *Hindu Pluralism: Religion and the Public Sphere in Early Modern South India*. Oakland, CA: University of California Press.

Fleet, J. F. 1988 [1882]. *The Dynasties of the Kanarese Districts of the Bombay Presidency from the Earliest Historical Times to the Musalman Conquest of A.D. 1318*. New Delhi: Asian Educational Services.

Foucault, Michel. 1973. *The Order of Things: An Archaeology of the Human Sciences, World of Man*. New York: Pantheon Books.

Geer, Alexandra van der, Michael Dermitzakis, and John de Vos. 2008. "Fossil Folklore from India: The Siwalik Hills and the Mahābhārata." *Folklore* no. 119 (1):71–92.

Gerow, Edwin. 1977. *Indian Poetics*. Wiesbaden: Harrassowitz.

Glasbrenner, Eva-Maria. 2015. "Cakra System and Tantric Ritual in Vīraśaivism." *The Journal of Hindu Studies* no. 8 (2):180–201.

Glucklich, Ariel. 1994. *The Sense of Adharma*. New York: Oxford University Press.

Glushkova, Irina. 2005. "*Dharma* and *Bhakti*: Marital Conflicts in the Vārkāri Tradition." In *In the Company of Gods: Essays in Memory of Günther-Dietz Sontheimer*, edited by Aditya Malik, Anne Feldhaus, Heidrun Brückner, and Günther-Dietz Sontheimer, 179–92. New Delhi: Indira Gandhi National Centre for the Arts in association with Manohar.

Gonāla, Aṅgappa. 2010. "Harihara-Rāghavāṅka Kāvyagaḷalli Jānapada Prajñe." In *Janamana*, edited by Aṅgappa Gonāla, 15–56. Gulbarga: Kannadanadu Prakashana.

Granoff, Phyllis. 1995. "Sarasvatī's Sons: Biographies of Poets in Medieval India." *Asiatische Studien/Études Asiatiques* no. 49 (2):351–76.

Granoff, Phyllis. 2009. Telling Tales: Jains and Śaivaites and their Stories in Medieval South India (unpublished conference paper). In *n/a*. Harvard University, Cambridge, MA.

Granoff, Phyllis. 2011. Marrying Outside the Faith: Buddhist and Jain Stories from Medieval India (unpublished conference paper). In *Lay Buddhism: An Old Issue Viewed in New Perspectives*. Vancouver, BC, Canada.

Guha, Dina Simoes. 1985. "Food in the Vedic Tradition." *India International Centre Quarterly* no. 12 (2):141–52.

Hallisey, Charles. 1988. *Devotion in the Buddhist Literature of Medieval Sri Lanka*. PhD diss., The University of Chicago, Divinity School, Chicago.

Hariharan, Githa. 2003. *In Times of Siege*. 1st American ed. New York: Pantheon Books.

Harlan, Lindsey. 1995. "Abandoning Shame: Mīrā and the Margins of Marriage." In *From the Margins of Hindu Marriage: Essays on Gender, Religion, and Culture*, edited by Lindsey Harlan and Paul B. Courtright, 204–27. New York: Oxford University Press.

Hawley, John Stratton. 1987. *Saints and Virtues, Comparative Studies in Religion and Society*. Berkeley: University of California Press.

Hawley, John Stratton. 1991. "Naming Hinduism." *The Wilson Quarterly (1976–)* no. 15 (3):20–34.

Hawley, John Stratton. 2005a. "Last Seen with Akbar." In *Three Bhakti Voices: Mirabai, Surdas, and Kabir in Their Time and Ours*, edited by John Stratton Hawley, 181–93. New Delhi: Oxford University Press.

Hawley, John Stratton. 2005b. *Three Bhakti Voices: Mirabai, Surdas, and Kabir in Their Time and Ours*. New Delhi: Oxford University Press.

Hawley, John Stratton. 2015. *A Storm of Songs: India and the Idea of the Bhakti Movement*. Cambridge, MA: Harvard University Press.

Heesterman, J. C. 1985. *The Inner Conflict of Tradition: Essays in Indian Ritual, Kingship, and Society*. Chicago: University of Chicago Press.

Hegewald, Julia A. B. 2015. "Śaiva-Jain-Liṅgāyat: Appropriation of Re-use of Sacred Architectural Space in Central and Southern India." In Sanmati: Essays Felicitating Professor Hampa Nagarajaiah on the Occasion of His 80th Birthday, edited by Luitgard Soni and Jayandra Soni, 239–84. Bangalore: Sapna Book House (P) Ltd.

Hess, Linda. 1988. "The Poet, the People, and the Western Scholar: Influence of a Sacred Drama and Text on Social Values in North India." *Theatre Journal* no. 40 (2):236–53.

Hess, Linda. 2001. "Lovers' Doubt: Questioning the Tulsi Rāmāyaṇ." In *Questioning Ramayanas: A South Asian Tradition*, edited by Paula Richman, 25–47. Berkeley: University of California Press.

Hess, Linda. 2015. *Bodies of Song: Kabir Oral Traditions and Performative Worlds in North India*. New York: Oxford University Press.

Hirst, Jacqueline Suthren. 2008. "Who Are the Others? Three Moments in Sanskrit-Based Practice." In *Religion, Language, and Power*, edited by Nile Green and Mary Searle-Chatterjee, 101–22. New York: Routledge.

Holdrege, Barbara A. 2015. *Bhakti and Embodiment: Fashioning Divine Bodies and Devotional Bodies in Kṛṣṇa Bhakti*. Abingdon, New York: Routledge.

Hopkins, Thomas J. 1968. "The Social Teaching of the Bhāgavata Purāṇa." In *Krishna: Myths, Rites, and Attitudes*, edited by Milton B. Singer, 3–22. Chicago: University of Chicago Press.

Hudson, D. Dennis. 1989. "Violent and Fanatical Devotion among the Nāyanārs: A Study in the Periya Purāṇam of Cēkkilār." In *Criminal Gods and Demon Devotees: Essays on the Guardians of Popular Hinduism*, edited by Alf Hiltebeitel, 373–404. Albany: State University of New York Press.

Ishwaran, K. 1983. *Religion and Society among the Lingayats of South India*. Leiden: E. J. Brill.

Ishwaran, K. 1992. *Speaking of Basava: Lingayat Religion and Culture in South Asia*. Boulder, CO: Westview Press.

Īśvaran, Hirēmallūra. 1971. *Hariharana Kṛtigaḷu: Ondu Saṅkhyā Nirṇaya*. Mysore: Prasārāṅga Mausīru Viśvavidyānilaya.

Kabir, Winand M. Callewaert, Swapna Sharma, and Dieter Taillieu. 2000. *The Millennium Kabīr Vānī: A Collection of Pad-s*. New Delhi: Manohar Publishers & Distributors.

Kalaburgi, Eṃ. Eṃ. 1970. *Śāsanagaḷalli Śivaśaraṇaru*. Dharwad: Sirigannaḍa Prakāśana, Karantaka University.

Kalaburgi, Eṃ. Eṃ. 2010 [1998]-a. "Kalyāṇa: Śaivadarmadinda Śaraṇadharmakke." In *Mārga: Saṃśōdhana Prabandhagaḷa Saṅkalana, vol. 4*, edited by Eṃ Eṃ Kalaburgi, 138–45. Bangalore: Sapna Book House (P) Ltd.

Kalaburgi, Eṃ. Eṃ. 2010 [1998]-b. *Mārga: Saṃśodhana Prabandhagaḷa Saṅkalana (Sampuṭa: Mūru)*. Edited by Eṃ Eṃ Kalaburgi. 6 vols. Vol. 3. Bangalore: Sapna Book House (P) Ltd.

Kalaburgi, Eṃ. Eṃ. 2010 [1998]-c. *Mārga: Saṃśōdhana Prabandhagaḷa Saṅkalana (Sampuṭa: Eraḍu)*. Edited by Eṃ Eṃ Kalaburgi. 6 vols. Vol. 3. Bangalore: Sapna Book House (P) Ltd.

Kalaburgi, Eṃ. Eṃ. 2010 [1998]-d. "Vīraśaiva Pada: Aitihāsika Beḷavaṇige." In *Mārga: Saṃśōdhana Prabandhagaḷa Saṅkalana, vol. 4*, edited by Eṃ Eṃ Kalaburgi, 197–204. Bangalore: Sapna Book House (P) Ltd.

Kalaburgi, Eṃ. Eṃ. 2010 [1998]-e. "Vīraśaiva Pada: Bhaugōlika prasāra." In *Mārga: Saṃśōdhana Prabandhagaḷa Saṅkalana, vol. 4*, edited by Eṃ Eṃ Kalaburgi, 205–11. Bangalore: Sapna Book House (P) Ltd.

Kalaburgi, Eṃ. Eṃ. 2011. "Ci. Mū Matto Vīraśaiva Vāda." *Prajāvāṇi*, January 20, 2011.

Karanth, G. K. . 2012. "Made Snana: Indignity in the Name of Tradition?" *Economic and Political Weekly* no. 47 (13):27–29.

Karnad, Girish Raghunath. 2005. *Collected Plays*. 2 vols. Vol. 2. New Delhi: Oxford University Press.

Kasdorf, Katherine E. 2013. *Forming Dōrasamudra: Temples of the Hoysaḷa Capital in Context*. PhD diss., Columbia University, New York.

Katkar, Sarjoo. 2012. *Annigeri Skulls Not a Result of Famine: Kalburgi*. Expressbuzz, August 14, 2011 [cited May 21, 2012]. Available from http://expressbuzz.com/topic/annigeri-skulls-not-a-result-of-famine-kalburgi/304029.html.

Kaul, Shonaleeka. 2010. *Imagining the Urban: Sanskrit and the City in Early India*. Ranikhet: Permanent Black.

Keune, Jon Milton. 2011. *Eknāth Remembered and Reformed: Bhakti, Brahmans, and Untouchables in Marathi Historiography*. PhD diss., Columbia University, New York.

Keune, Jon Milton. 2014. "Eknāth in Context: The Literary, Social, and Political Milieus of an Early Modern Saint-Poet." *South Asian History and Culture* no. 6 (1):70–86.

Keune, Jon Milton. Forthcoming. "The Challenge of the Swappable Other: A Framework for Interpreting Otherness in Bhakti Texts" In *Regional Communities of Devotion in South Asia: Insiders, Outsiders, and Interlopers*, edited by Gil Ben-Herut, Jon Milton Keune, and Anne E. Monius. London, New York: Routledge.

Killius, Rolf. 2003. *Drumming and Chanting in God's Own Country: The Temple Music of Kerala in South India*. London: Topic Records.

King, Stephen. 1987. *Misery*. New York: Viking.

Kinsley, David R. 1988. *Hindu Goddesses: Visions of the Divine Feminine in the Hindu Religious Tradition*. Berkeley: University of California Press.

Kittel, Rev. F. 1982. *A Kannada-English Dictionary*. Repr. ed. New Delhi: Asian Educational Services.

Kleinberg, Aviad M. 1992. *Prophets in Their Own Country: Living Saints and the Making of Sainthood in the Later Middle Ages*. Chicago: University of Chicago Press.

Kurtakoṭi, Kīrtinātha. 1995. *Kannaḍa Sāhitya Saṅgāti*. Hampi: Kannada University.

Lal, Amrith. 2017. "Why a 12th Century Bhakti Saint is Key for BJP in Karnataka." *The Indian Express*, May 15, 2017.

Leslie, Julia. 1989. *The Perfect Wife: The Orthodox Hindu Woman according to the Strīdharmapaddhati of Tryambakayajvan, Oxford University South Asian Studies Series*. Delhi, New York: Oxford University Press.

Leslie, Julia. 1998. "Understanding Basava: History, Hagiography and a Modern Kannaḍa Drama." *Bulletin of the School of Oriental and African Studies, University of London* no. 61 (2):228–61.

Liṅgaṇṇa, Si. 1979. "Harihara Kaviya Jānapada Prajñe." In *Rasikacakri Hariharadēva*, edited by Bi. Si. Javaḷi and Śāntarasa, 385–417. Hospet: Jagadguru Kotturuswami Matha.

Lorenzen, David N. 1988. "The Kālāmukha Background to Vīraśaivism." In *Studies in Orientology: Essays in Memory of Prof. A. L. Basham*, edited by A. L. Basham, Sachindra Kumar Maity, Upendra Thakur, and A. K. Narain, 278–93. Agra, India: Y. K. Publishers.

Lorenzen, David N. 1991. *The Kāpālikas and Kālāmukhas; Two Lost Śaivite Sects*. 2nd rev. ed. Delhi: Motilal Banarsidass.

Lorenzen, David N. 1995. "Introduction: The Historical Vicissitudes of Bhakti Religion." In *Bhakti Religion in North India: Community Identity and Political Action*, edited by David N. Lorenzen, 1–32. Albany: State University of New York Press.

Lutgendorf, Philip. 1991. *The Life of a Text: Performing the Rāmcaritmānas of Tulsidas*. Berkeley: University of California Press.

Madsen, Stig Toft, and Geoffrey Gardella. 2012. "Udupi Hotels: Entrepreneurship, Reform, and Revival." In *Curried Cultures: Globalization, Food, and South Asia*, edited by Krishnendu Ray and Tulasi Srinivas, 91–109. Berkeley: University of California Press.

Mallinson, James. 2011. "Nāth Saṃpradāya." In *Brill's Encyclopedia of Hinduism Vol. III*, edited by Knut A Jacobsen, Helene Basu, Angelika Malinar, and Vasudha Narayanan, 407–28. Leiden: Brill.

Mallison, Françoise. 2013. "Devotion Rewarded: The Attitude toward Wealth in the Religious Literature of Medieval Gujarat." In *Bhakti beyond the Forest: Current Research on Early Modern Literatures in North India, 2003–2009*, edited by Imre Bangha, 137–51. New Delhi: Manohar Publishers & Distributors.

Maridēvaru, Ec. 2011. "Basavaṇṇa Vīraśaivavavannu Oppi Vīraśaivavādare?" *Prajāvāṇi*, January 21, 2011, 1.

Mariguddi, Gurupāda. 2008. *Hariharana Liṅgabhēda Nirasana Ragaḷegaḷu.* Hampi: Kannada University.

McCormack, William. 1973. "On Lingayat Culture." In *Speaking of Śiva*, edited by A. K. Ramanujan, 175–87. Harmondsworth: Penguin.

McCrea, Lawrence. 2010. "Poetry Beyond Good and Evil: Bilhaṇa and the Tradition of Patron-centered Court Epic." *Journal of Indian Philosophy* no. 38 (5):503–18.

McGee, Mary. 2002. "Ritual Rights: The Gender Implications of *Adhikāra*." In *Jewels of Authority: Women and Textual Tradition in Hindu India*, edited by Laurie L. Patton, 32–50. New York: Oxford University Press.

Michael, R. Blake. 1982. "Work as Worship in Vīraśaiva Tradition." *Journal of the American Academy of Religion* no. 50 (4):605–19.

Michael, R. Blake. 1983a. "Foundation Myths of the Two Denominations of Vīraśaivism: Viraktas and Gurusthalins." *The Journal of Asian Studies* no. 42 (2):309–22.

Michael, R. Blake. 1983b. "Women of the Śūnyasaṃpādane: Housewives and Saints in Vīraśaivism." *Journal of the American Oriental Society* no. 103 (2):361–68.

Michael, R. Blake. 1992. *The Origins of Vīraśaiva Sects: A Typological Analysis of Ritual and Associational Patterns in the Śūnyasampādane.* 1st ed. Delhi: Motilal Banarsidass Publishers.

Michael, R. Blake. 2011. "Liṅgāyats." In *Brill's Encyclopedia of Hinduism*, edited by Knut A. Jacobsen, Helene Basu, Angelika Malinar, and Vasudha Narayanan, 378–92. Leiden, Boston: Brill.

Michael, R. Blake. 2012. "Basava." In *Brill's Encyclopedia of Hinduism*, edited by Knut A. Jacobsen, Helene Basu, Angelika Malinar, and Vasudha Narayanan, 177–84. Leiden, Boston: Brill.

Michael, R. Blake. 2015. "Virashaivism." In *Oxford Bibliographies Online*, DOI: 10.1093/OBO/9780195399318-0152. Oxford University Press.

Miller, Barbara Stoler, and Richard Maxwell Eaton. 1992. "Introduction." In *The Powers of Art: Patronage in Indian Culture*, edited by Barbara Stoler Miller, 1–16. Delhi; New York: Oxford University Press.

Mīrā, El. Ji. 2003. "Hariharana Ragaḷegaḷu: Ondu Strīvādi Adhyayana." In *Hariharana Ragaḷegaḷu: Sāṃskṛtika Mukhāmukhi*, edited by Vi. Śivānanda, 159–69. Hampi: Kannaḍa Viśvavidyālaya.

Monier-Williams, Monier, Ernst Leumann, and Carl Cappeller. 1986 [1899]. *A Sanskrit-English Dictionary Etymologically and Philologically Arranged with Special Reference to Cognate Indo-European Languages*. New ed. Delhi: Motilal Banarsidass.

Monius, Anne E. 2004a. "Love, Violence, and the Aesthetics of Disgust: Śaivas and Jains in Medieval South India." *Journal of Indian Philosophy* no. 32 (2–3):113–72.

Monius, Anne E. 2004b. "Śiva as Heroic Father: Theology and Hagiography in Medieval South India." *The Harvard Theological Review* no. 97 (2):165–97.

Monius, Anne E. 2009. "Purāṇa/Purāṇām: Modes of Narrative Temporality in Sanskrit and Tamil." In *Passages: Relationships between Tamil and Sanskrit*, edited by M. Kannan and Francois Gros, 217–36. Pondicherry, Berkeley: Institut Français de Pondichéry; University of California.

Monius, Anne E. 2011. "With No One to Bind Action and Agent: The Fate of Buddhists as Religious 'Other' in Tamiḻ Śaiva Literature." In *The Tamiḻs: From the Past to the Present*, edited by Peter Schalk, 153–78. Colombo: Kumaran Book House.

Mullatti, Leela. 1989. *The Bhakti Movement and the Status of Women: A Case Study of Virasaivism*. New Delhi: Abhinav Publications.

Nāgabhūṣaṇa, Si. 2000. "Dēvara Dāsimayya-Jēḍara Dāsimayya: Kelavu Saṅgatigaḷu." In *Śaraṇa Sāhitya Saṃskṛti Kelavu Adhyayanagaḷu*, edited by Si. Nāgabhūṣaṇa, 53–64. Bangalore: Kannada Sahitya Parishat.

Nāgabhūṣaṇa, Si. 2005. *Ēkāntada Rāmayya mattu Ādayya: Ondu Taulanika Adhyayana*. Bangalore: Basava Samiti.

Nagaraj, D. R. 2003. "Critical Tensions in the History of Kannada Literary Culture." In *Literary Cultures in History: Reconstructions from South Asia*, edited by Sheldon I. Pollock, 323–82. Berkeley: University of California Press.

Nāgarāj, Ḍi. Ār. 1999. *Allama Prabhu mattu Śaiva Pratibhe*. Heggodu: Aksara Prakasana.

Nandi, R. N. 1975. "Origin of the Vīraśaiva Movement." *The Indian Historical Review* no. 2:32–46.

Nandimath, S. C. 1979 [1942]. *A Handbook of Vīraśaivism*. 2nd. rev. ed. Delhi: Motilal Banarsidass.

Nandy, Ashis. 1995. "History's Forgotten Doubles." *History and Theory* no. 34 (2):44–66.

Nandy, Chandan. 2012. *C-14 Dating Gives Annigeri Skulls 638 Years*. Mysore: The Printers Private Ltd, May 9, 2011 [cited May 21, 2012]. Available from http://www.deccanherald.com/content/160243/c-14-dating-gives-annigeri.html.

Narasiṃhācār, Ḍi. El. 2008. "Hariharakavi mattu Avana Kelavu Ragaḷegaḷu." In *Heccina Barahagaḷu Bhāṣaṇagaḷu*, edited by Ṭi.Vi. Veṅkaṭācala Śāstrī, 148–55. Bangalore: B. M. Sri Smaraka Pratishthana.

Narasiṃhācārya, Ār. 2005 [1929]. *Karnāṭaka Kavicarite*. Vol. 1. Bangalore: Kannada Sahitya Parishat.

Narasimhacharya, R. 1988 [1934]. *History of Kannada Literature: Readership Lectures*. AES reprint ed. New Delhi: Asian Educational Services.

Narayana Rao, Velcheru. 1992. "Kings, Gods and Poets: Ideologies of Patronage in Medieval Andhra." In *The Powers of Art: Patronage in Indian Culture*, edited by Barbara Stoler Miller, 142–59. Delhi; New York: Oxford University Press.

Narayana Rao, Velcheru. 2004. "Purāṇa." In *The Hindu World*, edited by S. Mittal and G. R. Thursby, 97–115. New York: Routledge.

Narayana Rao, Velcheru, and David Dean Shulman. 2002. *Classical Telugu Poetry: An Anthology*. Berkeley, CA: University of California Press.

Narayana Rao, Velcheru, David Dean Shulman, and Sanjay Subrahmanyam. 2003. *Textures of Time: Writing History in South India, 1600–1800*. New York: Other Press.

Nāyaka, Hā. Mā., Ṭi.Vi. Veṅkaṭācala Śāstrī, and Ār. Vi. Es. Sundaram. 1977. *Kannaḍa Adhyayana Samstheya Kannaḍa Sāhitya Caritre (Nālkaneya Sampuṭa)*. 10 vols. Vol. 4. Mysore: Kannaḍa Adhyayana Saṃsthe Maisūru Viśvavidyānilaya, Mārāṭagāraru Prasārāṅga.

Nicholas, Ralph W. 1995. "The Effectiveness of the Hindu Sacrament (*Saṃskāra*): Caste, Marriage, and Divorce in Bengali Culture." In *From the Margins of Hindu Marriage: Essays on Gender, Religion, and Culture*, edited by Lindsey Harlan and Paul B. Courtright, 137–59. New York: Oxford University Press.

Nilakanta Sastri, K. A. 1960. "The Chāḷukhyas of Kalyāṇī and the Kalachuris of Kalyāṇī." In *The Early History of the Deccan*, edited by Ghulam Yazdani, 315–468. London, New York: Published under the authority of the Government of Andhra Pradesh by the Oxford University Press.

Nilakanta Sastri, K. A. 1976. *A History of South India from Prehistoric Times to the Fall of Vijayanagar*. 4th ed. Madras: Oxford University Press.

Novetzke, Christian Lee. 2008. *Religion and Public Memory: A Cultural History of Saint Namdev in India*. New York: Columbia University Press.

Novetzke, Christian Lee. 2011. "The Brahmin Double: The Brahminical Construction of Anti-Brahminism and Anti-Caste Sentiment in the Religious Cultures of Precolonial Maharashtra." *South Asian History and Culture* no. 2 (2):232–52.

Novetzke, Christian Lee. 2016. *The Quotidian Revolution: Vernacularization, Religion, and the Premodern Public Sphere in India*. New York: Columbia University Press.

Orr, Leslie C. 1998. "Jain and Hindu 'Religious Women' in Early Medieval Tamilnadu." In *Open Boundaries: Jain Communities and Culture in Indian History*, edited by John E. Cort, 187–212. Albany, NY: State University of New York Press.

Orr, Leslie C. 2005. "Identity and Divinity: Boundary-Crossing Goddesses in Medieval South India." *Journal of the American Academy of Religion* no. 73 (1):9–43.

Padoux, André. 2005. "Śaivism: Vīraśaivas." In *Encyclopedia of Religion*, edited by Lindsay Jones, Mircea Eliade, and Charles J. Adams, 8043–44. Detroit: Macmillan Reference USA.

Pande, Rekha. 2010. *Divine Sounds from the Heart: Singing Unfettered in Their Own Voices: The Bhakti Movement and Its Women Saints (12th to 17th Century)*. Newcastle upon Tyne: Cambridge Scholars Publishing.

Patel, Deven M. 2014. *Text to Tradition: The Naiṣadhīyacarita and Literary Community in South Asia, South Asia Across the Disciplines*. New York: Columbia University Press.

Pattanashetti, Girish. 2011. "At Annigeri, a Rare Find of Human Skulls." *The Hindu*, March 8, 2011.

Pattanashetti, Girish. 2017a. "Leaders, Seers Do Flip-Flop over Lingayat Issue." *The Hindu*, July 31, 2017.

Pattanashetti, Girish. 2017b. "Religion Tag for Lingayat: Why a Plea Was Set Aside Earlier." *The Hindu*, August 4, 2017.

Patton, Laurie L. 2002. *Jewels of Authority: Women and Textual Tradition in Hindu India*. New York: Oxford University Press.

Patton, Laurie L. 2007. "Telling Stories about Harm: An Overview of Early Indian Narratives." In *Religion and Vilolence in South Asia: Theory and Practice*, edited by J. R. Hinnells and R. King, 11–40. Oxon: Routledge.

Patton, Laurie L. 2008. "Ṛṣis Imagined Across Difference: Some Possibilities for the Study of Conceptual Metaphor in Early India." *Journal of Hindu Studies* no. 1 (1–2):49–76.

Patton, Laurie L., and Śaunaka. 1996. *Myth as Argument: The Bṛhaddevatā as Canonical Commentary, Religionsgeschichtliche Versuche und Vorarbeiten bd. 41*. New York: Walter de Gruyter.

Pauwels, Heidi. 2002. *In Praise of Holy Men: Hagiographiec Poems by and about Hariām Vyās*. Groningen: Egbert Forsten.

Pauwels, Heidi. 2009. "The Saint, the Warlord, and the Emperor: Discourses of Braj Bhakti and Bundela Loyalty." *Journal of the Economic and Social History of the Orient* no. 52 (2):187–228.

Pauwels, Heidi. 2010. "Who Are the Enemies of the Bhaktas? Testimony about 'Śāktas' and 'Others' from Kabīr, the Rāmānandīs, Tulsīdās and Harirām Vyās." *Journal of the American Oriental Society* no. 130 (4):509–39.

Pechilis, Karen. 1999. *The Embodiment of Bhakti*. New York: Oxford University Press.

Pechilis, Karen. 2008. "Chosen Moments: Mediation and Direct Experience in the Life of the Classical Tamil Saint Kāraikkāl Ammaiyār." *Journal of Feminist Studies in Religion* no. 24 (1):11–31.

Pechilis, Karen. 2012. *Interpreting Devotion: The Poetry and Legacy of a Female Bhakti Saint of India*. Abingdon, NY: Routledge.

Pechilis Prentiss, Karen. 2001. "On the Making of a Canon: Historicity and Experience in the Tamil 'Śiva-bhakti' Canon." *International Journal of Hindu Studies* no. 5 (1):1–26.

Peterson, Indira Viswanathan. 1992. "In Praise of the Lord: The Image of the Royal Patron in the Songs of Saint Cuntaramūrtti and the Composer Tyāgarāja." In *The*

Powers of Art: Patronage in Indian Culture, edited by Barbara Stoler Miller, 120–41. Delhi; New York: Oxford University Press.

Peterson, Indira Viswanathan. 1994a. "Tamil Śaiva Hagiography." In *According to Tradition: Hagiographical Writing in India*, edited by Winand M. Callewaert and Rupert Snell, 191–228. Wiesbaden: Harrassowitz.

Peterson, Indira Viswanathan. 1994b. "Tamil Śaiva Hagiography: The Narrative of the Holy Servants (of Śiva) and the Hagiographical Project in Tamil Śaivism." In *According to Tradition: Hagiographical Writing in India*, edited by Winand M. Callewaert and Rupert Snell, 191–228. Wiesbaden: Harrassowitz.

Peterson, Indira Viswanathan. 1998. "Śramaṇas against the Tamil Way: Jains as Others in Tamil Śaiva Literature." In *Open Boundaries: Jain Communities and Culture in Indian History*, edited by John E. Cort, 163–87. Albany, NY: State University of New York Press.

Pollock, Sheldon. 1993. "Ramayana and Political Imagination in India." *The Journal of Asian Studies* no. 52 (2):261–297.

Pollock, Sheldon. 1998. "The Cosmopolitan Vernacular." *The Journal of Asian Studies* no. 57 (1):6–37.

Pollock, Sheldon. 2001. "The Death of Sanskrit." *Comparative Studies in Society and History* no. 43 (2):392–426.

Pollock, Sheldon. 2004. "A New Philology: From Norm-bound Practice to Practice-bound Norm in Kannada Intellectual History." In *South-Indian Horizons: Felicitaion Volume for Francois Gros on the Occasion of his 70th Birthday*, edited by François Gros, Jean-Luc Chevillard, Eva Wilden, and A. Murugaiyan, 389–406. Pondicherry: Institut Français De Pondichery, and École Française D'Extreme-Orient.

Pollock, Sheldon. 2006. *The Language of the Gods in the World of Men: Sanskrit, Culture, and Power in Premodern India*. Berkeley: University of California Press.

Prasad, Leela. 2007. *Poetics of Conduct: Oral Narrative and Moral Being in a South Indian Town*. New York: Columbia University Press.

Prasād, Nallūru. 2001. *Saṅkṣipta Kannaḍa Nighaṇṭu*. 3rd ed. Bangalore: Kannada Sahitya Parishat.

Ramanujan, A. K. 1973. *Speaking of Śiva*. Harmondsworth: Penguin.

Ramanujan, A. K. 1981. *Hymns for the Drowning: Poems for Viṣṇu*. Princeton, NJ: Princeton University Press.

Ramanujan, A. K. 1989. "Talking to God in the Mother Tongue." *Manushi* no. 50-51-52:9–14.

Ramanujan, A. K., Vinay Dharwadker, and Stuart H. Blackburn. 1999. *The Collected Essays of A. K. Ramanujan*. New Delhi, New York: Oxford University Press.

Ramaswamy, Vijaya. 1996. *Divinity and Deviance: Women in Virasaivism*. Delhi: Oxford University Press.

Ramaswamy, Vijaya. 2007. *Walking Naked: Women, Society, Spirituality in South India*. 2nd rev. ed. Shimla: Indian Institute of Advanced Study.

Ramesh Bairy, T. S. 2009. "Brahmins in the Modern World: Association as Enunciation." *Contributions to Indian Sociology* no. 43 (1):89–120.

Rancière, Jacques. 2010. *Dissensus: On Politics and Aesthetics*. London, New York: Continuum.

Rao, Ajay K. 2011. "A New Perspective on the Royal Rāma Cult at Vijayanagara." In *South Asian Texts in History: Critical Engagements with Sheldon Pollock*, edited by Yigal Bronner, Whitney Cox, and Lawrence J. McCrea, 25–44. Ann Arbor, MI: Association for Asian Studies.

Reddy, Prabhavati C. 2014. *Hindu Pilgrimage: Shifting Patterns of Worldview of Srisailam*. New York: Routledge.

Ricœur, Paul, and Mark I. Wallace. 1995. *Figuring the Sacred: Religion, Narrative, and Imagination*. Minneapolis: Fortress Press.

Rinehart, Robin. 1999. *One Lifetime, Many Llives: The Experience of Modern Hindu Hagiography, AAR the religions*. Atlanta, GA: Scholars Press.

Ripepi, Tiziana. 2007. "The Feet of the Jaṅgama: Identity and Ritual Issues among the Vīraśaivas of Karnataka." *Kervan: Rivista Internationale di Studii Afroasiatici* no. 6 (July 2007):69–100.

Rodríguez, Guillermo. 2016. *When Mirrors Are Windows: A View of A. K. Ramanujan's Poetics*. New Delhi: Oxford University Press.

Rumāle, Mṛtyuñjaya. 2003. *Vacana Nighaṇṭu*. Gadag: Vīraśaiva Adhyayana Saṃsthe.

Śāmarāya, Ti. Es. ca. 1964. *Kannaḍa Sāhitya Caritre: Ondu Samīkṣe*. Mysore: T. V. Memorial Series.

Śāmarāya, Ti. Es. 2009 [1967]. *Śivaśaraṇa Kathāratnakōśa*. Mysore: Taḷukina Veṅkaṇṇayyasmāraka Grantha Māle.

Samartha, M. P. 1977. "Basava's Spiritual Struggle." *Religious Studies* no. 13 (3):335–47.

Saṇṇayya, Bi. Es. 2002. *Prācīna Kannaḍa Grantha Sampādne: 20neya Śatamānadalli, Ākara Granthamāle*. Bangalore: Karnāṭaka Sarkāra, Kannaḍda Pustaka Prādhikāra.

Saudattimath, S. D. 1988. *Harihara's Ragaḷes: A Linguistic Analysis*. 1st ed. Dharwad: Prasaranga, Karnatak University.

Savadattimaṭha, Saṅgamēśa. 1999. *Bhāṣālēkha: Kannaḍa Bhāṣāvaijñānika Saṃśōdhana Lēkhanagaḷa Saṅkalana Grantha*. 1st ed. Gulabarga: Ruparashmi Prakashana.

Savadattimaṭha, Saṅgamēśa. 2009. *Vīraśaiva Ākaragaḷu*. Balehonnuru: Shrimad Veerashaiva Sadbodhana Samsthe.

Savadattimaṭha, Saṅgamēśa. 2011. "Anya Bhāṣegaḷalli Haḷeya Dākhalegaḷu Labhya." *Prajāvāṇi*, January 18, 2011.

Schouten, Jan Peter. 1995. *Revolution of the Mystics: On the Social Aspects of Vīraśaivism*. 1st Indian ed. Delhi: Motilal Banarsidass Publishers.

Sen, Sudipta. 1996. "Passages of Authority: Rulers, Traders and Marketplaces in Bengal and Banaras, 1700–1750." *Calcutta Historical Journal* no. 17 (1):1–40.

Sharma, Krishna. 1979. "Bhakti." In *Problems of Indian Historiography*, edited by D. Devahuti, 61–71. New Delhi: D. K. Publications.

Sharma, Krishna. 1987. *Bhakti and the Bhakti Movement: A New Perspective: A Study in the History of Ideas*. New Delhi: Munshiram Manoharlal Publishers.

Shivaprakash, H. S., and K. S. Radhakrishna. 1990. *A String of Pearls: Selections from Kannada Poetry from Pampa to Present*. Bangalore: Karnataka Sahitya Academy.

Shulman, David Dean. 1980. *Tamil Temple Myths: Sacrifice and Divine Marriage in the South Indian Saiva Tradition*. Princeton, NJ: Princeton University Press.

Shulman, David Dean. 1984. "The Enemy Within: Idealism and Dissent in South Indian Hinduism." In *Orthodoxy, Heterodoxy and Dissent in India*, edited by S. N. Eisenstadt, Reuven Kahane, and David Dean Shulman, 11–55. Berlin, New York: Mouton.

Shulman, David Dean. 1991. "Fire and Flood: The Testing of Sītā in Kampaṉ's Irāmāvatāram." In *Many Rāmāyaṇas: The Diversity of a Narrative Tradition in South Asia*, edited by Paula Richman, 89–113. Berkeley: University of California Press.

Shulman, David Dean. 1992. "Poets and Patrons in Tamil Literature and Literary Legend." In *The Powers of Art: Patronage in Indian Culture*, edited by Barbara Stoler Miller, 89–119. Delhi, New York: Oxford University Press.

Shulman, David Dean. 1993a. "Book Review: Śiva's Warriors: The Basava Purāṇa of Pālkuriki Somanātha by Velcheru Narayana Rao; Gene H. Roghair." *History of Religions* no. 32 (3):312–4.

Shulman, David Dean. 1993b. *The Hungry God: Hindu Tales of Filicide and Devotion*. Chicago: University of Chicago Press.

Simmons, Caleb. 2011. "Yes Sir, That's My Devī: Authority and the Goddess in Nina Paley's *Sita Sings the Blues*." *Journal of Vaishnava Studies* no. 20 (1):133–56.

Singh, K. S. 2003. *People of India: Karnataka*. Vol. 26, Part Two. New Delhi: Anthropological Survey of India.

Singh, Ram Bhushan Prasad. 1975. *Jainism in Early Medieval Karnataka, C. A.D. 500–1200*. 1st ed. Delhi: Motilal Banarsidass.

Śivānanda, Vi. 1966–67. "Koṇḍaguḷi Keśirāja." *Prabuddha Karṇāṭaka* no. 48 (4):22.

Śivarudrappa, Ji. Es. 1976. *Samagra Kannaḍa Sāhitya Caritre: Sampuṭa 3*. 1st ed. 10 vols. Vol. 3. Bangalore: Bangalore University.

Smith, W. L. 2000. *Patterns in North Indian Hagiography*. Stockholm: Department of Indology, University of Stockholm.

Soneji, Devesh. 2012. *Unfinished Gestures: Devadāsīs, Memory, and Modernity in South India, South Asia Across the Disciplines*. Chicago, London: University of Chicago Press.

Śrīmati, Ec. Es. 2003. "Hariharana Ragaḷegaḷu: Strīvādi Ōdinalli." In *Hariharana Ragaḷegaḷu: Sāṃskṛtika Mukhāmukhi*, edited by Vi. Śivānanda, 100–109. Hampi: Kannaḍa Viśvavidyālaya.

Srinidhi, R. 2012. *Historian Unearths Sacrificial Sect Theory on Annigeri Skulls*. Mysore: The Printers Private Ltd, May 10, 2011 [cited May 21, 2012]. Available from http://www.deccanherald.com/content/160424/historian-unearths-sacrificial-sect-theory.html.

Srinivasan, Prema. 2000. "Ahara-Niyama: The Srivaisnava Dietary Regimen." *RES: Anthropology and Aesthetics* (37):186–204.

Stein, Burton. 1992. "On Patronage and Vijayanagara Religoius Foundations." In *The Powers of Art: Patronage in Indian Culture*, edited by Barbara Stoler Miller, 160–67. Delhi, New York: Oxford University Press.

Stewart, Tony K. 2010. *The Final Word: The Caitanya Caritāmṛta and the Grammar of Religious Tradition*. New York: Oxford University Press.

Stoker, Valerie L. 2015. "Darbār, Maṭha, Devasthānam: The Politics of Intellectual Commitment and Religious Organization in Sixteenth-Century South India." *South Asian History and Culture* no. 6 (1):130–46.

Stoker, Valerie L. 2016. *Polemics and Patronage in the City of Victory: Vyāsatīrtha, Hindu Sectarianism, and the Sixteenth-Century Vijayanagara Court*. Oakland, CA: University of California Press.

Thapar, Romila. 1992. "Patronage and the Community." In *The Powers of Art: Patronage in Indian Culture*, edited by Barbara Stoler Miller, 19–34. Delhi; New York: Oxford University Press.

Thapar, Romila. 2005. *Somanatha: The Many Voices of a History*. London, New York: Verso.

Thapar, Romila. 2008. "Somanatha: Narratives of a History." In *Demolishing Myths or Mosques and Temples? Readings on History and Temple Desecration in Medieval India*, edited by Sunil Kumar, 23–64. Gurgaon: Three Essays Collective.

Tulpule, S. G. 1991. "The Dog as a Symbol of Bhakti." In *Devotion Divine: Bhakti Traditions from the Regions of India: Studies in Honour of Charlotte Vaudeville*, edited by Diana L. Eck, Françoise Mallison, and Charlotte Vaudeville, 273–85. Groningen: Egbert Forsten.

Učida, Norihiko, and B. B. Rajapurohit. 2013. *Kannada-English Etymological Dictionary*. Tokyo: Research Institute for Languages and Cultures of Asia and Africa (ILCAA), Tokyo University of Foreign Studies.

Ulrich, Katherine E. 2007. "Food Fights." *History of Religions* no. 46 (3):228–61.

Urban, Hugh B. 2001. "The Marketplace and the Temple: Economic Metaphors and Religious Meanings in the Folk Songs of Colonial Bengal." *The Journal of Asian Studies* no. 60 (4):1085–114.

Vail, Lise F. 1985. "Founders, Swamis, and Devotees: Becoming Divine in North Karnataka." In *Gods of Flesh/Gods of Stone: The Embodiment of Divinity in India*, edited by Joanne Punzo Waghorne, Norman Cutler, and Vasudha Narayanan, 123–40. Chambersburg, PA: Anima.

Vamadeva, Chandraleka. 1995. *The Concept of Vannanpu "Violent Love" in Tamil Saivism, with Special Reference to the Periyapuranam*, Uppsala.

Veluthat, Kesavan. 1993. "Religious Symbols in Political Legitimation: The Case of Early Medieval South India." *Socail Scientist* no. 21 (1/2):22–33.

Veṅkaṭācala Śāstrī, Ṭi. Vi. 1978. *Kannaḍa Chandaḥsvarūpa* 1st ed. Mysore: D. V. K. Murti.

Veṅkaṭasubbayya, Ji. 2010 [1977]. *Kannaḍa Nighaṇṭu: Mūraneya Sampuṭa.* 8 vols. Bengaluru: Kannaḍa Sāhitya Pariṣattina.

Verghese, Anila. 1995. *Religious Traditions at Vijayanagara: As Revealed through Its Monuments.* New Delhi: Manohar: American Institute of Indian Studies.

Verter, Bradford. 2003. "Spiritual Capital: Theorizing Religion with Bourdieu against Bourdieu." *Sociological Theory* no. 21 (2):150–74.

Vidyāśaṅkara, Es. 2000. *Vīraśaiva Pāribhāṣika Padakōśa*. 1. Samskarana ed. Bangalore: Basava Samithi.

Vincentnathan, Lynn. 2005. "Nandanar: Untouchable Saint and Caste Hindu Anomaly." In *Untouchable Saints: An Indian Phenomenon,* edited by Eleanor Zelliot and Rohini Mokashi-Punekar, 109–19. New Delhi: Manohar.

Wagoner, Phillip B. 1996. "From 'Pampa's Crossing' to 'The Place of Virupaksha': Architecture, Cult and Patronage at Hampi Before the Founding of Vijayanagara." In *Vijayanagara: Progress of Research 1988–1991,* edited by D. V. Devaraj and C. S. Patil, 141–74. Mysore: Directorate of Archaeology and Museums.

Weber, Max. 1958. *The Religion of India: The Sociology of Hinduism and Buddhism.* New York: Free Press.

Wedemeyer, Christian K. 2013. *Making Sense of Tantric Buddhism: History, Semiology, and Transgression in the Indian Traditions.* New York: Columbia University Press.

White, David Gordon. 1995. "Predicting the Future with Dogs." In *Religions of India in Practice,* edited by Donald S. Lopez, 288–303. Princeton, NJ: Princeton University Press.

White, David Gordon. 2003. *Kiss of the Yoginī: "Tantric Sex" in its South Asian Contexts.* Chicago: University of Chicago Press.

Williams, R. 1963. *Jaina Yoga: A Survey of the Mediaeval Śrāvakācāras.* London, New York: Oxford University Press.

Yaravintelimath, C. R. 2006. *Vacanas of Women Saints.* 1st ed. Bangalore: Basava Samithi.

Zelliot, Eleanor. 1995. "Chokhāmeḷā: Piety and Protest." In *Bhakti Religion in North India: Community, Identity, and Political Action,* edited by David N. Lorenzen, 212–20. Albany: State University of New York Press.

Zelliot, Eleanor, and Rohini Mokashi-Punekar. 2005. "Introduction." In *Untouchable Saints: An Indian Phenomenon,* edited by Eleanor Zelliot and Rohini Mokashi-Punekar, 9–51. New Delhi: Manohar.

Zvelebil, Kamil V. 1986. "Brief Prolegomena to Early Tamil Literary History: Iṟaiyaṉār, Tarumi, Nakkīrar." *Journal of the Royal Asiatic Society of Great Britain and Ireland* (1):59–67.

Zydenbos, Robert J. 1985. "Jainism Endangered; The View of the Medeival Kannada Poet Brahmaśiva." *South Asian Digest of Regional Writing* no. 11:174–86.

Zydenbos, Robert J. 1997. "Review: Vīraśaivism, Caste, Revolution, Etc." Review of Revolution of the Mystics: On the Social Aspects of Vīraśaivism by Schouten, J. P. *Journal of the American Oriental Society* no. 117 (3):525–35.

Index

Abbalūru, 208, 212, 224n56
accountants, 48–50, 106–7, 110, 171, 180–81, 184
Ādayya, 209–17, 222, 226, 228
  Ragaḷe about (see *Ādayyana Ragaḷe* (Hampeya Harihara))
Ādayyana Ragaḷe (Hampeya Harihara), 59n41, 141n47, 155n2, 204n11, 209–13, 215n39
administrators at the king's court. *See* courtly politics
Ādyas ("first ones"), 166. *See also* Nāyaṉmār (Tamil Śaiva saints); *purātanagīte* ("songs of/about the elders")
Āgamas (ritual manuals), 7, 36, 132, 138
agonistic ritual, 207, 213
ahiṃsā (non-violence), 220
alaṅkāraśāstra (Sanskrit poetics). *See* Sanskrit language: poetics in the
Ali, Daud, 198
Allama Prabhu, 69–71, 214n37, 236
  Ragaḷe about (see *Prabhudēvara Ragaḷe* (Hampeya Harihara))
  vacanas of (see *vacanas*: of Allama Prabhu)
Ambedkar, B. R., 131n19
Ammavve, 112n56
Andhra Pradesh, 50n26
āṇe. *See* vow
aṅga (devotee's soul), 114n61. *See also* Śiva: and his devotees
Aṇṇigere, 204n11, 210
Āṇṭāḷ, 112n55, 117
anthologies, 9, 11n28, 43, 58, 63, 66
anubhava maṇṭapa. *See* "Hall of Experience"
Apayakulacekaraṉ, Rājarāja (king), 162
Appar, 221, 227n70. *See also* Tamil Śivabhakti literature
Ārādhyas, 12, 16, 126n2
ārati (worship with a lamp), 48, 217
Archaeological Survey of India (ASI), 209n26. *See also* epigraphy and archeology
archeology. *See* epigraphy and archeology
Arjuna, 83, 96, 148
ārōgaṇe (consecrated food). *See also* food, feeding, and cooking
artisans, traders, merchants, and markets, 99, 134, 137, 185, 197, 210, 224, 229
Ārūr, 162
assemblies of Śaiva devotees, 17, 18n43, 28, 35, 38, 92, 101n23, 108, 110, 115, 141, 167–68, 170, 186, 190, 202
astrology, 228